P2P Networking and Applications

The Morgan Kaufmann Series in Networking

Series Editor, David Clark, M.I.T.

For further information on these books and for a list of forthcoming titles, please visit our Web site at http://www.mkp.com.

P2P Networking and Applications

John F. Buford

Heather Yu

Eng Keong Lua

AMSTERDAM • BOSTON • HEIDELBERG • LONDON
NEW YORK • OXFORD • PARIS • SAN DIEGO
SAN FRANCISCO • SINGAPORE • SYDNEY • TOKYO

Morgan Kaufmann Publishers is an imprint of Elsevier

ELSEVIER

MORGAN KAUFMANN

Morgan Kaufmann Publishers is an imprint of Elsevier.
30 Corporate Drive, Suite 400, Burlington, MA 01803, USA

This book is printed on acid-free paper.

© 2009 by Elsevier Inc. All rights reserved.

Library of Congress Cataloging-in-Publication Data
Application Submitted

ISBN: 978-0-12-374214-8

For information on all Morgan Kaufmann publications,
visit our Web site at www.mkp.com or www.elsevierdirect.com

Printed and bound by CPI Group (UK) Ltd, Croydon, CR0 4YY

Transferred to Digital Print 2011

To my wife Gina and our daughter Jacqueline
JFB

To my lovely daughters Angie and Kiki
HY

To our adorable son Anthony
EKL

Table of Contents

Preface

Rationale
Peer-to-peer networking has emerged as a viable business model and systems architecture for Internet-scale applications. Although its technological roots trace back through several decades of designing distributed information systems, contemporary applications demonstrate that it is an effective way to build applications that connect millions of users across the globe without reliance on specially deployed servers. Instead, by combining the resources of each user's computer, these systems automatically self-organize and adapt to changing peer populations while providing services for content sharing and personal communications.

Public attention to peer-to-peer applications came first from highly popular file-sharing systems, in which decentralization was used to support a business model that needed to legitimize licensed content sharing. The subsequent success of the Skype Internet telephony application showed the generality of the peer-to-peer approach and its feasibility to provide acceptable service quality to millions of users.

Subsequently there has been growing interest in improving on these systems as well as considering new designs to attain better performance, security, and flexibility. Today it is anticipated that peer-to-peer technologies will become general-purpose, widely used vehicles for building a broad range of applications for social networking, information delivery, and personal communications applications in the future.

There are many important questions about the evolution of peer-to-peer technologies. What new applications will drive this evolution? Will P2P be used as a general-purpose technique for building any distributed application? How do trends in wireless networking, consumer electronics, home networking, high-definition content, digital rights management, and so forth intersect with peer-to-peer? Is P2P a panacea for designing large-scale applications, or if not, what are the characteristics of applications for which it is well suited? How should other architectures coexist with and adapt to peer-to-peer design? Will the P2P landscape be "Balkanized" by many incompatible peer-to-peer protocols and systems?

The topics covered in this book provide a comprehensive survey of both the practice of P2P and main research directions and are intended to frame the answers for these questions.

Organization and Approach
The first two chapters introduce the main concepts of peer-to-peer systems. We examine the operation of a basic P2P system, including behavior for self-organizing, routing, and searching. We also describe a number of representative commercial applications. The next four chapters describe the fundamental peer-to-peer overlay architectures, including both unstructured and structured overlays.

The last chapter in this group covers important implementation issues such as protocol design, NAT traversal, and peer capability assessment.

Detailed discussion of P2P mechanisms to support key applications follow, including chapters on search, content delivery, peercasting and overlay multicasting, and overlay-based Internet telephony. Important uses of peer-to-peer overlays that we describe here include different techniques for content search, delivery of real-time streaming content, and session initiation using the overlay. We then discuss in separate chapters how requirements for overlay performance, peer mobility, security, and management intersect with the P2P overlay design.

Throughout the book, to motivate and illustrate the material, we include examples of systems in use and describe important research prototypes. We also refer to open-source implementations for readers who seek a hands-on illustration of the ideas. In particular we use examples from OverlayWeaver, an open-source toolkit developed by Kazuyuki Shudo that supports a number of important peer-to-peer algorithms. Access to the open-source tools and updates to the book can be obtained via the companion Website at http://elsevierdirect.com/companions/9780123742148.

Audience

This book is intended for professionals, researchers, and computer science and engineering students at the advanced undergraduate level and higher who are familiar with networking and network protocol concepts and basic ideas about algorithms. For the more advanced parts of the book, the reader should have general familiarity with Internet protocols such as TCP and IP routing but should not need to know the details of network routing protocols such as BGP or OSPF. For some sections of the book such as discussions of mobility or multicasting, familiarity with mobility in IP and IP multicasting will be helpful but not required. The reader will also find it helpful to be familiar with notation for comparing algorithm performance, such as $O(n)$ or $O(\log n)$.

For instructors who want to use the book as a textbook in a class on peer-to-peer networking, a set of exercises for each chapter, with an answer key for selected exercises are available by registering at **http://textbooks.elsevier.com**

Peer-to-peer networking is generally seen as a new technology with a disruptive business model and many possibilities for further innovation. These trends make the subject matter in this book highly relevant to the technology community. We hope the book is a valuable starting point for readers who are new to the subject and an important reference to those who are active in the field. Throughout the book we conclude each chapter with suggestions for further reading for readers who would like to dig deeper into specific topics.

Acknowledgements

During the preparation of this book, many people provided help in reviewing portions of the text and the original book proposal. We greatly appreciate their suggestions and efforts in improving the quality of the book.

First, we would like to thank those individuals who reviewed the original proposal and made important comments about structure, topics, and emphasis: Germano Caronni, Google; Christos Gkantsidis, Microsoft Research; Wolfgang Kellerer, DOCOMO Euro-Labs; Xuemin (Sherman) Shen, University of Waterloo; and Xiaotao Wu, Avaya Labs Research. In addition, Wolfgang Kellerer, DOCOMO Euro-Labs, reviewed a substantial portion of the book and provided many useful suggestions.

We are also grateful to those who reviewed and commented on portions of the book: Yi Cui, Vanderbilt University; Anwitaman Datta, Nanyang Technological University; Aaron Harwood, University of Melbourne; Vana Kalogeraki, University of California Riverside; Mario Kolberg, University of Stirling; Ben Leong, National University of Singapore; Li Li, Communications Research Centre Canada; Lundy Lewis, Southern New Hampshire University; Muthucumaru Maheswaran, McGill University; Kurt Tutschku, University of Vienna; Mengku Yang, Eastern Kentucky University; Wenjun (Kevin) Zeng, University of Missouri-Columbia. The efforts and constructive comments of all the reviewers are greatly appreciated. Any mistakes that remain are the responsibility of the authors.

Thanks are due to the staff at Morgan Kaufman–Rick Adams, Senior Acquisitions Editor; assistant editors Gregory Chalson, Maria Alonso, and Lindsey Gendall; and our project manager, Melinda Ritchie.

Finally we thank our families for their support and understanding while we worked on this book.

John F. Buford, Princeton, NJ
email: buford@samrg.org

Heather Yu, Princeton, NJ
email: heathery@ieee.org

Eng Keong Lua, Japan and USA
email: eklua@computer.org

About the Authors

John F. Buford is Research Scientist, Avaya Labs Research, Basking Ridge, NJ. Previously he was Lead Scientist at Panasonic Technologies, VP of Software Development at Kada Systems, Director of Internet Technologies at Verizon, and Assoc. Prof. of Computer Science at University of Massachusetts Lowell. PhD in Computer Science, Graz University of Technology.

Heather Yu is Senior Manager of Media Technologies at Huawei Technologies USA, Bridgewater, NJ where she leads the research on multimedia content networking and digital media technologies. PhD in Electrical Engineering, Princeton University.

Eng Keong Lua is Faculty Member of College of Engineering, Information Networking Institute at Carnegie Mellon University, Pittsburgh, USA, and Systems Scientist, Carnegie Mellon CyLab USA and Japan. Previously he held research fellowship and industry consulting positions at the NTT Laboratories, Intel Research, Microsoft Research, and Hewlett-Packard R&D/Consulting. His research areas include Peer-to-Peer networks, Internet-scale P2P overlay multimedia communications, network security and future Internet. PhD in Computer Science, University of Cambridge, UK.

Introduction

Our discussion of peer-to-peer (P2P) concepts starts with an overview of the key applications and their emergence as mainstream services for millions of users. The chapter then examines the relationship of P2P with the Internet and its distinctive features compared to other service architectures. A review of P2P economics, business models, social impact, and related technology trends concludes the chapter.

P2P EMERGES AS A MAINSTREAM APPLICATION

The Rise of P2P File-Sharing Applications

Nearly 10 years after the World Wide Web became available for use on the Internet, decentralized peer-to-peer file-sharing applications supplanted the server-based Napster application, which had popularized the concept of file sharing. Napster's centralized directories were its Achilles' heel because, as it was argued in court, Napster had the means, through its servers, to detect and prevent registration of copyrighted content in its service, but it failed to do so. Napster was subsequently found liable for copyright infringement, dealing a lethal blow to its business model.

As Napster was consumed in legal challenges, second-generation protocols such as Gnutella, FastTrack, and BitTorrent adopted a peer-to-peer architecture in which there is no central directory and all file searches and transfers are distributed among the corresponding peers. Other systems such as FreeNet also incorporated mechanisms for client anonymity, including routing requests indirectly through other clients and encrypting messages between peers. Meanwhile, the top labels in the music industry, which have had arguably the most serious revenue loss due to the emergence of file sharing, have continued to pursue legal challenges to these systems and their users.

Regardless of the outcome of these court cases, the social perception of the acceptability and benefits of content distribution through P2P applications has been irrevocably altered. In the music industry prior to P2P file sharing, audio CDs were the dominant distribution mechanism. Web portals for online music were limited in terms of the size of their catalogs, and downloads were expensive. Although P2P file sharing became widely equated with content piracy, it also showed that consumers were ready to replace the CD distribution model with an online experience if it could provide a large portfolio of titles and artists and if it included features such as a search, previews, transfer to CD and personal music players, and individual track purchase. As portals such as iTunes emerged with these properties, a tremendous growth in the online music business resulted.

In a typical P2P file-sharing application, a user has digital media files he or she wants to share with others. These files are registered by the user using the local application according to properties such as title, artist, date, and format. Later, other users anywhere on the Internet can search for these media files by providing a query in terms of some combination of the same attributes. As we discuss in detail in later chapters, the query is sent to other online peers in the network. A peer that has local media files matching the query will return information on how to retrieve the files. It may also forward the query to other peers. Users may receive multiple successful responses to their query and can then select the files they want to retrieve. The files are then downloaded from the remote peer to the local machine. Examples of file-sharing client user interfaces are shown in Figures 1.1 and 1.2.

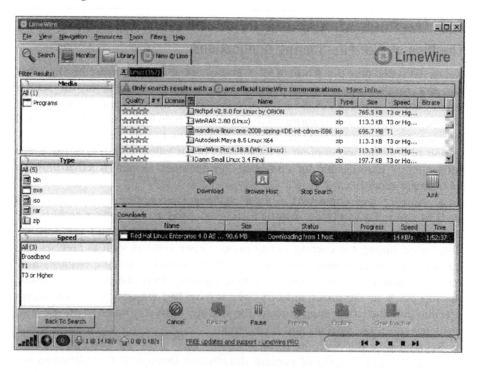

FIGURE 1.1 LimeWire client.

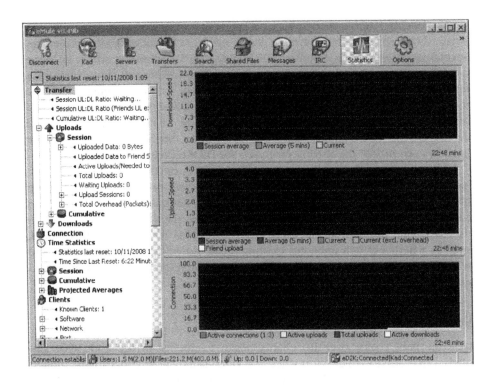

FIGURE 1.2 eMule client search interface.

Despite their popularity, P2P file-sharing systems have been plagued by several problems for users. First, some of the providers of leading P2P applications earn revenue from third parties by embedding spyware and malware into the applications. Users then find their computers infected with such software immediately after installing the P2P application. Second, a large amount of polluted or corrupted content has been published in file-sharing systems, and it is difficult for a user to distinguish such content from the original digital content they seek. It is generally felt that pollution attacks on file-sharing systems are intended to discourage the distribution of copyrighted material. A user downloading a polluted music file might find, for example, noise, gaps, and abbreviated content.

A third type of problem affecting the usability of P2P file-sharing applications is the *free-rider problem*. A free rider is a peer that uses the file-sharing application to access content from others but does not contribute content to the same degree to the community of peers. Various techniques for addressing the free-rider problem by offering incentives or monitoring use are discussed later in the book. A related issue is that of *peer churn*. A peer's content can only be accessed by other peers if that peer is online. When a peer goes offline, it takes time for other peers to be alerted to the change in status. Meanwhile, content queries may go unanswered and time out.

The leading P2P file-sharing systems have not adopted mechanisms to protect licensed content or collect payment for transfers on behalf of copyright owners. Several ventures seek to legitimize P2P file sharing for licensed content by incorporating techniques for *digital rights management* (DRM) and superdistribution into P2P distribution architectures. In such systems, content is encrypted, and though it can be freely distributed, a user must separately purchase an encrypted license file to render the media. Through the use of digital signatures, such license files are not easily transferred to other users. See this book's Website for links to current P2P file-sharing proposals for DRM-based approaches.

Other ventures such as QTrax, SpiralFrog, and TurnItUp are proposing an ad-based model for free music distribution. The user can freely download the music file, which in some models is protected with DRM, but must listen to or watch an ad during download or playback. In these schemes, the advertiser instead of the user is paying the content licensing costs. Questions remain about this model, such as whether it will undercut existing music download business models and whether the advertising revenue is sufficient to match the licensing revenue from existing music download sites.

Voice over P2P (VoP2P)

Desktop VoIP (voice over IP) clients began to appear in the mid-1990s and offered free desktop-to-desktop voice and video calls. These applications, though economically attractive and technically innovative, didn't attract a large following due to factors such as lack of voice quality and limited availability of broadband access in the consumer market. In addition, the initially small size of the network community limited the potential of such applications to supplant conventional telephony. This continues to be a practical issue facing new types of P2P applications—how to create a community of users that can reach the critical mass needed to provide the value proposition that comes with scale.

Starting in 1996 with the launch of ICQ, a number of instant-message and presence (IMP) applications became widely popular. The leading IMP systems, such as AIM, Microsoft Messenger, Yahoo! Messenger, and Jabber, all use client/server architectures.[6] Although several of these systems have subsequently included telephony capabilities, their telephony features have not drawn a large user community.

Skype is a VoP2P client launched in 2003 that has reached more than 10 million concurrent users. The VoP2P technology of Skype is discussed in Chapter 11. Compared to earlier VoIP clients, Skype offers both free desktop-to-desktop calls and low-cost desktop-to-public switched telephone network (PSTN) calls, including international calls. The call quality is high, generally attributed to the audio codec Skype uses and today's wide use of broadband access networks to reach the Internet. In addition, Skype includes features from IMP applications, including buddy lists, instant messaging, and presence. Unlike the file-sharing systems, Skype promises a no spyware policy.

FIGURE 1.3 Skype client.

The Skype user interface is shown in Figure 1.3. It includes a buddy list that shows other buddies and their online status. The user can select buddies to initiate free chat, voice, and group conference sessions. The user can also enter PSTN numbers to call, and these calls are charged.

P2PTV

The success of P2P file sharing and VoP2P motivated use of P2P for streaming video applications. P2PTV delivery often follows a channel organization in which content is organized and accessed according to a directory of programs and movies. Unlike file-sharing systems in which a media file is first downloaded to the user's computer and then played locally, video-streaming applications must provide a real-time stream transfer rate to each peer that equals the video playback rate. Thus if a media stream is encoded at 1.5 Mbps and there is a single peer acting as the source for the stream, the path from the source peer to the playback peer must provide a data transfer rate of 1.5 Mbps on average. Some variation in the playback rate along the path can be accommodated by prebuffering a sufficient number of video frames. Then if the transfer rate temporarily drops, the extra content in the buffer is used to prevent dropouts at the rendering side.

An attractive feature of peer-to-peer architectures for delivery of video streams is their *self-scaling* property. Each additional peer added to the P2P system adds additional capacity to the overall resources. Even powerful server farms are limited to the maximum number of simultaneous video streams that they can deliver. In a P2P network, any peer receiving a video stream can also forward it to a few other peers. If $D > 1$ peers are directly connected to the source peer and each peer can in turn support D peers, then up to $D^2 + D$ peers can receive a video stream within two hops from the source. Likewise, if each of the second-tier D peers can in turn support D peers, up to $D^3 + D^2 + D$ peers can receive the video stream in three hops. Note that each hop adds a small forwarding delay, which is usually not a problem in one-way video-streaming applications.

This simple model is good if all peers watching the specific video stream are viewing the same position in the stream close to simultaneously, equivalent to a broadcast television channel. However, in video-on-demand type applications, peers start viewing a stream at arbitrary times, and those peers that start viewing a stream concurrently may soon diverge in stream position due to user actions such as pause or rewind. To avoid transferring complete copies of video files to peers at playback, a method is needed for a peer to locate the next chunk of video in its playback schedule from some other peers in the P2P system. One technique used in BitTorrent [243] is for the source of the content to seed other peers with chunks of the content. These peers then access the *torrent* created by the source to identify each other and retrieve the content chunks directly from other peers. Such a group of peers exchanging chunks is called a *swarm*.

As is the case with other P2P applications, the volatility of peers could cause gaps in stream playback if the peer that is the source of the next segment of video suddenly leaves the P2P system. Since peers are user-controlled end systems, unpredictable and unannounced departures are an assumed hazard. Most P2P networks have specific protocols to recognize such departures and to continually locate new peers that are joining the P2P system. For video-streaming applications, mitigating the departure of a source peer can involve periodically searching for redundant sources (which are also volatile) and providing a sufficient buffer to reduce the impact on the user's viewing experience when a source peer departure does occur.

Outside of P2P video applications, a great deal of research has dealt with the issues of reliable network delivery of real-time video. Due to network congestion and network failures, packets may sometimes get dropped. P2P networks depend on the underlying physical network. Consequently, techniques already developed for reliable delivery of streams in packet networks are applicable in P2P overlay networks. Such techniques include adaptive video delivery, multiresolution video, and scalable video and are discussed in Chapter 8.

Several P2PTV applications are available. Examples include Babelgum, Joost, PPLive, PPStream, SopCast, TVants, TVUPlayer, Veoh TV, and Zattoo (see Figure 1.4).

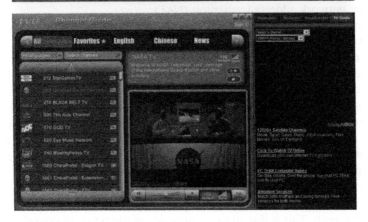

FIGURE 1.4 P2PTV applications, (A) Bablegum © 2008 Bablegum. Reprinted by permission, (B) Zattoo © 2007 Zattoo. Reprinted by permission, (C) TVU Networks © 2008 TVU Networks. Reprinted by permission.

P2P NETWORKING AND THE INTERNET

P2P Overlays and Network Services

Peers in P2P applications communicate with other peers using messages transmitted over the Internet or other types of networks. The protocol for a P2P application is the set of different message types and their semantics, which are understood by all peers. The protocols of various P2P applications have some common features. First, these protocols are constructed at the application layer of the network protocol stack. Second, in most designs peers have a unique identifier, which is the peer ID or peer address. Third, many of the message types defined in various P2P protocols are similar. Finally, the protocol supports some type of message-routing capability. That is, a message intended for one peer can be transmitted via intermediate peers to reach the destination peer.

To distinguish the operation of the P2P protocol at the application layer from the behavior of the underlying physical network, the collection of peer connections in a P2P network is called a *P2P overlay*. Figure 1.5 shows the correspondence between peers connecting in an overlay network with the corresponding hosts, devices, and routers in the underlying physical network. Later in this book we discuss important properties and details of P2P overlays. For consistency, when we want to talk about a system of peers using a common P2P application layer protocol, we will refer to it as a *P2P overlay* or simply an *overlay*. It might be convenient to think of a P2P system or P2P network as synonyms for P2P overlay.

The practice of overlay networks predates the P2P application era. For example, protocols used in Internet news servers and Internet mail servers are early examples of widely used overlays that implement important network services. These specialized overlay networks were developed for various reasons, such as enabling end-to-end network communication regardless of network boundaries caused by network address translation (NAT).

Another important reason for the use of overlays is to provide a network service that is not yet available within the network. For example, multicast routing is a network service that to date has been only partially adopted on the Internet. Multicast routing enables a message sent to a single multicast address to be routed to all receivers that are members of the multicast group. This is important for reducing network traffic for one-to-many applications such as video broadcasting or videoconferencing. Since multicast routing is not universally supported in Internet routers, researchers developed an application layer capability for multicast routing called *application layer multicast* (ALM) or *overlay multicast* (OM). These techniques, discussed in Chapter 9, use a type of overlay network to provide the multicast service for applications.

Another aspect of Internet routing is that some messages are not routed via the shortest path. This is due to the economics of the network providers that collectively provide the backbone of the Internet. These network providers establish network regions that connect at peering points to other network providers. The

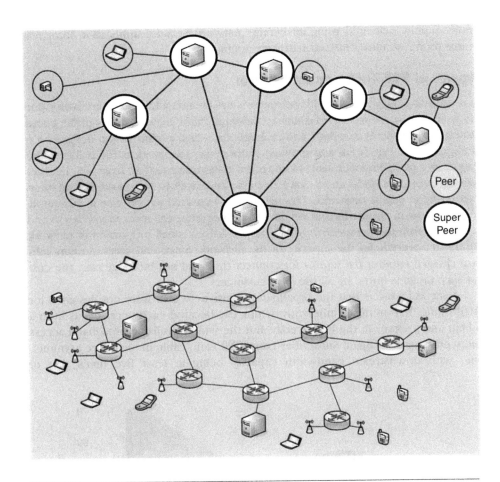

FIGURE 1.5 Peers form an overlay network (top) that in turn uses network connections in the native network (bottom). The overlay organization is a logical view that might not directly mirror the physical network topology.

traffic load at a peering point may be asymmetric. To maximize the value of the network to its customers, a network provider may route traffic coming into its peering point differently depending on the source of the packet. Consequently, different hosts sending messages to the same destination could see significantly different delays. *Resilient overlay networks* (RONs) are a type of overlay network that seeks to provide the shortest path in the physical network for a message. Such overlays are discussed in Chapter 11.

Finally, other examples of network services that can be supported using an overlay include secure delivery of packets, trust establishment between arbitrary endpoints, anonymous message delivery, and censorship-resistant communications. Such services are incompletely provided in today's Internet and can be more rapidly delivered using an overlay network because application layer features do not require network hardware upgrades.

Impact of P2P Traffic on the Internet

The growing popularity of P2P applications has created additional controversy due to its impact on network performance. Although traffic measurements of the global Internet are difficult to collect and evaluate, data such as that shown in Figure 1.6 indicate that a significant and growing proportion of network traffic is due to the popularity of P2P applications. More recent measurements[10] in large U.S. Internet service providers (ISPs) show that P2P traffic continues to be around 50% of Internet traffic in access networks. This situation is expected to continue as P2P applications grow in popularity and are used to deliver more and more video files to end systems. From the perspective of the ISP, a relatively small proportion of network users can overwhelm the capacity of the network. Since end users in many ISPs are charged either a flat rate or for connect time and not bit usage rate, the cost of such usage is borne by all the ISP's customers.

A second issue is that the broadband access networks were not designed for P2P traffic. P2P traffic is inherently symmetric because each peer acts as both a client and a server in the P2P overlay. But the widely available broadband access networks such as Digital Subscriber Loop (DSL) and cable modems are asymmetric, with downstream bandwidth capacity being at least five times that of

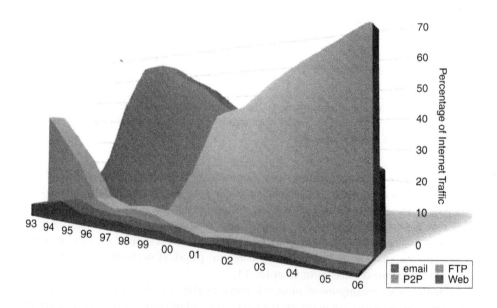

FIGURE 1.6 Relative percentage of Internet traffic by application category through 2006. (© 2006 Velocix, Reprinted by permission).

upstream capacity. Thus the networks of broadband ISPs are being overloaded by large volumes of upstream traffic produced by P2P applications.

The outcome of these conflicts between P2P applications and network providers depends in part on the continued popularity of P2P applications, particularly for media delivery versus the emergence of other distribution models that provide the same cost/benefit. A discussion of current approaches to ISP management of overlay traffic is found in Chapter 15.

MOTIVATION FOR P2P APPLICATIONS
P2P from the End User's Perspective

Though P2P applications have transformed the typical user's experience of getting content and communication services from the Internet, at the same time other popular Internet applications have not been built with P2P technology. Examples include social networking sites such as MySpace and content-sharing sites such as YouTube. Both P2P applications and these Web-based applications provide free services to large numbers of end users. But the owners of the Web-based applications generate revenue using inline advertisements. These Websites can measure ad viewership and click-throughs. Depending on the application, the Websites can also relate these statistics to user information that the Website gathers.

This revenue model has not been successfully integrated into popular P2P applications. Usage statistics gathering, which drives ad-based revenue, is more difficult in the P2P architecture because it is highly distributed. Additionally, as discussed in Chapter 15, the distributed architecture and dependence on user-controlled end system resources mean that it is more difficult to provide expected levels of service quality.

One might then argue that P2P is primarily a low barrier of entry, enabling technology for new applications. Once proven, such applications can be replaced with easier-to-manage and more reliable client/server technology. But P2P offers a uniquely self-scaling architecture, in which increased participation increases the capacity of the system. This plus the cost differential enabled by using end-system resources suggest that P2P should always be able to provide certain types of services at a cost level not achievable by client/server architectures. Further, popular applications that have reached a critical mass have been historically difficult to retire or replace, undermining the practicality of replacing P2P applications with corresponding client/server ones.

When a user interacts with an application, what features tell the user that it is implemented using a P2P overlay? There is no single function that can't be implemented in both architectures. But as the usage grows to a global community with significant information sharing, the difference in scaling properties means that, ideally, P2P should be able to support a much larger degree of interaction in terms of number of concurrent users and amount of content that can be mutually shared. For example, it is widely known that Web search engines index only a portion of the Web. Could a P2P architecture enable Web search to cover more content and provide more powerful semantic search capability? The answers to such questions will impact the future of P2P architectures.

Is P2P = Piracy?

P2P is not the first technological innovation to have its initial success due to somewhat less than ideal use. If P2P file sharing had from the start included ways for content owners to obtain licensing revenue, the role of P2P as a transformational technology would not have been obscured by the piracy association. Certainly, methods exist for protecting licensed content that can be applied in P2P file-sharing systems.

Consequently, we believe P2P is a disruptive technology that has important legitimate uses. In the case of music file sharing, early P2P systems demonstrated a large market for a new distribution model and new business model. This new distribution model uses global search, exchange of content directly between end users, high-quality audio, the capability to select individual tracks, and the ability to use the content on a variety of personal devices. Further, this distribution model is not restricted to content provided by the major labels. It is a low-barrier-of-entry means for independent artists and others to publish content for consideration by a wide audience, without the requirement to go through a music publisher. As for the business model, payment for indefinite personal use of track playback is widely accepted. Subscription models have shown viability. Others such as ad-driven models are in trial phases.

P2P Strengths and Benefits

Much of this book discusses the details of designing P2P applications and overlays. As a prelude to that, we should consider the benefits as well as the limitations of building and deploying an application using the P2P approach versus conventional client/server or Web-based approaches. Naturally, P2P might not be the best choice in many cases.

A P2P overlay is a collection of distributed networked hosts whose resources are available for use by the P2P applications associated with the overlay. These resources include computation, network capacity, and file storage. While their host is connected to the overlay, each end user shares in the cost of operating the overlay. This *cost sharing* by the participants lowers the barrier of entry to overlay providers. The *low barrier of entry* means that little hardware or network investment is needed to launch a P2P application.

As discussed earlier, the P2P architecture is inherently self-scalable, since each new peer adds additional capacity to the system. However, the developers of early P2P applications soon discovered that not all peers have equal capacity to contribute. For example, the host might be relatively limited in terms of CPU speed and memory capacity. Or the host might be behind a firewall, making it difficult for that peer to participate in the routing algorithm of the overlay. Or the host might be used for other applications that consume much of the available capacity. Consequently, some designs have organized peers into different categories depending on their capacity and reliability. The more capable or *super peers* might perform all the overlay operations, whereas the less capable peers play a more limited role.

The self-scaling property by itself doesn't necessarily translate into good performance under heavy loads since the load might not be uniformly distributed across the overlay. To illustrate, consider the well-known phenomenon of *flash crowds* that occurs when a very popular item is first available at a Website. As word spreads about the availability of this new item, large numbers of users simultaneously try to retrieve it using their Web browsers. This creates a sudden and excessive load on the Web servers that provide the object. Examples of objects that cause flash crowds include major news stories or new music or video releases by popular artists.

Flash crowds and less dramatic uneven loading can also occur in P2P overlays. On the Web, one technique to redistribute the load is to use Web caches that are distributed around the Internet. Caches are placed along the request path for a Web page and contain copies of objects that have been recently retrieved. When a browser requests an object, the request is first routed to nearby caches. If the object is located there, it will be returned to the browser without the request ever reaching the Web server. Some P2P overlay designs use a similar approach by keeping copies of objects that have been retrieved at intermediate peers along the search path. When another request for the object is routed along the same path, the intermediate peer will return the object before the request reaches the original peer serving the object. As discussed later in Chapter 11, such techniques don't work in all overlays. In addition, as objects lose popularity, a method is needed to replace old infrequently referenced objects with newer more popular ones.

The typical peer lifetime in a P2P overlay is short and of unpredictable duration. The lifetime of each peer is subject to local decisions of the user and is outside the control of the overlay designer. To successfully operate, an overlay must compensate for the variability in peer membership and dynamic behavior of participating peers. A key parameter affecting the design is the average rate at which peers join and leave the overlay, or the *churn rate*. An important feature of P2P overlays is the ability to self-organize in the face of this dynamic behavior. We'll discuss self-organization further in Chapter 2.

Volatility in peer membership effects peer *reliability*, another important property of P2P overlays. In general, reliability improves with increased redundancy. For example, if copies of an object are placed at multiple unreliable peers, it is more likely for some searching peer to locate the object than if a single unreliable peer stores the object. Likewise, peers need to identify a set of neighbors for routing messages to the rest of the overlay. A larger neighbor set can be useful for increasing the likelihood that at least one peer is online when a message is to be sent. On the other hand, redundancy increases state and maintenance overhead. P2P overlays use techniques such as redundancy to provide reliability and improve load distribution.

Finally, as we discuss in Chapter 3, P2P overlays can mimic the social interconnections of large communities. This has the advantage of leveraging well-known social group structure and relationships in information searching and sharing. Also, the P2P model can operate in both Internet-scale and ad hoc networks such as those formed spontaneously when a group of friends join their devices together.

P2P Open Issues

The potential benefits of P2P applications have spurred many research papers and industry proposals for improving the basic mechanisms. Much of the remainder of this book presents many of these ideas in detail.

The assumption of altruistic peers is idealized. In practice, peers can be expected to behave according to their own best interests. Thus peers may contribute only the minimum level of their own resources needed to access the shared resources of the P2P overlay. Peer participation is of unpredictable duration. Peers are heterogeneous in terms of both network and system capacity, meaning that some sets of peers subsidize other peers. Peers are autonomous and some peers could behave maliciously—for example, masquerading under multiple identities or interfering with the operation of the overlay.

Without centralized control, it is difficult to validate peer identity and trustworthiness. Such validation is required for enforcement of overlay behavior and validation of transactions. However, central control is contrary to the P2P model and may lead to scaling problems. These issues are discussed in more detail in Chapter 14.

P2P ECONOMICS
The P2P Value Proposition

The attraction of P2P overlays for delivering Internet applications includes the potential size of the customer base, a low barrier of entry, and high scalability. A certain critical mass is needed, however, and latecomers have had difficulty displacing those applications with a popular following. The large potential size of the customer base is due directly to the penetration of personal computers and broadband Internet access worldwide.

In addition, in many cases consumers pay a flat rate to access the Internet and have excess capacity on their computers and access network. As long as the P2P application resource use stays below a threshold, the user is likely to perceive a negligible cost in terms of contributing computer and networking resources that would otherwise not be used.

> The *P2P value proposition* for the user is to exchange excess computational, storage, and network resources for something else of value to the user, such as access to other resources, services, content, or participation in a social network.

We further observe that the value of a P2P overlay grows as a function of the number of participating peers. This is an application of Metcalfe's law that states that the value of a telecommunications network is proportional to the square of the number of users of the systems. In this case the P2P overlay is a virtual telecommunications network.

Barrier to Entry

Compare the costs of the client/server model with the P2P model for launching a new network application. For a number of significant applications, the relative software complexity is comparable. For large user populations, client/server requires a server farm, that is, a set of server-class hosts maintained in a data center with sufficient network capacity to carry the aggregated traffic from all the clients to the servers. For fault tolerance, the server farm is typically replicated at multiple locations. The servers are managed to provide 24×7 service. The servers are also monitored for faults, security, and utilization versus capacity.

In the P2P model there are no server farms. The client machines or end systems contribute resources. Systems are not managed. Service quality may be low. In real P2P deployments, servers can be used to download the initial client software, support the bootstrapping of the P2P overlay, and provide user account registration. These servers are typically modest in terms of costs compared to the server farms.

Revenue Models and Revenue Collection

The largest P2P applications today are embedded in a custom P2P overlay. In this case there are three basic revenue-producing scenarios. First, end users can be directly charged for use of the application. An example is some of the services provided by Skype. Second, if the application enables use of other services or licensed content, per-transaction fees might be extracted from these providers or licensors. For example, if a VoP2P application is installed on a wireless handset, every VoP2P call over the wireless network provider might produce a royalty to the VoP2P application. Likewise, if the P2P application is used to obtain content licenses for shared content, the licensors might pay a fee per licensing transaction to the P2P application. Third, advertising can be embedded into the application so that using the application user interface leads to advertisement presentation to the end user.

The P2P overlay must be able to monitor such transactions, collect them, and report them to the overlay operator. These steps must be done in a reliable and secure way. Users should be able to review their transactions and dispute them.

If third parties are used to provide some of the services, the P2P overlay must mediate all transactions between the end user's peer and the third party's systems. Transaction collection could be done by specific peers deployed by the overlay operator or by hosts at well-known addresses. The mechanism must scale as the size of the overlay and the transaction rate grow.

In the future, the P2P overlay could operate as an application platform, analogous to Web hosting and application servers. The P2P overlay then is designed so that third-party services can be added to the overlay. These services can be revenue generating, with the P2P overlay operator receiving a percentage of the proceeds. Suppose Vendor V builds a software Service S that runs on a P2P platform. Any number of peers might deploy Service S for other peers to use. Let's assume that the peers are incented to deploy such services, for example, by getting a better grade of service or discounts on their own use of the service. For a pay-per-use service, each time a peer uses Service S anywhere on the P2P overlay, the transaction record must be captured and delivered to V and the P2P overlay operator. For a subscription service, the accumulated use by a peer must be likewise captured and periodically delivered to V and the P2P overlay operator. In either case, the identity of the peer using the service must be traceable and nonspoofable. The transaction records must be nonrefutable.

Both the P2P overlay and any third-party services could also generate revenue by offering grades of services in which service quality varies in proportion to the cost of the service grade. A P2P overlay could provide premium overlay operation using specially deployed peers that are located in high-bandwidth networks. The hosts for these peers could also be high capacity, with a high percentage of uptime. Peers that subscribe to the premium service must be able to restrict their own message routing to the premium peers in the overlay. Another approach is to introduce priority classes so that messages from peers in the higher-priority class receive priority treatment compared to lower-priority classes.

In conventional networks the distinction between quality-of-service (QoS) classes for different traffic requires a network mechanism to route by class of service and to police the traffic in the priority classes. There is typically a way to measure actual service quality provided and compare it with the service quality that was delivered. There may be financial penalties if service quality falls below agreed-on levels. For future P2P overlays to make such stringent guarantees will likely depend on coupling the P2P overlay QoS mechanisms with the underlying network QoS mechanisms.

P2P Application Critical Mass

The attractiveness of P2P applications is affected by the number of participating peers. If the number is small, the service choices may be unappealing for new users to join. A P2P file-sharing application with only hundreds or thousands of users would typically offer a more limited range of content choices than an application with millions of concurrent users. Likewise, a VoP2P application with a small community of users offers fewer buddies with which to communicate.

The concept of *P2P application critical mass* refers to the level of participation in a P2P application in which the scale of membership and activity is sufficient to make it self-sustaining, either in terms of membership stability or economic viability. When a P2P application is operating below critical mass, some means to continually draw new users at a faster rate than existing users leave the P2P application is needed. Two advantages of the early P2P applications are the novelty factor and relatively open landscape. The success of the leading entrants now makes it more difficult for new entrants to leverage the novelty and newcomer status.

The *bootstrap appeal factors* are those aspects of a P2P application that produce a magnetic effect on potential users to join the P2P application's community during its precritical mass stage. For file-sharing systems these factors have included free content, wide selection, and convenient access. For VoP2P, factors have included low-cost international calls, free Internet telephony, and high-quality audio. For P2PTV, access to out-of-region programming and convenience while traveling have been important. A challenge for P2P entrepreneurs is to identify the right set of appeal factors—more a social and marketing dimension than an engineering problem.

ANATOMY OF SOME P2P BUSINESS MODELS
VoP2P

Consider an imaginary VoP2P provider that offers free unlimited P2P voice calls for all users. The free services are a way to attract users who will then be willing to pay for additional services, such as peer to PSTN calls and voicemail, charged on either a pay-for-use or subscription basis. Let's consider the costs for operating this service in two parts: fixed and per service use. As shown in Table 1.1, the VoP2P provider needs to maintain some server infrastructure so that it can manage user accounts and provide the charged services such as voicemail. Most likely these servers are hosted in multiple data centers for redundancy. There is some

Table 1.1 Example Costs Borne by VoP2P Provider

Fixed Costs	Costs Per Service Use
Development and maintenance of P2P software	Data center network use for transaction collection
Bootstrap and login servers	Per-call-minute access via PSTN gateway
Servers to mediate access to worldwide PSTN gateways for peer-to-PSTN calls	
Voicemail storage on servers	

per-service use of these services, such as storage use and network traffic in the data center. For free unlimited P2P voice calls, the costs to the VoP2P provider are primarily fixed. The provider develops and maintains the application software and operates some server infrastructure for overlay bootstrap and user account management.

A user downloads the VoP2P application and installs it on his machine. Typically the user will stay connected to the VoP2P overlay when not making phone calls so that he can receive calls and view the status of her buddies. Since the peer host is online, the VoP2P overlay uses such hosts for relaying traffic between other peers. As discussed in Chapter 12, relays can reduce end-to-end delay and increase throughput—important for voice traffic, particularly for calls between continents. In addition, some peers are behind NATs and require some peer with a public network address to mediate the connections on its behalf. As part of the VoP2P overlay, the peer will also perform overlay message routing and maintenance.

Since some peers are acting as traffic relays, they are receiving and forwarding voice packets for peers that could be anywhere in the Internet. The traffic relay peers are those peers that are not behind firewalls—for example, some home networks or university networks. The network providers for these networks in which the relay peers are located bear traffic-related costs for this relayed traffic. In addition, almost all VoP2P traffic is carried over the Internet backbone, so these ISPs also incur traffic-related costs. In effect, some network operators are subsidizing VoP2P voice call traffic that would otherwise be carried over voice networks. In addition, those open networks tend to subsidize the relay traffic flows for peers in closed networks. These costs are summarized in Table 1.2.

If all peers were behind NATs, the VoP2P overlay would have to provide its own servers to act as traffic relays and NAT traversal mediators. The number of servers needed to do this could be large. The relay peers are contributing disproportionately to the operation of the VoP2P overlay.

Today, VoP2P traffic is a small percentage of worldwide voice calls. The proportion of voice calls to other Internet traffic is relatively small. If VoP2P call volume grew to 50% of worldwide voice calls, the costs of network providers would increase substantially, and the economics of the PSTN might be effected as well.

Table 1.2 Example Costs Borne by Peers and Network Providers

Costs Borne by Peers	Costs for Network Providers
Traffic relaying by superpeers	Relayed traffic carriage in access networks
NAT traversal mediation by superpeers	VoP2P traffic carriage in backbone network
Traffic from originated or terminated calls	

File Sharing

Next consider a hypothetical P2P music file-sharing service, which supports free content and licensed content with legitimate access models for both. The free content could include song previews, songs licensed for a limited number of playbacks, or songs that are freely released to advertise a new artist or new album. The licensed content could include content in which a license must be acquired or content with embedded advertisements that produces advertising revenue for the content owner each time the song is played.

Suppose all the content is protected with encryption. Then a peer may freely distribute the media to any other peer, but playback of the media requires a license that includes the decryption technique. Figure 1.7 shows the initial acquisition of the content and license. A media distributor and licensor may operate separately from the P2P overlay to which Peer 1 belongs. Peer 1 obtains the media and a license for Peer 1's use of the media. Later Peer 1 can distribute the media to other peers. The ability to freely distribute protected media is referred to as superdistribution.

Many other peers may be interested in having this content, and these peers can share the content files without returning to the media distributor (see Figure 1.8A). If a license file is required to play the content, each peer can obtain

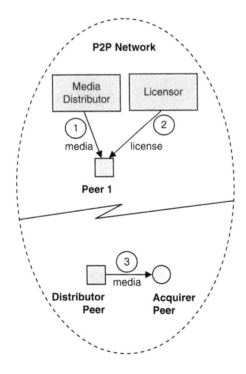

FIGURE 1.7 Licensed media acquisition for P2P redistribution.

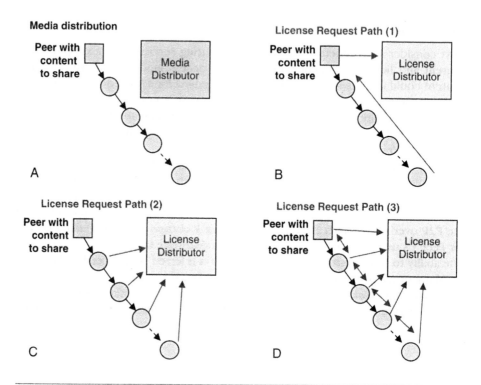

FIGURE 1.8 P2P superdistribution scenarios: (A) Media path and (B–D) license request paths.

a peer-specific license by either sending a request back through the distribution chain (Figure 1.8B), directly to a license distributor (Figure 1.8C), or opportunistically (Figure 1.8D). Prior to purchase of the license, there could be different policies for use of the protected content:

- None
- Unlimited use up to an expiration time
- A limited number of uses
- Preview only
- Compulsory advertisement per each use
- Offline use permitted until device connects to network which reaches content distributor; user must then either obtain license or pay for any usage done while offline

As in the previous example, we divide the costs of the P2P file-sharing provider into fixed and per service (Table 1.3). In addition to the costs for developing the application software and managing users on the P2P overlay, the provider needs additional capability to populate media files into the overlay and to

Table 1.3 Example Costs Borne by P2P File-Sharing Provider

Fixed Costs	Costs Per Service Use
Development and maintenance of P2P software	Data center network use for transaction collection
Bootstrap and login servers	Per-playback advertisement-viewing collection
Servers to access media files at media distributors' servers and push these media files into the P2P overlay	
Servers to integrate advertisements into media files	

integrate advertisements into the content. These functions could also be performed by other peers as well. The provider also needs to collect transaction records so that the provider's share of license revenue can be verified. Likewise, the viewing of advertisements must also be tracked.

In addition to exchanging media files with other peers, peers may also store media files for which they have no particular interest, simply to enable easier locating of content by other peers. The storage of these files and the network traffic to upload and download these files to other peers are costs borne by each peer (Table 1.4). Content providers may still face lost revenue due to pirated content, and they require servers to perform the content distribution and licensing. Finally, network providers in both access networks and the backbone network bear costs for media file transfer and the overlay operation.

SOCIAL IMPACT

Like other Internet trends such as Web publishing, blogging, virtual worlds, and RSS feeds, P2P carries the perception of empowerment of the end user and

Table 1.4 Example Costs Borne by Peers, Content Providers, and Network Providers

Costs Borne by Peer	Costs for Content Providers	Costs for Network Providers
Storage of media files	Lost revenue due to pirated content	Traffic carriage in access networks for peers acting as media repositories
Remote peer traffic to store and retrieve media files	Servers to handle media file distribution and licensing	Media file transfer traffic carriage in backbone network

leveling of the playing field. Each peer represents a user who at some level is an equal member of the peer community formed by the P2P overlay. As a paradigm, P2P implies symmetry among all participants. This is a powerful association because it can be used in the application design to create a sense of community among the members. This social dimension may also motivate increased participation. P2P doesn't have an exclusive lock on this social orientation. Many Web storefronts have long used user recommendations and feedback to create a community experience. However, in most cases, transactions are still between the individual and the storefront, or at least mediated by the portal. The P2P paradigm can be used to enable direct and unmediated interactions in the P2P community, which might have both positive and negative consequences.

Users who adopt this P2P paradigm may experience a sense of community and may be motivated at the social level to contribute to this community. Intuitively, it is possible to see how P2P systems can be used to create large communities of users. Many contemporary social networking sites also foster community. In most cases these communities are relatively small social groups that share common interests. Whether large P2P applications can catalyze large social communities remains to be seen. Factors such as the antisocial behavior of a minority and the anonymity of large groups that seem to foster such behavior as observed today in chat rooms and blogs are the kinds of impediments that might be difficult to overcome.

The P2P model is not restricted to applications such as file sharing and instant messaging. The P2P overlay can be separated from the specific application, similar to the principles of service-oriented architectures, and multiple applications could be delivered by one P2P overlay. Service-oriented P2P architectures have been proposed in which the overlay acts as a service delivery platform and in which each peer can offer specialized services to other peers. Peers seeking services use the overlay's search capability to perform *service discovery*. This is discussed further in Chapter 11. This potentially provides a new channel to deliver information and communication services. The potential for users to contribute new services is another kind of empowerment. Thus P2P is a vehicle for the end user to adopt the role of publisher and service offerer, not just a consumer role.

TECHNOLOGY TRENDS IMPACTING P2P

The question as to how the future adoption of P2P architectures evolves depends on the resolution of some of the technology issues raised earlier in this chapter. It also depends on trends in other technologies. Higher-capacity networks will enable larger-scale applications. Delivery of HDTV quality video over the Internet using techniques such as IPTV will likely spur the use of P2PTV approaches for delivery of HDTV.

The proliferation of broadband wireless networks and the increasing capacity of mobile devices means that in the future a large percentage of devices attached to the Internet could be mobile. Furthermore, many types of consumer electronics devices are likely to be network capable as well.

The emergence of pervasive sensor grids for a wide range of applications such as weather prediction, environmental monitoring, and safety and protection of society are another important trend. P2P networking may be a useful tool for coordinating and adapting the operation of such grids. Other interesting new P2P applications may emerge due to increasing availability of position and location-sensing devices such as GPS receivers.

SUMMARY

P2P is a disruptive technology for deploying applications that scale to millions of simultaneous participants. Because each user contributes computer and networking resources, it offers a low-barrier-of-entry platform with high scalability. Extensions to the basic model could offer different grades of service as well as address limitations of the basic model. These limitations are due to the decentralized character of the overlay and the unreliability of the peers.

As a disruptive technology, P2P raises important questions about the long-term impact on other approaches for video delivery, telephony, and other information delivery services. In addition, P2P applications to date have been primarily adopted in the consumer space. Requirements for further growth such as manageability, security, or ability to generate revenue may in the near term require hybrid variations of the basic model.

Today, deployed P2P applications demonstrate that it is feasible to launch an entry-point application at a low cost-quality operating point. As the application adoption grows, new services can be added and pricing can include service quality differentiation. The ability to incorporate reliable and secure transactions is still nascent.

FURTHER READING

The key ideas of P2P overlays can be seen as the confluence of a number of earlier concepts, including distributed systems, peer-to-peer protocols in local area networks (LANs), and specialized overlays developed for network services such as email and Internet relay chat (IRC). Consumer device technologies such as Universal Plug and Play (UPnP)[7] and Bluetooth enable devices to network peer to peer in a limited area. Because of the networking techniques used in these systems, they don't scale beyond home or personal area networks.

Clark et al.[1,2] have examined the impact of overlays on the technology and business of the Internet. Peterson et al.[3] present the benefits of network virtualization achievable through overlays.

The potential application of P2P search to Web search has been discussed by Li et al.[4] and Suel et al.[5]

Several industry consortia promote P2P technology, including the Peer-to-Peer Universal Computing Consortium (PUCC)[8] and the Distributed Computing Industry Association (DCIA).[9]

Peer-to-Peer Concepts

Looking beyond the popular P2P applications surveyed in the previous chapter, here we present a forward-looking view of the operation of a P2P system, where P2P encompasses mobile and other consumer electronics devices. We then discuss the principles of P2P overlays, such as self-organization and peer autonomy. Then we provide a sequence of sections giving various perspectives on the P2P model, including a graph theoretic perspective, a design space perspective, a routing performance perspective, and an implementation perspective.

OPERATION OF A P2P SYSTEM

The User View

A user downloads P2P application software from a Website on the Internet and installs it on his personal computer. Let's assume that the computer is connected to the Internet via a broadband connection. After the application is launched, it attempts to connect to certain hosts on the Internet that are configured in the software for bootstrapping purposes. It uses these connections to find other peers to connect to so that it can join the overlay. Initially it makes a few connections, gradually adding other connections. It may periodically change existing connections to new peers if the original peers leave the overlay or are unresponsive, or if the new peers provide better access to portions of the overlay.

Even if the user hasn't initiated any file searches or selected local files for sharing, the P2P application is most likely using the computer and its network connection for other peers. It may be responding to search requests from other peers or acting as a bootstrap peer for newly joining peers. It may be caching popular files on its disk drive to save search time for other peers. It could be proxying connections on behalf of peers that are behind firewalls. The user might not be aware of this use of his computer, or he might notice that the system is more heavily loaded now that the peer software is running. Network connections might appear slower. However, the details of how the P2P application uses the local machine and its resource, including what other peers are accessing its resources, are generally hidden from the user.

Later, when the user starts searching for files on the P2P network or publishes his own files for sharing with others, the P2P application will send messages to other peers to which it is connected. These messages may be further propagated to other peers if needed. The messages can contain search requests or carry information about the files the peer is sharing.

P2P Beyond the Desktop Computer

Though the majority of P2P applications today are running on desktops, the use of P2P technology is not restricted to desktop computing. In fact, P2P appears to be an even better fit for the capabilities and usage patterns of networked consumer electronics (CEs). For example, Figure 2.1 illustrates a P2P scenario involving streaming media with peercasting of live video to a set of different viewing devices.

On a limited scale, P2P is already being used for such personal devices. Because P2P means that a user's personal devices can interoperate without requiring a server, it is attractive to many consumers. Several industry specifications have been developed for devices to connect peer to peer and to share resources and services. For example, the Universal Plug-and-Play (UPnP) standard[12] defines protocols for devices in the home network to directly advertise their services to other devices and for other devices to discover and use these services. Bluetooth[13,14] is another standard for wireless devices to locate other devices and share services.

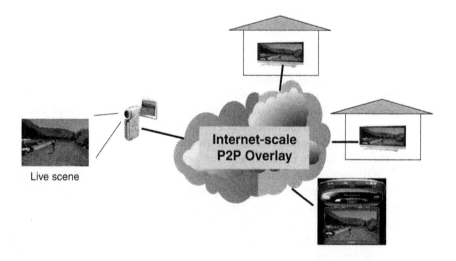

Live scene

FIGURE 2.1 A P2P streaming scenario involving networked consumer electronics devices as peers.

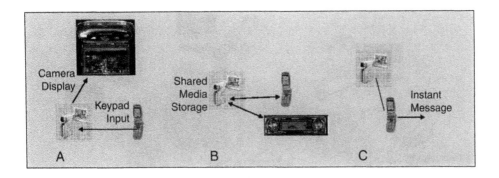

FIGURE 2.2 Peer-to-peer device composition.[15]

Sharing services between devices can expand the capability of the device without changing its form factor or cost (Figure 2.2). For example, the keypad of one device (Figure 2.2A) might be a more capable way of controlling a second device while displaying its output on a third device with a larger screen. Using local P2P connections, devices can also share storage (Figure 2.2B) or services such as instant messaging (Figure 2.2C).

Specifications such as UPnP and Bluetooth focus on home networks and near-field networking. In local area networks, peer-to-peer functions can be performed using existing broadcast protocols. But such protocols don't scale beyond local networks. If such protocols could be made to work in wide area networks, what kinds of capabilities would result? Applications that involve wide area networks include remote-to-home device control, wide area resource sharing, and location-based services. In remote-to-home device control, a consumer roaming outside the home uses a personal mobile device to connect to her home network and access information and services there. A consumer could retrieve video, photos, or music stored on the home media server or could control the home environment remotely.

In wide area sharing, a consumer accesses other device resources anywhere on the Internet. For example, let's say that a user scheduling a recording on a home personal video recorder (PVR) has a scheduling conflict (Figure 2.3). Is there a PVR elsewhere that could be used remotely to record the desired program? PVRs that are available advertise their availability and services using a wide area P2P network. When a program scheduling request occurs, the busy PVR discovers the available PVRs using a P2P discovery mechanism, schedules the recording request, and later obtains the media. If the media format needs to be converted to a specific format, other peers can perform the transcoding, again located using P2P advertisement and discovery.

In location-based services, a consumer uses a personal mobile device to access services and resources according to their geographic position. The services could be in the immediate vicinity, along a planned travel route, or in a specific area,

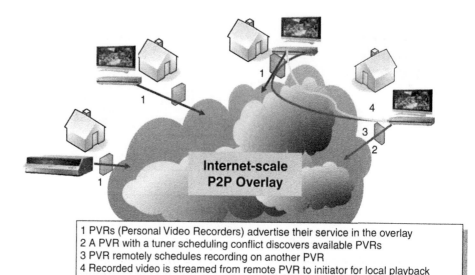

1 PVRs (Personal Video Recorders) advertise their service in the overlay
2 A PVR with a tuner scheduling conflict discovers available PVRs
3 PVR remotely schedules recording on another PVR
4 Recorded video is streamed from remote PVR to initiator for local playback

FIGURE 2.3 P2P sharing of PVR and media services in wide area networks.[16]

such as California wine country or Broadway in New York City. As we discuss in Chapter 11, location-based discovery uses geographic position or geographic area as one of the search criteria.

Overlay View

Let's assume that a device's capabilities are sufficient for it to participate in broadband networks, connect to the Internet, and support the message rates prevalent in P2P applications. Then how would such a wide area P2P network work? How is the network formed? How does it maintain its connectivity in the face of membership changes? How do applications use it for application purposes?

Initially there could be a small number of devices available to form a P2P network, but no P2P network is yet formed. At this stage we encounter the *bootstrap* problem. If there is no wide area P2P network, then, since these peers may be widely distributed on the Internet, they need some other way to discover each other and form the initial overlay. Possible ways of doing this include using a well-known server to register the initial set of peers, using a well-known multicast group address for peers to join, or using local broadcast to collect nearby peers, followed by progressively merging these peer sets into larger sets until the overlay is formed.

Once a sufficient set of peers are interconnected, then the *overlay* is formed. The overlay is a logical layer for message delivery between peers. If two peers aren't directly connected, they can use the overlay routing mechanism to send messages to each other indirectly via other peers. There is a wide range of schemes to organize the overlay. These schemes vary by how much state each peer has to keep, how much message overhead is needed to stabilize the overlay, and the message delivery performance that the overlay provides.

Peers are autonomous and may leave the overlay at any time. New peers may join the overlay. Fluctuations in overlay membership may ripple through the overlay, changing overlay peer relationships. For example, peers may change their adjacencies and neighbors in the overlay due to membership changes. The coordinated management of overlay routing state among the peers is called *overlay maintenance*. Since the peers are collectively coordinating the management of the overlay routing behavior without the use of a centralized overlay manager, P2P overlays are *self-organizing*.

Some peers store information or content that other peers would like to access. Peers search the overlay for the information of interest, perhaps using keywords. P2P search is different from Web search. Web search engines index a large number of Websites and store the indexed text in a set of servers that are then queried by users. In P2P search, the index itself is distributed across the entire P2P overlay. A query must be routed to the correct peer. Efficient search query routing is an important aspect of P2P design.

Overlay routing of messages and search are the building blocks for constructing many types of P2P applications. In the next section we discuss the principles of P2P overlays. Then we provide a sequence of sections giving various perspectives, including a graph theoretic perspective, a design space perspective, a routing performance perspective, and an implementation perspective.

PRINCIPLES OF THE P2P PARADIGM

A *peer-to-peer overlay* is a distributed collection of autonomous end-system computing devices called *peers* that form a set of interconnections called an *overlay* to share resources of the peers such that peers have symmetric roles in the overlay for both message routing and resource sharing. The P2P overlays of interest in this book have several inherent characteristics that we treat as the principles of the P2P paradigm: self-organization, role symmetry, resource sharing, scalability, peer autonomy, and resiliency.

The peers *self-organize* the overlay. Self-organization is a characteristic of many physical and social systems such that the organization of the system increases without being controlled by an encompassing agent or the environment. An overlay network design that is consistent with self-organization would not use a star topology or a broadcast topology to operate the peers or form the overlay. Instead the topology is likely to be decentralized such that the interconnectedness of any peer, referred to as the *degree*, doesn't dominate the overlay graph. Further, self-organization means that peers cooperate in the formation and maintenance of the overlay, with each peer using local state and partial information about the overlay.

The peers have *symmetric roles*. In contrast to client/server computing, where the roles of the endpoints are asymmetric, peers are functionally equal. Any peer can store objects on behalf of other peers, support queries, and perform routing of messages. In practice this idealized property is affected by peer lifetimes, variations of peers' hardware and network capacity, and networking issues such as Network Address Translation (NAT) that are discussed in Chapter 6. The relaxing of a strict interpretation of role symmetry has led to hierarchical schemes such as superpeers, as discussed in Chapter 5. Similarly, bandwidth capacity variations have led to proposals for variable-hop overlays, which are discussed in Chapter 13.

Peer-to-peer overlays are highly *scalable*. Several P2P applications operate today with millions of peers participating. An important dimension of scalability is the ability to operate the P2P overlay as the size grows by 100 times or more. Quantitatively, scalability means that the network and computing resources used at each peer exhibit a growth rate as a function of overlay size that is less than linear. The overlay should also scale geographically so that peers throughout the Internet can participate. Another key aspect of scalability is graceful degradation. As the performance limits of the overlay are reached, service levels fall off gradually. Early designs for some P2P applications that used controlled flooding were not scalable, because the message traffic grows exponentially with the number of peers.

Peers are *autonomous*. Each peer determines its capabilities based on its own resources. Each peer also determines when it joins the overlay, what requests it makes to the overlay, and when it leaves the overlay. Peer autonomy leads to unpredictability in the services offered by the overlay. A peer that searches for an object and doesn't find it might not be able to determine whether the object doesn't exist in the overlay or the peer storing the object has left the overlay. Peers may act to limit their resource contribution to the overlay, for example, by disconnecting from the overlay when not using it. Design techniques to counteract unpredictability include redundancy and incentives. Peer autonomy also means that peers may not have preexisting trust relationships. This exposes P2P overlays to a variety of security issues, discussed in Chapter 14.

A P2P overlay provides a *shared resource pool*. The resources a peer contributes include compute cycles, disk storage, and network bandwidth. There is a minimum resource contribution threshold for a peer to join the P2P overlay. Each peer's resources are used to support the operation of the overlay and provide application services to other peers. Resource contribution should be *fair*. A fair resource-sharing criteria might be that peer resource contribution never exceeds a certain bound. Another criteria might be that the average resource contribution of any peer should be within a statistical bound of the overall average of the P2P system. Resource contribution should be mutually beneficial. Users are incented to participate in P2P applications if the benefit is comparable to the resources being contributed. *Free riders* are peers who use the resources of the P2P overlay without contributing to the overlay. Nonuniform popularity of resources may lead to an imbalanced load on peers.

Peer-to-peer overlays are *resilient* in the face of dynamic peer membership, referred to as *churn*. Since peers have an incomplete view of the overlay topology and peer membership, the overlay depends on intermediate peers to forward messages to the correct region of the overlay. When peers leave or join the overlay, the routing paths are affected. The overlay graph structure or geometry contributes to resilience by enabling connectedness in the topology despite peer node changes. The graph structure provides multiple paths between every pair of endpoints. The connectivity of the graph is reflected at each peer in terms of its adjacencies to other peers. As the peer membership changes, adjacent peers have incorrect adjacency information. Mechanisms referred to as *overlay maintenance* are used to keep the peer state refreshed.

The principles of P2P overlays are generally not completely satisfied in any single system. Hybrid P2P systems may relax one of more these design goals. Some systems use central servers to authenticate peers; after peers are authenticated, the overlay itself operates without the central server. Improving the design of P2P overlays is an active area of research.

A GRAPH-THEORETIC PERSPECTIVE

Overview

We introduce a graph-theoretic notation to provide additional clarity to some concepts and terminology. In parts of several later chapters, a graph-theoretic view is helpful to explain functions such as overlay multicasting, mobility, and security that depend on the semantics of the overlay.

Another use of this section is as a step toward proving certain aspects of an overlay algorithm. Examples include:

- *Stability.* Does the rate of change of state of the peers follow the rate of membership change?
- *Convergence.* Is a message guaranteed to reach any peer in a bounded number of steps? Does the routing state stay within a certain accuracy bounds?
- *Boundary conditions.* At what churn rate does the algorithm become unstable or nonconvergent?

These questions are difficult to answer in general and have been studied in most cases for specific algorithms.

Overlay

A P2P overlay can be viewed as a directed graph $G = (V, E)$, where V is the set of nodes in the overlay and E is the set of links between nodes. Nodes are located in a physical network, which provides reliable message transport between nodes. Each node p has a unique identification number pid and a network address nid. An edge (p,q) in E means that p has a direct path to send a message to q; that is, p can send a message to q over the network using q's nid as the destination. It is desirable that G be a connected graph. Maintaining connectedness and a consistent view of G across all nodes is the job of the overlay maintenance mechanism.

Due to peers joining and leaving the overlay, the overlay graph G is dynamic. As an approximation (Figure 2.4), we say that the overlay proceeds through a temporal sequence $G_i(V_i, E_i)$, $G_{i+1}(V_{i+1}, E_{i+1})$, $G_{i+2}(V_{i+2}, E_{i+2})$, ... When a peer p' joins G_i at time i, the overlay join operation causes the overlay to become $G_{i+1}(V_{i+1}, E_{i+1})$, where $V_{i+1} = V_i \cup \{p'\}$ and $E_{i+1} = E_i \cup \{(p', m)\} \cup \{(n, p')\}$. That is, the join operation adds p' to the set of nodes and adds at least one incoming and at least one outgoing link between p' and some other node in the overlay. Likewise, when a peer p' leaves G_i at time i, the overlay join mechanism causes the overlay to become $G_{i+1}(V_{i+1}, E_{i+1})$, where $V_{i+1} = V_i - \{p'\}$ and $E_{i+1} = \forall m, n\ E_i - \{(p', m)\} - \{(n, p')\}$. That is, the leave step removes p' from the set of nodes and removes all incoming and outgoing links between p' and the remaining nodes in the overlay.

We treat overlay membership operations *join* and *leave* as part of the overlay maintenance mechanism. Peers p and q are adjacent in the overlay if they have an edge (p,q) or (q,p) in E. A join or leave operation by peer p directly affects peers to which p is adjacent and may indirectly affect the state of other peers. That is, there is a direct effect on node q if (q,p) is added to q's routing table as a result of p joining the overlay, or if (q,p) is removed from q's routing table as a result of p leaving the overlay. If there is no direct effect on q, there may still be an indirect effect on q that causes it to change the organization or contents of its routing table. Overlay maintenance is the management of these changes through the exchange of information about G between peers.

Peers p and q are neighbors in the overlay address space if pid_p and pid_q have a successor or predecessor relationship. Such neighbors are used to store object replicas in some designs. In some designs, neighbors are also selected as special adjacent peers.

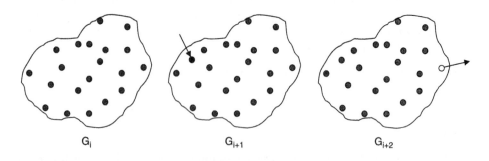

G_i G_{i+1} G_{i+2}

FIGURE 2.4 Overlay as a sequence of membership changes.

The preceding temporal sequence model of G is an approximation because it assumes that peer membership changes are sequenced and that the overlay maintenance for a specific membership change completes before the next join or leave begins. It is possible that several nodes may join or leave the overlay simultaneously. In a large overlay, it is usually the case that overlay maintenance operations due to a specific membership change will take an extended period of time and will overlap many other overlay maintenance operations. Also, if a large number of peers leave the overlay simultaneously, it could cause the overlay to form one or more partitions.

G is a global view on overlay node membership and routing. Each peer has a local view of overlay node membership and connectivity, which is its routing table. Ignoring dynamics, each peer has a routing table Rp (Vp, Ep) ⊆ G such that

$$Vp \subseteq V,$$
$$Ep \subseteq E,$$
$$Ep \equiv \forall (p,q) \in E \Rightarrow (p,q) \in Ep,$$
$$Vp \equiv \forall (p,q) \in E \Rightarrow q \in Vp \wedge \sim\exists q \in Vp \wedge (p,q) \notin E.$$

That is, p's routing table lists all nodes and edges to which it has a direct link. Each node entry in the routing table includes both its pid and nid. Given the approximated overlay dynamics (G_i, G_{i+1}, G_{i+2}, ...) previously stated, it is possible that two peers p′ and p″ could have routing tables that are out of sync not only with each other, that is, Rp″ ⊆ G_i and Rp″ ⊆ G_{i+1}, but also with respect to the current overlay state G_{i+n}. Further, Rp′ and Rp″ could have inconsistent views that are not subsets of any G_j. These inconsistent views are due to lack of global synchronization in the overlay and delays in propagating membership state changes throughout the overlay.

The routing procedure for peer p to send a message to some peer u is:

- If (p,u) ∈ Ep, then send the message directly to u.
- Otherwise, select one or more edges e = (p,q) from Ep according to a routing criteria that converges, that is, moves the message closer to the destination at each step.

Each edge from one peer to another peer that a message traverses in G is called a *hop*. Message path length from source to destination is frequently measured in terms of number of hops.

Graph Properties

Graph geometry affects routing performance, maintenance, and resiliency.[23,24,25,26] The graph geometry defines the basic static graph topology. Example geometries that have been used in various P2P overlay designs include rings, de Bruijin graphs, hypercubes, and butterflies. In Chapter 3 we discuss power-law graphs, random graphs, and the small-world model in the context of unstructured overlays. In this subsection we define several important graph properties.

The graph *diameter* is the maximum distance between any two nodes in the graph. From an overlay routing perspective, graph diameter provides a worst-case path length for sending a message between any two nodes in the overlay under static conditions. Consequently, graph diameter is an important parameter for comparing various geometries that might be used in an overlay.

Each peer in the overlay has a number of adjacent peers to which it has a direct connection. The number of such adjacencies is the *degree* of the peer. Outgoing degree is the number of adjacencies from the current peer to its neighbors. Incoming degree is the number of adjacencies to the current peer from its neighbors.

A *routing path* is the sequence of edges or hops from the peer sending the message to the peer which is the target of the message. The routing path is *recursive* (Figure 2.5A) if each successive peer along the path forwards the message to the next peer in the path. The routing path is *iterative* (Figure 2.5B) if each successive peer along the path replies to the sender with the next-hop information. The sender then forwards the message to the next hop. An iterative path, though less efficient than a recursive path in terms of number of messages, allows the sender to determine the progress of the delivery.

Object Storage and Lookup

A set of objects S is stored in the P2P overlay. Each object s has a unique identifier sid and a binding with the peer that stores it (p,s).

In a *distributed hash table* (DHT), the object ID space and the peer ID space are the same, and each peer p with predeccessor q is responsible for sids such that $pid_q < sid \leq pid_p$. On average, the number of objects p is responsible for is $|S|/|V|$. The DHT has at least two operations, insert(sid, s) and s = lookup(sid), which use key-based routing to store and retrieve objects in the DHT, respectively, according to their sid. In key-based routing, the object key or sid is used as the overlay address for the DHT messages. Thus an insert message with destination equal to sid_s is routed to that peer that is responsible for sid. Peers at intermediate hops forward the insert message using the sid as the destination address.

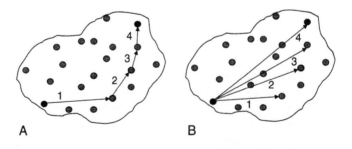

FIGURE 2.5 (A) Recursive and (B) iterative routing paths.

A DESIGN SPACE PERSPECTIVE

The designer of an overlay can view the design problem as selecting an operating point in a design space. Understanding the design space is important for finding solutions that might be advantageous for certain uses. Several researchers have proposed general-purpose frameworks or models. Here we'll follow the reference model proposed by Alima et al. later expanded in [20] and shown in Figure 2.6.

First there is an identifier space to which all object and peer IDs are mapped. The identifier space has size, an ordering relationship, a distance relationship, and an equality test. Since it is used for addressing, it must be efficient for storage and routing. The number of peers and resources that are represented in the identifier space could be very large, so it must be scalable. It must be location independent so that moving the device doesn't affect its addressability. For message routing to converge, the identifier space should support a metric such that at any position in the address space some distance to the target can be computed. At a minimum, this distance function should be 0 when the target is the same as the current node, and it should be greater than or equal to 0 if it is a different node.

As we discuss later in this chapter, the mapping of peers to the identifier space is important for locality properties of the overlay with respect to the underlying network. The mapping of peers to an identity in the identifier space is denoted by $F(P) \rightarrow I$. The mapping should be done so that each peer has a unique identity in the identifier space. Each peer is responsible for a subset of the identifier space. In practice, the usual approach is for a peer to cover the range down to its predecessor in the identifier space. If I_1, I_2, and I_3 are the identities of three adjacent peers, I_2 is responsible for the range $I_1 < I_2 \leq I_3$.

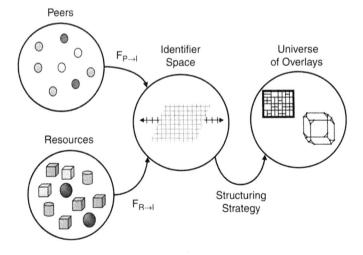

FIGURE 2.6 P2P reference model.

Mapping resources to the identifier space is done to facilitate discovery of those resources and is denoted by F(R) → I. A typical mapping scheme distributes resources randomly in the identifier space—for example, using a hash function. Other schemes could be used to produce locality or clusters for supporting range queries or enabling associative semantic search.

The overlay has *geometry*, the static structure of the graph. There is a wide range of possible geometries. Important properties guiding the selection of the geometry include the diameter of the graph, the connectedness of the graph, and the distribution of node degree across the nodes in the graph. The structuring strategy integrates the geometric model with a routing strategy and a maintenance strategy.

A ROUTING PERFORMANCE PERSPECTIVE
Routing Geometries and Resilience

The *overlay geometry* refers to the static model of the graph that the routing and maintenance algorithm constructs in the absence of churn. Such models have been widely studied in graph theory, and some examples are listed in Table 2.1, along with selected overlay algorithms Chord, CAN, and Pastry, which are described in Chapter 4.

Table 2.1 shows the degree and diameter for various graph models, where N is the size of the overlay. From this table we see that there are graph structures whose node degrees are independent of the size of the overlay and whose diameters grow more slowly as a function of overlay size than those of several proposed overlay designs.

For illustration, consider an overlay of 10^6 nodes. Table 2.2 compares the diameter of these same graph types for different values of k, the degree of each peer in the overlay. Looking at $k = 20$ row highlighted in the table, we see a substantial difference in the diameters of the graphs. Similar results hold for average distance in these graphs.

Table 2.1 Asymptotic Degree-Diameter Properties of Various Graphs[25]

Graph	Degree	Diameter
de Bruijin	k	$log_k N$
Trie	$k+1$	$2 log_k N$
Chord	$log_2 N$	$log_2 N$
CAN	$2d$	$\frac{1}{2} dN 1/d$
Pastry	$(b-1) log_b N$	$log_b N$
Classic butterfly	k	$2 log_k N(1-o(1))$

Table 2.2 Graph Diameter for an Overlay of 10^6 Nodes[25]

k	de Bruijin	Trie	Chord	CAN	Pastry	Classic Butterfly
2	20	—	—	huge	—	31
3	13	40	—	—	—	20
4	10	26	—	1,000	—	16
10	6	13	—	40	—	10
20	5	10	20	20	20	8
50	4	8	—	—	7	7
100	3	6	—	—	5	5

Note: — indicates that the graph does not support that node degree.

Tradeoff Between Routing State and Path Distance

If each peer had complete information about all other peers in the overlay, each P2P message would take at most one hop. However, all peers would need to maintain an O(N) routing table size, and each join and leave event would need to propagate to all other peers in the overlay, creating a large maintenance load. This maintenance load would grow with both the size of the overlay, N, and the churn rate. On the other hand, if a node knows only the link to its successor on a ring, routing state and maintenance load would be nominal but routing performance would be O(N).

Since neither of these two operating points is generally practical, there has been a great deal of interest in exploring the state versus overhead tradeoffs (Figure 2.7) of various algorithms. These tradeoffs are explored in detail in Chapters 4 and 5.

Churn and Maintaining the Overlay

The dynamic behavior of the peer population is an important aspect to the performance of the overlay. Peer lifetimes and arrival and departure rates can be assessed for existing overlays and used to evaluate new designs. Since P2P overlays are large and decentralized, such statistics are difficult to collect. Existing systems have been analyzed using crawlers. These measurements provide insights into peer behavior.

Overlay measurements have multiple uses for improving overlay design as well as for comparing designs. Uses include:

- Estimating the maintenance traffic needed to maintain the overlay routing state.
- Providing criteria such as previous session history and peer uptime, which can be used to determine which peers are likely to be long lived. Long-lived peers may be preferred by the overlay for certain roles (and thus elevated to

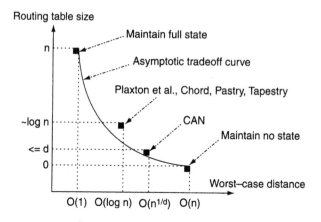

FIGURE 2.7 Asymptotic tradeoff between peer-routing table size and overlay diameter.[28] © 2003 IEEE.

superpeer) and may also be preferred by applications to render long-lived application services.

- Determining the data replication level to mitigate data loss.
- Determining path redundancy to mitigate routing failures.

Figure 2.8 shows the peer lifetime or session time distributions for three different file-sharing P2P applications: Gnutella, Kad, and BitTorrent. These distributions show a median peer lifetime of less than 1 hour and as little as 3 minutes. According to these measurements, as many as 2% of the peers will have a lifetime as long as one day.

Figure 2.9 shows measurements for the Skype P2P telephony application, which is discussed further in Chapter 12. These measurements were only collected for the Skype superpeers, that is, those nodes that, because they have more capacity and are not behind NATs, are able to act as relays for regular peers. Skype shows much longer median lifetime of about 5.5 hours. Since Skype is a personal communications application, users are motivated to stay connected for longer periods of time to receive calls. In typical file-sharing use, users download the desired content and then disconnect. About 1% of Skype supernodes have lifetimes exceeding eight days.

Figure 2.10 shows interarrival times for new peers joining two of the file-sharing systems used for measurements in Figure 2.8. Frequently an exponential distribution is assumed to model peer join rates. An exponential distribution is suitable for independent events that have a constant average rate of arrival. As Figure 2.10 shows, an exponential distribution doesn't fit the data well, possibly because the independence assumption is violated due to bursts of requests for a new release or temporal correlation.

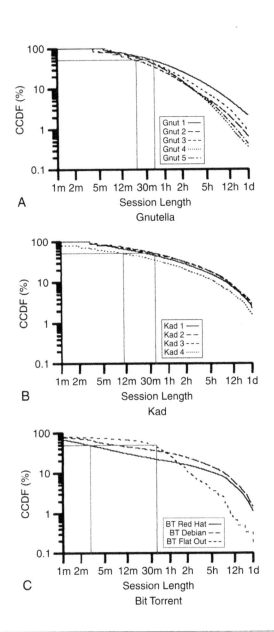

FIGURE 2.8 Peer session times for several file-sharing P2P applications.[18] © 2006 ACM, Inc. Reprinted by permission.

Locality

The performance of routing in the overlay is also strongly affected by the relation-

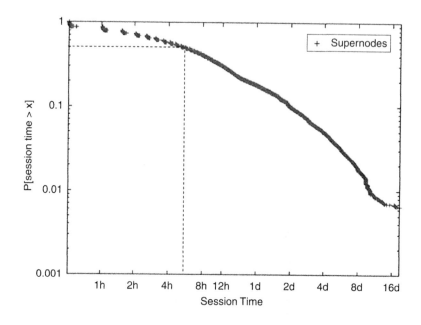

FIGURE 2.9 Session times for Skype superpeers.[29] © 2006 S. Guha, N. Daswani, and R. Jain.

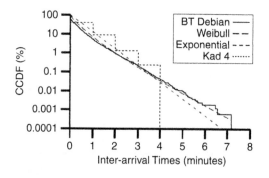

FIGURE 2.10 Interarrival times of peers joining BitTorrent and Kad, with corresponding exponential and Weibull distributions for comparison.[26] © 2006 ACM, Inc. Reprinted by permission.

considering the underlay, peers that are near in the overlay might be far away in the network. Consequently, each routing hop in the overlay might map to many network layer hops.

Figure 2.11 illustrates the difference between an overlay constructed with regard to the underlying network (Figure 2.11A) versus one that is not (Figure 2.11B). In general, assigning peers to the overlay according to their

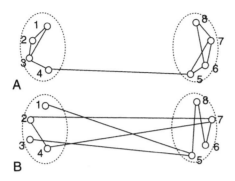

FIGURE 2.11 (A) Locality-aware overlay and (B) randomly connected overlay.[27] © 2004 IEEE.

position in the underlay will lead to much greater efficiency. However, it requires that network distance information be collected and may decrease reliability in designs that use neighbors to store replicas. Chapter 10 discusses measurement techniques needed to determine node locality.

AN IMPLEMENTATION PERSPECTIVE: OVERLAYWEAVER

OverlayWeaver[30] is an open-source P2P emulator and toolkit developed by Kazuyuki Shudo. It is designed for experimenting with peer-to-peer overlay algorithms and has an extensible design that is convenient for adding new routing algorithms. It includes a number of existing multihop overlay algorithms, including Chord, Pastry, Tapestry, and Kademlia.

OverlayWeaver runs on one or more computers and can be configured to emulate thousands of peers on each computer. Simple application behavior can be specified in text files called *scenario files*, which are loaded when the emulator is launched. Alternately, a developer can extend the behavior of OverlayWeaver by writing new Java classes. OverlayWeaver provides an API for the distributed hash table, which closely follows the design proposed in [31].

Figure 2.12 shows the architecture of OverlayWeaver. Specific routing algorithms are loaded by the routing driver and invoked using the routing runtime interface. The creation and parsing of messages between peers is handled by the messaging service, which is also integrated with the routing driver. The specific routing algorithm being used is transparent to the application, which uses the DHT interface to insert and look up objects.

In addition to the functions shown in Figure 2.12, the OverlayWeaver design has a distributed emulation framework that automatically launches and interconnects multiple emulators across a network of machines. Running within each

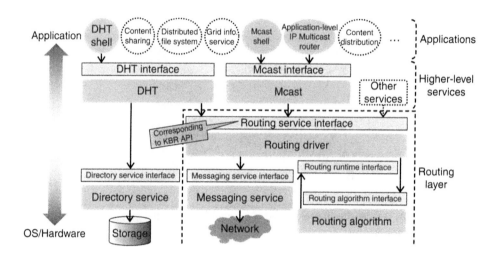

FIGURE 2.12 Architecture of OverlayWeaver emulator. Reprinted from [30], Copyright (2008), with permission from Elsevier.

emulator are one or more peers, as specified at startup time using scenario files. The peers use the usual virtual name space and overlay messaging, which is mapped by the emulation framework to the correct host and port on the network. Thus using OverlayWeaver it is possible to run thousands of peers on a small network of machines.

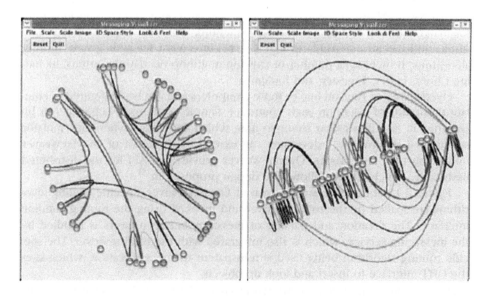

FIGURE 2.13 OverlayWeaver message visualizer tool. Reprinted from [30], Copyright (2008), with permission from Elsevier.

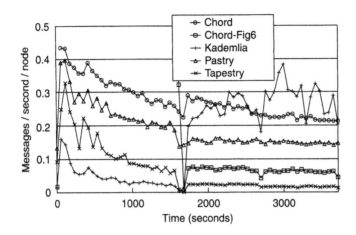

FIGURE 2.14 Message trace on a network of 196 computers running OverlayWeaver with various overlay algorithms. In this experiment, the first 1600 seconds are for overlay formation, and after 1600 seconds the remaining load is random *get* and *put* requests at 2-second intervals from each peer. Reprinted from [30], Copyright (2008), with permission from Elsevier.

OverlayWeaver also provides some tools for monitoring the operation of the overlay during an emulation session. Figure 2.13 shows screen shots of the message visualizer for small overlays of about 25 peers. Each node is a peer, and arcs between nodes are messages between those peers. The visualizer can be used to see routing patterns over time as the emulation runs.

Shudo et al. did an experiment (Figure 2.14) with OverlayWeaver on 196 computers. The message load shows an initial peak as the peers form the overlay and initialize their routing state. Peers join the overlay at intervals of 8 seconds, so the overlay is formed after about 1600 seconds. After the overlay is formed, each node randomly issues a DHT *get* and *put* request at 2-second intervals until the emulation completes.

SUMMARY

The idea of peer-to-peer communication has a long history with many interesting examples. The creation of self-organizing, decentralized, Internet-scale peer-to-peer overlays has a relatively short history but has garnered a significant amount of interest. The dynamic behavior of peers is perhaps the key factor complicating the optimization of P2P overlay design.

There are a number of ways to look at P2P overlays, from user to application developer, system designer, and researcher. Similarly, there are a variety of relevant conceptual, theoretical, and implementation perspectives to consider. In this chapter we have sampled some of the different perspectives for P2P overlays and laid some of the important conceptual foundations that will be needed in subsequent chapters.

FOR FURTHER READING

Schollmeier[17] presents definitions of peer-to-peer concepts. Various researchers have provided frameworks and reference models. Alima et al.[33] and Aberer et al.[20] define a P2P reference architecture that is discussed in Section 2.

Biskupski, Dowling, and Sacha[32] characterize self-organization in P2P systems. In their analysis, self-organizing systems exhibit properties of decentralization, localized consensus, and utility optimization. The mechanisms to achieve self-organization include partial views, feedback, decay, an evaluation function, and action selection. Many existing P2P systems including DHT designs are relatively static to be considered self-organizing in their model.

Graph-theoretic views of overlays are discussed further in Chapter 3, "Unstructured Overlays." Loguinov et al.[25] use a graph theoretic view of P2P overlays to evaluate overlay diameter and resilience. Other studies of overlay resilience include Gummadi et al.[23] and Wang, Xuan, and Zhao.[22] Kong et al. use a probabilistic failure model to develop the Reachability Component Model framework for evaluating overlay resilience.[24]

There has been growing realization that stochastic models of overlay churn and maintenance are more appropriate than analyses that start with a stable graph and use maintenance to repair it. This is due to the strong likelihood that large overlays never stabilize. An example stochastic analysis of Chord is found in [19]. This is discussed in Chapter 5.

A number of researchers have studied existing peer-to-peer systems for their dynamic characteristics. Stutzbach and Rejaie[18] use a particularly fast crawler, Cruiser, to collect measurements on three file-sharing P2P applications. They also provide a detailed analysis of the types of errors that occur in measuring large P2P systems.

Unstructured Overlays

Most deployed P2P applications have used unstructured topologies. Here we look at this important class of overlay in detail, starting with the basic routing mechanisms. Then we discuss the theory of various types of unstructured graphs such as random graphs, power-law random graphs, and scale-free graphs. Influential designs such as Gnutella, Freenet, Fastrack, and Gia are then discussed. Ideas from social networks, especially the small-world phenomenon, are related to unstructured topologies, and an overview of social overlays follows. The chapter concludes with a brief look at how an experimental overlay emulator implements its routing layer.

CONNECTING PEERS ON A GLOBAL SCALE

Envision a worldwide content-sharing system that permits any type of information to be discovered and shared among users. Of course, many file-sharing systems have been available for a number of years, but these existing systems—although highly popular—perhaps don't work optimally. It might be difficult to find specific files if the files are low in popularity, since there won't be many copies of the files in the network. The search request might take a long time to respond. Files that show up in the search might not be retrievable, because the host is no longer on the network. After retrieval the files might be found to be corrupted, truncated, or polluted. The use of the file-sharing software itself might lead to spyware or malware infesting a user's computer, and the performance of a user's computer and network connection might degrade substantially when connected to the file-sharing system. There could be a large number of matches to the search query, and it might be difficult to decide which version of the file is the best one to download. Information that a user wanted to share with only specific parties or under specific content-licensing terms might inadvertently be shared in an unrestricted fashion to all users of the file-sharing system.

These issues involve a variety of design dimensions, from security to distributed search and semantics or efficient and fair resource sharing. We can divide the problem into how the nodes interconnect (this chapter and next), how search criteria are specified and performed (Chapter 7), and how the system and its information are secured

45

(Chapter 14). In this chapter we look at the way file and similar information sharing works when the P2P application does not impose much if any structure on the interconnection of the peers. Such approaches are classified as *unstructured overlays*.

An important observation about the nature of information sharing in P2P applications compared to information delivery via the World Wide Web is that P2P involves primarily individuals as both information publishers and users. Thus there is a social dimension to P2P information sharing that is derived from the social relationships between the individuals who comprise the P2P system. These relationships might be explicit, as in sharing photographs with friends or family, or implicit, such as sharing based on common interests or common properties. Information sharing tailored according to common interests is successfully exploited by many recommender systems.

What are the important social relationships in information sharing, and how can they be exploited in a P2P system? More specifically, how can social relationships be reflected in the P2P interconnection structure? These social relationships might range from close friends with common interests, a small peer group with a shared common interest, or a larger community of interest to a large population in which subsets of individuals have common interests or social properties that are predictors of other information interests.

Another interesting question is, if nodes connect to other peers based on proximity in the network, as a result of successful queries, or based on social relationships, what kind of structure emerges? How does the number of nodes that are neighbor peers affect performance? What are the requirements for search on overlay topology, and how does topology affect various types of queries such as exact match, wildcard, range, and semantic lookup?

BASIC ROUTING IN UNSTRUCTURED OVERLAYS
Flooding and Expanding Ring

Let's assume that each peer keeps a list of other peers that it knows about. We can call these peers the *neighbors*. If neighbor relations are transitive, we have connectivity graphs such as the one shown in Figure 3.1A. In this particular graph, peers have between two and five neighbors in the overlay. The number of neighbors a peer has is called the *degree* of the peer. Increasing the degree of the peers reduces the longest path from one peer to another (the diameter of the overlay) but requires more storage at each peer.

Once a peer is connected to the overlay, it can exchange messages with other peers in its neighbor list. An important type of message is a query for specific information. The query contains the search criteria, such as a filename or keywords. Since we don't know which peers in the overlay have the information, we could try sending a query to every peer we know. If the neighbor peers don't have the information, they can in turn forward the request to their neighbors, and

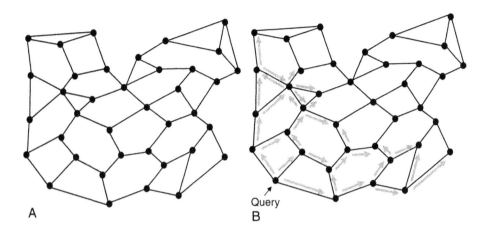

FIGURE 3.1 (A) Unstructured topology showing connections between peers and (B) query flooding to four hops.

so on. A few checks are needed to prevent messages from circulating endlessly. First, in case the message loops back or is received over more than one path, each peer can keep a list of message identifiers that it has previously received. If it sees the same message again, it simply drops the duplicate message. Second, so that peers don't have to remember messages for an arbitrary time, which would require a continuously growing amount of storage, each message has a time-to-live (TTL) value that limits its lifetime. The TTL value of a message is set by the message originator and decremented by 1 at each peer that receives the message. When the TTL value of a message reaches 0, it is no longer forwarded.

This simple query algorithm is called *flooding* (Figure 3.1B) and is shown in the following pseudo-code:

```
FloodForward(Query q, Source p)
    // have we seen this query before?
    if(q.id ∈ oldIdsQ) return // yes, drop it
    oldIdsQ = oldIdsQ ∪ q.id // remember this query
    // expiration time reached?
    q.TTL = q.TTL − 1
    if q.TTL ≤ 0 then return // yes, drop it
    // no, forward it to remaining neighbors
    foreach(s ∈ Neighbors) if(s ≠ p) send(s,q)
```

As mentioned earlier, each peer has a list of neighbors. It initializes its list of neighbors when it joins the overlay, for example, by getting a copy of the neighbor list of the first peer in the overlay that it connects to. Over time it can add and remove peers from its neighbor list. To refresh and update its neighbor list, it can send requests to current neighbors asking for their neighbors. It can also use queries from nodes it hasn't seen before to add to its neighbor list. It removes neighbors when they are unresponsive to keep-alive messages.

When the query is satisfied at some peer that receives the query message, a response message is sent to the requesting peer. If the object is found quickly, the flooding mechanism nevertheless continues to propagate the query message along other paths until the TTL value expires or the query is satisfied. Generally this creates substantial redundant messaging, which is inefficient for the network. One way to alleviate this redundant messaging is to start the search with a small TTL value. If this succeeds, the search stops. Otherwise, the TTL value is increased by a small amount and the query is reissued. This variation of flooding is called *iterative deepening*[77] or *expanding ring* and is particularly effective for significantly replicated objects. The pseudo-code for expanding ring is shown in Table 3.1 for both the peer sending the search request (left) and a peer receiving and forwarding a request (right).

If popular objects are frequently replicated throughout the overlay, the chance of finding a match to the query within a few hops is high. Objects that are sparsely placed in the overlay might not be found at all for some queries. The ability to guarantee that an object can be found if it exists in the overlay is an important feature for many applications and has motivated the structured overlay approach discussed in the next chapter. An alternate strategy taken in

Table 3.1 Pseudo-Code for Expanding Ring

Sending Peer	Forwarding Peer

ExpandingRingRequest(SearchTerm st)
    q.st = st
    q.TTL = minTTL // first try a small TTL
    // send search request to neighbors
    foreach(s ∈ Neighbors) send(s,q)
    // wakeup and do a retry if request fails
    lastTTL = minTTL
    setTimer(ERRequestRetry,100)
 	
ERRequestRetry()
    // have we exceeded the permitted TTL?
    // if so, then stop
    if (lastTTL > maxTTL) return
    // no, increase TTL and try again
    lastTTL = lastTTL + 1
    // send it to neighbors
    foreach(s ∈ Neighbors) send(s,q)
    // wakeup and do a retry if request fails
    setTimer(ERRequestRetry,100*
    (lastTTL-minTTL))
	ExpandingRingForward(Query q, Source p)
	    // is it an expansion of a previous query?
	    if(q.expansion = false) {
	        // no, have we seen this query before?
	        if(q.id ∈ oldIdsQ) return // yes,
	        drop it
	    }
	    // remember this query
	    oldIdsQ = oldIsQ U q.id
	    // expiration time reached?
	    q.TTL = q.TTL – 1
	    if q.TTL ≤ 0 then return // yes, drop it
	    // no, forward it to remaining neighbors
	    foreach(s ∈ Neighbors) if(s ≠ p) send(s,q)

unstructured overlays is to control the replication and placement of objects and the neighbor relationships to increase the likelihood of finding the objects. We discuss several approaches later in this chapter and describe overall search mechanisms in Chapter 7.

Random Walk

To avoid the message overhead of flooding, unstructured overlays can use some type of random walk. In random walk (Figure 3.2A), a single query message is sent to a randomly selected neighbor. The message has a TTL value that is decremented at each hop. If the query locates a node with the desired object, the search terminates and the object is returned. Otherwise the query fails, as determined by a timeout or an explicit failure message returned by the last peer on the walk. The initiating peer has the choice to reissue a query along another randomly chosen path. To improve the response time, several random walk queries can be issued in parallel (Figure 3.2B).

The key step in random walk is the random selection of the next hop, which avoids forwarding the query back to the node from which the query was received. The pseudo-code for RandomWalk follows:

```
RandomWalk(source, query, TTL)
    if (TTL > 0) {
        TTL = TTL − 1
        // select next hop at random, don't send back to source
        while((next_hop = neighbors[random()]) == source)
        send(source, query,TTL)
    }
```

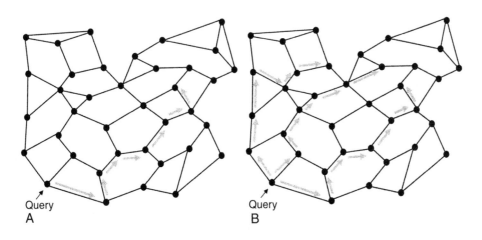

Query
A

Query
B

FIGURE 3.2 (A) Random walk and (B) k-way parallel random walk, k = 3.

UNSTRUCTURED TOPOLOGY CONSIDERATIONS
Types of Unstructured Graphs

As observed in Chapter 2, an overlay can be viewed as a graph in which peers are vertices and edges are overlay connections. Generally the approach used by an unstructured overlay to collect and maintain its neighbors affects important properties of the graph formed by the overlay. These properties include the degree distribution of nodes in the graph, which effects load distribution, and the diameter of the graph, which affects the hop count in query routing. Graph properties for networks found in many different phenomena—ranging from manmade networks such as the Internet and the hyperlink topology formed by the World Wide Web to social networks, epidemics, and physical systems—have been extensively studied. Surprisingly, there are important classes of graphs that can describe a large range of such real-world phenomena. As interest in the behavior and performance of overlay networks have grown, these graph models have naturally been used to assess the design of overlays. In particular, *random graphs* and *scale-free* or *power-law random graphs* are relevant to most unstructured topologies. In this section we very briefly summarize some of the key points about these models, and the reader is referred to [48] for a comprehensive recent discussion.

In addition, most P2P applications can be described in terms of social interactions and can be related to the social properties of the participating users. Consequently, properties of *social networks* have attracted the interest of P2P overlay designers. The *small-world model* is a well-known result related to social networks proposed by the psychologist Stanley Milgram[40] to explain degree of separation in society.

Random Graphs

A *random graph* is formed for a given set of vertices by adding edges between pairs of vertices chosen uniformly at random. The random graph $G_{n,p}$ is a class of random graphs in which p is the probability of an edge existing between any two vertices, independent of any other edge in the graph, and $1-p$ is the probability of the absence of an edge between any two vertices. Since the number of edges in $G_{n,p}$ is $n(n-1)p/2$, the average degree of a node in $G_{n,p}$ is approximately np.

Although random graphs are important for their analytical properties, they have been found to differ from real-world networks in two important ways. First, real-world networks exhibit clustering. *Clustering* is a property of a network such that two nodes are more likely to have an edge if they have a common neighbor. This can be measured using the clustering coefficient,[39] which is the probability of vertex clustering averaged over all pairs of vertices in the graph. In random graphs, edges are independently formed between nodes, so the value of the clustering coefficient is p, the probability of an edge being selected between two

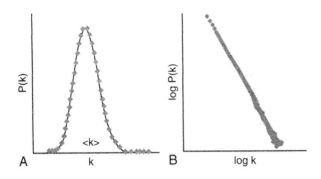

FIGURE 3.3 Node degree distribution for (A) a random graph and (B) a power-law graph.[64]
© 2001 Physics World.

nodes. In many real networks, the clustering values range from a few percent to as much as 50%.[35]

Second, the distribution of node degrees for most real-world networks follows a power-law function, meaning that a small portion of nodes have very large degree. Figure 3.3 shows the node degree distribution for a random graph (Figure 3.3A) and power-law graph (Figure 3.3B). The distribution for the random graph has a Poisson distribution with mean at $k = <k>$ and decays exponentially for large k. The distribution for the power-law graph does not have a peak and decays as a power law, $P(k) \sim k^{-\gamma}$. Such networks are also referred to as *scale-free* networks, a term introduced by Barabási and Albert.[36] *Scale-free* refers to the behavior of functions that satisfy the form $f(ax) = g(a)f(x)$, that is, an increase in the scale of x doesn't affect the density of $f(x)$ [42].

For a P2P overlay, scale-free networks offer the possibility that as the network becomes very large, it will still have very short diameter due to clustering, the existence of a small number of nodes with very high degree, or a few long-range connections. This property can be very important to limiting the hop count of query routing in unstructured overlays, provided it can be leveraged in the routing mechanism. For example, Figure 3.4 visually compares the level of reachability for a random graph and a scale-free graph with the same number of nodes and edges. The nodes with the largest degrees in each graph are effectively hubs that can be used to route to larger portions of the network. The five largest hubs in the random graph (Figure 3.4A) connect to 27% of the graph, whereas the five largest hubs in the power-law graph (Figure 3.4B) connect to 60% of the graph.

Power-Law Random Graphs

Given the benefits of scale-free graphs, we might ask what mechanisms could be used to construct the overlay organization to produce and maintain the power-law degree distribution. Further, how does such an overlay organization

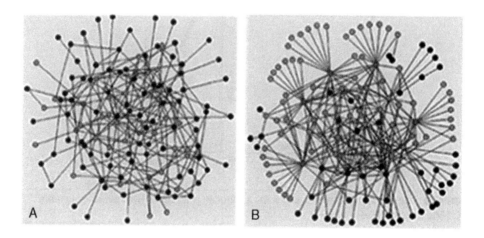

FIGURE 3.4 (A) A random graph and (B) a power-law graph. Each graph contains 130 nodes and 430 links. In each graph, the five nodes with the highest degree are depicted in white, and those nodes directly reachable from the white nodes are depicted in grey.[64] © 2001 Physics World.

interact with query routing, node capacity, object placement, and peer relationships?

Barabási, Albert, and Jeong[37] identified two characteristics of real-world networks to explain the occurrence of scale-free networks. First, most networks grow over time by connecting to existing nodes in the network. Second, new nodes tend to form connections with existing high-degree nodes, a property they refer to as *preferential attachment*. However, other competing explanations have also been proposed.

Adamic et al. analyzed two search strategies in power-law graphs, comparing random walk with query routing biased toward high-degree nodes. Biasing the query routing toward high-degree nodes outperforms random walk in terms of both search time and coverage of the overlay (Figure 3.5).

Scale-Free Graphs and Self-Similarity

Power-law, scale-free networks have received wide-spread attention because of their apparent universal applicability to a wide range of domains, yet there have been some criticisms of their use as models due to lack of precision in formulating the key properties of such graphs and questions as to their applicability to engineered systems such as the Internet.[34]

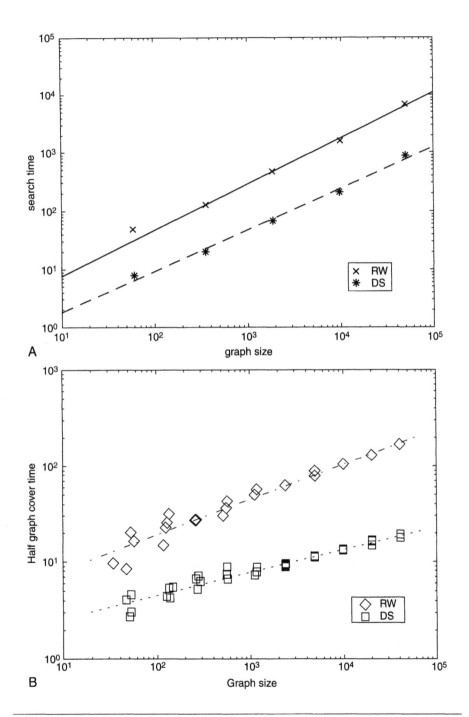

FIGURE 3.5 Comparison of random walk (RW) in a power-law random graph versus high-degree seeking (DS) strategy: (A) node-to-node search cost and (B) time to cover half the graph.[41] © 2001 American Physical Society. http://prola.aps.org/abstract/PRE/v64/i4/e046135.

Li et al.[42] have recently provided a more precise "scale-free metric" derived as follows: Let g be a graph with edge-set $= \varepsilon$, and let the degree at a vertex i be d_i. They define the metric:

$$s(g) = \sum_{(i,j) \in \varepsilon} d_i d_j.$$

For a given degree distribution, this is maximized when high-degree nodes are connected to other high-degree nodes. The following metric is in the range of 0 and 1, such that values close to 1 are scale free and values close to 0 are scale rich.

$$S(g) = \frac{s(g)}{s_{max}}$$

Here s_{max} is the maximum value of $s(g)$ for the set of all graphs with an identical degree distribution to g. Their analysis shows that scale-free networks (1) are created by random growth processes, (2) have a hublike core structure, and (3) are self-similar.

Social Networks and the Small-World Phenomenon

The intuitive notion that every person has some indirect connection through a small set of intermediaries to every other person is referred to as the *small-world phenomenon*. The idea was popularized by Milgram,[40] who performed a well-known experiment involving letter delivery between strangers in different regions of the United States. Using only local knowledge of immediate acquaintances, each participant was asked to forward the letter to a well-known acquaintance selected to bring it closer to the ultimate destination. The experiment showed that short paths, between five and six in Milgram's experiment, exist in large social networks and that using only local information, individuals can find these paths.[38]

Watts and Strogatz[39] were subsequently able to show the construction of random graphs that exhibit the small diameter of uniform random graphs and the clustering behavior of real networks. Starting with a random graph in which all edges are to nearby neighbors, called *short-range edges*, some edges are selected randomly and replaced with edges connecting the node to another node in a distant part of the graph. These new edges are called *long-range edges*, and the combination of short-range and long-range edges creates the required properties to support the small-world phenomenon.

The P2P model mirrors a social network because of the potential relationships between users of a P2P application. Consequently there is some interest in using a search approach similar to the social cues and context that people use in social networks. The intent is to mirror the familiar social phenomenon of finding information by contacting those in one's social circle who either are likely to know it or can find someone in their social circle who is likely to know it. We discuss some current approaches to this topic in a later section of this chapter.

EARLY SYSTEMS

Napster

Napster[65] is a file-sharing system that used a central server for storing and searching the directory of files, but performed the file transfer in a direct P2P fashion. After its launch in 1999, Napster achieved huge notoriety, first as the earliest and as an immensely popular file-sharing system and, subsequently, in a relative short period of time, as a legal test case for personal use of shared media. After losing on the legal front, Napster was shut down. In reaction to the legal issues Napster faced, subsequent file-sharing systems used a full P2P architecture for both the file directory and file transfer functions. The majority of these designs used an unstructured overlay mechanism. Although Napster is not a full P2P system, it popularized the P2P concept in the mass media and influenced subsequent file-sharing systems.

Gnutella

Gnutella was the first full P2P file-sharing system and has remained one of the more popular systems to date. The earliest versions of the Gnutella protocol, through version 0.4, used an unstructured overlay with flooding for query routing. After scalability became an apparent performance issue, the most recent version of the Gnutella protocol (version 0.6) adopted a superpeer architecture in which the high-capacity peers are superpeers and all queries are routed, using a flooding mechanism, between superpeers.

The Gnutella protocol is implemented in a variety of P2P clients and its messaging is described in Chapter 6. Gnutella has been the subject of many research analyses intending on improving the efficiency and effectiveness of the protocol design. The properties of the Gnutella network have also been the focus of various studies to determine, for example, whether the Gnutella network has a power-law distribution and what the peer lifetime distribution is. For example, [51] analyzes snapshots of the Gnutella network over a period longer than 18 months. As shown in Figure 3.6, the node-degree distribution is not power law but has an abrupt peak at about 30 edges. The range of node degree < 30 represents nodes that have recently joined and are in transition to the maximum connected state. The small tail > 30 represents either several nodes that are clustered behind a firewall or clients that have been modified for a higher level of connectivity.

FastTrack

FastTrack is another unstructured P2P overlay that appeared around the same time as Gnutella and was used by a number of file-sharing clients, including KaZaA, Grokster, and Imesh. It is a proprietary system that uses an encrypted protocol. FastTrack was analyzed in 2003[53] using a modified client and a protocol

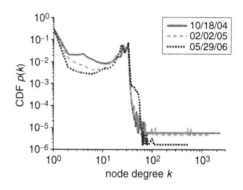

FIGURE 3.6 Superpeer degree distribution in Gnutella.[51] © 2001 IEEE.

decryption package developed by the giFT project. In this study, two sets of measurements were made separated by two months using specially instrumented clients and a packet sniffer platform.

FastTrack uses a superpeer architecture in which high-capacity peers are supernodes (SN) and low-capacity peers are ordinary nodes (ON). In an overlay of about 3 million nodes, the number of SNs is in the range of 25,000 to 40,000. Each ON maintains a connection with one SN. The SN provides its client ON with a list of other SNs, which the ON caches. After an ON issues a query to the SN and receives its responses, the ON disconnects from the current SN and reconnects to a new SN from its list. During reconnections to new SNs, it also receives a new SN list that it merges with the existing list.

An SN maintains about 40 to 50 connections with other SNs (Figure 3.7A). An SN on a residential broadband connection (Figure 3.7B) maintains connections to about 50 to 80 ONs. SNs with greater network capacity—for example, a university campus network—maintain connections with about 100 to 160 ONs at any given time. The average lifetime of an SN-SN connection is 34 minutes and an SN-ON is 11 minutes. Approximately 33% of the connections last less than 30 seconds.

The dynamics of the SN-SN and SN-ON connections appear to have several purposes, including load distribution across SNs, improving the locality of connections, and connection shuffling by ONs to increase the coverage of long searches over the overlay. High connection entropy also makes tracking of peer transfers more difficult, a potential motivation considering the legal battles of several of the file-sharing systems.

Freenet

Freenet was proposed by Ian Clarke[43] in 1999 as a distributed peer-to-peer file-sharing mechanism featuring security, anonymity, and deniability. The Freenet design discussed here is described in a paper published in 2000.[44] Both objects

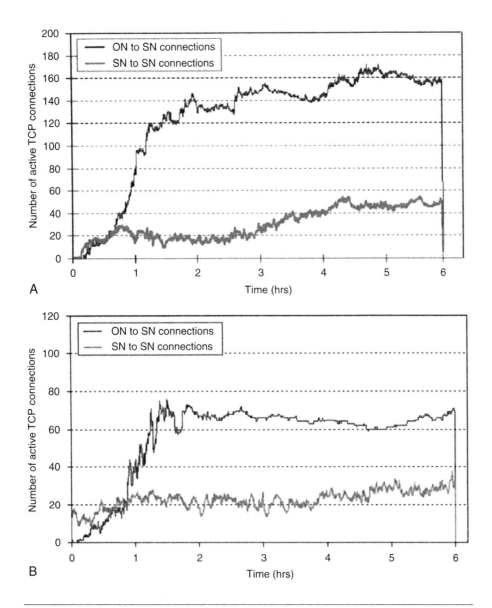

FIGURE 3.7 FastTrack supernode (SN) and ordinary node (CN) connectivity: (A) an SN located on a university campus network and (B) an SN located on a residential broadband connection. Reprinted from [53] © 2006, with permission from Elsevier.

and peers have identifiers. Identifiers are created using the SHA-1 one-way hash function. Peer identifiers are called *routing keys*. Each peer has a fixed-size routing table that stores links to other peers. Each entry contains the routing key of the peer. Freenet uses key-based routing for inserting and retrieving objects in the mesh. Requests are forwarded to peers with the closest matching routing key. If a request along one hop fails, the peer will try the next closest routing key in its routing table. The routing algorithm (Figure 3.8A) is steepest-ascent hill climbing with backtracking until the request TTL is exceeded. Consequently, depending on the organization of the links and the availability of peers, it is possible that requests could fail. Freenet counteracts this by caching objects along the return path both on lookup and insert requests. An object is stored at a peer until space is no longer available and it is the least recently used (LRU) object at that peer.

As shown in Figure 3.8B, performance grows logarithmically until the network reaches about 250,000 nodes.

Freenet is an open-source project. The evolution of the design of Freenet is described in [47].

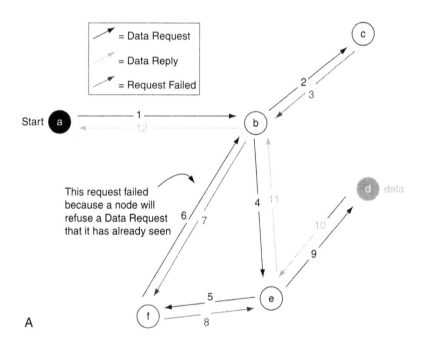

FIGURE 3.8 Freenet distributed key-based routing: (A) example routing path with backtracking on failure and

(Continued)

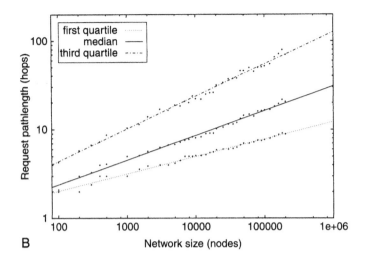

FIGURE 3.8—Cont'd (B) path length versus size of network.[44] (Figure 1 and 3) © 2000 Springer-Verlag, with kind permission of Springer Science and Business Media.

FastFreenet[45] is a proposed modification of the Freenet design to improve the request hit ratio by over six times compared to regular Freenet routing. In Fast-Freenet, each peer shares a fuzzy description of the files that it has with its neighbors. When a query is received, a node can tell which neighbors are likely to have the information, and forwards the query accordingly. The fuzzy description is an N-bit number in which each bit corresponds to $1/N$ segment of the key space. A 1 bit means that one or more files in that part of the key space are stored at that peer. A 0 bit means that no files in that part of the key space are stored at that peer.

Freenet caches objects that have been returned in response to earlier queries, to increase the likelihood of a successful query response. When the cache is full, space is made for new object query results by removing the LRU entry in the cache. An alternate policy is to prefer objects that are clustered around keys of interest. Objects that are furthest from the clustering key are removed first from the cache when new query results are available. Inspired by the clustering property of the small-world model, Zhang, Goel, and Govindan[46] show that this caching policy significantly improves Freenet's query hit rate. Since the cache policy is purely a local decision, no change to the Freenet protocol is needed to implement it.

The key clustering mechanism works as follows. Each node randomly selects a seed key that it uses to form the key cluster in its cache. When the cache is full, the key furthest from the seed key is removed. This is called *strict enhanced clustering*. A variation of this is called *enhanced clustering*, in which some cache entries far from the seed key are randomly retained in the cache. Figure 3.9A compares the two key clustering cache schemes with LRU. As the number of objects in the overlay increases, the clustering policies provide a substantial improvement to the hit ratio compared to LRU. For successful requests, the average number of hops using LRU is somewhat better than enhanced clustering and significantly better than strict enhanced clustering (Figure 3.9B).

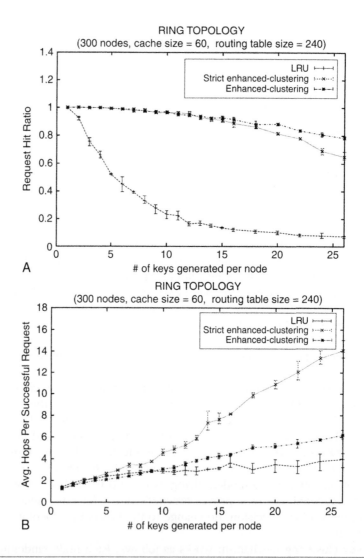

FIGURE 3.9 Impact of replacing Freenet's LRU cache replacement policy with key-clustering cache policies (A) hit ratio versus load and (B) average number of hops versus load. Reprinted from [46] © 2004, with permission from Elsevier.

IMPROVING ON FLOODING AND RANDOM WALK
Techniques

The basic flooding and random walk routing techniques have limitations. Flooding is inefficient and doesn't scale. Random walks could take a long time to find an object. In the unstructured overlay approach, what additional techniques are available to improve performance? The key choices include the overlay topology, object placement, caching, and query forwarding criteria.

In an unstructured overlay, each peer has control over the number of incoming and outgoing connections to other peers and to which peers such connections are made. There are many criteria that can be considered for determining these choices. Among them include the capacity of the peer, the type of content stored at the remote peer, and the connectivity of the remote peer. In addition, as discussed earlier, each peer's connectivity contributes to the average diameter of the overlay.

Clustering can be used to increase the route or object density with respect to some property. For example, *clusters* are formed in the topology when the probability of two vertices being connected by an edge is higher when these vertices have a common neighbor. Topology clusters can be based on proximity of the peers in the network, a preference for connecting with high-degree nodes, or shared properties of the peers or their local contents. Object clusters can be created by having each peer store objects that are close in some identifier or semantic space. Assume that a peer remembers those remote peers that returned results to previous queries. The existence of clusters can be used in future queries when a peer wants to locate objects similar to those that it found in the past. By routing such queries to related peers in a cluster, the chances of locating similar objects increase.

Object placement is the selection of nodes in the overlay where an object is stored. Factors influencing placement include object popularity and the query-routing mechanism. Distributing replicas of popular objects across the overlay can help distribute the search load and reduce the message cost to locate an object. Object placement may be accomplished by explicit push of objects to other peers or by caching the responses to previous queries.

Random walk forwards queries in the absence of any particular knowledge about where the object is likely to be. It may be possible to improve on random walk by informing the forwarding algorithm about the objects that are stored at neighboring peers. Neighboring nodes can exchange summaries of the types of objects that they store. These summaries can be cached and might need to be periodically refreshed.

Attractive properties of random walk and flooding are their relative simplicity to implement and minimal storage and computation overhead. As more intelligence is added to the query-routing algorithm, increased overhead is likely to result. A way to quantify the resource-performance tradeoff is needed. Various metrics are used to quantify performance, and these metrics are frequently evaluated using a query load that approximates real application use. The next section discusses several important metrics used in studying unstructured overlay algorithms.

Metrics

As a query is sent from one node to the next, a message is transmitted at the network level between the nodes. Each step of transmitting a message between neighboring peers is called an *overlay hop* or simply a *hop*, and the overlay hop may correspond to many network hops, depending on the proximity of the peers in the underlying network. The more hops a query uses to find an object, the more latency for responding to the request. Two query-routing techniques can be compared using *hops per request* and *hops per successful request*. Hops per request count the number of message hops a request accumulates, independent of whether the request is successful or not. Hops per successful request count the accumulated message hops for successful requests only. This answers an important question: If the object can be found, how quickly can it be found?

Increasing the number of successful requests is also desirable. An important component is the design of the query language used in the query request, and this is discussed in Chapter 7, "Search." Assuming that the query language is fixed, various query-routing techniques can also be compared using the *request hit rate*. The request hit rate is the ratio of the number of successful requests to the total number of requests issued. For a given message overhead and peer resources consumed, the higher-request hit rate is preferred.

To evaluate query-routing algorithms, a representative topology and workloads are selected. These values can be selected based on existing deployed P2P applications. During simulation analysis, the preceding metrics are computed for a given workload and then used to compare two or more algorithms.

Case Study: Gia

Gia[48] is an unstructured overlay that improves on the scalability of designs that use flooding or random walk. A key aspect of Gia is its ability to distinguish overlay nodes according to their capacity and to distribute load through the overlay according to the capacity of each node. In particular, node index state, connection degree, and permitted query rate are each regulated according to the available capacity of the node. The ability to recognize and adapt to node heterogeneity is a practical issue because large overlays will have a significant range of node bandwidth, CPU, and storage capacity. It also means that low-capacity nodes won't be overloaded.

Gia's design enhancements can be divided into the following four components:

- *Dynamic topology adaptation.* Gia forms an overlay in which the hub nodes, those with high connectivity degree to other nodes, are the high-capacity nodes. The mechanism is adaptive in that nodes actively seek more neighbors to satisfy their own capacity level.

- *Active flow control.* To prevent nodes from being overloaded with messages, nodes provide tokens to their neighbors to regulate the message rate.

Thus a node can only send a message to its neighbor when it has received a token from that neighbor. Tokens are assigned to neighbors in proportion to their capacity.

- *One-hop index replication.* Nodes send a copy of the index of the objects they store to their neighbors. When a node receives a query message, it looks in both its local index as well as the copies provided by neighbors to see if there is a match.

- *Biased random walk search protocol.* As a result of the previous three enhancements, high-capacity nodes are likely to have a high connectivity degree and have the index information for the largest numbers of peers. Further, these nodes are able to handle more of the query traffic. A peer forwarding a query preferably forwards it to a high-capacity neighbor.

For a given network size and peer capacity, the query rate can be increased until it reaches a saturation point, after which the performance degrades. The query level at which this saturation is reached is called the *collapse point.*[48] Larger values of the collapse point are preferred because they mean that the overlay has more capacity to support queries. Figure 3.10A shows the collapse point of Gia compared with three other unstructured query mechanisms for networks of size 5000 and 10,000 nodes. The three other mechanisms are random walk on a random topology (RWRT), flooding (FLOOD), and a superpeer architecture

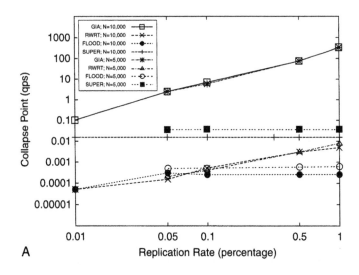

FIGURE 3.10 Gia performance versus random walk, random topology (RWRT), flooding (FLOOD), and superpeer topology (SUPER): (A) Total system capacity for queries per lookup

(Continued)

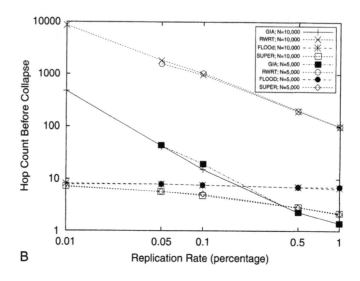

FIGURE 3.10—Cont'd (B) hop count.[48] © 2003 ACM, Inc. Reprinted by permission.

(SUPER). In the superpeer architecture, high-capacity peers form a backbone overlay and other peers connect only to superpeers. A query from a peer is sent to its superpeer, which propagates the query to other superpeers using flooding. As shown in Figure 3.10A, Gia provides significantly higher values for the collapse point, followed by the superpeer architecture.

For low replication rates, the superpeer architecture does provide a lower hop count value per query compared to Gia and other schemes (Figure 3.10B), where hop count measures the average number of hops in the overlay to reach the object being queried. A replication rate of 0.1% means that in an overlay of 10,000 nodes, each object would have 10 copies. So, at a replication level of 50 on a 10,000 node overlay, Gia and the superpeer architecture are comparable in terms of hop count.

Figure 3.11 shows the ability of Gia to distribute message load according to the node's capacity rating. In the figure, node capacities are 1, 10, 100, 1000, and 100000.

SOCIAL OVERLAYS
Using Similar Interests Among Peers

In the small-world experiment recounted earlier, individuals located other widely separated and previous unconnected individuals using a small amount of information about these remote individuals and leveraging only their immediate contacts. Generalizing, when looking for information that is not widespread knowledge, people often look in their social circle to find the best "expert" or someone who knows the best "expert." For example, a person traveling abroad for the first

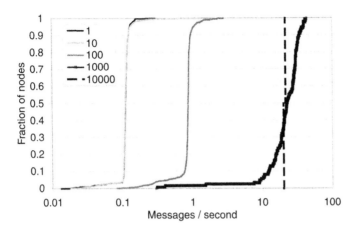

FIGURE 3.11 Load distribution in Gia by node capacity.[50] © 2005 M. Castro, M. Costa, and A. Rowstron. Used by permission.

time will seek someone else who has recently traveled to that same region for information. In a short period of time, a person could seek information from different individuals in their social circle on widely ranging and unrelated topics, from travel to cooking in a new cuisine to music recommendations. Individuals are able to use their social networks to find the nearest "expert" and search simultaneously for "experts" on unrelated topics without difficulty. They can find "experts" whose information or experience is likely to be close enough even if it is not an exact match. Further, one's social network is dynamic, changing due to chance encounters, introductions from peers, and life situation changes.

Peers in a computer network are agents for people who are typically acting on their own personal information goals. Although the social context in the peer-to-peer environment is usually not identical to the offline social network, many social applications form communities of interest. Thus the goal of social overlay design is for peers to interconnect in a way that mimics social networks and that can then be used for routing queries to neighbor peers who are likely to have the information. Unlike other overlays, such social overlays do not rely on network layer relationships between peers. Social overlays require ways to describe peers' interests, discover peers with similar interests, order multiple peers from most similar to least similar for both queries and overlay relationships, and revise peer relationships due to changes in interests.

Tribler

The goal of Tribler is to exploit social affinity between peers with similar preferences. Peers with similar tastes are likely to have files of interest to a peer that is searching for files. Several issues must be addressed for this approach to improve search time and reduce overhead. In a large overlay, only a small fraction of peers are likely to be close matches for similar tastes, and an efficient method to locate these peers is needed. For example, a recent survey of the social network Friendster.com[58] involving 27,000 users found that a user has on average 243 friends and 9,147 friends of friends (Figure 3.12). An efficient way to locate other peers with similar tastes is needed. Second, a way to describe a user's preferences and match preferences between users is needed. Such techniques have been developed for recommender systems and are used in many online e-commerce and social networking sites. Tribler peers exchange preference lists and use Bloom filters to reduce the amount of information each peer has to exchange.

To prepare for future searches being directed toward the most appropriate peers, each peer maintains several caches about other peers in the overlay. These caches contain the other peers' friends lists, peer neighbors, file metadata cache, and preference lists. This information helps the peer determine the parts of the overlay that should be explored and where to direct queries when new information is sought.

To keep the caches fresh, peers periodically exchange their preferences for certain files with other peers. These exchanges use an *epidemic protocol* called *buddycast*. Epidemic protocols, also called *gossip protocols*, mimic the flow of

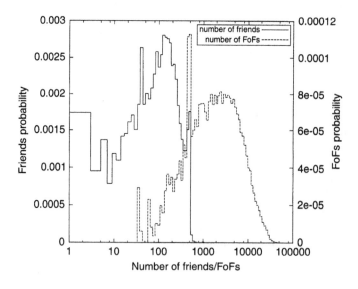

FIGURE 3.12 Distribution of friend and friend-of-friend relationships among 27,000 users of the Friendster.com social network.[58] © 2006 J. Pouwelse, et al. Used by permission.

viruses in social networks and, typically, the peer selected for information exchange is selected randomly. During the contact, both peers exchange information that affects the other peer's behavior. In the case of Tribler, peers update their preference lists in two phases. Then they can find other peers in the overlay that have similar tastes. In the exploitation phase, peers periodically contact peers already known to have similar tastes to collect new preference lists. In the exploration phase, peers periodically randomly select peers that they haven't previously contacted.

Lin et al.[57] evaluate a similar system that uses random walk to locate peers with similar preferences. Peers that have close matches are arranged as neighbors in the overlay. Then, during a search for a new object, query-routing proceeds to neighbors that are most likely to have the object based on preferences. This scheme was simulated using user preferences from a music playlist database of 1300 users. The similarity links improved both the success rate and the precision rate compared to flooding and random-walk queries in overlays with no similarity links but with increased messaging overhead.

INGA

INGA[56] creates a semantic social overlay in which each peer has four types of peer links. Each peer organizes a semantic index for its local content using the Resource Description Framework (RDF) ontology representation language. Information is associated with a topic, and topics are organized in a semantic hierarchy. The semantic hierarchy and topic set is shared across all peers. Queries for information are routed according to the associated topic and evaluated using a semantic matching function evaluating the topic against topics in the local index.

The four types of peer links are:

- *Content provider.* Each response to a query is remembered by the querying peer as a content provider shortcut. Subsequent queries for the same topic will be routed to these peers.

- *Recommender.* The source of each query that is routed through a peer is remembered by the receiving peer. Subsequent queries for the same topic will be forwarded to these recommender peers.

- *Bootstrapping.* These are links to hub peers that are also in the same content provider and recommender associations; hub peers have the largest in-degree and out-degree. Peers include their in-degree and out-degree in their queries, and as the query is routed in the overlay, intermediate peers extract the degree information.

- *Network.* As in Gnutella, a new peer connects randomly to a set of neighbors in the overlay. Using these connections, a peer can gradually form its other connection layers.

Query routing uses only the k best matching shortcuts, and content and recommender shortcuts have the highest priority. Some queries are forwarded to randomly selected peers to avoid having queries stuck in local minima and to help each peer adapt to changes in the overlay. Figure 3.13 shows performance comparison of INGA versus Gnutella-style lookup and a interest-based lookup design.

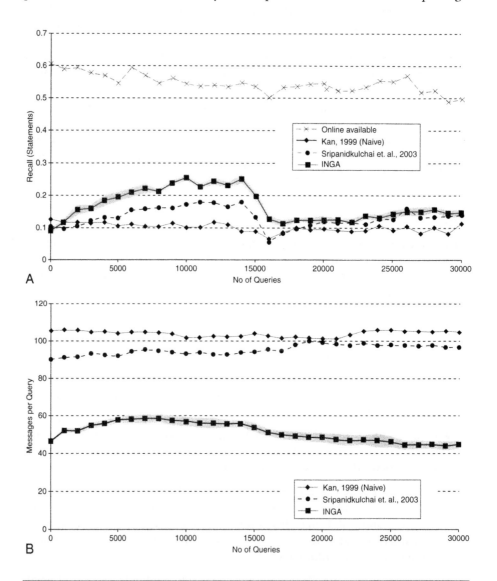

FIGURE 3.13 Comparison of INGA with Gnutella-style lookup (Kan, 1999) and IBL[59] (Sripanidkulchai et al., 2003) for an overlay of 1024 peers. The query topic shifts halfway through simulation: (A) recall rate and (B) message overhead.[56] © 2007 IEEE.

KEY-BASED ROUTING IN UNSTRUCTURED TOPOLOGIES
Overview

In this section we consider two unstructured overlays that use object keys in their query mechanism. In both examples, routing itself uses random walks. The use of object keys means that such overlays could support distributed hash table (DHT) semantics but with less strict guarantee on object lookup. In fact, the UDHT design presented here provides DHT operations put and get. Later, in Chapter 4, we look at key-based routing in structured overlays and DHTs with deterministic behavior.

Local Minima Search

Local Minima Search (LMS)[55] is an unstructured overlay that combines random walk with consistent hashing of object identifiers and node identifiers. A node in the overlay is called a *local minima* for a given object identifier if the node identifier is the closest match to the object identifier in a one- or two-hop vicinity around the node. LMS proactively replicates objects at randomly selected local minima in the overlay.

As with structured overlays, discussed in the next chapter, each node in the overlay is assigned a unique random identifier—for example, using SHA-1 hashing of the node's public key. Object identifiers are also unique and random in the same m-bit address space. The distance between an object identifier x and node identifier w is the arithmetic difference modulo 2^m, that is, $\min\{x-w \bmod 2^m, w-x \bmod 2^m\}$.

The basic protocol for inserting and locating an object consists of a probe message with the fields [initiator, key, walk_length, path]. Here initiator identifies the node that is the source of the message, key is the object identifier, walk_length determines the number of hops the random walk phase follows, and path is the accumulated record of nodes visited during the random walk. After the initiator sends the probe message to a randomly selected neighbor, the probe is forwarded as in the generic random walk algorithm described earlier. Each subsequently visited node adds its identifier to the path field and forwards the probe until the walk_length number of hops is reached. At that point, the random walk phase is finished and the deterministic walk begins. The node receiving the probe message computes the distance between the key and the identifier of each node in a specific k-hop radius around it. If it is the closest, the probe routing has completed. Otherwise it forwards the probe message to the closest node. The pseudo-code for the LMS forwarding algorithm follows:

```
LMSForward(initiator, key, walk_length, path)
  if (walk_length > 0) {
    // non-deterministic phase
    walk_length = walk_length - 1
    next_hop = neighbors[random()]
    send(probe, initiator, key, walk_length, path + this_node)
```

```
} else {
  // deterministic phase
  nearest = this_node
  foreach(node ∈ neighborhood)
    if (distance(node,key) < distance(nearest,key)) nearest =
    node
  if (nearest == this_node) // store or retrieve object
  else send(probe, initiator, key, walk_length, path +
  this_node)
}
```

One of the strengths of the LMS design is the proof of probabilistic bounds on lookup performance for a given replication factor and number of probe messages. The asymptotic performance bounds for search are $O((N \log N)/r \cdot d_h)$, where r is the replication factor and d_h is the size of the neighborhood. Table 3.2 shows LMS performance for a selected set of graphs, where the average number of probes issued per lookup is approximately equal to the number of replicas. Performance improves further when LMS is augmented with an additional optimization, labeled Bloom Filter in Table 3.2. In this technique, nodes create summaries of the objects that they store and propagate the summaries to nodes in their neighborhood. The summaries are computed using a Bloom filter. A Bloom filter is a compact bit vector representation of a set in which a 1 bit indicates the likelihood of an element being present in the set.

Unstructured Distributed Hash Table

An unstructured distributed hash table (UDHT)[54] is an overlay that supports both unstructured and structured overlay functionality in a single overlay. There are several rationales for such a design. First, the two types of overlays provide complementary search mechanisms. Unstructured overlays provide flexible query

Table 3.2 LMS Lookup Performance for Various Graphs[55]

Graph Type	Overlay Size	Average Degree	Number of Replicas	Number Visited (LMS)	Number Visited (LMS with Bloom Filters)
Power law	10K	4.11	3	17.7	4.4
Random	10K	4.11	22	131.1	21.8
Gnutella	61K	4.7	16	83.9	15.7
Random	61K	4.7	45	282.8	43.8
Random	100K	17	14	55.9	14.0
Random	100K	12	19	87.1	19.0
Random	100K	7	34	185.4	34.0

capabilities, whereas DHTs provide an exact match lookup that is guaranteed with high probability to find any object in the overlay. Second, since most overlay deployments today are based on unstructured overlays, UDHT could be used to transparently transition unstructured overlay deployments to structured overlays.

The unstructured routing in UDHT is similar to Gia, described earlier. UDHT also uses random walk, but rather than having each peer maintain a history of queries that it has seen, to avoid duplication a list of last n nodes visited is kept in the message itself. This mechanism is called an *embedded* n-*window*. UDHT uses one-way random walk and a TTL of 750 hops.

Each object is identified by its key K. To store an object in the overlay, a peer first queries the overlay for other objects with the same key. It does this by sending a get(K) message along a random walk. UDHT attempts to store objects with the same keys at the same peers. If no object is found, UDHT issues k-way parallel random walk to find k nodes to store the object. A typical object replication value for k is 5.

Figure 3.14A shows the frequency of successful lookup versus object replication factors for two different topologies. These topologies are taken from

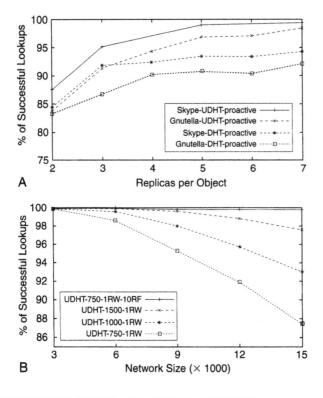

FIGURE 3.14 (A) Comparison of unstructured DHT (UDHT) with Chord (DHT) under topologies from Gnutella and Skype networks.[54] (B) Lookup success rate for UDHT as network size grows for several max hop-count variations for a single random walk.[54] © 2007 IEEE.

measurements of the Gnutella and Skype overlays and have respectively 1787 and 2100 peers in each. UDHT is compared with a conventional DHT based on the Chord design described in Chapter 4. Thus Figure 3.14A shows that DHT lookups over an unstructured topology can achieve comparable lookup success rates compared to a DHT. However, the average number of hops for UDHT lookups is about 200, whereas for Chord the maximum number of hops in an overlay of 3000 nodes is less than 12. Figure 3.14B shows that increasing the size of the overlay significantly reduces the lookup success rate unless the TTL or replication factor is substantially increased.

UNDER THE HOOD: AN OVERLAY EMULATOR
OverlayWeaver Routing Layer

Following [63], OverlayWeaver[30] separates the overlay operation into several layers starting with the lowest layer, which implements key-based routing according to the specified routing algorithm. On top of the key-based routing layer are the DHT, application multicasting, and generic messaging functions. To support the ability of the application to run different routing algorithms without modifying application code, OverlayWeaver separates the routing algorithm from the algorithm-independent portions of the routing layer using a modular design. This allows new routing algorithms to be easily added to the OW toolkit. The routing driver provides both recursive and iterative styles. Iterative routing can support α-way parallel requests for Kademlia and other parallel lookup algorithms.

The routing algorithm interface, specified in `ow.routing.RoutingAlgorithm`, includes the following methods:

- `closestNodes`. Returns a set of nodes from the routing table that are closest to the destination node, sorted in decreasing proximity. The calculation of closeness depends on the distance metric used by the specific routing algorithm.
- `adjustRoot`. Among the currently implemented algorithms, this method is used only by Chord. It is invoked at the last stage of routing to select the root node out of the list of neighbors.
- `join`. Invoked when a node joins the overlay. Routes a message in the overlay toward the identifier of the new node, causing the routing table of neighbors to be updated.
- `touch`. The specified node, which is the sender of an incoming message, is added to the routing table. This is an explicit feature of the structured overlay Kademlia discussed in Chapter 4; OverlayWeaver also implements this behavior for Pastry and Tapestry.
- `forget`: The specified node is dropped from the routing table, as when the node fails to respond to messages.

Each routing algorithm has a separate implementation in OverlayWeaver but relies on generic messaging operations, including:

- Routing an object request to the root node corresponding the object identifier
- Routing a message to the node nearest the specified identifier
- Checking another node's status
- Sending/receiving an algorithm-specific message

Unstructured Overlays in OverlayWeaver

Unstructured overlays can be built in OW using the messaging service. Algorithms described earlier for random walk and flooding can use the send primitive in the OW message service.

SUMMARY

Unstructured overlays have been used in several widely used file-sharing systems, despite their inefficiencies. In the research community there has been much effort to study the properties of these overlays using crawlers to measure the overlay network, peer, and content properties. In addition, many improvements have been suggested to increase their performance and reduce overhead. Since structured and unstructured overlays have somewhat complementary characteristics, there are proposals to create hybrid overlays that combine both types of routing algorithm. Patterning the overlay organization on power law and social networks has also drawn a great deal of interest.

FOR FURTHER READING

Random graphs and power-law graphs have been studied extensively. A recent collection of surveys of research in random graphs is found in [34].

An important design goal of Freenet is providing anonymized queries. Recently, Landsiedel et al.[62] developed an onion-routing scheme for multipath routing that provides anonymized routing in overlays.

The Gnutella2 protocol[52] is an offshoot of the Gnutella protocol and organizes the overlay into hub nodes and leaf nodes. A hub node is a high-capacity node that maintains a large number of connections to both other hub nodes and leaf nodes. Queries are routed from one hub node by successively contacting its neighbor hub nodes.

Other unstructured overlays include PROSA (P2P Resource Organisation by Social Acquaintances).[60,61]

Structured Overlays: Geometry and Routing

A second category of overlays, called *structured overlays,* emerged to address limitations of unstructured overlays by combining a specific geometrical structure with appropriate routing and maintenance mechanisms. Here we focus on geometry and routing; the next chapter is devoted to overlay maintenance. A large number of multihop designs have been studied, which we organize into prefix routing, ring with logarithmic degree mesh, and constant degree, such as butterfly, cubed-connected cycles, and de Bruijin graphs. In addition, O(1)-hop approaches offer lower hop counts but increased maintenance. The chapter concludes with discussion of criteria for comparing various designs.

STRUCTURED OVERLAYS
Motivation and Categories

The earliest peer-to-peer systems used unstructured overlays that were easy to implement but had inefficient routing and an inability to locate rare objects. These problems spawned many designs for overlays with routing mechanisms that are deterministic and that can provide guarantees on the ability to locate any object stored in the overlay. The large majority of these designs used overlays with a specific routing geometry and are called *structured overlays*. At the same time, many unstructured overlays have incorporated some degree of routing structure, such as clustering, near/far links, and semantic links to improve search efficiency. In addition to the structured and unstructured overlay categories, there are hierarchical models, which are discussed in Chapter 5.

Another difference between structured and unstructured overlays is that the former support *key-based routing* such that object identifiers are mapped to the peer identifier address space and an object request is routed to the nearest peer in the peer address space. Peer-to-peer systems using key-based routing are frequently called *distributed object location and routing* (DOLR) systems. A specific type of DOLR is a *distributed hash table* (DHT) in which the identifiers are computed using a consistent hash function[78] and each peer is responsible for a range of the hash table.

Within the category of structured overlays are several dimensions for distinguishing the many designs. These dimensions include:

- *Maximum number of hops taken by a request given an overlay of N peers.* The primary categories are multihop, one-hop, and variable-hop. We discuss multihop and one-hop designs in this chapter and variable-hop designs in Chapter 13.

- *Organization of the peer address space.* Typically the identifier space is large and peer address assignments are uniformly distributed. The primary categories of address space structure are flat and hierarchical. Hierarchical designs are discussed in Chapter 5.

- *Next-hop decision criteria.* For routing to converge to the correct destination, the distributed routing algorithm needs to ensure that the distance between the route progression and the endpoint is narrowing at each step. The criteria is often referred to as a *distance metric*, and computation of the distance metric in a routing context is done by a distance function. Distance metrics that converge include prefix matching, XOR metric, Euclidean distance in a *d*-dimensioned space, linear distance in a ring, and modulo bit shifting in de Bruijn graphs.

- *Geometry of the overlay.* Important graph properties for search such as the small-world model and power-law graphs were discussed in Chapters 2 and 3. Another important characteristic is how the node degree changes as the size of the overlay grows. This in turn reflects the growth of the routing table and maintenance traffic. Two important categories are logarithmic degree graphs and constant degree graphs such as butterflies and de Bruijn graphs.

- *Overlay maintenance.* Overlay membership changes due to peers joining and leaving the overlay require that routing tables be updated. Strategies for overlay maintenance include active versus correct on use. Overlay maintenance is discussed in Chapter 5.

- *Locality and topology awareness.* To improve overlay performance, many designs determine peer neighbor relationships according to the proximity and connectivity of the peers in the underlay. Chapter 10 discusses these techniques and their impact on overlay performance.

In this chapter we focus on the overlay geometry and the associated routing algorithms. The dynamics of overlay self-organization, including membership changes and overlay maintenance, are discussed in Chapter 5.

Geometry and Routing

Geometry defines the idealized static graph model for interconnecting peers. It constrains the available paths for sending a message between two peers, whereas a routing algorithm selects among these paths, depending on the distance metric.

During the design of an overlay, the selection of the overlay geometry should consider both static and dynamic conditions. Dynamic peer membership could cause a specific geometry to be unstable or expensive and complicated to maintain. Further, the important properties of the geometry that are realized when the overlay address space is completely populated might be unpredictably altered when the address space is sparsely populated, which would be the usual case in practice. Other geometry-related design goals to consider include reducing the maintenance bandwidth and lowering worst-case and average-case routing delay.

For a given geometry there may be multiple possible routing algorithms. The routing state used by an overlay routing algorithm is referred to as the *routing table*, but the actual organization of the routing state is algorithm dependent. Organization of the routing table for fast selection of the next-hop peers is an important aspect of the algorithm performance.

The routing behavior of a peer can be abstracted as a message-forwarding procedure as defined by the following `NextHop` function. The first step is to find candidate peers for forwarding the message. A special case is if the current peer is the intended destination of the message. Otherwise, there may be several choices, ordered according to their distance from the destination peer, using the distance metric and the current values in the routing table `RT`. Other elements not shown in this simplified `NextHop` function include whether the algorithm uses parallel lookups, uses intermediate responses to update the routing table state, or gathers overlay metrics.

```
NextHop(dest)
    if(dest == this_peer) return this_peer
    peer_choices = closest(dest,RT)
    return peer_choices
```

Later in this chapter we illustrate the `NextHop` pseudo-code for specific algorithms.

Roadmap for the Chapter

In the rest of the chapter we discuss a variety of multihop structured overlays in four categories: (1) logarithmic degree using prefix routing, (2) ring with embedded logarithmic degree mesh, (3) constant degree geometries, (4) some specialized distance metrics. Then we discuss several O(1)-hop (one-hop) structured overlays that show designs that use significantly more peer-routing state to reduce the number of routing hops. Table 4.1 identifies each of the systems and, where available, implementations and applications that have been created to demonstrate and validate the design. Further information on accessing implementations and Websites for these systems can be found on the Website for this book.

Table 4.1 Structured Overlays Discussed in This Chapter

Type	Systems	Applications	Implementations
Logarithmic mesh with prefix routing	PRR, S-PRR		
	Tapestry	Oceanstore, Bayeaux	Chimera, OverlayWeaver
	Pastry	PAST, Scribe	FreePastry,
	P-Grid	UniStore, PIX-Grid	OverlayWeaver
	Bamboo		P-Grid
	Z-Ring		OpenDHT
Ring with embedded logarithmic degree mesh	Chord	DHash, CFS	Chord, OverlayWeaver
	DKS		DKS
	Chord#		
Constant degree	Ulysses		
	Koorde		OverlayWeaver
	Cycloid		
Logarithmic degree with specialized distance metrics	CAN		
	Kademlia		KAD, OverlayWeaver
O(1)-hop	Kelips		
	OneHop		
	EpiChord		
	D1HT		

LOGARITHMIC DEGREE WITH PREFIX ROUTING
PRR

Prefix routing is used in many structured overlays, including Tapestry, Pastry, P-Grid, Cycloid, and Z-Grid. Plaxton, Rajaraman, and Richa (PRR)[79] presented the first algorithm for a peer-to-peer object location and routing system in a 1997 paper. By mapping object identifiers to the address space of peers, PRR enables key-based routing and is able to support read, insert, and delete operations on objects stored in the overlay. This principle is the basis for subsequent DHT designs.

PRR uses *suffix-based routing*, which is a symmetric case of prefix routing. Suffix and prefix-based routing match increasing portions of the destination address at each hop along the path until the destination is reached. For example, if the target address is the hexadecimal address 3A9F1, in suffix-based routing matching 4 bits at a time, successive hops along the path match xxxx1, xxxF1, xx9F1, xx9F1, and 3A9F1, where x is a wildcard. Tapestry uses a variation of PRR routing; other overlays, including Pastry and P-Grid, use prefix-based routing. Tapestry, Pastry, and P-Grid are described later in this section. The PRR algorithm doesn't deal with overlay formation or maintenance issues.

In PRR, peers are connected in a static overlay mesh network and each peer has a routing table to route messages. The routing table is organized in a fixed number of levels and within each level a fixed number of entries. The number of levels corresponds to the number of suffix match steps performed to route an address, and the number of entries corresponds to the number of digits in an address. So if addresses are 24 bits in length, and each hop matches the next 4 bits of the address, each peer needs $24/4 = 6$ routing table levels and $2^4 = 16$ entries at each level. Level 1 matches the suffix position S as in xxxxxS, level 2 matches the suffix SS as in xxxxSS, and so forth. At each level there are 16 possible digit choices to match; hence the 16 entries at each level. In general, suppose that identifiers are represented as a sequence of digits in some base b, with the number of digits equal to $B = 2^b$, and the number of nodes N in the overlay is a power of B. Then suffixes are matched b bits at a time at each hop, and the routing table at each peer has $(\log_2 N)/b$ levels and B entries per level.

In addition, in the PRR design, each entry has a cost value for routing between the peer and the corresponding destination. The lowest-cost neighbor at any (level, $i \in b$) position is the primary neighbor for that entry. If there are other neighbors that meet low-cost criteria for a given (level, $i \in b$) position, these are stored in the routing table as secondary links. If a node w is a primary neighbor of node x at entry (level, i), node w has a reverse link to x at the (i, j) position in its routing table.

Figure 4.1 illustrates suffix-based routing using 24-bit hexadecimal addresses matched 4 bits at a time at successive hops. On the left are the routing table levels at each of the six hops, showing only the primary neighbor entries; on the right is the path the message follows from starting node to destination node. Each routing table level contains the address of the current node, with the matched

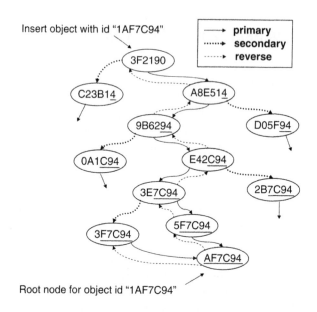

FIGURE 4.1 PRR suffix-based routing for 24-bit addresses matching 4 bits at a time.

hexadecimal digits highlighted in each row. The matching entry in each level is shown with an arrow connecting to the next hop.

Figure 4.2A shows a fragment of a PRR overlay with the primary, secondary, and reverse neighbor links. The insertion of an object with identifier 1AF7C94

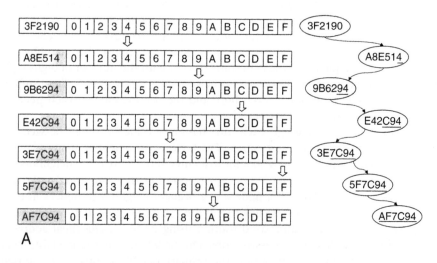

A

FIGURE 4.2 (A) Insertion of object with identifier 1AF7C94 in PRR overlay with root node AF7C94.

(Continued)

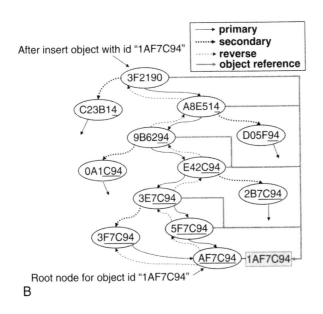

FIGURE 4.2—Cont'd (B) After object is inserted, object is stored at root node and references to the object are stored at nodes along the insertion path.

in the PRR overlay is directed along the primary neighbor links toward the root node for this object, with the root node address equal to AF7C94. The secondary links provide an alternate higher-cost path to the root node if the primary link fails for some reason.

For each object identifier A, there is some node r in the overlay that (1) matches the maximum sized suffix and (2) has the largest node identifier. This node is the root node for A and is unique in the overlay. The root node is where the object A is stored when it is inserted. Intermediate nodes along the path to r store references to A. Then when a query for A is routed along these paths, nodes that cache the reference to r can avoid further routing. If multiple copies of an object exist in the mesh, the reference to the closest object is saved at each hop to the root. The reverse-neighbor links are used to locate the references so that the references can be removed when an object is deleted at the root node.

For example, after the object 1AF7C94 is inserted at the root node, references to the object are stored at the nodes along the insertion path (Figure 4.2B). Each reference is a link to the object and contains the object identifier, the root node identifier, and the cost to reach the root.

When no node in the overlay matches the (i,j) position in a routing table, the largest node identifier matching (i,z) is chosen instead. PRR supports the operations read, insert, and delete as follows.

- read(A). The request starts at some node x in the overlay. The node does a local lookup in its routing table to select the primary link and forwards the request to the next hop. If x has a reference to A with cost k, it forwards the cost value k with the request to the next hop. If the node receiving the request is the root node, the object A is sent to x. If not, it checks with its primary and secondary neighbors to see if any neighbor has a lower-cost reference to A. If so, it updates its reference to A to refer to the new lower-cost location. Depending on which path provides the lowest-cost reference to A, the request either returns the local reference back to x or forwards the request to the next primary neighbor, which repeats the procedure until either the root node is reached or the lowest-cost reference A is found.

- insert(A). The request starts at some node x in the overlay. If an intermediate primary neighbor finds a new lower-cost path, it updates its reference to A and forwards the request along that path. Otherwise the insertion request is not forwarded.

- delete(A). The reference to object A at the current node is removed. After removal, the peer first checks with its reverse neighbors that share the suffix of A's identifier to see if any have a reference to another copy of A. If so, the current node adds a reference to this copy of A. Then the delete request is forwarded to the primary neighbor.

The PRR design is based on a static set of nodes. It does not consider dynamic node membership, and no mechanism for updating routing tables on node join or node leave is given. A simplified version of PRR called SPRR was subsequently proposed by Li and Paxton.[80] SPRR removed the locality criteria on neighbor selection and added algorithms for node join and leave. Tapestry extended PRR to support dynamic membership and is described next.

Tapestry

Tapestry[89] is based on PRR and adds algorithms for peer join, peer leave, and overlay maintenance. It uses prefix routing and, like PRR, organizes peer-routing tables into levels and entries per level based on the radix of the prefix. Figure 4.3A shows an object with identifier 4378, which is stored at two peers, 4228 and AA93, being inserted in the overlay. The two insertions are routed toward the root node 437A along different paths, and a reference link back to the object is stored at each hop along the path. When read operations for the object occur, as shown in Figure 4.3B for nodes 4664, 4B4F, and 57EC, these lookups are routed along the primary neighbor paths until they encounter a node with a reference to the desired object, at which point the request proceeds directly to the peer storing the object.

Message routing in Tapestry is done hop by hop.

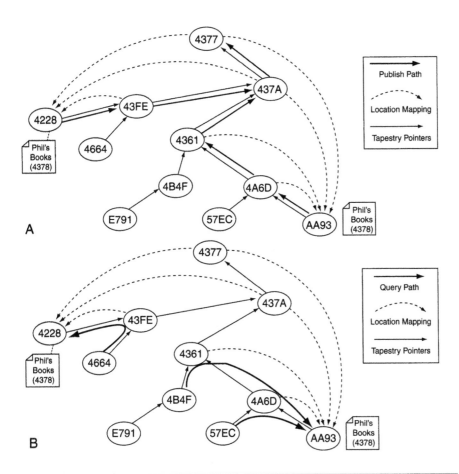

FIGURE 4.3 Tapestry object publish and lookup example. (A) Object 4378 is inserted into the overlay at two peers, and (B) three lookups for object 4378 are routed to nearest copy in the overlay, using the reference links to quickly locate the nearest copy.[89] © 2001 Springer-Verlag, with kind permission of Springer Science and Business Media.

```
NextHop(dest,n,G)

   if the prefix is completed {
      return this_peer
   } else {
      d is next digit in radix B
      e is the routing table entry at level n, digit d
      while e is null do {
   d = d + 1 mod B
   e is the routing table entry
      }
```

```
if e == self then return NextHop(dest,n+1,G)
    else return e
}
```

P-Grid

P-Grid (Peer-Grid)[92,93] also uses prefix routing (Figure 4.4). In this example, each key prefix is the responsibility of two different peers, for a replication factor of 2. The prefix tree shows which peers are responsible for the corresponding prefixes. For example, peers 1 and 7 store keys that start with the prefix 000, whereas 2 and 12 store keys that start with the prefix 11. Unlike other prefix routing schemes, the peer identifier itself is not used for associating keys. Instead, each peer has an assigned path prefix separate from its identifier, and it is this path prefix that is used for prefix routing. This allows P-Grid to use arbitrary size key identifiers for object identifiers.

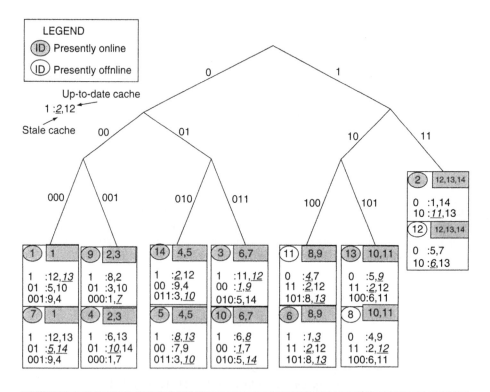

FIGURE 4.4 P-Grid overlay example with peers 1 .. 14. Each pair of peers is responsible for keys with the indicated prefix as shown in the labeled tree. In addition, each peer has a routing table or cache that associates key prefixes with other peers' identifiers. Some entries in the cache may be out of date.[92] © 2004 IEEE.

A P-Grid lookup uses the local routing table in the peer to match the closest prefix. If the indicated peer is not available, P-Grid will perform separate checking to see whether the peer is still online but with a separate IP address. After updating any routing table entries that are out of date, the P-Grid peer forwards the lookup with the longest prefix-matching entry. This continues until the key prefix is completely matched.

P-Grid has a number of interesting features, including a public key mechanism for authenticating peer-to-peer interactions, and a use-driven maintenance mechanism for updating its routing table when needed.

Pastry

Pastry[88] is a multihop structured overlay that uses prefix routing until the last hop, at which point it uses a separate list L of leaf nodes to finish the routing. The leaf nodes are a set of $|L|/2$ successors and $|L|/2$ predecessors in the address space, and are also used for placement of object replicas. Like PRR and Tapestry, the Pastry routing table has $\log_B N$ levels and $B = 2^b$ entries per level. Routing table entries have only a single peer address at each position, which, like PRR and Tapestry, is selected using a proximity mechanism. There are no secondary or reverse pointers. Pastry maintains a third set of nodes M called the *neighborhood set* that are the closest in terms of proximity to the current node. Each peer has a 128-bit randomly generated identifier. A typical value for L, M, and B is 16.

Pastry's NextHop algorithm shown below first checks the leaf nodes if the destination peer is in range, and, if so, selects the closest leaf node to the destination. Otherwise, the routing table is consulted for the entry which matches the next digit d in the destination address. If there is no such entry, then the node from any of the three sets (neighborhood, leaf, or routing table) which is closer than the current node and matches the same or more prefix digits is selected.

```
// return the peer closest to the destination peer 'dest'
NextHop(dest)
    // L.,L+ ∈ L are leaf set peers with the smallest, largest
      identifier
    if L. ≤ dest ≤ L+ {
        next = Li ∈ L such that |dest-Li| is minimal
        } else {
    // p is this peer, 0 ≤ r
    dest[r] is the r-digit prefix of dest that matches p[r]
    d is next digit in radix B of dest
            // e is the routing table R entry at level r, digit d
            if e = R[r,d] is not null {
        next = e
    } else {
        // rare case, there is no entry in the routing table
```

```
        // use leaf set L, neighborhood set M, and routing table R
        ∀ T ∈ L ∪ M ∪ R
        next = T where T[r+i] = dest[r+i], 0 ≤ i, and |T-D| ≤ |p-D|
    }
        }
    return next
```

Other Prefix-Routing Overlays

Bamboo[94] is the overlay used to implement the OpenDHT service on PlanetLab. Bamboo is similar to Pastry but with different mechanisms for join and neighborhood management. Overlay performance enhancements to OpenDHT are discussed in Chapter 6.

Z-Ring[104] uses a much larger base B = 4096 than Pastry, which increases routing state but reduces latency. Z-Ring uses a three-level address space in which each level is a group of peers that have full routing between them using Pastry prefix routing.

RING WITH EMBEDDED LOGARITHMIC DEGREE MESH
Chord

Chord[81,82] organizes peers on a logical ring, and peers maintain neighbor pointers spaced at logarithmic intervals around the ring. In addition, each peer has a link to its predecessor and successor peers on the ring. The Chord routing table is called a *finger table*. Figure 4.5 illustrates a Chord ring with eight peers. Peer 1's finger table consists of three intervals: from Peer 2 to 3, from Peer 3 to 5, and from Peer 5 wrapping around back to Peer 1. In addition to the finger table, each Chord peer maintains links to its successor in the address space.

Chord uses consistent hashing[78] to map keys to nodes. It can be shown that if the hash function has a random distribution, there is a high probability that K keys will be distributed across N nodes such that each node is responsible for, at most, $(1+\varepsilon)K/N$ keys. In addition, also with high probability, when a node joins or leaves an overlay of size N, only $O(K/N)$ keys move to or from the joining or leaving node. These characteristics are important for the load distribution and efficiency of the overlay under churn.

Chord's routing function uses its successor ring in the last hop and uses the finger table to maximize the size of the step toward the destination, as shown in the following NextHop function:

```
NextHop(dest)
    // if dest is in range of this peer and its successor, then
    // the successor is responsible
    if (dest ∈ (this_peer, successor]) return successor
```

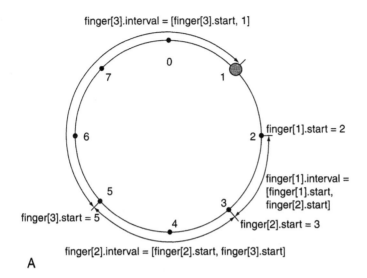

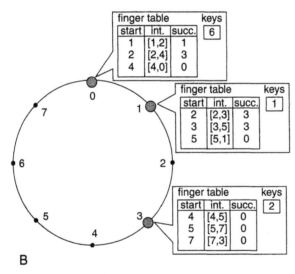

FIGURE 4.5 (A) Chord finger table intervals and (B) finger tables.[81] © 2001 ACM, Inc. Reprinted by permission.

```
// otherwise, search the finger table for
// highest predecessor of dest
for i = log₂ N downto 1
    if (finger[i] ∈ (this_peer,dest)) return finger[i]
return this_peer
```

DKS(N,k,f)

DKS[83,84] uses *distributed k-ary search*, in which the routing region at each hop is partitioned into k equal intervals until the final hop, at which point the partitions each contain only one element. Then the partition that contains the key of interest is used to resolve the key. DKS with $k = 2$ has similar routing characteristics to Chord. In DKS(N,k,f), N is the number of nodes in the overlay, k is the number of partitions at each level of search, and f is the replication factor for placing objects on multiple nodes.

Overlay maintenance in DKS assumes that the lookup rate dominates the churn rate so that there is enough traffic between peers to carry routing table updates. Otherwise, routing tables will gradually degrade, becoming less and less accurate. Like Kademlia,[95] discussed later in the chapter, peers in DKS exchange routing information during lookups rather than perform active stabilization by a separate maintenance mechanism. DKS's *correction-on-use* is based on the assumptions that peer routing tables will normally have out-of-date entries and that peers can provide more accurate routing information when exchanging lookup messages. It uses a lazy (as opposed to greedy) strategy of updating routing information only when it is needed.

Each peer has a $\log_k N$ size routing table. The routing table is organized into k-1 levels, and each level has k entries. Figure 4.6 shows a routing sequence from peer $x = 23$ to peer $z = 59$ in an overlay of size $N = 64$ with $k = 4$. The

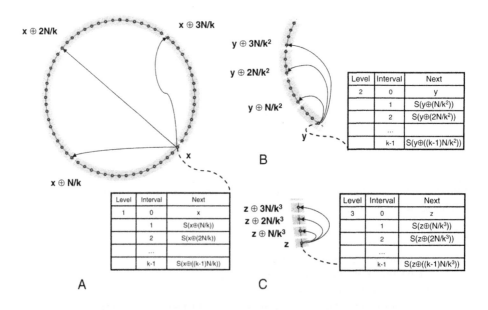

FIGURE 4.6 DKS k-ary search with $k = 4$, routing from $x = 23$ to $z = 49$ where $N = 64$.

notation $S(p)$ means the successor of peer p, and $a \oplus b$ means $(a+b)$ modulo
N. There are three levels to the route, labeled (A), (B), and (C) in the figure. At
each level, the first interval is owned by the current node, for example, peer x
in Level 1. Each interval at a given level has size N/k^L, where L is the level number. The first node in each interval is responsible for that interval on behalf of
the peer referencing it.

Routing starts at the first level (a), where interval 1 is selected and the request
is forwarded to the peer $S(x \oplus (N/k))$, that is the owner of the first interval starting from this peer or Peer 39. The request is forwarded to Peer 39, which does
the second level lookup in its routing table. Interval 2 is selected, which is owned
by the peer defined as $S(y \oplus (2N/k^2))$. In this case, that is Peer 47, and the
request is forward to Peer 47. Peer 47 matches the destination address to Interval
2 and forwards it to Peer 49, completing the routing.

Routing takes $\log_k N$ steps and proceeds as follows.

```
NextHop(dest,k,level)
1 if dest is between this_peer and this_peer's predecessor, then
  next = this_peer
2 // otherwise, lookup in the routing table
3 // compute the interval for the current level
4 t = (dest - this_peer) modulo N
5 partition_size = N/k^level+1
6 j = t / partition_size
7 next = RT[level,j]
8 return next
```

Chord#

Chord#[86,87] is a modification to the Chord algorithm, which reduces the cost of
updating a routing table entry from $O(\log N)$ to $O(1)$ and which provides a tight
bound on lookup performance. The latter is illustrated in Figure 4.7, which shows
average lookup latency versus bandwidth used by the peer. The use of bandwidth
as a cost criterion is discussed in the performance evaluation section of this
chapter.

In addition, Chord# supports range queries, which are discussed in Chapter 7,
"Search." Unlike Chord, Chord# does not use consistent hashing but instead uses
a key-order preserving function to generate object identifiers. In Chord and many
other P2P overlays, keys that are lexicographically adjacent are randomly
distributed in the overlay due to the consistent hashing function. As discussed
earlier, this has the benefit of distributing K keys across N nodes such that
each node is responsible for at most $(1+\varepsilon)K/N$ keys but makes range queries inefficient. Because Chord# does not use consistent hashing, keys are likely to be
distributed nonuniformly across the overlay, leading to load imbalances unless
key redistribution is performed periodically.

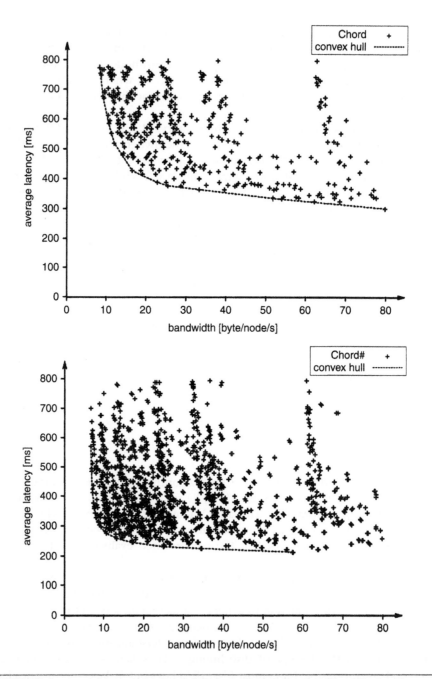

FIGURE 4.7 Average latency versus bandwidth for lookups comparing Chord (top) and Chord#, where each point represents a different configuration setting of the algorithm and the convex hull corresponds to the best configurations.[86] © 2006 IEEE.

CONSTANT DEGREE

Features of Constant Degree Graphs

Unlike logarithmic-degree graphs in which each peer's interconnections grow at an $O(\log N)$ rate, in a constant degree graph each peer has a fixed maximum number of interconnections, independent of the overlay size. This has the benefit of fixed-size routing state and potentially low overlay maintenance costs. Offsetting these benefits are complexity in routing and maintenance. The overlay address space is typically large and sparsely populated, requiring that the geometry structure be adapted. The dynamics of overlay membership require that the geometry be maintained. Because of these issues, several designs "simulate" or "approximate" constant degree graphs.

In the following subsections we describe three constant degree graphs: de Bruijn, butterfly, and cube-connected cycles (CCC), examples of which are shown in Figure 4.8. A de Bruijn graph has 2^b number of nodes, where b is the number of bits in the binary representation of the key. There is an edge from every node a to neighbors b_1 and b_2 such that $b_1 = 2 \cdot a \bmod 2^b$ and $b_2 = 2 \cdot a + 1 \bmod 2^b$. Routing to a key k from node x in a de Bruijn graph involves successive shift of the bits of k into the rightmost bit of x. So, for $k = k_1 k_2 k_3 k_4 \ldots$, successive routing steps are $p_1 = 2 \cdot x + k_1 \bmod 2^b$, $p_2 = 2 \cdot p_1 + k_2 \bmod 2^b$, $p_3 = 2 \cdot p_2 + k_3 \bmod 2^b$, and so on. The de Bruijn graph can be extended[96] from base 2 to base B, and each node has out-degree B and the graph has diameter $\log_B N$. An example de Bruijn graph is shown in Figure 4.8A.

A butterfly graph is specified with diameter r and degree d and has $N = r \cdot d^r$ number of nodes. Each node in the graph has a unique address (row, level), where row is an r-digit value in base d and $0 \leq \text{level} \leq r-1$. For any vertex (x, y) where $x = x_0 x_1 \ldots x_{k-1}$ and $y < r-1$ there are directed edges to vertices in level y+1 that connect to all nodes ($x_0 x_1 \ldots x_i z x_{i+2} \ldots x_{k-1}$, y+1) where $0 \leq z \leq r-1$. When $y = r-1$, the graph wraps back to level 0: ($x = z x_1 x_2 x_3 \ldots x_{k-1}$, 0). A two-level butterfly of eight nodes is shown in Figure 4.8B. Routing from any node (x, y) to another node (e, f) uses successive transitions from level i to i+1 to transform the ith digit in x to the ith digit in e. After all digits in x are transformed to the corresponding digits in e, taking at most r level transitions, routing continues along row e until level f is reached. For example, for a two-level eight-node butterfly the route (10,0) $\Rightarrow$ (01,1) involves the steps (10,0) $\Rightarrow$ (00,1) $\Rightarrow$ (01,0) $\Rightarrow$ (01,1).

A CCC graph has d dimensions. It is constructed as 2^d cycles, each cycle containing d nodes. Each node in a cycle is connected to a node in a different cycle, and the edges connecting the cycles form a d-dimensional cube. Thus the total number of nodes in a d-dimensioned CCC graph is $d \cdot 2^d$. The construction of a CCC graph for $d = 3$ is shown in Figure 4.8C. Each node is uniquely referenced by its cycle index i and cube index j, where $i \in [0..d-1]$ and $j = [0..2^d]$. Routing from any node (i, j) to another node (e, f) is done

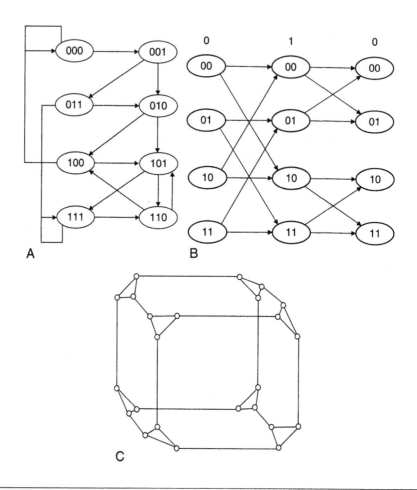

FIGURE 4.8 Static topologies for constant degree graphs: (A) an eight-node de Bruijn, (B) a two-level butterfly, and (C) cube-connected cycles (CCC) for d = 3.

as follows. If j = f, the nodes are on the same cycle and the message can be sent along successive cycle edges until the destination is reached. If j ≠ f, a path through the cube edges is followed until the destination cycle is reached, at which point the message is sent along successive cycle edges until the destination is reached.

Next, for each of these three types, we discuss specific overlay designs, focusing on the static models that deal with sparsely populated address spaces and their routing algorithms. Later, in Chapter 5, we discuss overlay maintenance.

Koorde

Koorde[96] constructs a de Bruijn graph embedded in a Chord-like ring. Since one of the outgoing edges in a de Bruijn graph is the same as the successor link in a Chord ring, this embedding adds no additional edges to the nodes. Because the overlay address space is usually sparsely populated, a method is needed to affect de Bruijn routing when a node along the path is missing from the overlay. Koorde handles the sparse address space by routing to the nearest predecessor of the intended de Bruijn node, effectively simulating de Bruijn routing. Koorde reduces the routing distance to $O(\log N)$ hops by selecting the starting node of a lookup to be some node i between the current node and its successor. The node i is selected so that the address of i contains as its low-order address bits the top $(b- (2 \log N))$ bits of the key k, where b is the number of bits in a Koorde address. This reduces the number of routing steps to $O(\log N)$ bits.

Koorde uses Chord's join algorithm, successor list, and stabilization algorithm. Koorde's ability to self-stabilize like Chord is unknown.[96] Koorde can also support base-B de Bruijn graphs for $B > 2$.

Ulysses

Due to the sparse population of the address space, to retain the butterfly routing characteristics Ulysses[98] needs a way to map all identifiers in the overlay address space to actual nodes in the overlay. Each actual node is assigned an identifier (P,h), where P is the row identifier and h is the level. Each (row, level) identifier in the static butterfly is mapped to $(P,1)$ as follows. There is a direct correspondence between level and h. Each possible node address $(x_0 x_1 \ldots x_{k-1})$ in the overlay is mapped to bits i, i+k, i+2k,..., i+(k-1)k in P. Let $P = a_0 a_1 \ldots a_h$ and the arithmetic progression extraction of P be defined as $AP(P,\{i\}) \equiv a_i a_{i+k} a_{i+2k} \ldots a_h$. For example, if k = 5 and $P = a_0 a_1 \ldots a_{12}$, we have

- $AP(P,\{1\}) = a_1 a_6 a_{11}$
- $AP(P,\{2\}) = a_2 a_7 a_{12}$
- $AP(P,\{3\}) = a_3 a_8$
- $AP(P,\{4\}) = a_4 a_9$
- $AP(P,\{5\}) = a_5 a_{10}$

Objects are also mapped to identifiers (α,h) using a uniform hash function. Row identifier α is m bits in length so that the object space $k \times 2^m >> N$ is large enough to assign unique keys for all objects to be indexed. Then if k = 5 and $B = b_0 b_1 \ldots b_{12}$, $AP(B,\{0,2,3\}) = b_0 b_2 b_3 b_5 b_7 b_8 b_{10} b_{12}$.

Then a node with identifier (P,h) stores all keys (α,h) where P is a prefix of α. The edge construction for Ulysses follows the static butterfly structure described earlier. Each node with identifier (P,h) has links to all $(P', h+1)$ nodes such that P and P' overlay in all dimensions except the i+1 dimension.

Then routing for key (α, h) in Ulysses proceeds in a similar fashion to the static butterfly. Starting at some arbitrary node (P, h), it proceeds $(P, h) \Rightarrow (P',\ h+1) \Rightarrow (P'',\ h+2) \Rightarrow \ldots$ where each successive stage matches the node row identifier at the hth digit to α until α is completely matched.

Cycloid

Cycloid[101,102] constructs a sparse CCC graph and uses Pastry-like prefix routing to locate keys in the graph. As in the CCC graph, peer addresses consist of two parts: a cyclic index and a cubical index. Figure 4.9 shows the neighbor relationships for node (4-,101-1-1010) in a seven-degree Cycloid graph. Each peer has two cyclic neighbors and one cubical neighbor, which are labeled in Figure 4.9. Like Pastry, Cycloid has additional links called *leaf sets*.

In Cycloid there are two categories of leaf sets for each peer: inner leaf set and outer leaf set, which are also labeled in Figure 4.9. Cycloid organizes peers that have the same cubical index into an additional cycle. To distinguish this cycle from the CCC cycles that are peers with the same cyclical index, we refer to the additional Cycloid cycle type as a cubical cycle. Peers use the inner leaf set to link to the predecessor and successor peers on their local cubical cycle. Peers use the outer leaf set to link to other cubical cycles. The entire set of cubical cycles is organized into a ring that uses the outer leaf sets to refer to the successor and predecessor cubical cycles.

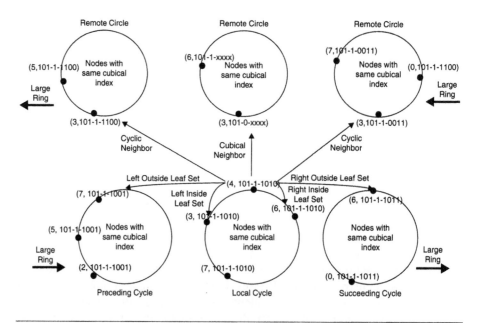

FIGURE 4.9 Cycloid node routing links, based on [101].

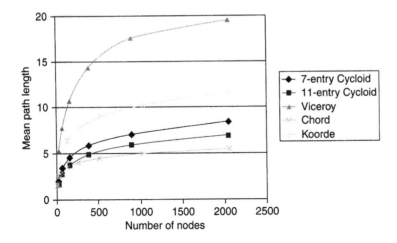

FIGURE 4.10 Path lengths of lookup requests, comparing several fixed-degree overlays and Chord.[101] © 2004 IEEE.

Given this structure, Cycloid routing has three phases: ascending, descending, and traverse. In the ascending phase, it routes to the nearest cubical index for the desired destination using the outside leaf set. In the descending phase, the inside leaf set is used to find the closest cubical and cyclic index. In the traverse phase, if the destination is in the local cubical cycle, the message is routed using the inside leaf set. Otherwise it is routed using the outside leaf set.

The mean path length of Cycloid is compared with several other overlays in Figure 4.10 as a function of increasing overlay size. Cycloid with 11 entries adds predecessor and successor entries to its inner and outer leaf sets, reducing the mean path length.

OTHER DISTANCE METRICS
Content Addressable Network (CAN)

Content Addressable Network, or CAN[90,91] is a constant-degree structured multihop DHT that organizes peers in a d-dimensional Cartesian coordinate system. Like the other systems we discuss, CAN peers and objects have identifiers from the same virtual address space. Each peer's position in the d-dimensional space and the boundaries it shares with other peers determine the extent of the *zone* of the space for which the peer is responsible. An example two-dimensional space with dimensions [0, 80] x [0, 80] is shown in Figure 4.11A. In the figure, three peers are highlighted: x, y, and z. The extent of the zone for each peer is shown to the right of the figure. Objects are hashed to keys in the same space and

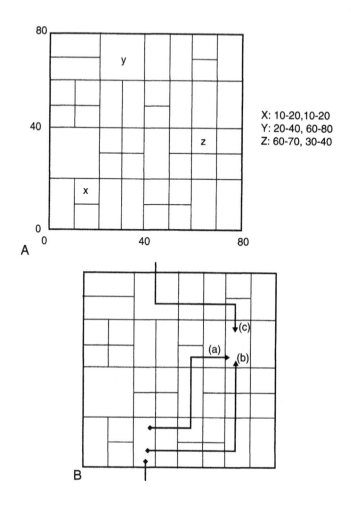

FIGURE 4.11 (A) Two-dimensional CAN coordinate system with 42 peers total, three of which are labeled. (B) Example routing paths in CAN.

stored at the peer whose zone assignment contains that key. For example, object t with key [65, 35] would be in peer z's zone.

Peers in CAN maintain information about neighboring peers that abut them in each of the d dimensions. When a message is being sent, a neighboring peer that is the closest to the target is selected. Figure 4.11B shows three possible routing paths in the two-dimensional space example. Notice that the space wraps around, making a d-dimensional space a d-torus for d > 3. The number of hops for the paths are as follows: *a* has six hops, *b* has seven hops, and *c* has five hops.

Assuming that the space is divided into equal zones, the average routing path length is $(d/4)(n^{1/d})$, where d is the number of dimensions and N is the number of peers in the overlay.

To join the overlay, a new peer performs three steps. First, it locates some peer already in the CAN. Second, it randomly selects a peer whose zone will be split to accommodate the new peer, and it sends a join request to it via the first peer. Third, split the existing zone and notify the neighbors of the split zone so that the routing decisions include the zone changes. In a d-dimension space $[d_1, d_2, \ldots, d_d]$, zones are split in a fixed order of the dimensions. Merging of zones when a node subsequently leaves the CAN is done in reverse order. These steps are highlighted in Figure 4.12. When a zone is split, the original peer retains those key-value pairs that fall within its new subdivided zone. The remaining key-value peers go to the joining peer. Similarly, the joining peer inherits the neighbors of the original peer that abut the edges of the zone for which the new peer is responsible. Both the new peer and the original peer become neighbors, and the original peer prunes its neighbor list and notifies its neighbors accordingly.

Neighboring peers exchange heartbeat messages to verify that they are still connected to the overlay. If missing heartbeat messages indicate that the peer is no longer available, the neighbors of the leaving peer need to coordinate to determine which peer will assume ownership of the zone held by that peer. A message exchange is conducted so that the neighbor with the smallest zone assumes ownership of the orphaned zone.

Kademlia

Kademlia[95] is a multihop overlay that uses a non-Euclidean distance metric, the exclusive-or (XOR) function, which is defined as the bitwise Boolean exclusive-or operation. The routing table is organized into log N buckets, where each

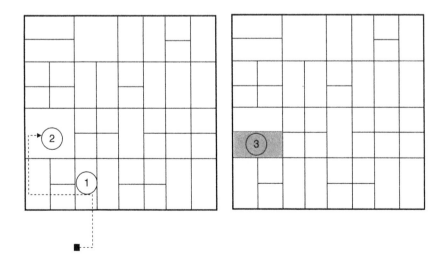

FIGURE 4.12 Peer join sequence in CAN: (1) Contact an existing peer in the CAN, (2) route to the zone that will be split, and (3) split the zone and update the neighboring peers.

bucket holds up to k entries such that entries in the ith bucket are a distance $[2^i...2^{i+1})$ from the current peer. Each routing table entry in turn includes the host IP address, its peer identifier in the overlay, and the time of last contact with that peer. Contact times are used to maintain a least recently used (LRU) replacement policy when new peers are discovered.

Kademlia introduced two new mechanisms into overlay routing: parallel lookup requests and exchanging routing table entries during lookups rather than in separate maintenance requests. An example lookup is shown in Figure 4.13 with three-way parallel requests in an address space of 64 peers. Peer with identifier $= 38$ issues a FIND_NODE 49 in parallel to the three closest peers in its routing table—43, 47, and 54. Each peer receiving the FIND_NODE message looks in its routing table for matching entries and returns k entries from the bucket corresponding to Peer 49. The requesting peer uses these responses to update its routing table and selects those peers that will be sent the next stage of parallel requests until an entry for Peer 49 is obtained.

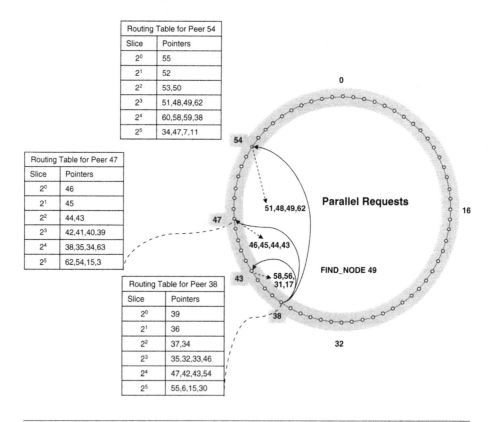

FIGURE 4.13 Kademlia node lookup using $\alpha = 3$ to nodes in k-bucket $i = 4$, that is, nodes whose distance is in the range $[2^3..2^4)$, and each bucket has a maximum size of $k = 4$.

In general, during a lookup, a peer computes the XOR distance to the destination peer, looks in the corresponding k-bucket in its routing table to select the α-closest nodes that it knows of already, and transmits parallel requests to these peers. Responses return closer nodes because the routing tables are organized to have higher density in the vicinity of the peer. Kademlia iteratively sends additional parallel requests to the α-closest nodes until it has received responses from the k-closest nodes it has seen. A typical value of α is 3 and a typical value of k is 20.

O(1)-HOP ROUTING
Multihop Versus One-Hop

Though many multihop designs have demonstrated a high degree of scalability and robustness, even with proximity-aware designs the performance might not satisfy all applications. As discussed in Chapter 2, one-way response time can be improved at the cost of increased routing state and maintenance overlay. An interesting question is, When is multihop necessary? Rodrigues and Blake[105] summarized the tradeoffs between multihop and one-hop, as shown in Figure 4.14. An O(1)-hop (or simply one-hop) overlay maintains sufficient routing information to approach constant hop routing independent of the size of the overlay. To do this, peers must have enough storage capacity to store the routing table and enough upstream and downstream bandwidth capacity to propagate the majority of join and leave events to all peers in the overlay. As the churn rate decreases (the y axis in Figure 4.14), required bandwidth falls, and as the number of

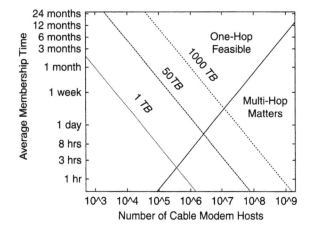

FIGURE 4.14 Feasible performance region for one-hop overlays.[105] © 2004 Springer-Verlag, with kind permission of Springer Science and Business Media.

peers in the overlay increases (the x axis in Figure 4.14), the required bandwidth rises. Further, the overlay is used to store and retrieve data objects. The more bandwidth that is used for data movement, the less that is available for stabilizing the overlay, as shown by the diagonal lines labeled 1, 50, and 1000 TB (Terabytes). Thus the boundary between feasibility of one-hop overlays and multihop overlays depicts the operating points where there is insufficient bandwidth, based on existing residential broadband capacity, for the one-hop stabilization to be met.

In the next subsections we survey some of the designs for O(1)-hop overlays. As observed in a number of the multihop designs, the base can be increased to increase the size of each routing decision, at the cost of additional routing state. If the base were set to $N^{1/2}$, the worst-case number of hops is $\log_{\sqrt{N}}(N)$ $= \log_{\sqrt{N}}((\sqrt{N})^2) = 2$. This is the routing state used in Kelips[106] and Tulip [120]. If the base is set to N, the number of hops is $\log_N(N) = 1$, as approached by One-Hop and EpiChord, discussed later in this section. Another recent one-hop overlay is D1HT.[110,111]

Kelips

Kelip[106] is a O(1)-hop overlay that uses an epidemic multicast protocol to exchange overlay membership and other peer states between peers. The epidemic multicast protocol consists of two subprotocols:[107] (1) a multicast data dissemination protocol and (2) a gossip protocol to exchange message history for reliability purposes. A gossip protocol is the periodic exchange of small amounts of information between nodes.

The multicast data dissemination protocol is either IP multicast or random spanning trees over the multicast group formed by unicast connections. However, available IP group multicast protocols don't scale to the number of groups that would be needed in large overlays.[112] Unicast connections don't leverage the packet savings in multicast protocols.

The Kelips epidemic multicast heartbeat protocol maintains state in each peer by gossip exchanges to peers in its own group and to contacts in other groups. Each group size is less than $\sqrt{N}$, and each node has two multicast groups in a given gossip round. Intragroup targets for gossip are weighted toward neighbors. Intragroup multicast groups are reused in subsequent rounds until the neighbors change. Intergroup targets vary round by round, so intergroup multicast group membership changes each round at each node. In a given gossip round, Kelips requires $O(N)$ number of multicast groups.

OneHop

OneHop[109] is an active stabilization one-hop overlay. The overlay is organized into slices, and each slice is decomposed into units. Each unit has a leader and each slice has a leader. Join and leave events are forwarded to unit leaders, which then forward them to slice leaders. Consequently, OneHop places a disproportionate load on unit and slice leaders. The OneHop topology is shown in Chapter 15 (Figure 15.2).

EpiChord

EpiChord[108] is a one-hop overlay that uses an opportunistic routing table maintenance algorithm. The EpiChord routing table is organized in slices. Slices are organized in exponentially increasing size as the address range moves away from the current peer's position. This leads to a concentration of routing table entries around the peer, which improves convergence of routing. EpiChord doesn't maintain a completely accurate routing table. It achieves close to one-hop performance by combining parallel requests with increasing routing table accuracy in the vicinity of each peer.

EpiChord adopts two techniques from Kademlia: p-way requests directed at peers nearest to the node and passing back routing table entries in response to lookup requests. More details about the opportunistic routing table stabilization mechanism used in EpiChord are given in Chapter 5.

COMPARISON AND EVALUATION
Analytical Performance Bounds

At this stage a reasonable question to ask is, How do all these overlay designs compare, and which ones perform best? The answer to this question depends on the types of application the overlay is to be used for. Also, when designs have similar performance characteristics, other less tangible attributes may be considered, such as relative complexity and available implementations.

Considering performance, we can examine several different dimensions of overlay operation.[96] We divide these into two categories: algorithm correctness and operational metrics. Correctness of performance includes two aspects:

- *Convergence.* Is the routing algorithm guaranteed to reach the destination in a practically bounded hop limit?
- *Stability.* Is the overlay provably stable under churn? At what churn rate does the overlay destabilize?

Performance metrics have to do with the amount of state, bandwidth, and other resources consumed under a given workload. Metrics of interest include:

- *Node degree.* The number of neighbors with which a peer is in continuous contact, which is proportional to routing table size and overlay maintenance overhead.

- *Hop count.* The number of overlay hops to send a message from a source to a destination. There is worst case and average case.
- *Degree of fault tolerance.* The percentage of nodes that can fail without losing data or causing message failures.
- *Maintenance overhead.* The bandwidth consumed at a peer for overlay maintenance traffic and its relationship to peer churn rate.
- *Load balance.* Are a random set of keys uniformly distributed among the peers, and is message-routing load uniformly distributed among the peers?

These metrics are interrelated, and there are tradeoffs between several, such as node degree and hop count. Metrics can be evaluated both analytically and through measurement in a simulation or deployment. Analytical evaluation usually focuses on asymptotic behavior—for example, as the size of the overlay N grows large. Analytical metrics are not available for all overlay designs. Table 4.2 lists the analytical metrics for some of the overlays discussed in this chapter.

A related question is, How close are these existing overlay designs to the theoretic optimal performance? This question has been studied by Xu, Kumar, and Yu,[99] who give the asymptotic limits for number of hops in an overlay of size N. Although the majority of multihop overlays have $O(\log N)$ lookup performance and $O(\log N)$ routing table size, they show that the optimal graph diameter is in fact $O((\log_2 N)/(\log_2 (\log_2 N)))$. However, they also show that graphs

Table 4.2 Comparison of Structured Overlays

Type	Design	Peer Insert Cost (*whp*)	Per-Peer Space	Object Lookup Hops
Prefix routing				
	PRR	—	$O(\log N)$	$O(\log N)$
	Tapestry	$O(\log^2 N)$	$O(\log N)$	$O(\log N)$
	Pastry	$O(\log^2 N)$	$O(\log N)$	$O(\log N)$
Ring with embedded logarithmic degree mesh				
	Chord	$O(\log^2 N)$	$O(\log N)$	$O(\log N)$
	DKS(N,k,f)		$O(\log k\, N)$	$O(\log k\, N)$
Fixed degree				
	Ulysses		$O(\log N)$	$O(\log N)/(\log \log N)$
	Koorde		≥ 2	$O(\log N)$
	Cycloid		7	$O(d)$
	CAN	$O(d\, N^{1/d})$	d	$d\, N^{1/d}$

Note: Data based on [148][169]. whp = with high probability. N = number of nodes in the overlay. d = number of dimensions.

meeting this optimal diameter don't satisfy certain uniformity conditions on network load between peers, whereas existing DHT algorithms such as those in Table 4.2 do meet these uniformity requirements.

Measurement Through Simulation

Most of the designs discussed in this chapter have been the subject of analysis through simulation. Typical simulations range from 1000 nodes to 100,000 nodes. Due to the large number of different designs, there are no simulation results directly comparing more than a few of the designs. Different simulations might not be directly comparable due to different sizes of networks, different workloads, and different churn rates. The performance versus cost (PVC) framework[114] shown in Figure 4.15 is proposed as a way to directly compare overlays using a single cost metric: bandwidth.

In a PVC study,[114] five protocols were compared by simulating a 1024-node overlay. Each protocol was measured for various combinations of operating parameters. For example, Tapestry can be tuned by changing the base, the stabilization interval, the number of backup nodes, and the number of nodes contacted during repair. The best-performing combination of parameters for each algorithm is plotted for average lookup latency versus average number of bytes sent by each peer per second. This gives a cost-performance comparison basis for a given topology and lookup load. Note that the bandwidth consumption includes both lookup and maintenance traffic. Thus an algorithm that has the best lookup efficiency might still perform worse than an algorithm that is more efficient with respect to overlay maintenance, depending on the relative mix of lookups and node churn in the workload.

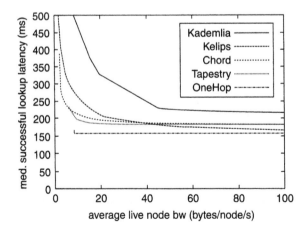

FIGURE 4.15 Cost-performance comparison of five structured overlays.[114] © 2005 IEEE.

At low bandwidth, Chord performs the best of the five because it has a low-maintenance ring structure to use when bandwidth is insufficient to maintain the normal routing table. As bandwidth increases beyond 25 bytes per second, the algorithms performance differences narrow, but the OneHop overlay provides the lowest lookup latency.

SUMMARY

In the design of structured overlays, the geometry of the overlay is a key design decision. To be effective for P2P use, the geometry must meet several criteria, including:

- The overlay must be fully connected for resiliency to peer failure.
- Peers throughout the peer population, must have uniform degree to avoid load imbalance.
- There must be support for at least one type of distributed routing function that converges.
- Efficient and easy construction and maintenance of the overlay routing state and topology using a distributed algorithm are required.

To organize the large space of structured overlays, we have used the following criteria: multihop versus O(1)-hop, logarithmic degree versus constant degree, and routing using prefix, Euclidean distance, and XOR metrics. Some overlay designs might fit more than one criteria, so we also considered historical significance and grouping by essential characteristics.

Performance analysis is analytic, through simulation, or through implementation.

FOR FURTHER READING
Surveys and Frameworks

Milojicic et al.[66] provide the earliest survey of peer-to-peer computing. Many peer-to-peer systems and issues are discussed in a 2004 survey of content distribution technologies.[67] Lua et al.[68] provide a thorough survey of structured and unstructured overlays with an extensive bibliography. Alima et al. propose a reference model for structured overlays which characterizes the design space.[69] An extended version of this reference model is given in [70]. Risson and Moors[71] provide a comprehensive discussion of search methods in overlays and provide a precise delineation of early research work leading up to distributed object location and routing. El-Ansary and Haridi[72] provide a recent survey of multihop structured overlays. Li et al.[113,114] describe a PVC framework for comparing different overlays. A group theoretic framework based on Cayley graphs for comparing DHTs is presented in [73].

History of Distributed Hash Tables

Early versions of distributed hash tables were studied by Devine,[77] which appears to be the first published use of the term. Litwin et al.[75] proposed Scalable Distributed Data Structures (SDDS) that would scale when implemented across a large number of computers. They analyzed a specific instance an SSDS, a distributed linear hash table called LH* [75] [76]. LH* could grow as computers were added to the system.

Other Structured Overlays

Many interesting designs for structured overlays could not be discussed in this chapter due to space constraints. These include Broose (de Bruijin),[97] Cactus (2 tree combined with cube-connected cycle),[115] D2B (de Bruijn),[116] FissionE (Kautz graph),[117] HiPeer (multiring de Bruijin),[118] HyperCup (hypercube),[119] Symphony (ring with links at harmonic intervals),[103] Tango (logarithmic degree),[85] Tulip (2-hop),[120] and Viceroy (butterfly on a ring).[100] SkipNet and Skip Graphs are discussed in Chapter 7.

Routing and Geometry in Computer Networks

Overlays have many similarities with the design of computer networks, and many schemes for network routing have been explored over the years. For example, CIDR uses prefix routing, and the Internet uses hierarchical routing. See [74] for a thorough discussion of network routing.

Structured Overlays: Maintenance and Dynamics

5

We continue the discussion of structured overlays begun in the previous chapter, here focusing on the methods by which the peers form a structured overlay and maintain its geometric and routing properties, a process referred to as *overlay maintenance*. The discussion is again organized into different overlay categories: prefix routing, ring with logarithmic degree mesh, and constant degree graphs. In addition, a stochastic model of overlay maintenance under churn is presented. The chapter concludes with a discussion of hierarchical and federated overlay architectures.

PEER CHURN

Churn in a P2P overlay network means that peers join and leave the overlay arbitrarily and do not stay in the overlay for a predictable time. To ensure dependability of the overlay, peers with neighbor links to the joining or leaving peers require updates. If peers' routing tables lose accuracy, the system's latency increases due to messages being sent to unavailable peers, leading to timeouts. As the churn rate increases, this problem intensifies. As the churn rate increases further, the overlay network eventually partitions, causing lookup queries to return inconsistent results and significant degradation in the overlay's service quality.

Overlay maintenance mechanisms require efficient methods to find stale routing table entries and replace them with new entries in a way that retains the desired routing behavior. Since the lookup query traffic and overlay maintenance traffic both compete for the underlying network bandwidth and resources, maintenance traffic should be constrained to that needed for target routing table accuracy. Intuitively the maintenance traffic per peer should be proportional to the churn rate of its neighbors.

Therefore, overlay maintenance algorithms have to be devised to include efficient features that are able to handle peer churn. For example, Kademlia[121] maintains several neighbors for each routing table entry. They are ordered by the length of time they have been neighbors. If there is churn in the set of neighbors, newer peers will replace existing neighbors to mitigate the effects of high "infant mortality."

Overlay maintenance algorithms have to cater to the fact that a P2P overlay network is evolving continuously[122] and that many peer join and leave operations are happening concurrently. What happens as the churn rate changes? Will the maintenance rate increase to keep the overlay stable, or will the system accept an increase in latency to maintain the bandwidth used by the overlay to some limit? An overlay maintenance protocol has to ensure that the amount of per-peer bandwidth consumed due to the maintenance messages would not grow excessively as the network size increases. Otherwise, the access bandwidth of the overlay peers could be overwhelmed and the system become impractical. More important, the overlay maintenance algorithms have to work efficiently and properly even though the P2P overlay system is no longer in its ideal state during peer churn.

A metric is defined[122] to quantify the performance of the overlay maintenance algorithm. The performance metric of an overlay maintenance protocol is the *rate* at which each peer must expend network resources in the system for maintenance. The consumption of the resources needed for overlay maintenance should be kept as small as possible, since these resources are therefore unavailable for useful work by the P2P application. What is the minimum update rate that each peer in the P2P system must achieve to keep the system in an ideal state? How much work is required to provide a proper routing state so that lookup queries are correct and fast?

We use Figure 5.1 to answer these questions. Here a peer's *session time* is the elapsed time between joining and subsequently leaving the system. A peer's *lifetime* is the time between joining the P2P overlay system for the first time and leaving the system permanently. The total of a peer's session times divided by its lifetime is its *availability*. Peer session time is an important metric[123] with respect to the lookup functionality of a DHT. The temporary loss of a routing neighbor weakens the correctness and performance of a DHT. The unavailability of neighbors reduces a peer's overlay connectivity, causing it to choose suboptimal paths that both affect lookup latency and increase the inefficiency of the overlay maintenance in future churn events. When peers are volatile, with short and unpredictable session times, remembering such neighbors is of little value in performing lookup queries.

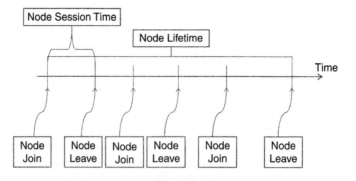

FIGURE 5.1 Metrics of peer churn.

Another overlay maintenance framework[124] uses a *cost/performance* metric to quantify peer churn effects, specifically treating lookup messages to absent peers as a latency penalty. The communication cost is the average number of message bytes sent per second by the live peers. This includes lookup queries, peer join, and maintenance of the overlay routing table. The performance is the average lookup latency including timeout penalty and lookup query retries.

APPROACHES TO OVERLAY MAINTENANCE

The degree of performance degradation of a DHT due to churn depends on its ability to detect join and leave events from other peers and its ability to select fresh entries for its routing state. Two approaches to overlay maintenance are called *active* and *opportunistic*.

Active Maintenance

In *active maintenance*, a peer handles the failure or departure of an existing neighbor (or the new joining peer added to its neighbor table) by sending a copy of its new neighbor set to other peers in the system. To save bandwidth, a peer can send differences from the last state of the system, but the total number of state is still $O(k^2)$ for a neighbor set of k peers. This algorithm converges quickly. Pastry uses a more complex variant of active maintenance[127] that is bandwidth efficient. Cycloid (which makes use of Pastry), Tapestry and D1HT also adopt such active maintenance overlay operation. We describe them in a later section.

Active maintenance runs the risk of creating a positive feedback cycle as follows: Consider the case whereby a peer's access link to the network is sufficiently congested, which causes timeouts for the peer to believe that one of its neighbors has failed (left the system). If the peer is recovering in an active mode, maintenance operations will begin. This operation will add even more packets to its existing congested network link, which will increase the likelihood that more other peers will mistakenly deduce that other neighbors have failed in the system. As this process continues, congestion collapse on its access link may eventually happen.

Under low peer churn, active maintenance is efficient and scalable because maintenance messages are only sent in response to actual overlay membership change events. As the churn rate increases, however, this process becomes more expensive. A peer sees more churn when its neighbor set gets larger in size.

Opportunistic Maintenance

In *opportunistic maintenance*, a peer periodically shares its neighbor set with each of the members of that set, which responds in kind with its own neighbor set. This process takes place independently of the peer detecting changes in its neighbor set. A peer picks one random member of its neighbor set to share state with in each period of optimization. This change saves bandwidth but still converges in $O(\log k)$ stages, where k is the size of the neighbor set. Similar opportunistic maintenance algorithm is currently used by Bamboo and Ulysses, and the periodic nature of this algorithm is also adopted by Chord and its variants such as Koorde and EpiChord, to keep track of its successor list in terms of its correctness and overlay maintenance. We describe them in a later section.

By decoupling the rate of maintenance from the discovery of peer churn, opportunistic maintenance prevents the feedback cycle described. In addition, by lengthening the maintenance period with the observation of system state time-outs, this method will introduce a negative feedback cycle, which further improves resiliency. Such a process can be more conservative in detecting peers to mitigate the instability associated with active maintenance. One drawback with this technique, however, is that neighbors that have actually departed the overlay remain in a peer's routing table for some period of time. Query lookups that would route through these staled neighbors are thus delayed, resulting in long query latencies. To solve this problem, a peer stops routing through a neighbor after seeing some specified number of consecutive system timeouts to that neighbor. In addition, some overlays use parallel lookups to compensate for having some inaccurate routing table entries.

Under low peer churn, opportunistic maintenance becomes wasteful. However, when a peer's neighbor set becomes larger as the system size grows, the set of other peers that it must notify about the resulting churn in its own neighbor set gets larger opportunistic maintenance aggregates all churn events in each period of time into a single maintenance cycle. Thus, the bandwidth consumed under high churn rate and large neighbor size is controlled to a scalable level.

OVERLAY MAINTENANCE ALGORITHMS

The following subsections discuss overlay maintenance algorithms in each category of structured overlays, parallel to the text organization in Chapter 4.

Logarithmic Degree with Prefix Routing

Pastry

Pastry implements a periodic routing table maintenance protocol[127] to actively repair entries of the routing table due to peer churn and to prevent gradual deterioration of the locality properties over a long period of time. Pastry uses a constrained gossiping algorithm via which peers send probes to measure the distance to peers to update the routing tables based on a Proximity Neighbor Selection (PNS) strategy. As shown in Figure 5.2, the implementation of Pastry's overlay maintenance algorithm[127] (`probing_receive`$_i$`()`) uses variables to keep track of peers being probed by peer i (`peer_probing`$_i$) and the number of probe entries sent to each peer (`peer_probe_retries`$_i$`(j)`) and a set of peers that are faulty (`peer_failed`$_i$). Note that a peer i has a routing table R_i and a leaf set L_i (total number of peers in leaf set is l); the Boolean variable `peer_active`$_i$ indicates whether peer i is active.

function **probing_receive**$_i$ (j,{MSG-PROBE,MSG-PROBE-REPLY},L, $peer\_failed_i$)
// The joining peer probes all the nodes in its leaf set to ensure
consistency.
$peer\_failed_i = peer\_failed_i - \{j\}$
L_i.add($\{j\}$)
R_i.add($\{j\}$)
for each $a \in L_i \cap peer\_failed_i$
    do peer_probe$_i$(a)
L_i.remove($peer\_failed_i$)
$L' = L_i$
L'.add($L - peer\_failed_i$)
for each $a \in L' - L_i$
    do peer_probe$_i$(a)
if (message = MSG-PROBE) then
    send([MSG-PROBE,i, L_i,$peer\_failed_i$]) to j
else
    complete_probing$_i$(j)

function **peer_probe**$_i$ (j)
// Sending probes to peers to measure distance to peers.
if ($j \notin peer\_probing_i$ AND $j \notin peer\_failed_i$) then
    send [MSG-PROBE,i,L, $peer\_failed_i$] to j
    $peer\_probing_i = peer\_probing_i \cup \{j\}$
    $peer\_probe\_retries_i(j) = 0$

function **complete_probing**$_i$ (j)
// This function removes peer j from the set of peers being probed.
$peer\_probing_i = peer\_probing_i - \{j\}$
if($peer\_probing_i = \{ \}$) then
    if (L_i.complete) then
        $peer_active_i = $ TRUE
        $peer\_failed_i = \{ \}$
    else
        if ($|L_i.left| < 1/2$) then
  peer_probe$_i$($L_i.leftmost$)
        if ($|L_i.right| < 1/2$) then
  peer_probe$_i$($L_i.rightmost$)

function **peer_probe_timeout**$_i$ (j)
// Peers are marked faulty (failed) if they do not receive a probe
reply within T_{out} seconds (timeout).
if ($peer\_probe\_retries_i(j) < max\_probe\_retries$) then
    send[MSG-PROBE, i, L_i, $peer\_failed_i$] to j
    $peer\_probe\_retries_i (j)++$
else
    L_i.remove(j)
    R_i.remove(j)
    $peer\_failed_i = peer\_failed_i \cup \{j\}$
    complete_probing$_i$(j)

FIGURE 5.2 A simplified version of an overlay maintenance algorithm in Pastry.

Peer Joining

The joining peer i sends a join request to the *seed* peer (the overlay peer that is the nearest neighbor derived from the nearest-neighbor algorithm to seed the join process), which routes the join message to i's nodeID. The peer i obtains the rth row of its routing table from the peers along the overlay route whose nodeID matches peer i's in the first $(r-1)$ digits. The joining peer becomes inactive until it first probes all the peers in its neighbor set to ensure consistency. When a peer received a neighbor set probe from peer j (the MSG-PROBE message is sent by peer j and contains a copy of j's L and peer_failed$_i$), it adds peer j to its neighbor set and routing table. It then sends probes for peers in the neighbor set that are in faulty state. These identified peers are removed from its neighbor set. To ensure no false positives, these removed peers are probed to confirm their faulty state. That is, the peer i creates a clone L' of its leaf set and adds nonfaulty peers from L_i to L'. The peers in L' that are not in L_i are peers for inclusion in i's leaf set are probed before inclusion. Last, the peer i sends a MSG-PROBE-REPLY message back to peer j. After the processing of a probe reply from peer j, a peer invokes the complete_probing$_i$(j), which removes peer j from the set of peers being probed.

Peer Leaving (Failure)

If a peer i does not receive a probe reply from peer j within T_{out} seconds (timeout) in time, a timeout state occurs; the peers are marked faulty in peer_probe_timeout$_i$(j). To reduce the case of marking a live peer faulty, probes are retried a few times with a large timeout. Once it's confirmed that peer j is faulty, it is marked faulty, removed from the routing state, and added to the faulty state. If there are no outstanding probes and the neighbor set is incomplete, a repair is involved by probing the neighbor set. The intuition in the algorithm is to have probing iterates toward the correct side (leftmost or rightmost side) of the neighbor set while notifying the probed peers about the probing peer. In this way, a peer never inserts another peer into its neighbor set without receiving a message directly from that peer. Thus, the problem of probes propagating the dead peers is prevented. In addition, the routing tables are used to aid repair so that the maintenance process is efficient even when simultaneous peer churn occurred.

Tapestry

Tapestry has a number of overlay maintenance mechanisms to maintain routing table consistency and ensure object availability.[125,126] The majority of control messages described here in the system require acknowledgments and are retransmitted where required.

New Peer Joining

There are four key maintenance operations for a new peer i joining a Tapestry overlay network, as illustrated in Figure 5.3:

function **peer_join** (*gatewayIP, newpeerIP, newpeer_name*)
// The peer join process starts by contacting a gateway node in the
Tapestry network. The object pointers are then transferred and the
neighbor table optimized.
(*surrogateIP, surrogate_name*) ← get_primary_surrogate(*gatewayIP,
newpeer_name*)
a ← largest_commonprefix(*newpeer_name, surrogate_name*)
obtain_neighbortable(*surrogateIP*)
multicast_acknowledged(*surrogate_IP, a, pointers_correction_root
(newpeerIP, newpeer_name*))
optimize_neighbortable(*newpeer_name, newpeerIP, surrogate_name,
surrogateIP*)

FIGURE 5.3 New peer insertion in Tapestry overlay network.

- The new peer *i* begins by contacting a surrogate peer with the ID closest to its own in the Tapestry network and obtains a copy of the surrogate's neighbor table. Using the multicast_acknowledged() function,[125,126] the new peer contacts the peers that the peer *i* fills a null entry in their neighbor table. It sends out a Multicast-Acknowledged message to reach the set of all existing peers that share the same prefix by traversing a tree based on their nodeIDs and the first list of the nearest-neighbor algorithm.

- A near-optimal routing table is constructed for new peer *i*.

- Peers that are near the new peer *i* are notified so that they can consider using new peer *i* in their routing tables as an optimization process in such a way that the new peers joining the Tapestry overlay network do not fail to notify each other about their existence.

- If new peer *i* becomes the new object root for existing objects in the system, pointer links to those objects must be moved to new peer *i* to maintain object availability. The pointers_correction_root() function ensures correctness of pointers to objects by making the object pointers that should be rooted at the new peer and removing pointers that are no longer on the existing current peer. By redistributing the object pointers, it would make the objects to be located optimally.

Existing Peer Leaving Voluntarily

As shown in Figure 5.4, if an existing peer *i* leaves the Tapestry overlay network voluntarily, the set *D* of peers in peer *i*'s backpointers and a replacement peer for each routing level from its own routing table are notified of its intention. The notified peers each send object republish traffic to both peer *i* and its replacement. Removing a peer of its links to peer *i* could end up leaving this peer with a wrong hole in the neighbor table. Therefore, replacements' information can

function **peer_leaving_voluntary (*i.pointer*)**
```
// Peer i volunteers to leave the network; it removes itself and
permits seamless object location by following its backpointers to
notify corresponding nodes that it is leaving the network.
for i.pointer ∈ {i.backpointers}
     routing_level = get_routing_level(i.pointer)
     leave_network(obtainIP(i.pointer),i.nodeID, routing_level,
     obtain_nearest_neighbor(i.pointer,routing_level))
for i.pointer in {neighbors ∪ i.backpointers}
     remove_link(obtainIP(i.pointer),i.nodeID)
```

FIGURE 5.4 Voluntary peer removal operation in Tapestry overlay network.

maintain a correct neighbor table by running the nearest-neighbor algorithm periodically. After the peer *i* has contacted all its backpointers, the objects rooted at peer *i* can be located through new surrogates. Finally, the peer *i* informs those peers in its backpointers and forward pointers that it is leaving the network, and it removes all links.

Existing Peer Leaving Involuntarily

Tapestry improves object availability and routing in a dynamic churn environment by building redundancy into routing tables and object location references, for example, by having backup forwarding pointers for each routing table entry. Peers use periodic beacons to detect link and peer failures to trigger repair of the routing mesh and initiate redistribution and replication of object location references, augmented by soft-state republishing of object references. Tapestry is able to retain nearly a 100% success rate at routing queries to peers in a continuous churn environment.

Ring with Embedded Logarithmic Degree Mesh

Chord

Chord makes use of the successor pointers and fingers operations to handle the unexpected events of peer joining and leaving the system concurrently.[122]

New Peer Joining

The algorithm in Chord to handle peers joining the system is as follows: When a new peer *i* joins the system, it must set i.successor to point at its immediate successor peer *s* on the Chord ring. The new peer *i*'s immediate predecessor will update its successor pointer to point to new peer *i*. Its finger table entries and some other peers have to also update the fingers to point to new peer *i*. To handle simultaneous joins, as shown in Figure 5.5, an optimization process[122] is carried out whereby each peer stores an *additional* predecessor pointer that is used

```
function i.optimize( )
// Verify i's successor s and inform s of i. Run only after join process.
x = successor.predecessor
if (x ∈ (i,successor)) then successor = x
successor.notify(i)
```

function i.inform (i')
```
// i' think it might be the predecessor.
if (predecessor = null OR i' ∈ (predecessor,i)) then predecessor = i'
```

FIGURE 5.5 Algorithm for peer-joining operation in Chord.

to record the closest predecessor that the peer has learned. That is, peer i will update its successor to (i.successor).predecessor when its successor is between i and i.successor. This optimization function is done periodically, including updates to the finger table.

Peer Departing (Failure)

Chord handles both cases whereby the peer i departs the system voluntarily and due to unexpected failures. This is illustrated in Figure 5.6. To handle a peer's successor failure, each peer keeps a successor list of the first r peers following it on the Chord ring. In the event of peer failures, Chord's operation will check the operation of forwarding search to a live peer instead of failed peers and considers the peers in the successor list for the next routing hop on the search path. In searching for a node, the i.closest_peer_search() function checks that the search is to a live peer instead of failed peers along the search path. A peer's successor list is maintained by repeatedly obtaining the successor list of its immediate successor s as well as periodically confirming that its predecessor is alive.

function i.closest_peer_search (nodeID)
```
// Search the local table for the highest predecessor of the peer nodeID.
return (largest peer u that is alive in finger[1,...,m] OR successor_
list so that u ∈ (i,nodeID))
```

function i.update_successor_list( )
```
// Reconcile with successor's successor list periodically.
[s₁,...,sᵣ] = successor.successor_list
successor_list = [successor,s₁,s₂,...,sᵣ]
```

function i.update_successor( )
```
// Updated failed successor pointer periodically and if necessary.
if (succesor = faulty) then (successor = small live peer u in finger
    [1,...,m] OR successor_list)
```

function i.update_predecessor( )
```
// Confirms predecessor is alive periodically.
if (predecessor = faulty) then predecessor = null
```

FIGURE 5.6 Algorithm for peer-leaving (failure) operation in Chord.

Constant Degree

Koorde

Koorde[128] is a new distributed hash table (DHT) based on Chord[122] and de Bruijn graphs.[129] Similar to the finger pointers in Chord, Koorde's de Bruijn pointer is an important performance optimization. So Koorde can utilize the successor property in Chord's join algorithm. In addition, to keep the overlay connected in case peers leave the overlay network, Koorde uses Chord's successor list and stabilization algorithm. The extension of Koorde to degree-*k* de Bruijn graphs is to trade off degree for hop count. A de Bruijn graph will have a peer for each binary number of *b* bits, whereby a peer and a key have identifiers that are uniformly distributed in an $n = 2^b$ identifier space, as illustrated in Figure 5.7.

Figure 5.8 shows the lookup routing algorithm in Koorde peer *m*, whereby *k* is the key, `kshift` is the key shifted by previous iterations (initial `kshift = k`), and *i* is the imaginary de Bruijn peer. Each peer *m* keeps track of two peers: the first peer, *j*, consists of the predecessor of 2m (*m*'s first de Bruijn peer), and `successor` contains the successor set of *m* on the ring. The predecessor for the second de Bruijn peer (2m+1) is *d* because the de Bruijn peers follow each other directly on the ring. The nodes are represented using `concatenation` mod 2^b, that is, *m o 0 = 2m mod 2^b* and *m o 1 = 2m+1 mod 2^b*. A peer *m* has a link to peer (*m o 0 = 2m mod 2^b*) and another link to peer (*m o 1 = 2m+1 mod 2^b*). That is, a peer *m* links to the peers that are identified by shifting a new low-order bit into *m* and dropping the high-order bit. The lookup routing algorithm[128] hops from imaginary peer *i* to imaginary peer (*i o topBit(k)*), shifting in *k*.

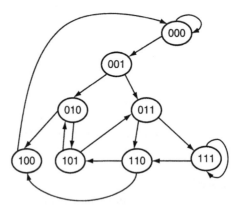

FIGURE 5.7 A de Bruijn graph with $b = 3$.

*function m.lookup(**k, kshift,i**)*

```
// Koorde maintains O(log n) peers immediately following a peer m and
   routing can be done by following live successor pointers to the
   correct peer.
if (k ∈ (m,successor]) then
    return(successor)
else
    if (i ∈ (m,successor]) then return
    j.lookup(k,kshift<<1,i o topBit(kshift)))
else
    return (successor.lookup(k,kshift,i))
```

FIGURE 5.8 The Koorde lookup query algorithm[219].

Rather than having peer m maintain only its immediate successor as in Chord's successor list maintenance protocol, Koorde maintains the $O(\log n)$ peers immediately following it (for n peers in the overlay). In this way, at least one of the peers in each successor list can stay alive with high probability and routing can be possible by following live successor pointers to the correct peer. Koorde also points at $O(\log n)$ peers on the ring immediately preceding 2m. Unlike successor pointers, predecessor pointers may become incorrect by pointing at peers that have initiated the Chord join protocol but have not completed the operation; this will make lookup query operations incorrect.

Instead, peer m uses a lookup to find the immediate predecessor p of $2m - x$, where $x = O(\log n/n)$, and $O(\log n)$ peers occupy the interval between $2m - x$ and $2m$. Even if half the peers fail with high probability, m will have a pointer to the immediate predecessor of address $2m$. The estimate of n is easily obtained by considering the distribution of a peer's successors. Such an attempt to gain fault tolerance and maintenance has eradicated the constant degree of Koorde. However, Koorde can work with a base-$O(\log n)$ de Bruijn graph that has fault tolerance benefit and the routing hops are optimal at $O((\log n/\log\log n))$.

Ulysses

Ulysses[130] allows the routing to stabilize on peer joins and leaves as well as ensuring correct routing while stabilization is occurring. In a Ulysses network with k levels, each peer represents a zone in the name space identified by a tuple $(P,1)$, where P is a row identifier and l is the level, $0 \le 1 \le k-1$.

New Peer Joining

- *Find a row.* A new peer i will first randomly generate a key $(\alpha,1)$ (the search key in Ulysses of k levels is mapped to this tuple using one or more uniform hash functions; l corresponds to the level and α is the row identifier of m bits long, where m is a constant such that $k \times 2m$ is large to assign unique keys for all objects in the DHT) and sends a lookup query for this key through an existing peer X in the Ulysses overlay network. This operation will route to reach the peer O with identifier $(P, 1)$, which is responsible for the key $(\alpha, 1)$. Then peer O splits its zone into two and assigns one half of the responsibility to the new peer n. The peers n and O are *buddies* because they differ only in their last bit of the identifiers.

- *Update the routing tables.* As described previously, the new zones of peers n and O are subsets of the original zone of responsibility of the peer O. So their routing tables are the subsets of peer O's original routing table. The peer O informs the new peer n about its original neighbors in its routing table. In turn, the peers in the preceding level of $1 - 1$ that include peer O as the neighbor, are informed of this split of zones.

Peers Departing

- *Graceful departures.* A leaving peer with identifier $(P, 1)$ hands over its keys to another peer at the same level. The zones of these two peers have to be merged. However, it is possible with small probability that the zone of the leaving peer's original buddy has been split into multiple zones. This is illustrated in Figure 5.9. The leaving peer A is split into multiple zones. The peer B with the smallest zone is promoted to take over the leaving peer's zone, and the peer C merges with peer B's zone. Similarly, the peers in the previous level $1 - 1$ will be informed of the departure.

- *Ungraceful departures.* The detection of ungraceful peer departures is done by asynchronous mechanism; a peer detects that its successor has failed due to unsuccessful lookup query operation. Once detected, it initiates the housekeeping operations as described previously.

Cycloid

Cycloid[131] is a constant-degree P2P overlay network that combines Pastry with a Cube-Connected-Cycles (CCC) graph of d-dimensional cube, with replacement of each vertex by a cycle of d peers. There are $d.2^d$ peers in a Cycloid system, and

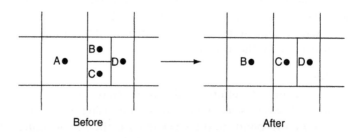

Before   After

FIGURE 5.9 Merging of zones during peer departures[221] © 2003 IEEE.

each lookup takes $O(d)$ hops with $O(1)$ neighbors per peer. It uses consistent hashing to map keys to peers, which have identifiers that are uniformly distributed in a $d.2^d$ identifier space. Each peer is represented by a pair of indices $(k, a_{d-1}a_{d-2}...a_0)$ where k is the cyclic index and $(a_{d-1}a_{d-2}...a_0)$ is a cubical index.

New Peer Joining

A new peer $X = (1, b_{d-1}b_{d-2}...b_0)$ joining the Cycloid network will first contact a live peer in the system, $A = (k, a_{d-1}a_{d-2}...a_0)$. Peer A's joining message will be routed to existing peer Z, whose *identifier* is numerically closest to the X's identifier. X's neighbor sets are updated with Z's neighbor sets (both inside and outside neighbor sets):

■ If X and Z are in the same cycle and Z is the X's successor, Z's predecessor and Z are the left peer and right peer in the X's inside neighbor set, respectively. Otherwise, Z and Z's successor are the left peer and the right peer.

■ If X and Z are not in the same cycle, X's outside neighbor set is initiated in accordance with Z's outside neighbor set. For the case when Z's cycle is the succeeding remote cycle of the X, Z's left outside neighbor set peer and the primary peer in Z's cycle would be the left peer and the right peer in X's outside neighbor set. Otherwise, Z's right outside neighbor set peer and the primary peer in Z's cycle would be the left peer and the right peer in X's outside neighbor set.

To initialize the three neighbors in X's routing table, it searches for a neighbor in the local cycle in decreasing order of the peer cyclic index. Its neighboring remote cycle is searched if the neighbor is not found. Once the peer joined the system, the peers in its inside neighbor set and outside neighbor set (if it is the primary peer of its local cycle) are notified of the join.

Peer Departing

When a peer leaves the Cycloid, it notifies the peers in its inside neighbor set. Since a peer has outgoing links only and no incoming links, a leaving peer cannot make notification to those peers who are their cubical neighbor or cyclic neighbor. It is the responsibility of the system stabilization to update the cubical and cyclic neighbors. The peers in the inside and outside neighbor sets update themselves after receiving the peer departure notification. Cycloid assumes that the peers must make notification before leaving.

$O(1)$-Hop **Routing**

EpiChord

Similar to Kademlia, EpiChord[132] uses *p-way* requests directed to peers nearest the peer so that it can improve the success of lookups. Figure 5.10 shows the detailed model of EpiChord's request and probe mechanism. A peer maintains

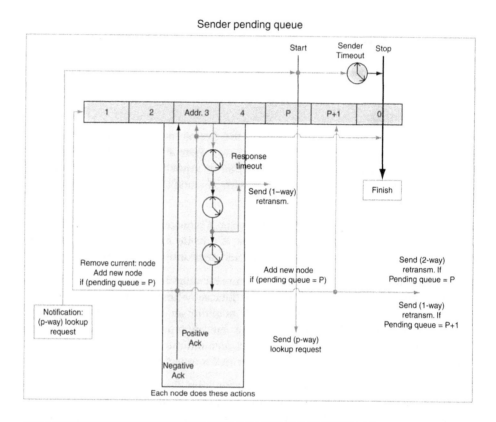

Sender pending queue

FIGURE 5.10 EpiChord pending request queue states and actions[132] © 2007 IEEE.

at least two active entries in each slice of its routing table when high churn occurs. If the number of entries in a slice falls below two, the peer issues parallel lookup messages to identifiers in the slice. The responses to these lookup queries are used to add entries to that slice in the routing table.

p requests are initially sent and are placed in the pending queue. A Unicast request is resent to that peer after a first or second timeout. On the third timeout or if a peer responds with a NAK, the peer is removed from the pending queue. If the pending queue is of size $p-1$, two new peers are sent with two-way requests and are added to the pending queue. This increases its size to $p+1$. When an ACK is received, the lookup query terminates. The tradeoff of this algorithm is that the amount of parallelism in practice is not simply p due to the Unicast retransmissions and two-way messages used by EpiChord to NAK responses. In addition, the proportion of Unicast retransmissions and two-way messages are dependent on the churn rate and the level of accuracy in the routing table.

D1HT

D1HT[133,134] defines the active overlay maintenance algorithm EDRA whereby it propagates all events (join/leave actions) throughout the system in logarithmic time. For n number of peers in the system, each join/leave event is forwarded to $log_2(n)$ successor peers at relative positions $log_2(0)$ to $log_2(x)$, where $x = [log_2 n]$. Propagated events are those directly received and those received from predecessors since the last event message.

As defined in [133], the notations of Θ is the time interval at which a peer p propagates events to its successors (p_{succ}) in the ring and $\rho = [log_2 n]$ is the maximum number of messages a peer sends in the time interval. Each message has a time to live (TTL) and it is acknowledged. If there are no events to report, only messages with TTL = 0 are sent. For message $M(x)$ where x is the TTL value, only events received in incoming messages with TTL $\leq$ x are included, and peer p sends $M(x)$ to $succ(p, 2^x)$. (For any $i \in \mathbb{N}$ and $p \in \mathbb{D}$, the ith successor of peer p is given by the function $succ(p, i)$, where $succ(p, 0) = p$ and $succ(p, i)$ is the successor of $succ(p, i-1)$ for $i > 0$, and $i \geq n$, $succ(p, i) = succ(p, i-n)$. Similarly, the ith predecessor of peer p is given by the function $pred(p, i)$, where $pred(p, 0) = p$ and $pred(p, i)$ is the predecessor of $pred(p, i-1)$ for $i > 0$.[132]

Figure 5.11 shows incoming messages to a peer in an overlay of size n, and Figure 5.12 shows the outgoing messages.

A joining peer is placed in quarantine for an interval Tq to reduce the impact of churn. Quarantined peers route their queries through the nearest nonquarantined peer.

- *Explicit join interval.* To fix the routing table errors due to the update propagation delay when a peer p joins the overlay, a join interval $\Theta \cdot \rho$ is defined in which the closest peer p_{RT}, which is selected from the successor peer p_{succ}'s list of other peers, forwards events it receives after sending its routing table to peer p. If this closest peer p_{RT} leaves the ring before the peer join interval is complete, peer p selects a new p_{RT} as join proxy.

- *Forwarding of unacknowledged events.* In propagating an event, a reporting peer pR might not get an acknowledgment from the destination peer pD that it selected from its propagation path. This is due to the situation that the peer

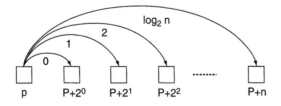

FIGURE 5.11 Incoming messages from predecessors of peer p with corresponding TTLs[133]
© 2007 IEEE.

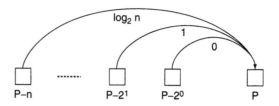

FIGURE 5.12 Outgoing messages from peer p to its successors, each containing the recent events and corresponding TTLs[133] © 2007 IEEE.

pR might not have yet received a peer-leaving event for peer pD. Then peer pD's successors will also not receive this event message. To resolve this situation, peer pR can proxy for peer pD by forwarding the event with TTL $= t-1$ to those peers that would receive the event directly from pD if it were still in the ring. It can continue to proxy events during an interval $\Theta \cdot \rho$, which is the maximum time for pD to propagate to it during a peer-leaving event. Its routing table should be updated by removing the entry for pD.

- *Handling of duplicate events.* The peer receiving the duplicate message can ignore the event. Otherwise, the peer can send the event with the same TTL to its predecessor and successor as a recovery mechanism. A peer seeing this event ("recovery from duplicate message") for the first time processes it for forwarding as usual but not to its successor who sent the message. A high routing table accuracy may still occur even because forwarding to immediate successor and predecessor peers corrects single routing table errors. The routing table accuracy can be dynamically evaluated by looking at the number of lookup timeouts it receives. Lookup traffic can be used to exchange routing table updates between peers.

- *Concurrent adjacent events.* When a new peer p joins the overlay, it contacts both its successor peer p_{succ}, which is responsible for reporting the new join events, and its predecessor p_{pred}. When the predecessor of p (p_{pred}) is notified of p's existence by its own predecessors, it is required to notify p. Thus, if p is not notified about its own peer-join event in period $\Theta \cdot \rho$ interval, it should initiate the reporting of its own peer-join event by itself.

- *Maintenance concatenated in lookups.* The EDRA is further augmented with any events received in the last $\Theta \cdot \rho$ interval would be included in the DHT requests and responses. When a peer received any message from any other peer due to maintenance, lookup, or the like, it would add that peer to its routing table.

- *Routing table recovery using lookups.* The extensions to EDRA as described previously are preventive because any missed event not prevented by these extensions will propagate as more routing table errors occurr over time. Similar to EpiChord, background lookup traffic is added to recover from routing table errors. However, this lookup traffic is randomly distributed in the overlay.

STOCHASTIC MODELING OF PEER CHURN

It is still an active research area to provide good performance of P2P overlays in a dynamic network environment, especially at high churn rates. Recent work in [135] proposes a novel maintenance strategy based on the dual roles of short-range and long-range connections where maintenance overhead in P2P DHT-based overlay approaches the theoretical lower bound necessary to prevent partitioning of the P2P overlay. The proposed stochastic long-range connection method is to define a parameter for maintenance actions. The definition of this parameter involves the sequence of long-range connections of a peer in the one-dimensional Kleinberg model as a stochastic process in one-dimensional Euclidean metric space. Such a stochastic process can be derived from a stationary Poisson process by an exponential transformation. It is shown that the communication overhead of long-range connection maintenance per peer and per system half-life is $O(\log n)$, where n is the size of the network. This maintenance overhead proposed in [122] was $O(\log^2 n)$, which is the lower bound for maintenance traffic to ensure connectivity of the overlay.

The Network Model

The network model used for the proposed stochastic maintenance is adapted from [135] using the terminology and reference model of [136] and illustrated in Figure 5.13. Peer identifiers are mapped onto a one-dimensional Euclidean

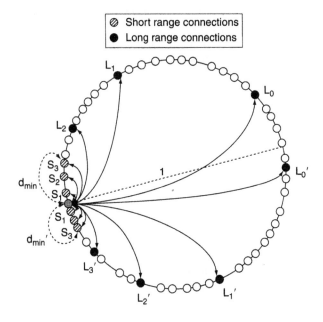

FIGURE 5.13 The network model used for stochastic maintenance, Reprinted from [135], © 2008, with permission from Elsevier.

metric space wrapped around in a ring with bidirectional connections and bidirectional routing in the network.

Each peer has a $2N_S$ of fixed number of short-range connections to the $N_S = 3$ (in the figure) closest neighbors in both directions. It also has a variable number of long-range connections in decreasing distance order at the left and right sides of the peer (defined as $N_L + N_L'$). The short-range connections are constant, whereas long-range connections satisfy the probabilistic requirements, whereby the probability of having a long-range connection between two peers is inversely proportional to their distance.

Stochastic Model for Long-Range Connections

The sequence of long-range connections in both directions as a Y_i stochastic process is shown in Figure 5.14.

X_i is a stationary Poisson process of rate λ given by the sequence of arrival times. The stochastic process Y_i is derived from X_i by transforming each arrival time x_i into an arrival time y_i. Thus it is possible to transform well-known properties of a stationary Poisson process to a long-range connection distribution. The derived stochastic process Y_i is defined in one-dimensional Euclidean metric space. The Poisson process-based model allows definition of connection density as the rate λ of the original Poisson process and it determines the lookup performance as well as in maintenance algorithms.

A last short-range connection, which is shown as an empty circle in the figure, ends the stochastic process Y_i with a distance d_{min} (a random variable depending on the distribution of peer identifiers in the metric space) from the own ID of the peer. This end point maps to a distance of $-\ln(d_{min})$ in the X_i Poisson process. The number of long-range connections (at one side of the ring) follows a Poisson distribution:

$$P(N_L = k) = \frac{\left(-\lambda\ln(d\,_{min})\right)^k}{k!} e^{\lambda\ln(d_{min})} = \frac{\left(-\lambda\,1\,n(d\,_{min})\right)^k}{k!} d_{min}^\lambda$$

The derived Y_i stochastic process exhibits inverse power-law distance distribution necessary for logarithmical routing, which can be used to describe the sequence of long-range connections.

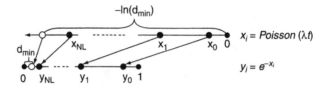

FIGURE 5.14 Stochastic process corresponding to the sequence of long-range connections, Reprinted from [135], © 2008, with permission from Elsevier.

Maintenance of Short-Range Connections

The short-range connection maintenance is opportunistic. That is, each peer periodically sends messages to a randomly chosen peer of its short-range peers. Since the short-range relations are bidirectional, the messaging ensures failure detection in bounded time. This method is similar to neighbor set maintenance in Bamboo[122] and self-stabilizing maintenance algorithm in [136].

Maintenance of Long-Range Connections

The proposed algorithm creates initial long-range connections in according to the desired power-law distribution with only $O(1)$ maintenance overhead per connection. Connections are created in decreasing distance order; from the furthest identifier (ID) and approaching the ID of the peer in bidirectional. The fastest (first) lookup hit (ID) matching the determined range is used. As shown in Figure 5.15, d_i is the distance from the ith long-range peer and d_{i+1} is the distance drawn to create the next long-range connection. A range $[d_{i+1}/c, d_{i+1}.c]$ is defined whereby $c = 1 + \varepsilon$ (constant parameter). If $d_{i+1} > d_i$, the range at d_i is truncated so that the next long-range connection is always closer in the metric space.

Creation of long-range connection has the advantage of self-adapting the number of long-range connections to the network size. The long-range connection establishment is completed when there are no peers available in the given next-closer range. During the final step of the peer-join process, the short-range connection is established.

The sequence of long-range connections created during the peer-join process is described by a Poisson process of rate λ. New incoming connections can be considered as the superposition of another Poisson process to the Poisson process that describes initial long-range connections of the peer. Deletion of connections as a result of peers failing or leaving the network can be described as random selection from a Poisson process. Such operations result in a Poisson process of different rate. So, network dynamism does not affect the inverse

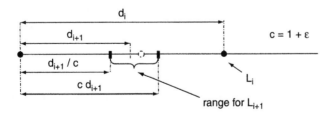

FIGURE 5.15 Range definition for initial long-range connections, Reprinted from [135], © 2008, with permission from Elsevier.

power-law nature of long-range connections. However, the parameter defining the density of long-range connections will change as the network evolves.

The connection density corresponds to the λ rate of the generator Poisson process. The maintenance operation should attempt to keep the connection density within a given range. The rate of a Poisson process is estimated as the number of arrivals per interval, and connection density can be estimated from the number of connections and the length of process: $\lambda = N_L/\ln(d_{min})$. The upper and lower bounds for connection density are defined as $\lambda_{min} < \lambda_{opt} < \lambda_{max}$, and the connection density is always within this range. New connections are created until $\lambda > \lambda_{opt}$ if the estimated connection density falls below λ_{min}. If the estimated connection density exceeds λ_{max}, some connections are deleted until $\lambda < \lambda_{opt}$. Random deletion of arrivals from a Poisson process results in another Poisson process of smaller rate.

Comparison with Existing DHT Overlay

As described, the transformation model[135] provides theoretical foundations for stochastic long-range connection maintenance. This is a good tool to analyze and compare the choice of long-range connections in other DHT-based overlays. The long-range connections of one DHT peer in the original (lower line) and the inverse transformed (upper line) metric space for each DHT overlay are illustrated in Figure 5.16 (parameter b is the number of bit lengths in the routing table for Pastry-like ring topology, and k is the maximum bucket size for Kademlia).

It is possible to define a long-range connection density parameter λ for each DHT overlay independent of the distance and network size. We can observe the differences in the degree of determinism. Each connection is deterministic in Chord, whereas Pastry is more flexible because each routing entry may consist of any peer from a given range. Kademlia allows the choice of any peers (maximum number of k) from a given range. The proposed loose and stochastic long-range connection maintenance mechanism in [135] achieves low maintenance overhead in large networks with high churn rates without affecting routing performance because long-range connections in the underlying network model do not impose any of the previously described constraints.

FEDERATED OVERLAY TOPOLOGIES

With increasing pervasive deployments of various P2P overlay architectures, federation is used to connect and interoperate among these P2P overlay architectures in differing administrative domains. This is done so that service advertisement, discovery and binding to bootstrap services can be carried out in

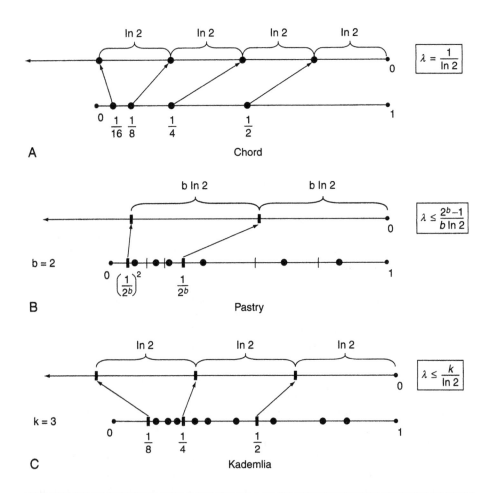

FIGURE 5.16 Comparison with Chord, Pastry, and Kademlia, Reprinted from [135], © 2008, with permission from Elsevier.

these P2P overlays. The challenge is thus to design scalable mechanisms to bootstrap multiple P2P overlays providing differing services: advertise and discover services, binding to bootstrap service, contact peers and service code, and so on.

There are three basic approaches to federating P2P overlay architectures:

- Universal overlay
- Hierarchical overlay
- Concentric nested rings of overlays

Universal Overlay

A universal overlay can provide a scalable infrastructure to bootstrap multiple service overlays[137], bind users with code necessary to install the service on peers, and perform service advertisement and discovery mechanisms so that a user is allowed to deploy and find services of interest. That is, it is an overlay that all participating peers in other separate overlays join. The peers in these other separate overlays that are created dynamically are a subset of the peers in this universal overlay architecture. In [138], Pastry is used as the structured universal P2P overlay, although other structured P2P overlays such as Tapestry could be utilized, as long as the infrastructure is self-organizing, fault tolerant, and able to scale to a large number of peers.

The universal overlay provides an indexing service that allows users to find services of interest by performing Boolean queries; multicast service to distribute software updates and coordination among members of a service overlay; persistent store and distribution network that allows users to obtain the code needed to participate; and finally, a contact service that allows new users to join a service overlay. The operation defined in Pastry (or specified DHT-based P2P overlay) is utilized to handle peers leaving the universal overlay.

A new joining peer needs to obtain a `nodeID` that is assigned by some certification authority such as VeriSign to join the universal ring. In addition to the `nodeID`, the certification authority signs a `nodeID` certificate that binds the `nodeID` with a public key for a specific amount of time. The certification authority charges the peers for the certificates issued so that it is difficult for an attacker to control many virtual peers in the universal overlay. The peer can authenticate itself to other peers in the overlay by the use of the private key that corresponds to the public key. Then the new joining peer obtains the address of a contact peer in the universal overlay. Such a contact peer can be chosen by some form of controlled flooding method, or servers with well-known domain names are used.

To join a specific service overlay within the universal overlay, a peer first needs to obtain the address of a contact peer in the service overlay. In each service, a small list of contact peers is inserted in the universal overlay under the service key. The peer looks up the service certificate in the universal overlay and chooses at random one of the peers in the list to be its contact peer. The oldest member of the list will be replaced by the joining peer to ensure that the contact list remains fresh. For redundancy of the contact list, some copies of the contact list can be cached in the universal overlay path to the peer that stores the service key. This will attempt to prevent peer overloading.

Due to the randomization of the `nodeID`, there is a high chance that the contact peer is not close to the joining peer. The algorithm described in Pastry can solve such a problem; it uses the contact peer and traverses the service overlay routing tables bottom up to find a good approximation to the service overlay peer that is closest to the joining peer in the overlay. This new joining peer can be used to start the joining algorithm.

Hierarchical Overlays

Hierarchical overlay[139,141,142] consists of two-tier overlays whereby the peers are organized into disjoint groups. The overlay routing to the target group is done through an intergroup overlay; then intragroup overlay is used to route to the target peer. The hierarchical overlay architecture of the Internet offers several important advantages over the flat DHT-based P2P overlay:

- It reduces the average number of peer hops in a lookup query. Fewer hops per lookup query means that less overhead messages. The higher-level overlay topology consisting of stable superpeers will have more stability. This increased stability allows the lookup query to achieve optimal hop performance, for example, on average, $\frac{1}{2}logN$ for Chord, where N is the number of peers in the Chord overlay.

- It reduces the query latency when the peers in the same group are topologically close. The number of groups will be smaller than the total number of peers being query routed and the stability of the higher-level superpeers will help cut down the query delay.

- It facilitates large-scale deployment by providing administrative autonomy and transparency while enabling each participating group to choose its own overlay protocol. Intragroup overlay routing is totally transparent to the higher-level hierarchy. If there were any changes to the intragroup routing and lookup query algorithms, the change is transparent to other groups and higher-level hierarchy. That is, any churn events within a group are local to the group in terms of changes, and routing tables outside the group are not affected.

In [139], a general framework is presented for hierarchical DHT overlays whereby each group maintains its own overlay and uses its intragroup for overlay routing of lookup queries. A higher-level overlay is defined among the groups. Within each group, there is a subset of "superpeers"—analogous to gateway routers in hierarchical IP-based networks—to route messages among groups. So, peers in the same group are close in locality. The work in [139] proposed a scalable algorithm for assigning peers to groups, identifying superpeers and overlay maintenance. As shown in Figure 5.17, the hierarchical overlay routing of messages is achieved through the higher-level overlay network to some superpeer and then routed at the next level below through its "local" overlay network (within the group) until the messages finally arrive at some peers at the lower level.

Within the intragroup level, the groups can use different overlays. Each peer in the group could keep track of all the other peers in the group based on their IDs and IP addresses. The group could also use CARP[143] or consistent hashing[144] to assign and locate keys within the group. Since each peer runs a local hash algorithm to determine the peer within a group that is responsible for a key (g_2), the complexity of the intragroup lookup query in the target group is $O(1)$, as illustrated in Figure 5.18. The superpeers could also track all the peers in the group

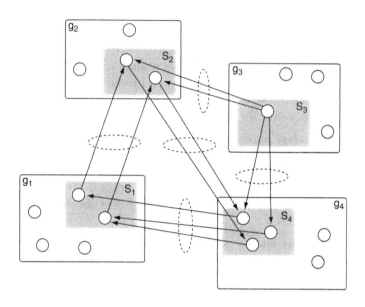

FIGURE 5.17 Intergroup communications through selected superpeers[139] © 2003 Springer-Verlag, with kind permission of Springer Science and Business Media.

if the group is not large. This is achieved by forwarding a lookup query to a local superpeer; in turn, a peer can do a local lookup query in $O(1)$ steps, as shown in g_1 in Figure 5.18. On the other hand, for large group, a DHT such as Chord, CAN, Pastry, or Tapestry can be deployed within the group (g_3 and g_4 in Figure 5.17). The number of steps in such a local lookup query will be $O(log\ M)$, where M is the number of peers in the group.

Hierarchical Group Management

In the two-tier hierarchical DHT, consider a new peer p joining the hierarchical DHT overlay. The assumption made is that p is able to obtain the ID g of the group it belongs to. The procedures are as follows:

- p contacts and asks another peer p_0, which is a member of the P2P overlay network, to look up p's group using key g.
- On hierarchical lookup routing, p_0 locates and returns the IP address of the superpeer(s) of the group responsible for key g.
- If the group ID of the superpeer(s) is g, then p joins the group using regular join mechanisms of the intragroup overlay protocols. p also notifies the superpeer (s) of its resources such as bandwidth and CPU.

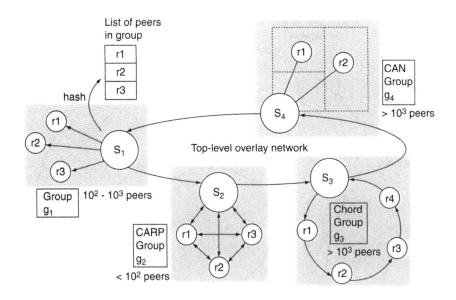

FIGURE 5.18 A ring-like overlay network with one superpeer per group and different intragroup lookup services (CARP, Chord, CAN)[139] © 2003 Springer-Verlag, with kind permission of Springer Science and Business Media.

- If the group ID is not g, a new group is created with ID g and p as the only superpeer.

The first m peers to join a group g can become the superpeers of that group. They are expected to be the most stable and powerful group peers. The superpeers keep an ordered list of superpeer candidates that present good characteristics; this list is periodically sent to the regular peers of the group. The longer a peer remains connected with higher resources, the better a superpeer candidate becomes. When a superpeer fails or leaves the overlay, the first normal peer in the list becomes a superpeer and joins the top-level overlay. All the peers in its group are informed of its arrival as well as the superpeers of the neighboring groups. Stability is attained at the higher-level overlay using multiple superpeers; most stable peers are promoted to become superpeers; and repair is done on the infrequent departures of superpeers.

Concentric Nested Rings

HiPeer[140] is a concentric multiring overlay topology that provides effective and efficient resource discovery and distribution methods for a fault-tolerant P2P resource-sharing environment. The concentric rings topology is navigated from the middle (smallest) ring to the surface (largest) ring, as shown in the Figure 5.19. The peers are represented by the identification of d-based integer of length $D \geq 1$,

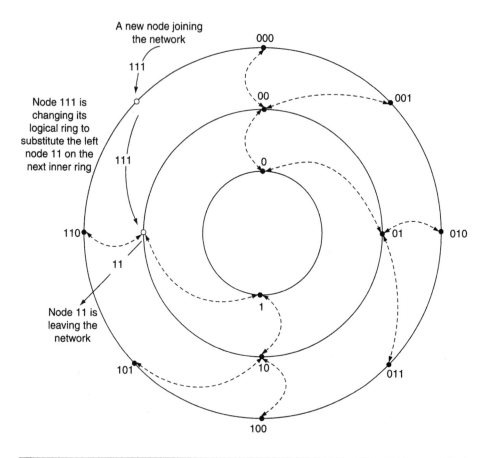

FIGURE 5.19 Concentric nested rings[140] © 2005 IEEE.

with D expanding from the innermost to outermost ring. The function $ring(x) = D_x$ is the ring identifier (RID) for which peer x resides on the concentric multiring topology.

New Peer Joining

The outermost ring is considered the entry point to the network. New peer x asks for an ID from a contact peer on the outermost ring. If the outermost ring is full, a new outermost ring is created and peer x will become the member of the list of contact peers on the new outermost ring. Otherwise, the new peer x is attributed an ID in the middle of the next larger space on the outermost ring, and this operation requires at most $D_{HiPeer} = log_d(N(d-1)+d)-1$ peers (number of N peers in the network of (degree,diameter)-tuple (d, D) topology) to forward the join request message. A peer x joins the network, and the join operation divides the space between peers 110 and 000 in two spaces that are equal in distance, and new peer x is assigned ID 111. The new peer x notifies its neighbors, distributes its resources, and constructs its routing tables. So the number of messages generated as a result is $d+3$ (one message to determine the RID of the outermost ring, one resource location message, and at most $d+1$ messages to update the routing table), which is at most D peers for forwarding.

Peers Departing

A peer x leaving the network notifies its ambassadors based on the WARAAN protocol[145]. It chooses a successor peer x_{out} so that x_{out} exists on the outermost ring with RID D_{max}. That is, it chooses a successor to inherit its ID on the ring because the ring is always fully constructed. Peer x then sends its routing tables to its successor for update and then it leaves the network. In addition, the successor abandons its own resource location table and adopts the resource location table of peer x. The following two cases apply for nonexistence of peer x_{out}:

- If peer x is on the outermost ring with RID D_{max} and it is one of the contact peers, the closest neighbor x_{left} or x_{right} becomes the successor. If the peer x is any peer other than the contact peer, it simply notifies its neighbors.
- If peer x is on the inner ring with RID $D_{max}-1$ and the peer with ID x_{out} on the outermost ring does not yet exist in the network, any peer x_{out} that is closest is chosen to move to the inner ring.

The successor becomes the new peer x, which differs from the old peer x in the IP address and the provided resources. Once the new peer with ID x is on the new ring, the peer publishes its resources to ambassadors on the same ring and on the next inner ring and updates the routing entries of its de Bruijn neighbors. Thus, each peer leaving the network generates at least $d+2$ messages.

SUMMARY

This chapter summarized the characteristics and behaviors of peer churn dynamics deployed in structured overlays and federated overlay topologies. It is clear that current structured overlays exhibit less than desirable performance at a high rate of peer churn. However, much of the structured overlay research has been directed toward designing tradeoffs in overlay maintenance algorithms to handle the effects of high rates of peer churn and provide overlay stability.

FOR FURTHER READING

Churn dynamics in P2P overlays is discussed in [146], which characterizes and compares aspects of peer dynamics in three classes of P2P system: an unstructured overlay (Gnutella), a torrent (BitTorrent), and a structured overlay (Kad).

They identify several measurement pitfalls such as biased peer selection and false negatives, leading to measurement error:

- Overall dynamics are similar across the three systems.
- A large population of active peers are stable, whereas the rest of the small number of peers turn over quickly.
- The peer session lengths are correlated and not exponential.

Peer-to-Peer in Practice

The goal of building large-scale P2P systems is challenging from an implementation perspective. Here we survey some of the key lessons that come from experience with existing overlays as well as general knowledge about network programming and protocol design for distributed systems. Details of protocols for Gnutella, BitTorrent, and structured overlays are discussed, followed by solutions to the crucial problem of NAT traversal. Practical techniques are presented for a peer to determine its capability and for bootstrapping a peer, needed for peers to self-organize and join an overlay. The chapter concludes with a review of P2P networking support in Microsoft Windows.

P2P BUILDING BLOCKS

In previous chapters we focused on the concepts, algorithms, and abstractions of P2P networks. Here we are concerned with the design of a peer as a system and the associated implementation issues. What are the key elements or modules of a peer? Are there common features that different approaches share? What are the hard problems in developing a robust and deployable system? What components and interfaces should a peer provide to application developers?

In widely used software systems, principles and structures have emerged over time for the key functional areas. Examples include operating systems as resource managers, multistage compilers, network protocol stacks, graphics pipelines, and component architectures for middleware. For peers, let's first consider a minimalistic view in which the application supported by the P2P overlay is content sharing and there is no security enforcement. We divide the functions into three areas:

- Overlay routing and messaging
- Search and content storage
- Configuration and peer role selection

In addition, the generic peer provides APIs for the messaging and search functions. In the overlay routing and messaging component, each peer maintains some connection state to neighboring peers in the overlay; maintaining this state could include neighbor discovery and other overlay state maintenance. It has a bootstrap mechanism for locating other peers by which it can join the overlay. The steps for joining and leaving the overlay are enabled using a join/leave protocol. The application layer can exchange messages with other peers in the overlay using the overlay messaging API, and messages received from other peers can be forwarded toward their destination using the message-forwarding function (see Figure 6.1).

Shared content is stored locally for access by other peers as well as the application interface on this peer. The content must be organized for searching, such as providing one or more search indices and a query interface. In addition, the storage area must be managed so that space is allocated to higher-priority objects when space is limited and old unused objects are purged when no longer needed.

The third functional area concerns how the peer self-organizes both its local resources and its role in the overlay. The peer determines the available system and network resources at startup and may monitor them periodically for changes, in case the user changes the peer configuration or other applications change their utilization. The peer self-selects its role(s) in the overlay based on its capability assessment. Peer roles such as superpeer and relay depend on capabilities such as system and network resources, stability of the peer as might be indicated by past churn rate, and public address in the underlying network.

Figure 6.1 can be refined, for example for structured overlays, as shown in Figure 6.2. Here the search API is based on the DHT functions of `put` and `get`. In addition, the routing layer in this case uses key-based routing.

From this basic architecture, a variety of extensions are possible (see Figure 6.3). Existing protocols for session management and media transport can be integrated

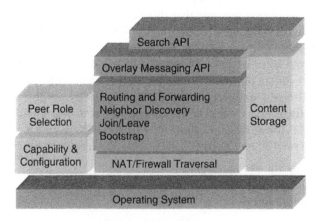

FIGURE 6.1 Generic peer architecture.

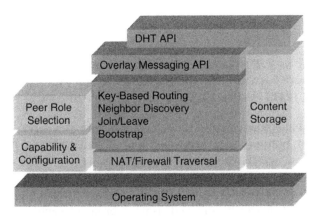

FIGURE 6.2 Basic components of peers for structured overlays.

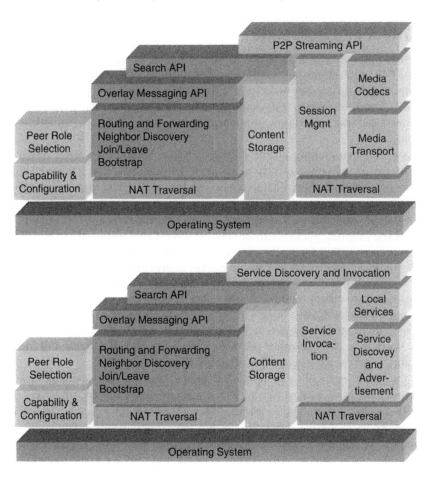

FIGURE 6.3 The basic peer architecture extended for (top) streaming and (bottom) service discovery.

into the overlay for P2P streaming applications (Figure 6.3, top). Such protocols in use today in IP networks include Session Initiation Protocol (SIP) and Real-Time Protocol (RTP). VoP2P applications and protocols are discussed further in Chapter 12.

The peer architecture can also be extended for use as a service-oriented platform (Figure 6.3, bottom). Local services can be advertised for use by other peers, and each peer can search for services offered by other peers. The service discovery and advertisement can use existing protocols such as UPnP, Bluetooth, and SLP. It can also use the overlay search API, as discussed in Chapter 11. Once a service is discovered, it can be invoked using a protocol such as Simple Object Access Protocol (SOAP).

NETWORK PROGRAMMING

The basic P2P concept is attractive for its simplicity, but what issues face developers of P2P applications and deployments of P2P overlays on real networks? The implementation issues can be considered in various dimensions, such as network programming (discussed in this section) and topics such as overlay protocol design, NAT traversal, and application programming interfaces, discussed in subsequent sections.

Network programming in P2P concerns issues common to other distributed applications. Peers communicate using network protocols that have well-known performance and reliability characteristics and tradeoffs. The underlying network can exhibit large variations in delay due to network traffic, and packets could be lost in transit. Available end-to-end bandwidth also fluctuates.

Over the Internet, packets can be sent between peers using either unreliable or reliable transport. Reliable packet delivery uses end-to-end (E2E) acknowledgments and flow-control mechanisms. Reliable packet delivery is desirable but comes with more overhead. Because these mechanisms affect throughput and E2E delay, P2P applications may create multiple parallel connections between peers to get more bandwidth. Considered in a large-scale context with millions of peers, such techniques may increase link saturation and complicate congestion control in the network. Peers may also use other peers as relays to reduce E2E delay and increase throughput. Relays are discussed in Chapter 12.

If the peer protocol uses unreliable packet delivery for sending messages between peers, it might never know that a message was delivered. If confirmation is needed, a typical design is for the peer receiving the message to send an acknowledgement message immediately after receiving it. If the initiating peer does not receive an acknowledgement within a specified time limit, it can resend the message after each timeout. After a certain number of retries fail, the initiating peer can assume that the other peer is no longer available and may remove it from its connection list. The sending peer needs to keep a copy of the message until it is acknowledged and needs a retry counter and a timer for receiving an acknowledgment. The receiving peer should be prepared to receive duplicate messages that might on occasion be due to a misrouted message or if the acknowledgment was not received by the initiating peer. The access network in many cases is asymmetric, usually with more capacity downstream than upstream. This is a particularly important constraint on the ability of peers to contribute network capacity to the overlay. Such capacity is needed by other peers for relaying media streams, participating in torrents, and responding to queries. The asymmetry means that such peers will have significantly more capacity to receive content than to serve it to other peers. In common DSL and cable modem installations, this disparity can be a factor of four or more.

In addition, many users connect to the Internet through a router or gateway that performs network address translation (NAT) and may have a firewall. This particularly affects P2P applications because peers must support both inbound and outbound connections with other peers. Both NAT and firewall functions interfere with an external peer's ability to reach a peer with a translated addressed or filtered packets. Due to the wide variety of NAT implementations, there is no single solution to creating inbound connections to a NATed peer. Many solutions involve probing the kind of NAT present in the local network and using an external peer with a public address to act as a bridge to other peers beyond the NAT. We discuss some common approaches later in this chapter.

It should be pointed out that NAT and firewall functions are network administration choices. NATs are used to permit a number of networked computers to share a single public IP address. Firewalls are a security function to prevent unwanted incoming traffic. Thus the ability of P2P applications to circumvent NATs and firewalls may be viewed as violations of local network administration policy.

OVERLAY PROTOCOL DESIGN

General Protocol Issues

A protocol is a set of messages, the rules for exchanging the messages between endpoints, and the semantics for the interpretation of the messages. The importance of having a published protocol with well-defined syntax and meaning is that independent implementations of the peer software can interoperate.

Each message includes a message type that identifies its meaning to the recipient. There may be attributes to affect the operation of the message. Typically these attributes are placed in the message header. Rules include message sequencing, timing, and error handling. Network protocols are organized by layers, and an overlay is an application layer protocol. A protocol has a syntax and encoding. Encodings may be binary or in human readable formats such as XML.

Protocols are sometimes separated into control and data transfer functions. The frequency and size distribution of these different packet sizes can vary, and by separating them, the protocol can optimize their transport and delivery. In a

P2P overlay, control messages include overlay routing table maintenance and measurement of network distances. Data transfers messages include application layer multicasting and DHT operations.

For IPv4, UDP packets can carry up to 65,507 bytes in the payload or data field, which is much larger than most overlay messages require. Thus a single UDP packet could carry multiple overlay messages, improving the efficiency of the network. For example, a number of structured overlays exchange recent routing table changes with DHT request and response messages. This bundling of multiple overlay messages in a single packet is referred to as *piggybacking*.

Unstructured Overlay: Gnutella

In Gnutella, peers are referred to as *servents*, which is a combination of the words *server* and *client*. Later versions of Gnutella introduced *ultrapeers,* which are high-capacity and stable peers. Each ultrapeer maintains connections to a set of other ultrapeers. The Gnutella protocol[150] consists of a set of basic messages (Table 6.1) and an optional set of extensions.

Each Gnutella message has the following fields:

- *Message ID.* A 16-byte field contain a globally unique message ID for (1) correlating response messages with the original query, (2) routing query hits from remote peers back over the original connection, and (3) detecting duplicate or misrouted messages.
- *Payload type.* A 1-byte field containing the message type.
- *Time to Live (TTL).* A 1-byte field that is decremented by each peer when it receives the message until the TTL reaches 0, at which point the message is no longer forwarded. Typically TTL is no larger than 3.[149]
- *Hops.* A 1-byte field incremented by each peer receiving the message and that indicates the number of hops the message has traveled so far.
- *Payload length.* A 4-byte field containing the number of bytes in the remainder of the message.
- *Payload.* A variable-length field, the contents of which are message dependent.

After a `QueryHit` is received, selected files can be downloaded out of network. That is, a direct connection between the source and target peers is established to perform the data transfer. The protocol for this direct connection is typically HTTP.

Figure 6.4 shows a simplified Gnutella messaging sequence for a set of peers P1 to P6. The messaging is divided into three groups: connecting a new peer to the network, exchanging connectivity information using `Ping` and `Pong`, and query routing.

First, P1 connects to the Gnutella network by exchanging messages to peer P2. How peer P1 initially locates peer P2 is the bootstrap problem discussed later in this chapter. During this phase, the peers exchange information about which version of the protocol they support and what extensions they implement. The extensions are described in capability headers. Peer P2 could reject the

Table 6.1 Basic Message Types for Gnutella v.0.6

Message Type	Meaning
Ping	Discover other hosts that are in the Gnutella network and basic information about connecting to them. If TTL=1 and Hops=0 or 1, treat the request as a direct probe of the receiving host. If TTL=2 and Hops=0, treat the request as a "crawler" ping that is collecting information about the neighbors of this host.
Pong	Reply to a ping. Provides the IP address and part number of the host and extensions supported by the peer. It may include pong responses cached from other peers. Cached entries are peers that are likely to be alive and are spread across the network; for example, by varied connections and hop-count values, these pongs are cached.
Query	Search for a file. Specifies the minimum transfer speed of the peer and the search criteria. The search criteria is text, such as a string of keywords. Search criteria of " " means return an index of all files shared by the peer. A peer forwards incoming queries to all its connected peers.
QueryHit	Response to a query. A peer returns query hit responses to previously forwarded queries back along the connection from which the query was received. Contains the number of hits in the result set and, for each hit, a list of [*file index, file size, file name, and list of extensions*].
Push	Download a request for firewalled peers.
Bye	Tell the remote host that the connection is being closed.

connection request, for example, if it does not have sufficient resources or is going offline. But in this case, peer P2 indicates, similar to HTTP messaging, a 200 OK status.

Now that peer P1 is connected to the Gnutella overlay, it may probe the network to find other neighbors to connect to. P1 issues a crawler Ping to P2 to obtain information about other neighbors. P2 responds with a Pong containing connectivity information about itself and its two neighbors P3 and P4.

Later, using a flooding query, P1 issues a Query with TTL = 3 to P2. P2 responds with a QueryHit and forwards the Query to its neighbors P3 and P4 after decrementing TTL. P3 and P4 in turn return QueryHit responses to P2, and P4 forwards the Query to its neighbor P5. Since TTL = 0 at P5, the Query is not propagated any further. P5's QueryHit is returned to P4, which forwards it back along the path that it came, namely P2 and then P1.

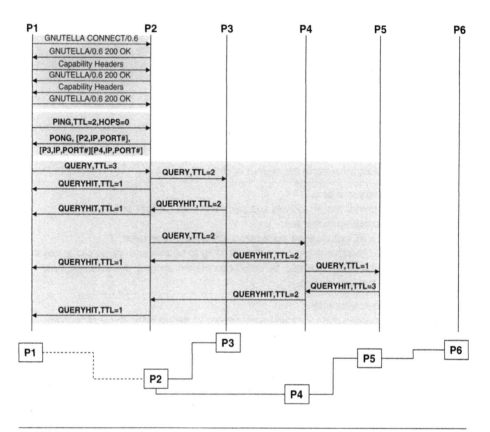

FIGURE 6.4 Example Gnutella messaging using flooding-style query.

During the initial handshake, when a peer connects to another peer in the Gnutella network, each peer exchanges a list of protocol extensions that it supports. The common extensions are listed in Table 6.2. In Table 6.2, headers such as `User-Agent`, `Accept-Encoding`, and `Content-Encoding` are reused from the HTTP 1.1 specification.[151] In addition, the peers will exchange a list of vendor-specific messages that are supported. For more information about vendor-specific messages, see the handshake discussion in [149].

Current versions of Gnutella implement dynamic querying,[149] described in Chapter 3 as expanding ring search. In dynamic querying, the query is successively resent with increasing TTL values until the query is satisfied. For example, an ultrapeer initially sends the query to its leaf peers with TTL = 1. If the leaf peers don't have the file of interest or if the hit count is too low, the requesting ultrapeer sends the query to its ultrapeer neighbors, a step called a *probe query*. Each ultrapeer receiving the query will search its local files and its leaf peers. If the hit response is too low within a specified time period, the initiating ultrapeer enters a third step, called *controlled broadcasting*, in which the TTL is increased

Table 6.2 Gnutella Capability Headers[149]

Header	Example Value	Description
User-Agent	LimeWire/4.10.9	The vendor and version number of the application software
X-Locale-Pref	en	The preferred language of the client, as in en for English
X-Requeries	false	If false, client indicates it won't issue the same query twice
X-Version	4.9	Software version for automatic software updating
Listen-IP	217.254.98.153:6346	IP address and port number of the responding peer
Remote-IP	68.37.233.44	IP address that the request came from, in case the requesting peer doesn't have it due to the presence of a firewall
Accept-Encoding	deflate	If deflate, the responding peer can receive compressed data
Content-Encoding	deflate	If deflate, the requesting peer can send compressed data
X-Ultrapeer	True	If true, responding peer is an ultrapeer; otherwise it is a leaf
X-Try-Ultrapeers	217.254.98.153:6346	A list of other ultrapeers
X-Degree	32	The number of other ultrapeers this ultrapeer connects to at any time
X-Query-Routing	0.1	Indicates support for the Gnutella Query Routing Protocol (QRP) version 0.1
X-Ultrapeer-Query-Routing	0.1	Indicates support for the Gnutella Query Routing Protocol (QRP) version 0.1
X-Dynamic-Querying	0.1	Indicates support for dynamic querying version 0.1
X-Ext-Probes	0.1	Indicates ability to forward query probe messages used in dynamic queries version 0.1
Vendor-Message	0.2	Vendor-specific messages are supported
GGEP	0.5	The Gnutella Generic Extension Protocol (GGEP) version 0.5 is supported
Pong-Caching	0.1	Peer indicates that it automatically forwards its pong cache
X-Max-TTL	3	Messages with TTL values greater than specified will rejected

to 2 or 3 and the query is sent to one or a few ultrapeer neighbors. The larger TTL value causes the query to be sent deeper into the Gnutella network. Sending only to one or a few ultrapeer neighbors limits the amount of query traffic compared to flooding. The TTL value and number of neighbors depend on whether the results of the previous probe query indicated that the file is popular or rare.

Since these repeated query messages use the same message ID, an ultrapeer supporting dynamic querying can't discard messages coming with the same message ID as seen previously. This capability is enabled if the ultrapeer supports the probe query extension and sees a subsequent query message with a larger TTL value.

BitTorrent

BitTorrent[152] is a protocol designed for distributing large files in pieces using mutual distribution of the pieces between a set of peers called a *swarm*. If the swarm is sufficiently large, this offloads the Web server that is the primary source of the content. Generally peers join a swarm to download a specific file and leave the swarm shortly after the file download completes.

The file to be downloaded is available at a Web server called the *seed*, which also provides a torrent file corresponding to the content file. The torrent file identifies the individual fixed-size pieces of the large content file and specifies a host that monitors the peers, called the *tracker*. Peers that want to access the pieces of the content file contact the tracker to determine other peers that have already joined the swarm. Thereafter, peers directly communicate with one another using the peer list provided by the tracker, without requiring the tracker to participate further. In some designs, the tracking is done using a DHT. A trackerless DHT design using the Kademlia algorithm is specified in 153].

A peer seeking to download a file first obtains the torrent file and a URL to the tracker. The tracker returns a list of peers randomly selected from the swarm that are currently downloading the file. Each peer requests pieces to download in random order from its neighbor peers. Each time a peer has successfully retrieved a piece of the file, the downloading peer announces the download to the other peers in the swarm to which it is connected.

The goal of each BitTorrent peer is to maximize its piece download rate in a reciprocal manner. Several policies are implemented in the protocol to achieve fairness, provide incentives for mutual exchange, avoid overloading, and find better peers with which to exchange pieces. Each peer should avoid being overloaded by requests for piece transfer. For this reason and for good TCP performance, each peer limits the number of simultaneous active connections, typically four. These active connections are placed by the peer in the unchoked state, while the other neighbor connections are placed in the choked state. Frequent changes in neighbors' choked state, known as *fibrillation*, are limited to specific time intervals, currently 10-second intervals. Exchanges with neighbors should be fair, that is, each peer should reciprocate by supplying pieces to peers that provide downloads to it. Finally, each peer should try other peers periodically to see if the download rate is better than the current active set.

To achieve the fairness and performance goals, each peer follows several strategies.[154] First, it favors a rarest-first prioritization of pieces to download. It knows which pieces have already been downloaded by its neighbor peers in the swarm. By selecting pieces that have been infrequently downloaded, it increases the likelihood of other peers wanting to exchange pieces with it. Second, it favors peers that have higher capacity based on previous data transfer rates with each neighbor peer. Third, it opportunistically tries other peers periodically to see if better transfer rates can be obtained. This opportunistic unchoking changes peers every 30 seconds.

BitTorrent uses a rate-based tit-for-tat (TFT) strategy in which the download peer chooses other peers based on the capacity of that peer to download the piece of interest. Each download peer has two flags per connection with other peers in the swarm: choked/unchoked and interested/uninterested. An unchoked peer is one in which the download peer considers suitable to send pieces to, based on previous download rates. By sending pieces, the peer increases the chances of receiving pieces from those peers receiving the pieces. Those peers that don't reciprocate with sufficient pieces during a TFT round are subsequently choked. A peer indicates it is either interested or uninterested in receiving exchanges from a neighbor peer in the swarm.

When data is being transferred, download peers queue several piece requests at once to get good transport performance, a technique called *pipelining*.

The BitTorrent peer protocol has the following message types:

- `Choke`. The initial state of a peer, which signifies that it is not sending data to the neighbor peer.
- `Unchoke`. The neighbor peer is to receive pieces from this peer.
- `Interested`. The peer is willing to receive pieces from this neighbor.
- `Not interested`. The peer is not willing to receive pieces from this neighbor.
- `Have`. The piece that this peer has most recently downloaded and verified.
- `Bitfield`. A bitfield that has a 1 bit in each position, indicating pieces already sent by this peer.
- `Request`. Identifies a piece being requested for download.
- `Piece`. Identifies a piece being sent by a neighbor peer.
- `Cancel`. A flow control mechanism to cancel previously requested pieces, typically used near the completion of a file download.

Peers that have a complete copy of the content file and continue to serve other peers are called *seeds*. Peers that are downloading the file are called *leechers*. An example of the population of seeds and leechers is shown in Figure 6.5, which plots the tracker log of the torrent for the Linux RedHat 9 distribution. The data were collected over a nine-month period in 2003. Demand peaks during the first five days, a type of flash crowd effect.

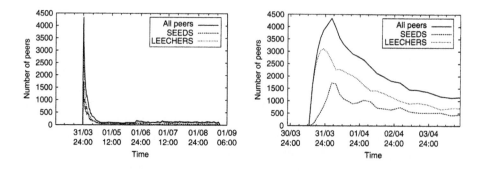

FIGURE 6.5 Trace of swarm population in a torrent: (left) over a five-month period and (right) the first five days.[155] © 2004 Springer-Verlag, with kind permission of Springer Science and Business Media.

Structured Overlays

Most file-sharing systems used unstructured overlays, but the eDonkey system led to the development of two file-sharing overlays based on Kademlia. The original eDonkey system used servers to provide file indexing. Later this was replaced with a structured P2P protocol called Overnet. Overnet used the Kademlia multihop overlay algorithm discussed in Chapter 4. Overnet is no longer operating; an unofficial description of the Overnet protocol is found in [160]. Separately, the eMule application software for the eDonkey network also developed a Kademlia-based overlay network called Kad. The protocol used by eMule is defined in [161]. Currently the Kad network support in eMule is in test phase.

Several experimental systems have created protocols to support a variety of structured overlays. For example, both Overlay Weaver[162,163] and OverSim[164,165] support a variety of multihop structured overlays in a common messaging layer. In this section we discuss the experimental P2PP proposal defined in [166], which is currently being considered as a component of the P2P-SIP specification discussed in Chapter 12. Table 6.3 shows message types for a universal P2P message protocol for structured overlays.

Each peer has an overlay address, typically in an address space of 128 bits or more. To avoid two peers selecting the same address, the address space should be much larger than the number of peers participating in the overlay at any one time, and each peer should randomly select its address. An effective way to accomplish this is to use a cryptographic function on a unique value. Since this function will also be used to generate keys in the DHT, it should be efficient to compute. A common implementation choice is the SHA-1[167] encryption algorithm, since it already implemented on many platforms to support SSL and TLS security protocols.

Several protocol techniques have been studied in the OpenDHT testbed for improving performance of multihop DHTs to counteract transient conditions at

Table 6.3 Example Structured P2P Message Types[166]

Message Category	Message Type	Meaning
Startup	Enroll	Enables the user to become a member of an overlay
	Authenticate	Authenticates the user and creates a binding of the user and/or peer ID to the peer's public certificate
	Bootstrap	Peer locates other peers via which it can join the overlay
Maintenance	Join	An authenticated peer joins the overlay by connecting to one or more other peers already in the overlay
	Leave	Peers departing the overlay notify their neighbors
	KeepAlive	Peers signal their heartbeat to neighboring peers
	LookupPeer	Finds information about a peer for the routing table
	ExchangeTable	Exchanges some part of the routing table with another peer
	Replicate	Replicates resource objects on other peers for redundancy
	Transfer	Transfers ownership of resource objects to another peer, typically after a join or a peer departure
Date storage and retrieval	PublishObject	Publishes or refreshes a resource object for other peers to access
	LookupObject	Searches for a resource-object
	RemoveObject	Removes the resource object
Connection management	Tunnel	Encapsulates an application layer protocol message for transfer over the P2P overlay
	Connect	Initiates a NAT traversal
	Invite	Promotes a client or ordinary peer to superpeer status
	Query	Determines the services or resource objects provided by a peer
Overlay migration	UpdateSoftware	Obtains and transitions to a new version of peer software
	MigrateProtocol	Transitions to a new version of the protocol

peers that can cause long delays in response times.[168] Since peers are shared with other applications, there may be unpredictable changes in workload that affect the peer's processing time. In addition, requests routed through a series of peers may encounter congestion. These techniques include:

- Proximity awareness (discussed in Chapter 10)
- Delay-aware routing (discussed in Chapter 11)
- Iterative routing
- Parallel requests

In *delay-aware routing*, each peer retains the latency of previous communications with its neighbors. New requests are routed toward those neighbors with minimal expected latency. Delay-aware routing can incorporate other factors. First, the progress of the request in the overlay address space can be considered relative to the latency, so that the neighbor that offers the maximum overlay distance per latency will be preferred. This is consistent with the goal of maximizing the progress of the request toward the destination at each hop while accounting for different latency characteristics for the alternative paths. Second, delay-aware routing can be selectively used such that expected latencies below the median of the overlay simply route to maximize the overlay distance covered in the next hop; otherwise the hop is also selected according to the best delay.

In *iterative routing*, first used in Kademlia, the response at each hop is sent back to the originating peer. The originating peer can then select the peer that will be selected for the next hop. The response at each hop will include the set of neighbors for the next hop and their latency. Iterative routing is an alternative to recursive routing, in which the peer at each hop selects its neighboring peer and directly forwards the request to its neighbor. Iterative routing has more message overhead than recursive routing but can more easily be combined with the next technique, *request parallelism*. Accordion, described in Chapter 13, is an overlay that combines parallelism and recursive routing.

In *parallel requests*, the request is sent to multiple peers at the same time. The first response that is received then triggers the next set of parallel requests to its neighbors, and so on. This reduces the impact on nodes that are heavily loaded or may have recently left the overlay, at the cost of greater message overhead. DHTs using request parallelism include Kademlia, EpiChord, and Accordion.

NETWORK ADDRESS TRANSLATION AND P2P OVERLAYS
How NAT Effects P2P Connectivity

A common networking element called a network address translator (NAT) causes significant problems for P2P applications because it, in combination with the network's firewall, typically prevents incoming application connections from reaching their destination host. Enabling peers to circumvent NATs requires some networking acrobatics, referred to as *NAT traversal*. These techniques, particularly important to VoP2P, which involves two-way connections, but are generally applicable to any P2P overlay which spans multiple networks.

A typical use of a NAT in a home or small business network with multiple computers is to allow these computers to share a single public IP address for all connections to the Internet. Otherwise each computer would need a separate public IP address, which must be obtained from an ISP. Instead, with a NAT, each computer has a separate private IP address. As packets leave the local network to a destination address on the Internet, the NAT translates the private source IP address and, depending on the type of NAT, the TCP/UDP port of outgoing packets to a single public IP address and usually a different port. In most protocols this translation is transparent to either of the endpoints. Incoming packets are translated by the NAT to the appropriate private address and port and forwarded by the NAT to that computer. In many cases, the NAT is integrated with the edge router by which the network connects to the ISP network.

The specification of IPv6 with 128-bit addresses to replace the 32-bit addresses of IPv4 was expected to eliminate the need for NATs. But the slower-than-expected conversion of the Internet to IPv6 indicates that NATs will likely be a common fixture on the Internet for some time to come. Currently it is estimated that upward of 70% of hosts are behind NATS.[172] The wide use of NATs complicates the operation of client-to-client protocols such as those used in peer-to-peer applications, since a computer with a private address cannot be directly reached by any computer outside that private network. Figure 6.6 compares an outbound and inbound connection via a NAT. Four computers have private addresses in a small network and reside behind a NAT. When one computer application connects to a Web server on the Internet, the packet contains a private source address and a public destination address. The NAT translates the private source address to its own public address and forwards the packet to the public destination address.

However, when a P2P application running on a computer elsewhere on the Internet wants to connect to a P2P application running on one of the four computers behind the NAT, several problems arise. First, the private address of the

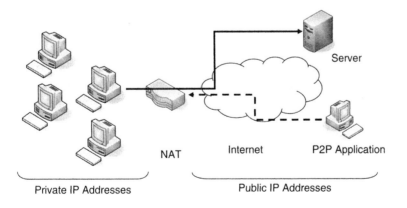

FIGURE 6.6 Effect of NAT on client-to-client connections.

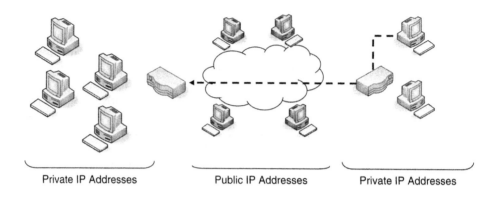

Private IP Addresses   Public IP Addresses   Private IP Addresses

FIGURE 6.7 P2P applications in separate private networks.

target computer can't be used to route the packet through the Internet. Second, if the packet is sent to the public address of the NAT, the NAT can't translate it to the destination computer's private address, since on inbound connection setups there is no way to distinguish which local computer is intended as the destination. On the outbound connection to the server, the NAT remembers the endpoints of the connection so that when the server sends packets in response to the request, the NAT can forward these packets to the proper endpoint. But on inbound connections, the NAT doesn't have the local endpoint address. In addition, most NATs are operating with a firewall, which typically blocks incoming connections for security reasons.

This problem is compounded when each endpoint is behind a NAT, as shown in Figure 6.7. Now both endpoints have private addresses and cannot directly address each other.

NAT Traversal

One way to enable computers behind NATs to receive incoming connections is to explicitly configure the NAT so that an external source address is mapped to a specific private address and port. This approach has the disadvantage that it can be difficult to administer for users who operate their own home or small business networks. For peer-to-peer applications, this is impractical because of the large number of peers that participate in the overlay and the difficulty in knowing which peers will be involved in connections to a given peer. It might be possible for the P2P application itself to dynamically configure the NAT. For example, the UPnP Forum's Internet Gateway Device control protocol,[176] or something like the SIMCO[175] experimental protocol might be used. However, few NATs support such protocols, and there are security issues in permitting applications to control NATs, since network intruders might use the application to open the network to other attacks.

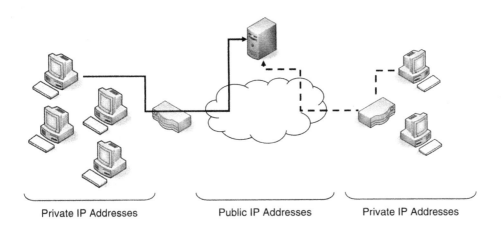

Private IP Addresses   Public IP Addresses   Private IP Addresses

FIGURE 6.8 NAT traversal using an intermediate server.

Consequently, creative application designers have devised ways for their applications to establish client-to-client connections when one or both of the clients are behind NATs. The techniques are referred to as *NAT traversal*. Frequently, NAT traversal involves an intermediate server with a well-known public IP address, as shown in Figure 6.8.

One way to use the intermediate server for NAT traversal is for the server to act as an application relay, forwarding packets between the two endpoints. Since the server has a public IP address, each private client can make a direct connection to it. For large numbers of peers, this doesn't scale, because the load on the server grows according to the number of connections it supports.

Alternately, the public server can use its connectivity between the two endpoints to create a second direct connection between the endpoints. This second, direct connection is used for the actual application packet flow between the endpoints. Even with this improvement, a single server would not scale sufficiently to be used in a large peer-to-peer overlay. In the next subsection we discuss some of the details of the NAT traversal approach, using the Internet Connective Establishment (ICE) protocol[178] as a case study. Later we discuss some issues for using an ICE-like approach in a peer-to-peer overlay.

NAT Traversal with ICE

ICE is intended to enable session-oriented protocols to establish end-to-end connections between endpoints that might be behind NATs. Two important assumptions in the ICE design are that endpoints can't determine their own network topology and that there is a signaling channel already set up between the endpoints. The first assumption means that ICE relies on external servers to determine whether it is behind a NAT and, if so, what its public address is. Following the second assumption, ICE uses the signaling channel to convey the candidate addresses that are available for each endpoint.

There are two phases to ICE's operation. In the first phase, each endpoint performs the same steps. In the second phase, one of the endpoints controls the selection of the connection path from the validated choices obtained by the first phase. Phase one includes these steps (see Figure 6.9): (1) collect the candidate addresses, (2) prioritize the candidates, (3) send the candidates and the priority information to the other endpoint using the signaling path, and (4) validate the candidates received from the endpoint in priority order by four-way handshake. Since more than one pair of candidates may be validated, in the second phase the controlling endpoint selects the nominated candidate and informs the controlled endpoint of the selection.

Figure 6.9 shows the possible addresses that a connection may use to reach an endpoint. There are three cases: (1) the direct network interface, (2) the public address and port of the outermost NAT, and (3) the address and port of a public server that implements the TURN protocol.[180] During the candidate collection step, each endpoint sends a query packet to its designated server. From this packet, the server can determine the endpoint's public address and port for the outermost NAT between the endpoint and the server. The server is able to do this because it receives the packet after its source address has been translated by the NAT, if one is in the path. The server then passes this address as well as an address-port allocation on the server itself back to the endpoint.

The public address of the NAT can be used in a NAT traversal technique known as hole punching. The TURN server address can be used for relaying traffic. For UDP traffic, hole punching is preferred because it is a more direct path, but it depends on the type of NAT.

For session-oriented connections in which endpoints exchange many packets over an extended period of time, the overhead of ICE is a marginal cost compared to the session duration.

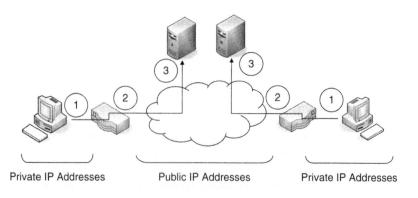

Private IP Addresses   Public IP Addresses   Private IP Addresses

FIGURE 6.9 Candidate address collection in ICE for NAT traversal.

NAT Traversal in a P2P Overlay

In a large overlay, peers can be spread over many private networks behind NATs as well as throughout the Internet. For brevity, we'll refer to peers behind NATs as *NATed peers*. As shown in the previous discussion, a NAT traversal mechanism is needed for any host to be able to participate in the overlay protocol as a full peer.

An alternative design is to designate peers that are NATed as clients of the overlay. In this case, only those peers with public addresses are part of the overlay. Clients can issue requests to the overlay by sending them to one of the public peers. This approach is called the *superpeer model*. The success of this approach in general depends on the availability of sufficient numbers of peers that want to act as resource servers for a potentially large population of client peers.

As discussed earlier in the book, peers in structured overlays maintain routing tables for forwarding messages between peers. These routing tables map overlay addresses to routable IP addresses for the given peer. Considering the three types of addresses used by ICE, generally only Type 2 (the NAT public address) or Type 3 (a public relay supporting the TURN protocol) would be of use for overlays spanning the Internet and multiple private networks.

Relayed connections (Type 3) could be used to make NATed peers full-fledged members of the overlay. However, either a large collection of TURN servers would be needed or those peers with public addresses would be required to offer TURN-like services to the NATed peers. The relayed NAT traversal model for NATed peers thus exhibits the load distribution properties of the superpeer architecture, with additional complexity for supporting a NAT traversal protocol such as ICE.

Hole punching can be used for many NATs if Type 2 addresses are known. However, a large number of NATs don't support hole punching,[171] and there are limits on the number of separate incoming connections the NAT can support. The message-routing mechanism and routing table maintenance mechanisms of most structured overlays would need to incorporate dynamic NAT traversal mechanisms. This could be a significant cost, offsetting the benefits of load sharing across a larger set of peers.

PEER CAPABILITY DETERMINATION
Overview

As part of determining its role in the overlay, each peer evaluates the capacity of the local system and network resources needed to perform the role. The *peer capability* is the available resources at a peer relevant to its role in a peer-to-peer overlay, specified as a set of capacities and system attributes. For conventional operating systems, there are well-defined system APIs and local management agents that an application can access to determine the state of most potential resources. We can divide these into static and dynamic capabilities. Static capabilities include CPU type and speed, installed memory, and network interface speed. Dynamic capabilities include the current memory, network, and CPU utilization.

Most hosts are used for other applications in addition to the P2P application. The "good citizen" rule means that the peer cooperates with other applications in sharing the system resources and won't attempt to allocate all available resources to itself. Peer applications may provide an interface for the user to configure how much system resource should be used by the P2P application. Further, a peer should be able to limit incoming message flow and system usage by other peers. This requires that the overlay protocol includes mechanisms for throttling and redirecting message flow and that each peer has a means to measure the system and network resource utilization due to other peers' requests.

After startup, at any time the peer should have a snapshot of its current capabilities and may maintain some historic values for determining longer-term averages. Such averages can be used to determine, for example, whether a sudden change in capacity is an anomaly. Given the capability snapshot, we define the *peer capability assessment* as an algorithmic decision as a function of peer capability as to whether a peer satisfies the criteria for a specific role such as supernode status. There can be different assessments for different roles.

It may be convenient to exchange capabilities with other peers. When a peer is searching for a resource or service, it could prefer to access the resource or service at a more capable peer. This requires a format for encoding capabilities and their values.

Network Capacity

A peer has a network interface that has a maximum bandwidth capacity for sending and receiving packets of information from other nodes in the network. The bandwidth capacity of the network interface is generally not a good estimator of the actual available end-to-end bandwidth that a peer can achieve in communicating with another peer anywhere in the network. First, the actual access network the peer is connected to may have much lower bandwidth. For example, existing Fast Ethernet network interfaces support 100 Mbps and higher data rates, whereas most DSL and cable modem broadband access networks have data rates that are asymmetric and typically less than 5 Mbps. Second, other packet traffic in the network reduces the available bandwidth and, if the network is heavily congested, may cause packets to be lost or dropped.

One technique for estimating bandwidth between two endpoints is called a *packet train*. In a packet train, a sender node sends a series of fixed-length packets at the maximum rate it can to the destination node. When the destination receives the first packet, it starts a timer. When the last packet in the packet train is received at the destination, the total payload of the series of packets divided by the elapsed time from first to last packet is the available bandwidth between the two endpoints. The packet train estimates bandwidth in one direction only. If measurement is needed in both directions, the source and destination must reverse roles and do a separate packet train measurement in the opposite direction. In addition, since network conditions change from time to time, the endpoints can periodically repeat the bandwidth measurement to maintain an accurate estimate.

In some cases it may matter whether the bandwidth estimation is performed in-band versus out of band. An in-band measurement is performed by sending the packet train over the same network connection that the application data follows. A packet sent in-band is more likely to follow the network route that the actual application data packets follow, thus giving a more reliable measurement. However, in-band measurement requires that the endpoints flagged the measurement packets so that they are not confused as application data.

Peer Lifetime

Peer roles such as superpeer and relay generally prefer peers that are likely to be connected to the overlay for higher-than-average time periods because the departure of such peers has a greater impact on more peers.

Some studies of actual overlays have found that node lifetime is heavy tailed, meaning that peers whose lifetime exceeds the mean peer lifetime are likely to stay connected to the overlay for a much longer time. When a peer first joins the overlay, it can start a timer to measure its lifetime. When the timer reaches a certain time value, the peer can use that as an indicator that its lifetime is likely to persist. The peer can also keep a history of previous session durations to determine whether the recent history shows a pattern of longer-than-average sessions. Further, it can also examine the system uptime to determine how frequently the host is restarted or brought offline. System uptime history is accessible on conventional operating systems.

BOOTSTRAPPING AND PARTITIONS
Finding a Rendezvous Peer

Bootstrapping is the mechanism by which a newly joining peer identifies a peer already in the overlay to which it can issue the join request. Since it is not yet part of the overlay, it can't use the search mechanisms of the overlay itself to locate a peer with which to connect. The alternatives include:

- Bootstrap server
- Broadcast or multicast discovery
- Bootstrap overlay
- Cached entries from previous sessions

Let's call a peer that receives the join request a *rendezvous peer*. The rendezvous peer may not have the capacity to accept another peer as a neighbor. If it does not, it can respond with a rejection, which includes a referral list of other rendezvous peers. Ideally, the bootstrap method should distribute the join request load across a large set of rendezvous peers so that rendezvous peers don't become overloaded and so that rejections are minimized. In addition, the list of rendezvous peers should be fresh so that join requests don't experience timeouts. Finally, depending on the overlay, it may be desirable that the rendezvous peer be close to the joining peer.

In the bootstrap server approach, one or more servers with well-known addresses are configured to provide a list of rendezvous peers. If all joining peers first contact a bootstrap server, it is easy for the bootstrap server to maintain a list of rendezvous peers and to tailor that list so that successive referrals are distributed across the overlay. The bootstrap server removes peers from its list when such peers leave the overlay or fail to provide a keep-alive message. A disadvantage with the bootstrap server approach is that it requires that one or more servers be available for the overlay to operate. An advantage is that it is less susceptible to the formation of overlay islands or partitions than a distributed scheme.

A joining peer can issue a broadcast or multicast discovery request to discover a rendezvous peer. Rendezvous peers listen on a well-known broadcast or multicast address and respond by sending information to the requesting peer regarding details of making a connection to the rendezvous peer. Alternately, each rendezvous peer can periodically broadcast an advertisement containing this information, and joining peers can listen for such advertisements. Broadcasts flood the network and are not suitable for large area discovery or advertisement. Consequently, if a rendezvous peer and the joining peer are not near each other in the network, broadcast discovery will fail. Group multicast protocols are not universally supported on the Internet, so multicast discovery may not be reliable.

Peers can cache a list of rendezvous peers from previous sessions in the overlay. If the list is sufficiently large, it increases the probability of locating an active rendezvous. Though caching doesn't solve the problem of how a first time peer locates a rendezvous point, it can substantially reduce the load on other mechanisms, more so as the overlay's churn rate grows.

A universal overlay could be operated in which peers in every other overlay are members.[183] Rendezvous peers in each overlay store their connection details in the universal overlay. Joining peers search the universal overlay for rendezvous peers in the overlay of interest. The entries in the universal overlay need to be periodically refreshed to avoid stale entries. If the universal overlay is a DHT, the indexing method for discovering rendezvous peers should distribute the request load to avoid overloading individual peers.

Merging Partitions

An overlay partition is the separation of two or more sets of peers into separate overlays. Partitions can occur due to sudden failure of connections between the two sets of peers, due to a network failure, sudden massive churn, or a denial-of-service attack on the overlay itself. A partition could also be formed during overlay creation if, for example, respective rendezvous peers are in separate regions of the network and cross-connections between peers in separate regions are not created. A partition is undesirable since the collective resources of the full set of peers cannot be achieved.

To merge two overlays requires that the partition must first be detected and then that peers in each partition obtain connection information for their counterparts. One technique is to force each peer in one partition to rejoin the other partition by sending join requests to rendezvous peers in the continuing overlay. Sometime after joining the new partition, each peer from the dropped partition would put its shared objects into the overlay. This approach could create a massive amount of routing table changes in the continuing partition. A side effect is that each join leads to data movement as peers in the continuing overlay adjust their index storage to new neighbors. If the joining peers from the dropped partition immediately reindex their data objects in the continuing overlay, these objects will likely contribute to further data movement during the merge period.

The volume of messaging could be mitigated by controlling the rate at which peers from the dropped partition can join to the continuing overlay. Such rate control will mean that some peers are penalized with significant delays in being able to access the continuing overlay.

P2P NETWORKING SUPPORT IN MICROSOFT WINDOWS

Starting in Windows XP, Microsoft has added capabilities to the operating system to support P2P applications.[182] These new capabilities include peer identity, distributed peer name resolution, connectivity with other peers, formation of secure peer groups, and search.

Peer Identity

The structure of the Peer Name Resolution Protocol ID (PNRP ID) shown in Figure 6.10 enables each peer to create multiple IDs for itself, each ID being unique and securely authenticated using the peer's public key. Each PNRP ID

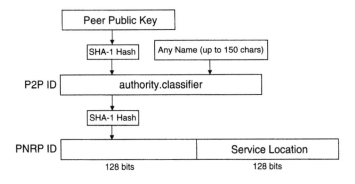

FIGURE 6.10 Peer identity construction.

can be associated with a separate application, using the classifier component of the P2P ID. If a peer has more than location in a network area, these can be distinguished using different values for the service location field.

Peer Name Resolution Protocol

Using the Peer Name Resolution Protocol (PNRP), any PNRP ID can be resolved to its IPv6 address and a self-signed digital certificate called the Certified Peer Address (CPA). The CPA itself contains IP address, port numbers, and protocol IDs for communicating with the peer. PNRP is a decentralized protocol that doesn't require use of the server-based Distributed Name Service (DNS) used on the Internet to resolve hostnames to IP addresses.

Each peer maintains a cache of PNRP IDs. Each cache entry includes the IP address of the peer and the CPA corresponding to the PNRP ID. When a peer wants to use a service on another peer for which it has the PNRP ID but no IP address, it uses the PNR protocol to resolve the ID into an IP address. PNRP is an iterative protocol that selects the closest ID in its cache. It sends a request to peer with the closest ID. The requested peer looks in its cache to find either the requested ID or an ID closer than its own. In either case, it returns the ID to the requesting peer; otherwise it returns a negative result. The requesting peer continues searching if the ID was not found, by sending the request to the closest ID returned by the previous peer or, if none, by sending the request to the next closest ID in its own cache.

PNRP ID caches are organized hierarchically with a limit of log N levels, each level containing no more than 20 entries, where N is the number of peers in the network. The lowest level contains entries nearest to this peer's ID. To ensure that PNRP converges, each time a peer adds an entry to the lowest level of its cache, it floods a copy of the entry to all the peers already in the last level of the cache. Cache entries are periodically refreshed, and stale entries are removed.

The PNRP resolution sequence, combined with the hierarchical cache structure, makes the protocol similar to lookups performed in multihop DHTs using iterative routing. Further information about other features of PNRP including cache organization, cache initialization, and APIs is available at [181].

Peer Overlay

The peer overlay in the Microsoft design is called a *graph*, and the function of managing the peer's participation in the overlay is called *graphing* (see Figure 6.11). This figure also shows the other key pieces of the Microsoft peer functions, including Grouping for managing peer groups, Identity Manager for managing secure peer identities, and the Name Service Provider (NSP), which in this context is the interface to the PNRP.

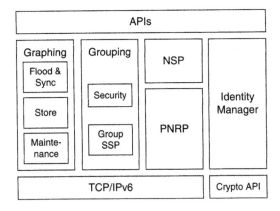

FIGURE 6.11 Peer components in Windows.

Data are shared and replicated between peers by flooding updates across the graph. Thus the current Microsoft P2P model for data sharing can be described as an unstructured overlay with flooding.

Each peer has a data store in which to maintain shared data. Each data item has a globally unique ID (GUID), a version number, and a timestamp. When data are changed, they are flooded across the graph to all other connected peers to keep all peers' data stores in sync.

Each graph is identified by the lowest peer ID that is part of the graph. If the graph becomes partitioned, it can be detected by determining whether the lowest peer ID has changed.

When joining the graph, a joining peer determines the peer to connect to using PNRP or DNS to locate the peer. If the peer has sufficient capacity to accept a new peer connection, it will accept the connection. Otherwise, it provides a referral list of other peers in the graph, which may accept the join request. The joining peer selects a peer randomly from the referral list and sends a join request to it. Each peer periodically manages its connections with other peers to eliminate those with low utility in providing unique or timely information.

Grouping

Within a graph, any subset of peers may form a secure relationship, called a *group*. Management of groups is handled by the Grouping function (see Figure 6.11). The group is a mechanism to enforce private and secure communication and data sharing between peers in the group. Each group has a creator and a unique ID. Peers join the group by invitation. The definition of the group includes permissions for which peers have access rights to modify data objects shared within the group.

The security features of a group can be tailored by an application, including:

- Connection authentication, confidentiality, and integrity
- Encryption of messages for message/record confidentiality
- Validation of messages between peers

In the default implementation, groups and group members are identified using a secure peer ID. Each peer ID is backed by a private key, which only the peer holds. The peer signs its CPA using its private key, which any other peer can verify using the peer's public key. The same method is used to name groups. When a group is created, the creator also generates a new public and private key pair for the group. It also produces a Group Root Certificate (GRC), which is signed using the group private key. The GRC is used to validate the membership of peers in the group by acting as the root of the certificate chain for each member. The group ID is registered using PNRP. The group owner also establishes group security policies.

Each peer that is a member of the group is given a Group Membership Certificate (GMC) when it is invited to join the group by the group owner. The GMC is an X.509 digital certificate signed by the group's private key. The GMC contains the peer name identifying the member in the Subject Alternate Name property of the certificate. The peer name is a secure peer name validated by the peer's CPA. GMCs may be given an expiration time.

The new group member connects to the group using PNRP to resolve the group ID and obtain the address of a group member. It then attempts to establish a secure, mutually authenticated TLS connection with the current group member. Mutual trust is based on the GMCs that each peer holds and that can be validated using the GRC. After joining, the new group member receives the existing group data records from the peer to which it is connected. It can subsequently connect to other group members using the graph management methods described earlier. The Group Security Service Provider (SSP; see Figure 6.11) is used to establish secure connections between group members.

Identity Management

Each peer has a unique identity in the graph and uses self-signed digital certificates conforming to X.509 to authenticate itself to other peers. The use of self-signed certificates means that each peer acts as its own certification authority (CA). This allows the graph to operate independently of access to an external hierarchy of CAs, but it has the limitation that the identity of the peer is not validated by any external agency.

The Identity Manager (Figure 6.11) performs the creation and management of peer identities.

Search

In the current design, peers can search their local data stores using keyword search with Boolean operators. Both content search and metadata search are supported. Groups automatically replicate all shared records to all group members. Search queries are not currently sent to other group members.

SUMMARY

Challenges in describing the practice of peer-to-peer implementation are the ad hoc state of some implementations, lack of detailed documentation, and proprietary closed systems. Important issues common to many systems can nevertheless be identified, including NAT traversal, bootstrapping, dynamic resource assessment, and protocol design. Some items such as routing table organization have been omitted from discussion because these details seem too specific to particular algorithms.

The emergence of platform support, such as P2P networking services in Microsoft's Windows XP and Vista, may lead to regularized middleware-based P2P applications in the future.

FOR FURTHER READING

Application programming interfaces for DHTs have been described in [147], [148], [162], and [168].

The incentive mechanism in BitTorrent has been studied in [156], [157], [158], and [159].

Strauss et al.[185] provide survey tools for available bandwidth measurement and report on a comparison of various tools over a large number of Internet paths.

To support rapid merging and splitting of overlays, Jelasity et al.[184] propose a bootstrapping service. The bootstrapping service is built on a sampling service that maintains a random sampling of reachable nodes. During a reformation of the overlay, all participating peers exchange a list of peers from the sampled set to recreate the overlay.

Windows P2P networking support relies on IPv6 and uses Intra-Site Automatic Tunnel Addressing Protocol (ISATAP)[186] and 6to4[187] to provide IPv6 interoperability in IPv4 environments. NAT traversal support is based on Teredo.[188]

Search

7

Search is an intrinsic function of most P2P overlays, and the overlay geometry and routing protocol is often designed to make search efficient. There are many types of search mechanism, from keyword and simple pattern matching to information retrieval and content-based retrieval. This chapter looks at the intrinsic search capability available in different P2P architectures, including search in unstructured overlays and hash-based indexing in DHTs. Various types of search queries, including keyword, range queries, and semantic search, are also discussed. A look at the state of the art of content-based retrieval and pattern matching in P2P overlays concludes the chapter.

OVERVIEW

Efficient search is essential in many aspects of today's digital entertainment and enterprise and personal applications. Search, according to Webster's Dictionary,[189] means "to look into or over carefully or thoroughly in an effort to find or discover something." The quality of a searching scheme is governed by the recall rate, precision, and speed to locate the desired object or data. These metrics have been long used in information retrieval, where recall rate is the fraction of documents that are relevant to the query that are actually retrieved and precision is the fraction of objects retrieved that are relevant to the query. Thus, an efficient searching scheme needs to take storage, indexing, query, and retrieval into consideration. In other words, how and where objects are stored and the way the objects are indexed, queries are formulated and matched, accurate queries are matched, and fast objects are retrieved can have substantial impact on the efficiency and effectiveness of a system's data searching capability.

P2P networks use the computation, storage, and bandwidth resources of peer nodes. Consequently, information retrieval in a P2P network must take into account the network model as well as the characteristics of the information being acquired, stored, and transmitted. Ideally, a P2P search algorithm should achieve high recall and high precision query results while supporting complex queries, low cost, high robustness and reliability, and fast query response. Many studies on improving

163

routing efficiency to increase the speed of query returns, reducing routing maintenance cost, and improving fault-tolerance capabilities can be found in the research literature. Notably, most existing P2P systems support simple key- or ID-based object lookup. This is especially true for structured P2P networks. Unstructured P2P networks can handle more complex queries, such as keyword-based search. Semantic search, where queries are expressed in natural language instead of simple keywords, poses significant challenges, especially in structured P2P networks. In this chapter, we look at some existing indexing and query schemes to understand the requirements, approaches, and challenges in designing P2P search schemes. Data storage schemes, routing scalability, and reliability, although having significant impact on searching efficiency, are discussed in other chapters of this book, so those will not be covered in this chapter.

CENTRALIZED VS. LOCALIZED VS. DISTRIBUTED INDEXING

Most existing P2P indexing schemes can be categorized into local, centralized, distributed, or hybrid indexing types. Figure 7.1 illustrates centralized, local, and distributed types of indexing systems. Sample hybrid indexing configurations are shown in Figure 7.2.

Centralized Indexing

With a centralized index (see Figure 7.1A), the index is kept on a centralized server. Object lookup is done by searching over the index on the central server to obtain the location of the target object. Napster,[190] the father of today's P2P content distribution system, is a classical example of centralized indexing. In

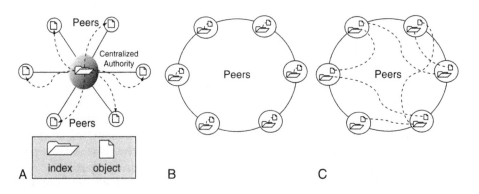

FIGURE 7.1 Illustration of (A) centralized index, (B) local index, and (C) distributed indexing.

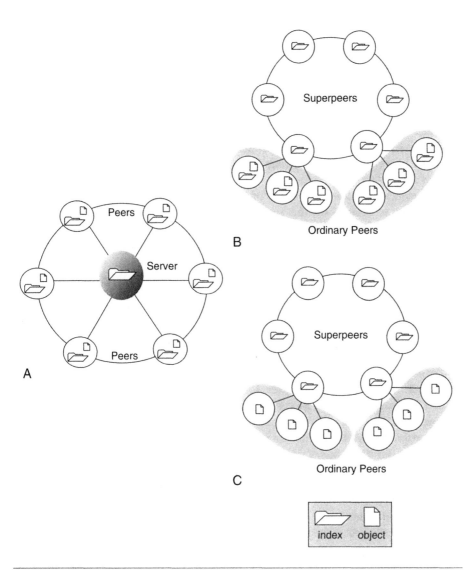

FIGURE 7.2 Illustration of sample hybrid indexing configurations.

Napster, peers share MP3 files stored locally on their hard drives. Text-based content description, such as the title of a song, is then generated, indexed, and stored by the Napster server. Each peer in the Napster network uses the Napster client software to connect to the centralized Napster server. Peers connected to the Napster server can submit keyword-based queries for a particular audio file. A list of matching files along with the description and location of the file is sent to the peer from the server. The peer then tries to connect to the peer with the desired audio file and transfers the target content in a P2P fashion. iMesh[191] is another example of a centralized indexing P2P system with the capability to serve any type of file.

The most noticeable drawbacks of a fully centralized indexing system include vulnerability to attacks on the server and the possibility of a bottleneck at the server. Research in centralized P2P indexing has been limited since Napster was shut down and due to the advantages of distributed search discussed next.

Localized Indexing

In a local index-based system (see Figure 7.1B), each peer keeps the directory of its own data objects locally. The early Gnutella[192] design is a typical example of local index-based P2P system. Local object indexing can be used to support complex query search. When a peer generates a query, it conveys the query to peers in the network to locate the desired object, most often through flooding or random walk, as discussed in Chapter 3. Forwarding of query messages is stopped when the desired object is found or when the Time-to-Live (TTL) value expires.

Compared to centralized indexing schemes, localized indexing can create more network load since queries potentially have to be sent to many peers in the overlay. But since query processing is distributed across many peers in parallel, there is inherent scalability. If any peer node is faulty, it affects the objects stored locally but not the overall search mechanism of the network. Thus localized indexing offers advantages over centralized schemes in terms of system scalability and reliability. It has led to the development of many Gnutella-based systems, including Bearshare,[193] Shareaza,[194] and Limewire,[195] since the protocol was first released in 2000.

Theoretically, with suitable query modeling and searching algorithm, any kind of complex query can be supported in this kind of system. However, purely localized P2P indexing systems suffer from the high cost often associated with query flooding and low object retrieval efficiency. FastTrack tackles the problem via a hybrid P2P architecture. Peers are divided into two classes: superpeers and ordinary peers. Indices may be kept on each peer locally. Peers with significant computational power and larger bandwidth serve as superpeers, which are connected together to create an overlay network that acts as a hub processing all query requests received from ordinary nodes within the network. When a peer issues a query, it submits the query to the superpeer; the query message is then propagated to other superpeers, which then deliver it to the connected ordinary peers. Like Gnutella, message propagation is terminated once the target object is found or a predefined TTL is reached. Once the object is found, it is transferred directly from the target peer to the querying peer.

Distributed Indexing

Distributed index (see Figure 7.1C), on the other hand, distributes the index over all peers. Pointers to a single object may reside in multiple indices located in different peer nodes, most often in neighborhood peer nodes. Freenet[196] is one of the earliest P2P systems in this category. It uses content hash keys to identify files. Queries are forwarded to neighborhood peers based on a peer routing table until the target object is found or the TTL threshold is reached. One disadvantage posed by Freenet is its long startup time at peer joining. Subsequently, Mache[197] proposed to place additional index entries on successful queries. Freenet offers only key-based indexes, but FASD[198] suggests to cache lists of weighted keywords and to use Term Frequency Inverse Document Frequency (TFIDF)[199] measures along with inverted indexes[200] to offer keyword-based searching capability in distributed indexing systems. It is worth mentioning here that an inverted index is a popular data structure used in databases and information retrieval. It maps a search key such as a word to a list enumerating documents containing the key. The list may also comprise the locations of occurrence within each document. Inverted indexing allows efficient implementation of Boolean, extended Boolean, proximity, relevance, and many other types of search algorithms. It is one of the most popular index mechanisms used in document retrieval. Noticeably, an inverted index is not limited to distributed indexing for P2P systems.

The Foreseer P2P system also employs distributed indices.[201] Cai et al. claim their approach improves efficiency in decentralized unstructured P2P systems using two orthogonal overlays, which they term *neighbor* and *friend overlays*. Foreseer is based on the idea that everyone has neighbors and friends. People tend to get to know their neighbors over time as they become more settled within their environment and make friends through social interactions. Taking advantage of this observation, Foreseer constructs its two orthogonal overlay-based system accordingly. In query search, neighbor peers help reduce response time and lower resource consumption; friend peers offer better temporal locality.

Today, distributed indexing is one of the most popular P2P indexing schemes seen in the literature. Many search algorithms that we discuss later in this chapter use a distributed index.

Hybrid Indexing

Hybrid indexing intends to take advantage of the query efficiency of centralized indexing and the scalability of localized and distributed indexing. For instance, Figure 7.2C presents an example of hybrid indexing under a hybrid P2P overlay. In this case, superpeers (supernodes) maintain the indices in a distributed manner. A query from an ordinary peer is sent to its superpeer to retrieve the location of the desired object. The superpeer forwards the query to other superpeers if it does not find the desired object in its own index. Information about the desired object is sent back to the ordinary peer via its superpeer. Thereafter, the query issuer may directly contact the peer with the desired object.

HASHING-BASED INDEXING AND LOOKUPS

DHT-based P2P systems are one of the best known types of P2P systems in which searching processes are more finely controlled. With strong theoretical foundations, DHT-based P2P systems offer efficient key- or ID-based exact match lookups: given a key- or an ID-based query, the system can guarantee the return of results if they exist. In a DHT-based P2P system, each data object and each peer is uniquely identified using a numerical key or an ID h that is generated via a one-way hash function $H(\ )$ of a unique description f of the object or peer ob:

$$h_i = H(f(ob_i))$$

The hash of objects and peers are within the same identifier space, with each peer responsible for all keys in a certain portion of the identifier space. DHT-based P2P systems can be classified into hierarchical and flat categories.[202] Flat DHT map a flat address space to a variety of geometries, including ring, hypercube, mesh, and de Bruijin graph, as disccussed in Chapter 4. Chord,[203,204] CAN,[205] Pastry,[206] and Tapestry,[207] for instance, are four example systems of this kind. Hierarchical DHTs organize peers into different groups or sets. Each group forms its own overlay and together they construct a hierarchical overlay based on DHT. Hierarchical overlays are discussed in Chapter 5.

Searching in a Flat DHT

Chord employs a ring topology. A consistent hashing function, such as SHA-1, is used to generate peer and object IDs known as *keys*. The peer ID may be created using the peer IP address and port; the object ID can be generated from its text description. Every object key k is assigned to the peer whose ID is larger than or equal to the hash value of k. In Chord, peer IDs increase clockwise. Chord uses a hashing function designed to distribute object keys evenly throughout the ring topology. Every peer keeps a routing table with the information about its successor, with queries passed from successor to successor. When the query hash value is greater than or equal to the hash value of the peer ID, the peer can map the query to an object key in its responsibility. To overcome the need to traverse every peer, a peer can attempt to find the predecessor using a finger table.

CAN is another distributed system that maps keys onto values, self-organizes, and routes queries using the DHT concept. CAN forms a P2P overlay network that stores chunks of a DHT (object IDs) known as *zones*. The protocol is based on a virtual d-dimensional Cartesian coordinate space. This space is dynamically partitioned among all the peers in the system. Every peer owns its own zone within the global coordinate space. Object IDs, hash values of descriptions of the objects, are mapped into the partitioned space. A peer is responsible for all object IDs resides in its zone. A CAN peer maintains a routing table that holds its neighbor's IP address and its coordinate zone. A peer routes a query message toward its destination using a simple greedy forwarding to the neighbor peer that is closest to the destination coordinates.

Pastry and Tapestry both use Plaxton-like prefix routing. Pastry peers are identified in the network space using a 128-bit identifier, known as the nodeId. The nodeId indicates a peer's position in the circular nodeId space. The nodeIds themselves are assigned randomly when the peer first connects to the Pastry network. Many mechanisms can be used to derive the nodeId, including a peer's public key or IP address-based hashing. Peers within Pastry maintain their own routing tables and a neighborhood set that contains information about the peers closest to the local peer. The routing table holds the set of peers with numerically closest but larger nodeIds and numerically smaller nodeIds, relative to the present peer's nodeId. A prefix-routing algorithm is used to forward query messages until the target object is found.

All three schemes discussed here use greedy routing to move the query closer to the destination. Compared to these algorithms,[208] de Bruijn graphs[209] can achieve better routing efficiency since they can achieve an asymptotically optimal diameter that impacts query delay and aggregated lookup load.

Searching in Hierarchical DHTs

Hierarchical DHTs organize peers into different sets or groups, most often into two to three hierarchies. Kelips divides the peers into k virtual affinity groups with group IDs of $[0, k\text{-}1]$. To search for an object, the querying peer A in group G hashes the file to the files belonging to group G'. If G' is the same as G, the query is resolved by checking the local intragroup data index. Otherwise, A forwards the query to the topologically closest contact in group G' until the target object is located.

A more popular hierarchical DHT scheme classifies peers into superpeers and ordinary peers based on the peers' processing power, bandwidth, or other resources or capabilities. Object lookup starts with the superpeer SA connected to the querying peer A. If SA is responsible for key K, SA locates and returns the query results to A. Otherwise SA forwards the query to other superpeers according to a specific routing algorithm until the target object is located. KaZaA,[210] for example, employs the two-tier hierarchical structure with the superpeers indexing the files in their managed groups.

Discussion

With guaranteed search results and high search speed along with its high scalability, DHT-based P2P protocols are said to provide considerable benefits over early centralized and fully decentralized P2P protocols. The tradeoff is the routing table maintenance cost because the network topology is continually changing. Therefore, managing a consistent DHT requires considerable effort. In an attempt to leverage the benefits of DHT but also minimize some of its inherent limitations, the JXTA[211] specification has tried to create a balance by creating a hybrid system that uses a loosely consistent DHT.[212] The JXTA overlay network acts as a virtual hash table containing the index of all the published objects that they call advertisements in JXTA.[213] Peers are classified into two categories: ordinary peers, called *edge peers* in JXTA, and superpeers, called *rendezvous peers* in JXTA. Shared resource distributed index (SRDI) is used to create and maintain a conceptual index of resources in the network through a set of specified XML attributes. The distributed index maintained resembles a hash table, with the indexed attributes as hash keys and the hash values mapping back to the source peer containing the actual advertisement. Queries can then be made anywhere in the rendezvous network based on these attributes. In this way, SRDI can answer advertisement queries in the network by locating the peer that has the required advertisement. An edge peer can query the hash table at any time by supplying a set of attributes—the hash keys in the table. The query is resolved by the network (actually, the rendezvous superpeer network) by hashing the key to the required value (that is, the peer containing the requested advertisement). That is, the rendezvous peers form a rendezvous network that maintains a DHT. Because the set of rendezvous peers cooperating to implement the DHT may come and go (albeit less frequently than edge peers) in a P2P network, the DHT cannot be maintained in a perfectly consistent fashion at all times. When a rendezvous goes away, the chunk of index that it is maintained by it becomes unavailable for a period of time (until the responsible peers publish it again). This loosely consistent DHT helps deal with the transient nature of peers in a P2P network.

Recall that Chord, Pastry, and CAN rely on more costly mechanisms to keep the network view consistent. Although JXTA can reduce the maintenance cost via a less costly mechanism that ensures the network view is only loosely consistent, the inconsistency may be permanent and hence cause problems at query retrieval.

A second most noted weakness of DHT-based systems is that this type of system usually cannot support keyword or complex queries. In most applications, obviously, keyword-based searches and complex queries are more useful than key- or ID-based exact match searches. Later in this chapter we look at some schemes that tackle this problem.

SEARCHING IN UNSTRUCTURED OVERLAYS
Flooding-Based Search

Flooding-based search was a popular approach in early unstructured P2P networks. In this approach, the querying peer sends the query request to all or a subset of its neighbors. Each neighbor that receives the query request processes the request and returns the result if a match is found. If no match is found, the neighbor forwards the query request to its neighbors, and so on. The process continues until a fixed TTL threshold is reached. Basically, a flooding-based search floods the query request through the P2P network, with the querying peer being the center of the flood. Clearly, this type of search mechanism is high in cost and inefficient due to the massive amount of query messaging being transmitted for a single query.

Gnutella used breadth-first search (BFS) and fixed TTL to limit the number of hops each query may have, in an attempt to reduce query bandwidth cost. The downside of it, though, is the reduction of the probability of a target object being found. Thus, many improved searching schemes for unstructured P2P networks were proposed. These include iterative deepening, guided search, random walk, bloom filter-based search, and adaptive probabilistic search, to name a few. In the following, we look at these approaches to further understand the challenges of content searching in unstructured P2P networks.

Iterative Deepening

To improve the recall rate in a flooding-based search, Yang and Garcia-Molina[214] proposed iterative deepening, whereby a growing ring is used to iteratively deepen the query flooding range until the target object is found. If a query is satisfied within a first iteration, the query is stopped. Otherwise, a second query message is issued to a large ring, that is, it reaches more nodes in the network. Noticeably, iterative deepening does not reduce the number of duplicated messages.

Random Walk-Based Search

Random walk is another popular scheme without duplication of query messages. The querying node forwards (walks) the query message (walker) to one randomly selected neighbor, which randomly selects its neighbor to forward the query message. The walk goes on until the target object is located. Certainly random walk reduces the number of duplicated messages, with a penalty of long search delays. This can be a significant problem in many real-world applications. To reduce searching delays, k-walker,[215] where the querying node forwards the query message to k randomly selected neighbors instead of one neighbor generating k walkers is proposed. Since the number of nodes reached by k random walkers in h hops is the same as in one random walk over kh hops, a k times reduction in query delay can be expected. Other variations of random walk also exist.[202]

Guided Search

Guided search rests on the idea that "guidance" on where the query message should be forwarded can improve query efficiency. In routing index-based guided search,[216] each peer maintains a routing index that gives "direction" toward objects. On receiving a query, the "goodness" of its neighbor is evaluated using the routing index to determine where the query should be forwarded. To keep track of the "goodness" of neighbors, a node needs to keep track of statistics, such as the number of query results returned through the neighbor, on all its neighbors.

With a similar idea, Yang and Garcia-Molina[214] used a directed BFS scheme to reduce the routing cost of BFS. A subset, instead of all neighbors of a peer, receives the query messages. Each node maintains a set of statistics of its neighbors to estimate the "goodness" of them. Neighbors are selected based on their "goodness" for query forwarding.

A more intelligent guided search[217] uses keyword vector, query similarity function, peer ranking, and profile to guide the query forwarding. It's based on the assumption that peers that answered certain queries are likely to answer similar queries with higher probability. At object search, the querying peer first evaluates the past performance of all its neighbors to find those neighbors that have answered similar queries. The query message is forwarded to only those with a high ranking value at evaluation. The query message is then forwarded similarly until a predefined TTL is reached or the target object is found. To answer query requests, each peer needs to store a profile that keeps track of queries it answered. The efficiency of this kind of approach is largely dependent on the accuracy of the query similarity function.

Adaptive probabilistic search (APS)[218] extends the k-walker random walk scheme using probabilistic forwarding. Probability values are computed once a query request is received at a peer node based on the results of previous queries and are updated thereafter. Query messages are forwarded to the neighbor with highest probability value along the path of each k walker. Although the bandwidth cost of APS is the same as its predecessor, k-walker random walk, it offers a better recall rate.

Another guided search scheme takes advantage of a hierarchical structure to improve search efficiency. Similar to the hierarchical DHT-based scheme, the dominating set-based scheme[219] also classifies peer nodes into two categories. A selected set of nodes forms a connected dominating set (CDS) overlay. A one-hop ranking value is calculated at each CDS peer using the sum of the number of objects on the peer node and the number of objects on the peer's neighbor with the most objects. Query requests are forwarded to the connected CDS peers with the highest one-hop ranking or an ordinary node if it has the most objects among all neighbors of the source peer until the object is found or until the query reaches an ordinary peer.

Hybrid-Based Approaches

Most existing searching mechanisms for unstructured P2P networks suffer from high cost or high delay. To offer query scalability and adaptability with more efficiency, some have proposed schemes that take advantage of both the efficiency of the structured P2P system and the richer query capability of an unstructured P2P system. For instance, Loo et al. introduce a hybrid-based P2P search system whereby unstructured search is used to find largely replicated objects and structured search is employed when searching for rare objects. Castro et al. proposed Structella,[235] a hybrid structured and unstructured system with Gnutella built on top of Pastry. These systems present an interesting approach in an attempt to support efficient searching capabilities to a wide range of queries.

KEYWORD SEARCH

Earlier we mentioned a second drawback of early DHT-based P2P systems: their inability to support keyword or more complex searches. Yang et al.[232] offer keyword search capability in the DHT-based P2P networking approaches via Proof that utilizes advances in information retrieval research. The Proof system comprises a crawler, a database, an index generator, and a distributed P2P system. The P2P system has N peers and uses a consistent hash function to assign an identifier to each peer, whereas the index generator produces an inverted index and a summary inverted list (SIL), which are periodically distributed in the P2P system. Each SIL entry for a keyword contains the document ID, a page rank value similar to that used by Google, and two other values for query processing and evaluation. Given a keyword-based query, the querying peer requests all other peers that are responsible for the inverted lists of query keywords to report the length of its SIL. The query is then forwarded from the peer with the shortest SIL to that with the longest one. A Bloom filter is then used to evaluate the query in Proof. Yang et al. argue that Proof has a number of advantages: It reduces cost since the query chooses the shortest inverted list; and Bloom filter precision makes the Bloom membership query more accurate.

Other keyword-based searching schemes exist in different types of P2P systems. For example, earlier we mentioned FASD[198] as one approach that offers keyword-based searching capability in distributed indexing system. FASD caches lists of weighted keywords and uses Term Frequency Inverse Document Frequency (TFIDF)[199] measures along with inverted indexes[200] to offer keyword-based searching capability in distributed indexing systems.

RANGE QUERIES

In general, a *range query* is a query that describes a region (range) in space and asks for a subset of object points that belong to the region. In content search applications, for example, a user may pose an inexact query that gives a range in space. The simplest approach to the range search algorithm is to partition the range query into n independent queries and retrieve corresponding points in the region one by one. However, this works only if the number of independent queries is reasonably small. In centralized P2P indexing systems, a range query may be implemented using a top-down tree. The query starts at the root of the index tree and traverses recursively down every subtree for which the bounding region intersects the query range. Other methods to resolve range queries in classical database problems can also be easily imported. In localized or distributed P2P indexing systems, though, the problem is amplified. Today, range query is a challenging problem in the P2P search domain. Many open research issues exist. In the following, we look at several sample schemes found in the literature.

Non-DHT-Based Approaches

Mercury[223] suggests that we group peers into logical routing hubs. Each routing hub is responsible for one attribute, and any peer can be part of multiple logical hubs. Peers within a hub are arranged into a circular overlay of nodes. Objects are placed on the ring, with each node responsible for a range of values for the particular attribute. An object in Mercury is stored in all hubs for which it has an associated attribute. Queries, a conjunction of predicates with varying degrees of selectivity, are passed to the hubs corresponding to the attributes that are queried. In this hub, a query is routed to the first value appearing in the range, and then the contiguity of range values is used to spread the query along the circle, as needed. To minimize cost and avoid wildcard predicates being flooded to every node, it is important to send the query only to the hub that is most selective. In Mercury, query selectivity is resolved using a classical canonical solution that employs approximate histograms of the number of records per bucket. Mercury uses random sampling to estimate the density of nodes in different parts of the routing hub and hence the average load. The querying peer sends off a sample request message with a small TTL. Every node along the path selects a random neighbor link and forwards it. When the TTL expires, the last node reached sends back a sample. Each node within a hub gathers the histogram of the distribution of nodes using random sampling. Histograms of other hubs may be pulled through the interhub links. These histograms are then used to determine the selectivity of a subscription for each hub.

Range Queries in DHTs

Though non-DHT-based schemes seem to be natural choices to support range queries, range queries in DHT-based P2P systems are also studied because DHT-based indexing is popular in the P2P world. The first question we might ask is, Can DHT-based indexing support range queries? Intuitively, DHTs are constrained to single-key, exact-match queries. The randomized property of DHT indexing works against the range query. Recall that most DHT-based schemes rely on numerical keys to index and query objects in the P2P network. Object searching is accomplished using key distance and routing toward the peer that has the closest key to the querying object key. This implies the possibility of range-based hashing to offer range query capability. If the hashing algorithm can offer range-attuned numerical keys to objects in the database, range query could be supported. One straightforward approach is to use partition-based indexing in which an index over the stored data partition ranges is built. However, partition location in a distributed indexing-based P2P system with range selection is very hard to solve exactly.[224] Gupta et al.[225] tackle the problem using locality sensitive hashing (LSH) to hash similar data partitions to nearby identifiers and similar ranges to the same peer with high probability. Gupta uses the LSH scheme given by min-wise independent permutations. Given a domain D, consider a random permutation π of D. Assume that the elements of D are totally ordered. Given a range set $Q \subseteq D$, the hash function h_π is defined as:

$$h_\pi(Q) = \min \{\pi(Q)\}$$

which satisfies

$$pr_\pi[h_\pi(Q) = h_\pi(R)] = \frac{|Q \cap R|}{|Q \cup R|}.$$

The disadvantage of the scheme lies in its low scalability when the number of partitions grows significantly large.

Andrzejak and Xu[226] proposed Space Filling Curve over CAN construction to deal with range queries in DHTs. In their system, nearby ranges are mapped to nearby CAN zones. If a range is split into two subranges, the zone of the primary range is partitioned into two zones of subranges. For a range query whose lower and upper bounds are l and u, the query is first routed to the peer that owns the middle point $(l+u)/2$. The query is then recursively propagated to neighbor peers until all the zones that intersect the query are visited. This is just like a localized flooding, which is simple to implement and works without changes if single attribute values are sought. Andrzejak and Xu proposed three flooding algorithms: brute force, controlled flooding, and directed controlled flooding. However, other flooding algorithms can also be used here.

Skip Graphs

A skip graph-based approach is another direction that has caught noticeable attention among researchers. SkipIndex[227] is one of the schemes that offers solutions to range queries in P2P networks. SkipIndex includes the following key mechanisms:

1. The system partitions the search space into a hierarchical tree and organizes the leaf partitions using a skip graph-based distributed data structure. Even though the underlying skip graph supports only one-dimensional keys, SkipIndex supports high dimensional range and similarity queries while requiring only a logarithmic number of peer pointers and a logarithmic number of overlay hops.

2. The system provides an approximate query mechanism, where the user gets to specify the desired level of search accuracy and the system intelligently controls the number of nodes interrogated to satisfy the error-bound.

3. Diverse data sets with differing dimensionalities and distributions can be stored in the distributed infrastructure at the same time.

4. The system allows the high-dimensional feature space to be partitioned dynamically among participating index nodes in a load-balanced manner. It uses a CAN-like construction with a one-dimensional key associated with each region. This key captures the hierarchical manner in which the region was created. The keys are then used to store the leaf regions in a searchable skip graph.

The skip graph is used to support insertion and lookup based on a one-dimensional key. Range queries are supported with a range-limited "multicast" operation. Range queries are multicast to all the nodes whose regions intersect the query range. SkipIndex guarantees a logarithmic bound on the number of multicast steps for such queries. Recall that in a centralized P2P indexing system, a range query may be implemented using a top-down tree with the query starting at the root and traversing recursively down every subtree. SkipIndex deals with range query in a similar manner, with the variation that each node maintains only a partial view of the region tree to achieve distributed indexing. To locate a region containing a data point, the query is routed through the skip graph in a way such that the distance to the target region, measured in terms of the total order, is probabilistically halved in every routing step. With appealing results on small P2P networks, this scheme awaits testing of its reliability and scalability over large P2P networks.

SEMANTIC QUERIES

According to Zhu,[222] semantic search is a content-based, full-text search, whereby queries are expressed in natural language instead of simple keyword matches. Existing work on semantic search particularly focuses on extending information retrieval algorithms such as Vector Space Model (VSM) and Latent Semantic Indexing (LSI)[228] into the P2P domain. In the following, we look at the algorithms introduced in [222] as examples to understand the requirements and challenges of semantic queries in P2P systems.

Semantic Search in Structured Overlays

Here we look at two algorithms introduced in [222]. The first one is pSearch.[229] It introduces the concept of *semantic overlay* on top of a DHT (i.e., CAN) to implement semantic search. The semantic overlay is a logical network in which documents are organized under their semantic vectors such that the distance (e.g., routing hops) between two documents is proportional to their dissimilarity in semantic vectors.

Two basic operations are involved in pSearch: indexing and searching. Whenever a document D enters the system, pSearch performs the indexing operations as follows:

1. Use LSI to derive D's semantic vector V_d.
2. Use a rolling index to generate a number p of DHT keys (k_i, $i = 0, \ldots, p - 1$) from V_d.
3. Index D into the underlying DHT using these DHT keys.

Whenever a query Q is issued, pSearch performs the search operations as follows:

1. Use LSI to derive Q's semantic vector V_q.
2. Use a rolling index to generate a number p of DHT keys (k_i, $i = 0, \ldots, p - 1$) from V_q.
3. Route Q to the destination nodes that are responsible for these DHT keys.
4. On reaching the destination, Q is either flooded to nodes within a radius r or forwarded to nodes using content-directed search.
5. All nodes that receive the query do a local search using LSI and return the matched documents to the query originator node.

The second algorithm, developed by Zhu, is an LSH-based semantic search system built on top of DHTs.[231] To support semantics-based access, it adds two major components to an existing P2P system: (1) *a registry of semantic extractors and* (2) a *semantic indexing and locating utility.*

The functionality of semantic indexing is to index each object automatically according to its semantic vector (SV) whenever an object is created or modified. The functionality of semantic locating is to find similar documents for a given query.

The index table is fully distributed. When an object is created or modified, its SV is extracted. The system then hashes the SV to an integer number called semID. The DHT uses this semID as a key to put an index entry (a pointer to the original object) into the P2P system. Note that the original locations of documents are not affected. Given a query, the system generates a semID based on the query's semantic vector. The semantic locating utility then uses the semID to locate the indices of similar documents stored in the P2P systems.

The key here is to make sure that two semantically close documents (which have similar semantic vectors) will be hashed to the same semID so that the underlying DHT can locate the indices. However, this is not possible in many traditional hashing functions that try to be uniformly random. As a result, two documents that are similar but slightly different (e.g., different versions of the same document) will generate different hashing results. Their system, on the contrary, relies on a very special class of hashing function called *locality sensitive hashing* (LSH). If two documents are similar, it is likely that they will generate the same hashing result. Moreover, the higher the similarity between the two files, the higher the probability that the hashing results are the same.

While LSH is proposed for semantic P2P search, its value in keyword-based search and range query deserves evaluation. However, LSH cannot guarantee that two similar documents will always have the same hashing result. To increase the probability, they use a group of n LSH functions to generate n semIDs (n is a small number, about 5 to 20). If the probability of generating a matching result from a single LSH function is p, the probability of generating at least one matching result from n LSH functions will be $1 - (1 - p)^n$ The locating utility then uses the resulting n semIDs to search the DHT. Their initial results indicate that with n set to about 10 to 20, their system can find almost 100% of semantically close documents. As a result, their system is very efficient: Instead of sending the query to tens of thousands of nodes in the system, they need to send it to only n nodes.

Evidently, supporting semantic search with high efficiency and accuracy in structured P2P is nontrivial. Continued study on this domain is expected.

Semantic Search in Unstructured Overlays

In this section we look at one scheme, ESS,[230] discussed in [222]. The design goal of ESS is to improve the quality of search (e.g., high recall) while minimizing the associated cost (e.g., the number of nodes visited for a query). The ESS design philosophy is to improve search efficiency and effectiveness while retaining the simple, robust, and fully decentralized nature of Gnutella.

In ESS, each node has a *node vector*, a compact summary of its content. Each node can have two types of links (connections), namely *random links* and *semantic links*. Random links connect irrelevant nodes, whereas semantic links organize relevant nodes into semantic groups. The topology adaptation algorithm is first performed to connect a node to the rest of the network through either random links or semantic links, or both. The goal of the topology adaptation is to ensure that (1) relevant nodes are organized into the same semantic groups through semantic links, and (2) high-capacity nodes have high degree and low-capacity nodes are within short reach of higher-capacity nodes.

Given a query, ESS's search protocol first quickly locates a relevant semantic group for the query, relying on selective one-hop node vector replication as well as its capacity-aware mechanism. Then ESS floods the query within the semantic group to retrieve relevant documents. ESS will continue this search process until sufficient responses are found. The intuition behind the flooding within a semantic group is that semantically associated nodes tend to be relevant to the same query.

Unstructured P2P systems are capable to support arbitrarily complex queries by nature. In unstructured P2P systems, node churn causes little problem. The main problem facing semantic search systems built on top of unstructured P2P networks is, still, the search inefficiency problem: A query might probe a very large fraction of nodes to be answered.

ADVANCED TOPICS

Distributed Pattern Matching System (DPMS)

To address the flexibility and efficiency challenges, Ahmed[233] proposes their Distributed Pattern Matching System (DPMS). DPMS is based on Bloom filter-based pattern matching distributed throughout the P2P network. Given a search pattern Q, DPMS tries to find peers containing some pattern P that matches Q, that is, the 1 bits of Q for a subset of the 1 bits found in P. DPMS peers can act as either a leaf peer or an indexing peer, where the former resides at the bottom level of the indexing hierarchy. This type of peer advertises its indices representing the content the peer wants to share. Indexing peers store indices received from other peers; these peers may be leaf peers or indexing peers.

Peers join various levels within the hierarchy and can act both as leaf peers and indexing peers. Within this hierarchy, indexing peers disseminate index information using repeated aggregation and replication. Replication is used for disseminating patterns from leaf peers to a large number of indexing peers. To overcome increased traffic load, DPMS combines replication with lossy aggregation. Advertisements provided by different peers are aggregated and propagated to peers in the next level along the aggregation tree. Based on repeated lossy aggregation, the information content of the aggregates is reduced as you move toward the top of the indexing hierarchy. This helps balance the system and improve fault tolerance. Furthermore, peers can route queries toward a target without having any global knowledge of the overlay topology. It also helps minimize query-forwarding traffic.

DiffSearch

The difficulty with protocols such as Gnutella and FastTrack is that they rely on flooding or random walk for content search, with messages propagated to every peer. This results in increased costs and network traffic. Wang et al.[234] aim to alleviate these limitation using their proposed Differential Search (DiffSearch) algorithm. DiffSearch improves search efficiency of unstructured P2P networks by giving higher querying priority to peers with high query/reply capabilities, known as *ultrapeers*. Ultrapeers form an overlay and serve visiting peers known as *leaf peers*. The indices of leaf peers are uploaded to ultrapeers, allowing all shared content to be searched within the first round. Based on tests using Gnutella, Wang et al. argue that 1% of peers answer the main portion of queries. Consequently, by routing queries to these peers, it is possible to save up to 90% of query traffic. Using counters to track files that answer queries, which they call *effective files*, a matrix is created that allows ultrapeers to be self-aware by counting the number of shared files that have been visited. If the number of shared files exceeds a threshold, a peer can promote itself to ultrapeer status. This results in an overlay in which members have higher priority depending on where they reside in the hierarchy. To further decrease traffic, DiffSearch hitchhikes query/ response messages to perform network management tasks, for example, allowing ultrapeers to advertise themselves to leaf peers, and vice versa.

Content-Based Search

Most existing P2P systems provide very limited content search capabilities. Content-based search[237] is desirable for querying multimedia data when text annotations and metadata cannot offer the level of detail the target query desires. For multimedia data that contain text, audio, and video streams, multimodal search that relies on linguistic, acoustic, and visual information can be applied to find content more effectively. MIRACLE[238] is an ongoing research project at AT&T Labs aimed at creating automated content-based media processing algorithms and systems to collect, organize, index, mine, and repurpose video and multimedia information. This video search engine combines existing metadata with content-based information that is automatically extracted from the audio and video components. The MIRACLE search engine currently operates on an archive of more than 32,000 hours of video that have been collected and automatically indexed over a 10-year period. The Informedia II[239] digital video library at CMU is another pioneering multimedia database system that consists of more than 1,500 hours of video. Informedia combines speech recognition, image understanding, and natural-language processing technologies to automatically transcribe, segment, index, and summarize the linear video.

Content-based multimedia indexing and search also attract significant attention from standards organizations. MPEG-7, formally named Multimedia Content Description Interface, is a standard sponsored by the International Organization for Standardization (ISO) for describing multimedia content. TRECVID is sponsored by the National Institute of Standards and Technology (NIST) to stimulate research in automatic segmentation, indexing, and content-based retrieval of digital video.

Applying content-based search in P2P systems has important application value, yet is also challenging. PeerSearch[240] supports content and semantic search in P2P networks. It extends existing information retrieval methods, the vector space model (VSM) and latent semantic indexing (LSI), to work with the efficient routing mechanisms in a content-addressable network (CAN). In PeerSearch, semantic vectors are used as the key to store the document index in CAN such that the indices stored nearby in CAN are close in semantics. That is, instead of semantic-free keys, PeerSearch uses semantic keys to index objects to offer semantic and content-based search capability. Other approaches[241] explore content-based resource selection and document retrieval algorithms in P2P networks.

A content-based P2P music retrieval system is described in [242]. In this system, each audio document is converted into a stream of characteristic sequences, a *vector*. Each vector represents a short segment of music data. All vectors are indexed using the LSH scheme such that similar (in terms of human perception) vectors can be hashed into the same hash value with high probability. To improve the search efficiency in a P2P environment, a two-phase search protocol is employed. First, the query peer broadcasts a small subset of query vectors to all potential peers; then peers with a higher chance of a hit will conduct the more rigorous search.

The multimedia semantic gap and the large data rate of content-based querying pose significant challenges for content-based P2P search.

SUMMARY

We enumerated a handful of schemes on P2P search in this chapter. They represent only a subset of the numerous schemes proposed in the research literature. This brief exercise nevertheless offers implications on the need of application-driven and more efficient and effective schemes for P2P search today. For example, it might be necessary for a P2P system to support a set of rich queries that ranges from simple semantic free ID lookups to keyword search or Structured Query Language (SQL) like queries. To date, the ability to effectively and efficiently retrieve information for a given application with approximate, incomplete, or vague information queries remains a challenging problem in P2P networking.

FOR FURTHER READING

Many P2P search-related technical papers can be found in the literature. The following three survey papers are among the most comprehensive articles on the topic:

- Survey of research on robust peer-to-peer networks: Search methods by Risson and Moorse[221]
- Searching techniques in peer-to-peer networks by Li and Wu[202]
- Semantic search in peer-to-peer systems by Zhu and Hu[222]

Interested readers are encouraged to refer to these three articles for more information on P2P content search.

Peer-to-Peer Content Delivery

8

P2P technologies offer a new approach to content delivery networks that combines improved system scalability with low implementation cost. P2P content delivery is thus an important technique for commercial systems such as IPTV. In this chapter we look at the design issues of P2P content delivery networks, including topology, delivery path selection, push versus pull, and control strategy for content flow. In addition, various approaches for content caching are discussed and some example systems are used to illustrate the approaches. The chapter concludes with a discussion of hybrid P2P-CDN designs.

CONTENT DELIVERY

In the past few years, we have witnessed an astonishing increase in the number as well as the functionality of content delivery systems. A Google search of *content delivery system* results in 69,400 results. From Internet music to Internet video, broadcast video to Video-on-Demand (VoD), premium content to user-generated content, and Internet TV to mobile TV, various content delivery services are offered throughout the networked world.

This new and exciting content-rich networked world is rooted in the availability of low-cost broadband networks and advanced computing, communications, and media compression technologies. These put forward new and exciting opportunities for both consumers and content providers in terms of multimedia content access and distribution. Today Internet end users are consuming digital media at an abundant and continuously escalating level. To offer services that can accommodate the large and growing number of audiences and traffic levels, content providers have tried to deploy networks and systems that can provide increased scalability, reliability, and quality of services. The Content Delivery Network (CDN) is one of the solutions born in the late 1990s. Basically, CDN is an overlay network that employs technologies, such as caching, load balancing, scheduling, and request routing, to push replicated content close to the network edge. A properly funded content publisher/server can easily reach a reasonably large number of customers via a commercial CDN. However, those who cannot afford the cost are often limited in the type of content they can serve and its capability to reach a desirable number of audiences. In the history of the Internet, mirroring has played a significant role in helping those publishers to reach more audiences. Organizations with good network connectivity have long known to offer mirror services for static content. And yet, the size of audiences largely depends on the number of volunteer mirror sites. The scalability is very limited.

To reduce the cost of content delivery, today many companies are seeking or are offering peer-to-peer-based solutions in both personal and enterprise applications. In the following, we look at some popular approaches and technology directions relating to P2P content delivery.

Classification of P2P Content Delivery Schemes

Various Delivery Methods

Content delivery, based on the way the content is transported and consumed, can be categorized into downloading and streaming modes. *Streaming* refers to the delivery method whereby content is played at the client side while it is being transported. *Downloading*, on the other hand, requires that the entire content be received at the client side before it can be played out. Compared to the streaming mode, downloading is less restrictive and relatively easier to implement. Just as in client/server-based systems, P2P content delivery can also be classified into downloading and streaming modes. Gnutella,[243] Kazaa,[244] BitTorrent,[245] and eDonkey,[246] for example, are all popular P2P file-sharing systems that support downloading. Most existing P2P file-sharing systems use block-based downloading delivery. That is, each content file is partitioned into blocks. The delivery and reception of the blocks are not sequential, making it impractical to play back before all the blocks of the content file reach the client side. An obvious advantage of downloading-based content delivery is that the quality of content playback is independent of the network bandwidth. Although it could take a long time, even hours, to download a video file today, the playback quality can always be guaranteed if the download is successful.

Streaming offers a new way for consumers to enjoy content playback without waiting for the entire content being downloaded, with a possible sacrifice in terms of playback quality. Even though a client-side buffer is used to preload a certain number of content segments before the content is played back, the available bandwidth and network dynamics can often limit the terminal device's capability to fetch enough data to offer the desired the quality of experience. Rate control and error control mechanisms are thus extremely important in streaming media services. Akin to traditional client/server-based streaming services, P2P streaming services[247,248,249,250,251,252] also share the same requirements. Further discussions on P2P streaming can be found in Chapter 9. Interested readers can also refer to the case study presented later in this chapter.

Streaming

Streaming can be further classified into delay-bounded and nondelay-restricted classes. In a delay-bounded application such as gaming and conferencing, an upper bound on the maximum delay has to be satisfied to offer suitable quality of service and user experience. The upper bound can be relaxed to a certain extent in a nondelay-restricted application, such as Internet TV. Even though most delay-bounded applications today only require support for small-scale P2P systems, they still impose significant challenges.

Depending on when the content is generated, streaming can also be further categorized into live and on-demand streaming. Live streaming identifies services for which the content is being streamed while it is being created, whereas on-demand streaming characterizes services being streamed as prestored content on the server or serving peer.

A protocol and sender/receiver size-based classification puts streaming further into (one-to-one) unicasting, one-to-many multicasting, and many-to-many multicasting. Definitions and techniques for each of these content delivery types are delineated in Chapter 9.

Topology Constraints

Data can be delivered via flooding, random walk, or a topology-defined specific route in a P2P overlay network. That is, the data delivery route maybe deterministic in one P2P overlay and nondeterministic in another. This is dependent on the topology of the P2P overlay network. Recall that Chapters 3 and 4 addressed the fundamentals of unstructured and structured P2P overlays. In a majority of P2P networks, flooding or random walk is deployed in unstructured P2P overlays, whereas a unique key is assigned to data items and peers for content delivery in structured P2P overlays. A structured graph maps each key to the peer that stores the data block or content. Since structured overlays depend on a globally maintained protocol for content delivery, it is commonly believed that the maintenance cost is much higher than that of unstructured overlay. Furthermore, as was discussed in Chapter 3, unstructured P2P overlays are more resilient to peer join and departure dynamics. Thus, flooding and random walk-based content delivery methods have higher fault tolerance capability under churn. The major disadvantage of such kinds of schemes is the lower probability of guaranteed successful delivery. Another drawback is the large amount of signaling traffic caused by message or content flooding. To overcome the limitations of both structured and unstructured overlays, a hybrid system[253] was proposed. In such systems, flooding or random walk is used for content searching, whereas a structured graph is used for deterministic data placement. Since unstructured topology offers complex querying support and the churn resilience capability and structured topology guarantees a content object can be found if it exists, the hybrid system is intuitively more scalable and more content friendly.

Categories of Data Topology and Delivery Path

Tree and mesh are two widely studied data topologies in P2P networks. In a tree-based content delivery system, data are delivered along a distribution tree that is rooted at the source peer that stores the data. It is not difficult to see that this data topology cannot take full advantage of the network resources and the system can easily become unbalanced because the bandwidth of the leaf peers is not utilized. Moreover, the system is vulnerable to peer churn since any intermediate peer departure will disconnect all descendents of the peer from the content delivery tree. To overcome this limitation, a multiple tree-based data topology[252] was invented. Content may be partitioned into multiple strips, each distributed over a different tree. That is, the leaf peers of one tree are made intermediate peers of another tree to construct a better-balanced system that could potentially take advantage of all the resources in the P2P network. Once the P2P overlay is determined, the data topology is decided, and thus the path, from the sender to the receiver, through which each block of the content will travel, is fixed. Obviously, when the number of substrips is not very small, the algorithm complexity to calculate such a balanced network and to construct a near perfect multitree distribution system is very high.

Though adaptation in tree-based delivery is done globally, another approach takes advantage of local adaptation to lower cost and implementation complexity. That is called *mesh-based content delivery*. Content blocks flow through the network with a mesh topology that is more resilient to peer churn and network dynamics. This is because real-time status information may be acquired at each peer and used to decide the delivery path of the content block on the fly. That is, in mesh-based content delivery systems, delivery decisions are made locally at each peer. These characteristics are very welcome in real-world applications, and subsequently mesh-based systems are widely deployed in many popular P2P applications today. BitTorrent,[245] PPLive,[249] and UUSee,[250] for example, are all mesh-based systems.

Various Delivery Initiators

Depending on who initiates the content delivery, it can also be grouped into push-based and pull-based types of delivery model. When the sender initiates the content delivery, it is called *push delivery*. In contrast, *pull delivery* indicates that the content transport is started by the receiver. A system that employs both push and pull for content delivery is called a *hybrid push-pull* or a *joint push-pull*. Later in this chapter we discuss each of these delivery methods in more detail.

Characteristics of Content Flow Control Strategy

Here are two additional questions to ask in designing a P2P content delivery system:

- Which peer should the current peer select to pull or push the content?
- Which content block should be delivered next?

The answers to these questions largely affect the performance of the content delivery system. Resource availability, efficiency, fairness, and fault-tolerant capability should all be taken into consideration. Tit-for-Tat, used by BitTorrent and described in Chapter 6, is a fairness-based peer selection strategy. This strategy can effectively prevent free riders. A resource availability-based strategy has a better result when quality of service is one of the performance measurement metrics. The answer to the second question is comparably less complex. Most popular content block flow control strategies include random order-based, sequential order-based, and popularity-based strategies, which are all straightforward to implement.

Design Criteria

Cost, implementation complexity, efficiency, robustness, scalability, quality of service and experience are some of the key design criteria for P2P content delivery services. For instance, in a videoconferencing service, the system has to meet the delay-bound constraint to offer an acceptable customer experience. In an Internet video service, system scalability is directly associated with system capability. System capability to cope with churn and network dynamics is imperative in any P2P content delivery system. An efficient system that can take advantage of the P2P network resources in a fair and balanced way can have a strong impact on system scalability and performance.

P2P CACHING

Caching is a well-known strategy in many networked applications. The capability to:

- Reduce origin server load and bandwidth requirement
- Reduce network bandwidth usage
- Reduce client-side latency

leads to improved scalability and performance with lower cost. For example, caching is used by ISPs to accelerate Web content delivery. Proxy caches may be placed between the server and the clients (see Figure 8.1A). A client's request for content is first directed to a proxy cache. At a cache miss, the proxy contacts the server to satisfy the client's request. Caching helps move the content closer to the edge of the network, reducing both server and network bandwidth requirement.

Popular caching schemes include just-in-time (JiT) caching and precaching (PreC). In JiT, the cache pulls the content from the server with the content sent to the cache and the requesting client simultaneously immediately after a request is received from the client. In PreC, content is cached before a request is received at the proxy. For dynamic content, how to maintain the freshness of caching copies of the content is a common issue.

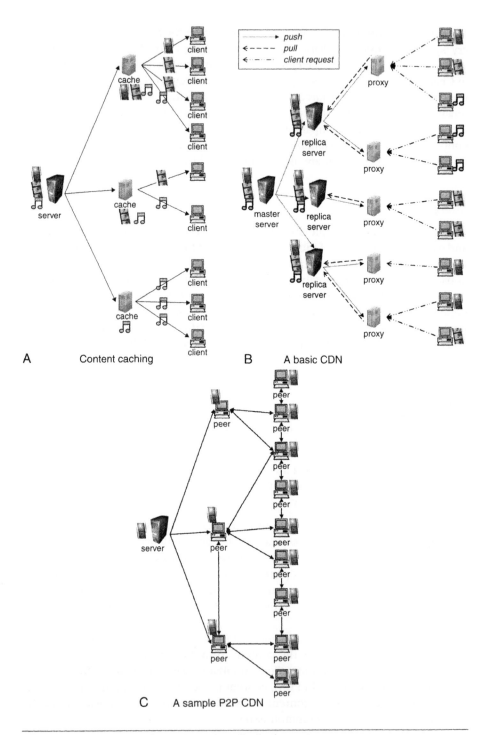

FIGURE 8.1 Architectures of sample content distribution systems.

Caching is also used in combination with server replication in classical CDNs to improve system scalability and reduce access latency. A multilevel replication-plus-caching mechanism is shown in Figure 8.1B. Similar to the caching scheme, the effectiveness of a replica-based scheme is limited by the number of available caches and replicas and the dynamism of content. These bring up scalability, reliability, cost, and other issues.

Today Internet traffic is often dominated by P2P traffic. Unlike Web objects, P2P content is often significantly larger in size and more dynamic in nature. These challenge the application of traditional Web caching schemes for P2P file-sharing applications. Here we look at how P2P caching can facilitate content delivery.

Unlike traditional CDN systems, where active content replication is used to improve system capability and performance, content replication takes place passively in P2P-based systems where peers request and copy content from one another. Caching in P2P networks refers to the case of caching copies of the content in peers as the content passes through them to reach other peers in the P2P network. For instance, at an initial request, when peer P_i in Figure 8.2 succeeds in locating a content C, C is transmitted through multiple peers $P_2, P_3, \ldots$, until it reaches P_j. Copies of C may be cached in the intermediate peers $P_2, P_3, \ldots$, along

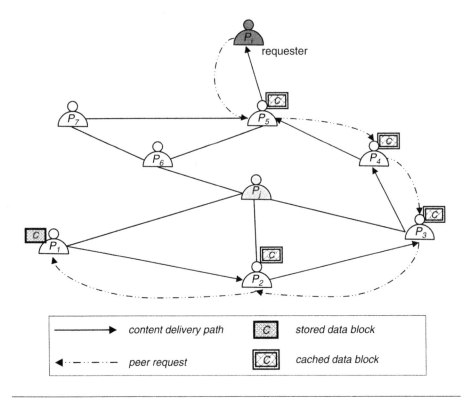

FIGURE 8.2 Caching in P2P networks.

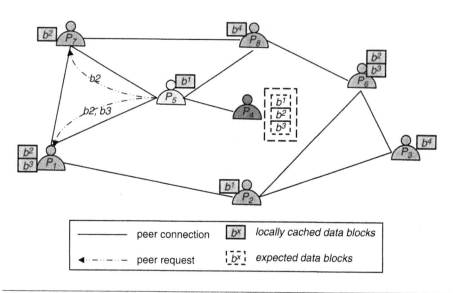

FIGURE 8.3 An example of P2P caching.

the transmission pass. In a future request issued by other peers, such as P_j, the availability of content C with respect to requester P_j is increased while the latency to retrieve content C and send back to P_j may be reduced.

In Figure 8.3, a set of peers are self-organized into an overlay P2P network. Each peer P_i has a local cache. In this P2P network, one media content data stream Cd, such as a video data stream, is often partitioned into small data blocks $B(Cd) = \{b^1, b^2, b^3, \dots\dots b^N\}$. A peer P_i participating in the P2P network may cache some or all of the data blocks, that is, a subset of the content data blocks $B_i = \{b_i^1, b_i^2, b_i^3, \dots\dots\} \subseteq B(Cd)$. The P2P network implements certain mechanism to publish its locally cached contents and other necessary information. When P_j, which is connected to P_i, requests content blocks b^k, P_i may answer the request locally if it has the required data block. It propagates the request to its neighbors otherwise. Using Figure 8.3 as an example, peer P_4 wants to get content blocks b^1, b^2, and b^3. It is connected to P_5 (solid line denotes connections between peers). Assuming P_5 already has b^1 in its local cache, but not b^2 and b^3, it sends a request for b^2 and b^3 to its neighbors P_1 and P_7. P_7 has b^2 in its local cache, whereas P_1 has b^2 and b^3 in its local cache. Once receiving the request, P_1 and P_7 compute an estimated cost for retrieving and transmitting the results to P_5. Meanwhile, b^2 and b^3 may be transmitted directly to P_4 with a suitable P2P network connectivity scheme and protocol. The estimated cost may be used to determine whether P_1 or P_7 or both will be offering block b^2. This again may depend on the system connectivity scheme and protocol. In this system, the P2P network acts as a combined virtual cache. All peers offer resources (here, the resource offered is memory) in collaboration to achieve lower cost and latency for content delivery.

Caching and replication in structured P2P[254,255,256,257] can be tricky. Some of the structured P2P systems discussed in Chapter 4 associate objects to the object identifier that is also the key to discovering the location of the object. Effective caching and replication of objects require additional mechanisms. In Tapestry,[257] replica roots identified with random keys that are generated using a replication function are used for object replication. A similar idea is used in CAN[255] as well.

Design Issues

Care has to be taken in designing a P2P caching scheme. Hit/miss rates, cache replacement strategies, fault tolerance capability, impact on bandwidth requirement, and the like should all be taken into consideration.

Data Consistency and Synchronization

One immediate issue that arises with P2P caching is associated with its fully distributed nature. By replicating content at many peers in the system, data consistency and synchronization issues need to be handled properly. Assume that P_7 in Figure 8.2 is requesting content C from P_5. If C in Figure 8.2 is modified at P_1 and becomes C' while the cached copies C on other peers are not updated, the acquired copy at P_7 is outdated. To get an updated copy, C', P_7 has to reissue a request for C'. If a proper scheme is available, P_7 may eventually get C', though, with added message flow and thus an increased bandwidth requirement. If no proper mechanism is implemented, it is possible that P_7 will not even be able to get the updated copy C'.

Synchronization through flooding is an intuitive approach that could offer high fidelity. A version number, for example, can be used to indicate a content change of a file. At a specific time or on the modification of the original copy of the content, the original owner broadcasts an update notification message that is propagated through the P2P network. The broadcast may be stopped when the message hits all peers or a predefined TTL is reached. Once receiving the updating message, a peer checks its cache and invalidates the content block or file if the version number of the content block in the cache does not match the one in the updating message. Variations of the scheme can also be used in a flooding-based data synchronization. Noticeably, the drawback of such kinds of schemes is the additional communication cost. Updating message flooding can significantly increase bandwidth requirement. This is especially a problem for dynamic contents.

On the contrary, synchronization on demand, whereby synchronization occurs at the request of a replica or caching peer, has much less bandwidth overhead. Yet it might offer only a weak guarantee. Assuming that peers with cached content will connect the owner or originator of the content to determine whether a replica is fresh, an algorithm that determines when and how to query the owner has to be defined. Care has to be taken in designing the algorithm to avoid over- or underquerying. An adaptive approach whereby the time and frequency of query are adjusted based on the dynamism, updating history, and so on can reduce the probability of too frequent or too infrequent queries.

To further enhance replication and caching consistency, joint push and pull schemes can be used. Gtk-Gnutella[258] is one example that utilizes such a mechanism. Push-based broadcasting is done just like in a push based scheme. In addition, peers occasionally query the owner for update information. The algorithm is designed in a way that TTL, peer churn, and peer neighborhood size are taken into consideration to determine when a peer will pull.

Increasing the Hit Rate

To amplify the hit rate, some classical caching schemes can be employed. For example, prefetching, whereby peers keep downloading content data blocks to anticipate future peer requests, can reduce the average number of peers referenced for certain requests. It could also reduce the average hops for content downloading. However, when all peers in the P2P network continuously perform prefetching, a significant amount of bandwidth needs to be budgeted for it. This tradeoff has to be considered in designing a P2P caching scheme.

Other factors can also affect the cache hit rate and thus the P2P caching scheme design. For instance, in any P2P network, churn could affect system performance significantly. In the system depicted in Figure 8.3, when P_1 is faulty or offline, P_5 will not be able to get the requested content block b^3 from P_1. A cache miss occurs. A new request may have to be issued for b^3. Or it may eventually get b^3 from P_6 via P_8. In either case, additional latency is introduced. In P2P caching, obviously, churn could drastically increase the cache miss rate.

Active Caching

In the system discussed earlier, peers support partial caching and are active in the sense that they can actively request missing content blocks from their neighbors. A passive P2P cache in which the peer cache cannot originate download requests will need a full P2P caching scheme or alternative protocol support. Otherwise, the cache miss rate could escalate dramatically.

Dynamic Replication

When replicas are placed dynamically using certain placement strategies, it is called *dynamic replication*.

Cache Replacement Policies

The cache often has limited size. When the cache becomes full, some objects or content blocks must be removed to make room for new ones. A system has to take many factors into consideration for cache replacement. This is referred to as a *cache replacement* policy. Cache replacement policies for Web caching have been studied extensively.[259,260,261,262,263,264,265,266] In general:

- Size of the cached object
- Time of the last reference made to the cached object
- Frequency of the requests made to the object

- Time of last modification
- Cost to fetch the object from its original server

are all important factors in designing a cache replacement policy. Randomized strategy, function-based strategy, frequency-based strategy, object size-based strategy, and freshness-based strategy are some of the popular strategies used in practice. A least recently used (LRU) cache replacement policy, where the least fresh object is removed, is a typical freshness-based mechanism. A minimum size (MinS) cache replacement policy takes object size into consideration. The smallest object is removed first. Opposite MinS is another straightforward object size-based strategy, namely a maximum size policy (MaxS) whereby the largest object is considered for elimination first. A least frequently accessed (LFA) policy looks at the frequency of the objects being requested to determine the order of removal. That is, those objects that are being accessed frequently will be kept, whereas those that are not will be considered for deletion first. More sophisticated schemes will take into consideration several of these attributes. A cost function can be used to construct the priority list.

Similar to Web caching, P2P caching needs to consider replacement policy as well. In P2P caching, in addition to those factors considered in Web caching design, peer (i.e., cache) availability, churn rate, range issues, and the like are additional issues that cannot be ignored. When a peer P_i is disconnected from the P2P network, its cache is detached as well. The objects (content blocks) cached in P_i's cache disappear from the network along with P_i. In a function-based cache replacement strategy, the replacement function will have to offer mechanisms that deal with the churn rate and the object distribution among neighborhood peers to minimize lost performance due to churn.

Other Issues

How to design a P2P caching scheme that does not instigate unsustainable bandwidth cost is also an important issue. The number of requests issued to neighbor peers for a particular content block and the frequency of cache replacement, for instance, can affect the number of messages and network traffic pattern. To avoid flooding the network with request messages, specifying a threshold, such as a maximum hop number or TTL, is a simple approach.

Interested readers are also directed to Chapters 3, 4, and 5 on issues related to P2P overlay design. Many issues discussed in those chapters should be taken into consideration when designing a P2P caching scheme.

Example P2P Caching Systems

PeerOLAP

The PeerOLAP[267] architecture for supporting online analytical processing queries with a large number of low-end clients takes advantage of P2P caching to reduce system cost. Peers are connected through an arbitrary P2P network, with each containing a cache with the most useful results. It employs three cache control policies that impose different levels of cooperation among the peers. If a query cannot be answered locally (i.e., by using the cache contents of the computer where it is issued), it is propagated through the network until a peer that has cached the answer is found. An answer may also be constructed by partial results from many peers.

FastTrack Cache Replacement

Wierzbicki et al. studied FastTrack[268] and Kazaa[244] cache replacement policies in [269] and [270]. Their evaluation of the cache replacement policies that were successful for Web traffic indicates the need for new policies specialized for P2P networks.

Let's look at Kazaa, a popular P2P file-sharing network utilizing the FastTrack protocol. In this hybrid P2P system, supernodes serve as referral nodes for files. Supernodes register the list of cached files on those ordinary nodes with which the supernode is connected. An ordinary node A connected to supernode S1 communicates with S1 to issue requests. S1 uses its local database and collaborates with other supernodes to compile a list of other ordinary nodes that store the file and sends this list back to A. A then communicates directly with those ordinary nodes that are on the list to request the content blocks/files they desire. Delivery of the content blocks/files occurs thereafter. At last, A informs S1 of new availability of the file it just acquired once the entire file is obtained.

Wierzbicki et al.[269,270] analyzed Kazaa traffic and found that the percentage of recurrently popular files is stable at about 30%, whereas the percentage of files that are popular in all observation periods stabilizes at about 15%. Splitting a single file download into multiple, independent file-range downloads is a central feature of the FastTrack protocol and thus the Kazaa protocol. In Kazaa, a file stored in a cache may consist of several ranges with gaps in between. To design a more FastTrack-friendly cache replacement policy, Wierzbicki defines three additional attributes, specifically maximum size, transmitted bytes, and scaled access time. *Maximum size* denotes the maximum size of an object. *Transmitted bytes* delineates the number of bytes of an object that has been sent to peers. *Scaled access time* weighs the last access time with the portion of the object that has been requested. The study shows that the best performance in terms of byte hit rate was obtained using a policy that employs the transmitted bytes attribute. Wierzbicki et al. call the policy *least-sent byte*. The policy considers churn information. Intuitively, since files are split into ranges, if a cache stores almost the entire file, it has a better chance of serving a range request for that file. That is, the larger the percentage of a file that is stored in the cache, the more chance a cache hit will be achieved. Consequently, minimum relative size (MinRS) instead of the minimum size policy is more suitable for FastTrack/Kazaa. With this cache replacement policy, those have the smallest cached size relative to the entire file size are taken away first. Similarly, since a cache needs to have the entire requested range to serve the request, cache entries that are large will have a better chance of serving a request, that is, with a higher hit rate. This implies that policies that remove large cache entries are likely to perform poorly in Kazaa, and vice versa.

Wierzbicki et al. found in their simulation that high byte hit rates can be obtained by caching, since the set of popular objects contains a subset of all-time favorites that remain popular over a long period of time. Thus a suggestion to target on this data set using specialized cache replacement policies as a future research direction is given. Furthermore, "range requests are short and can ask for any portion of the file. Additionally, user aborts tend to increase the number of small requests."[269] And yet traditional cache replacement policies do not exploit these characteristics. This further indicates the need for P2P-specific cache replacement policies. Understanding the behavior and dynamics of the P2P network, including peer behavior pattern, traffic pattern, file and object travel pattern, and various statistics, is helpful for caching design (certainly as well as for the P2P file-sharing system design).

Wierzbicki's study also suggests possible performance improvement in Fast-Track via some protocol extension. Comparing full hits with partial hits, they further found that partial hits could improve byte hit rate. This suggests a possible extension of the FastTrack protocol to add a partial hit notification message. When an ordinary node is notified of a partial hit, it could initiate a new request for the missing parts of the range.

Summary

P2P caching is one of the solutions to address P2P content delivery and the problem of P2P network traffic growth caused by the increasing amount of content being delivered over P2P networks. It utilizes peer caches in the P2P network to cache and serve P2P content. The P2P network thus acts as a large distributed cache, which amplifies the benefits of traditional client-side caching. However, P2P networks retain different characteristics. Specialized caching schemes that take advantage of the characteristics of each P2P network are expected to offer better performance gain.

CONTENT PULL AND CONTENT PUSH

Pull and push are two different content delivery models in a network (see Figure 8.4). *Push* refers to the model whereby the sender initiates the delivery and the receiver passively accepts the traffic. In contrast, in the *pull* model, the receivers can initiate and regulate if and when they want to receive traffic.

In a peer-to-peer content delivery network, a push model (as illustrated in Figure 8.4B), sometimes also called the *sender-driven delivery model*, grants the sender the capability to push content data to selected peer or peers, whereas the receiver gets to control the content data flow in the pull model (as shown in Figure 8.4A) by pulling content data blocks from its peer(s). *Receiver-driven delivery model* is another name for the pull model, as you can easily understand.

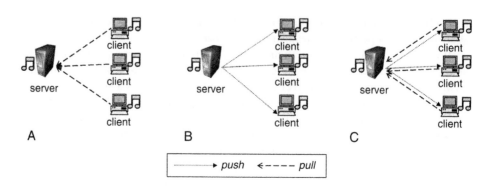

A   B   C

·····▶ push   ◀ ─ ─ ─ pull

FIGURE 8.4 Pull versus push.

In a third model, both sender and receiver may take the initiative to deliver the content. This is called a *hybrid* or *joint sender/receiver* delivery model (see Figure 8.4C).

The tree-based P2P delivery, where peers push content to their children along the tree, is one good example and a popular type of push delivery. The key advantages of this push-style approach include simplicity and statelessness. In mesh-based overlays, the push mode is slightly different. The sender has to consult or negotiate with the receiver to push a content block to the receiver. The receiver may also reject the delivery. This ping-pong process could cause delivery delays. In either case, though, the advantage of efficient utilization of the uploading bandwidth of the sender is obvious.

Unlike a push-based approach, in which the sender is responsible for the content data delivery, a pull approach places the burden on the receiving peers. Pull is a popular delivery method in mesh-based system like BitTorrent. Often, a receiving peer needs to gather certain information, such as content block availability and resource availability, from its neighbors and then determine from which neighbor it will pull the content.

Joint push-pull mechanisms, also called *hybrid push-pull mechanisms*, intend to take advantage of the pros from both sides to achieve the best performance and cost-optimized content delivery. GridMedia,[271] for example, uses pull at first join and push in subsequent redelivery to neighbor peers.

Case Study

Push-Pull Gossiping

Khambatti[272] introduces push-pull gossiping to facilitate a more efficient gossiping operation. Peers are categorized into influential and ordinary peers. Gossiping is achieved via a push phase followed by a pull phase. In the push phase, the content for delivery is multicast to the influential peers. Ordinary peers then retrieve the content via a pull phase.

Prior P2P gossiping approaches have sent messages through all or selected neighbors and up to a certain depth. Unlike these approaches, the push-pull technique introduced here involves a discovery phase to gather data on peers. Thereafter, the push phase of P2P gossiping involves a multicast of that information to specially selected peers (called *seers*) based on the discovered data. As long as the discovered data are available and recent, the push phase can be repeated with new information numerous times. Whenever required, a peer will retrieve the information from a nearby seer via a pull phase. Unlike conventional P2P gossiping approaches, the push-pull gossiping approach can achieve better performance in terms of average hops for content delivery. In a small P2P network of 5000 to 10,000 peers tested in [272], a two-hop performance with more than 80% of its members is achieved when 5% or more peers in the network are influential peers.

A similar strategy is also introduced in the P-grid system to improve system updating efficiency.[273]

CoolStreaming

Coolstreaming,[274] a live streaming application system built on top of a data-driven P2P network called DONet, is one of the first pull-based P2P streaming systems that was tested in actual deployment. The design of DONet focuses on three key criteria: implementation simplicity, content delivery efficiency, and robustness. It achieves its implementation goal via a smart scheduling algorithm that deals with the bandwidth differences of peers, a membership manager that helps the peer maintain a partial view of other overlay nodes, and a partnership manager that establishes and maintains the partnership with other peers.

In CoolStreaming a video stream is divided into segments of uniform length (see Figure 8.5). A buffer map is implemented at each peer to represent the availability of the segments in the buffer of the peer. Each peer periodically exchanges its buffer map with all its partners and schedules the segment to be fetched from its partner accordingly. Scheduling takes into account the playback deadline for each segment and streaming bandwidth of each partner. Since peers periodically exchange buffer maps, detection of neighbor (partner peer) failure becomes easy. Furthermore, it uses gossiping to announce graceful departure of itself or the detection of a partner failure. By allowing active establishment of partnership, the system is better stabilized at peer churn. CoolStreaming fully exploits the benefits of a mesh-based P2P overlay and pull-based content delivery for live video streaming.

CoolStreaming introduces a parameter called a *continuity index* to measure the quality of experience, that is, the continuity of video stream playback at each peer. A continuity index measures the rate of segments that arrives in time for playback. Over a test of 10 to 100 nodes with each peer having two to six partners, a continuity index of approximately 90% to 98% with up to 15% improvement over a tree-based overlay was observed. On average, a >1 hop reduction over tree-based overlay was also experienced.

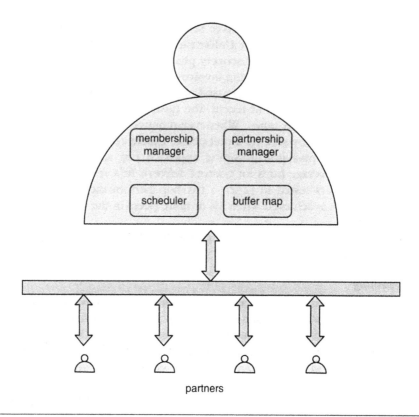

FIGURE 8.5 CoolStreaming peer functional modules.

HYBRID CDN AND P2P ARCHITECTURES

The low cost, scalability, and fault tolerant characteristics make P2P networks more and more attractive for media content delivery today. Yet current P2P technologies still suffer from many disadvantages in supporting high-quality content distribution. For example, the high data rate of video traffic and the bursty arrival and departure of end users are causing significant problems on ISP links. Popular P2P video streaming services such as PPLive and UUSee are also experiencing long startup delay and channel-switching delay of seconds to minutes. Additionally, unpopular programs, those with few peers watching simultaneously, are often poor in quality. Skevik[275] further found in their simulation that the performance of P2P-based systems can be considerably affected by the presence of firewalls, which reduce the load distribution gain of P2P streaming nearly to the level of client/server-based systems.

Overview

To overcome the limitations of P2P-based streaming systems, approaches based on hybrid CDN-P2P architecture were proposed. A generic hybrid CDN-P2P network is illustrated in Figure 8.6. The basic idea is to overcome the limitations of P2P streaming systems with replicas and proxy-caching mechanisms.

Case Study

In [275] and [276], a CDN-P2P hybrid streaming protocol was proposed. It comprises four logical levels in the system structure. Figure 8.7 shows the idea. The client application at the peer communicates with the local host cache at the client side to request or send out content. The local host cache, placed outside the client firewall, corresponds with the server-side content proxy to retrieve content data. It also shares data with other local host caches in the network. The local host cache is responsible for timely retrieval of data blocks and for monitoring communications with other peers as well. The server-side proxy cache talks to the master server, which has the original copy of the content. It also serves content to many local host caches on the client side. The system retains caching at both the client side and the ISP level, making it possible to exploit the advantages of CDNs. The system places the server-side proxy outside

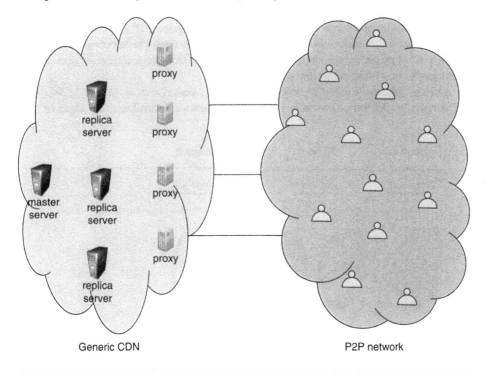

FIGURE 8.6 Hybrid CDN, a conceptual illustration.

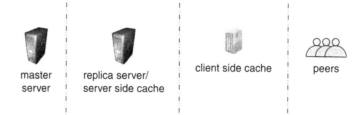

master
server

replica server/
server side cache

client side cache

peers

FIGURE 8.7 A four-level architecture.

the server's firewall. This ensures that external peers have a host to connect to, eliminating the firewall problem in a pure P2P system.

By implementing the P2P operations at the local host cache, system management is simplified at the client side. The local host cache has the capability to serve content even when the client application is not in use by the peer. Since the local host caches can share data directly at the lowest level of the content distribution tree, the load and overhead on the server-side proxy can be substantially reduced. The use of a CDN structure at the server side offers network administration capability that ensures the communication between local hosts is efficient and possibly secure. More important, the use of a proxy in this system eliminates the unavailability problem caused by firewalls in a pure P2P system.

One issue to be addressed here is how to manage multiple server-side replicas/caches. Communications security and efficiency between different server-side replicas/caches must be addressed.

Another hybrid CDN-P2P streaming system described in [277], [278], and [279] takes a different approach. Figure 8.8 reviews the fundamental ideas of this

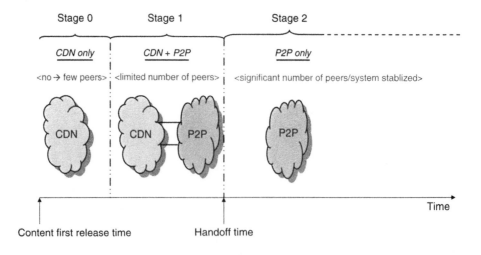

FIGURE 8.8 Stages of the content distribution process in [277].

system. When the media content is first released, it is published in the CDN server. Since there are no peers at this time, the CDN server relies on the CDN only to deliver the content to requesting clients (Stage 0 of Figure 8.8). After a streaming session, the CDN server registers the client that has just received the streaming service. Information regarding the client capability, resources, and so on is also recorded. The client is transformed into a supplying peer of the content distribution system after the registering process.

Now the system becomes a CDN/P2P coexisting content distribution system with the CDN sharing the streaming load with the supplying peers (Stage 1 of Figure 8.8). After a while, the P2P streaming capacity for the specific media content becomes big enough. The CDN steps out of the picture at this point (Stage 2 of Figure 8.8). CDN-based streaming for this particular content will no longer be provided, releasing the CDN server capacity to support other media content streaming. When the number of peers drops under a threshold, the CDN may be directed to rejoin the distribution of this specific media content (back to Stage 1). This way, the problem of low quality delivery of unpopular content of a pure P2P-based system is resolved. Notice, though, that this time-based hybrid system alone does not offer solutions to the ISP stress, firewall, and channel-switching delay problems. Other mechanisms are needed to tackle those problems. Combining the two solutions discussed in this section is a possibility, though care has to be taken in managing the system to avoid high complexity and management cost.

SUMMARY

One of the key challenges of content distribution is delivering increasingly distributed and large amounts of complex data to an increasingly expanding Internet population. P2P technologies are valuable for improving system scalability with low implementation cost. Today network and telecommunication companies are looking into the possibility of integrating P2P technologies into their commercial content distribution systems, such as IPTV and Internet video application systems. IPTV and Internet video heavily rely on video-streaming technologies. To date, video streaming, one of the most popular means for content distribution, still suffers from several drawbacks when built on top of a fully distributed P2P overlay. These include high stress on the ISP links, dependency on high-bandwidth peers, uneven quality distribution, lack of content security mechanisms and authentication capability, and long startup delay and channel switching delay. To take advantage of the P2P network's scalability and low implementation cost properties, the industry is looking into hybrid solutions that are expected to reduce ISP stress and improve security as well as performance. It is clear, though, that one way or the other, the industry is determined to offer high-quality video-streaming services, including IPTV and Internet video services on a wide scale in the very near future.

FOR FURTHER READING

In the beginning of this chapter, generic caching and replication mechanisms for content delivery were briefly introduced. For additional information and advanced caching and replication mechanisms, interested readers can refer to the following publications. Several books on content delivery networks[281,282,283,284] are available. Together they provide a comprehensive coverage on content delivery network architecture, modeling, caching, load balancing, management, and security issues. Furthermore, Venkatesh[285] reviews the consistency mechanisms for caching and replication-based content delivery systems; Saroiu[286] reviews and compares four content delivery systems: HTTP Web traffic, the Akamai content delivery network, the Kazaa P2P file-sharing system, and the Gnutella P2P file-sharing system; Dilley[287] describes the well-known Akamai content delivery network system and its deployment mechanisms; Vkali[288] reviews CDN architecture and popular CDN service providers; and so on.

The following papers provide comprehensive reviews on P2P content delivery:

- J. Li, on peer-to-peer (P2P) content delivery[289]
- S. Androutsellis-Theotokis and D. Spinellis, a survey of peer-to-peer content distribution technologies[290]

Security and privacy are crucial aspects to consider in designing any content delivery system. Chapter 14 of this book is dedicated to P2P security. Interested readers are encouraged to refer to Chapter 14 for related discussion.

Several books listed in the reference sections and discussed in this chapter also serve as good references to further understanding content delivery technologies,[281,282,283,284] caching techniques,[266] and streaming media.[291,292]

Peercasting and Overlay Multicasting

Streaming content over the Internet to a user desktop is a mainstream application today, and using a P2P overlay to peercast streaming content is an important use of P2P technology. When groups of users receive a stream at the same time, it is possible to use multicast techniques to improve efficiency of delivery. Multicast service implemented at the overlay network layer is called *overlay multicast*. This chapter compares native multicast with overlay multicast and reviews the key elements of overlay multicast, including multicast tree formation, group management, and tree management. Techniques for improving overlay multicast performance are discussed, followed by a case study.

INTRODUCTION

The Television Paradigm Shift

In the last 50 years, TV has had major impact on our cultural and daily lives. Today we are witnessing a major shift in the distribution model of TV programs. The conventional scheduled one-to-many broadcasting distribution model that we have been trained to expect is being transformed into a many-to-many, user-centered, "I create," "I find," "I select," "I schedule," "I interact," and "We redistribute" paradigm with potential end-user accessibility to an infinite pool of contents from an endless pool of producers. Real-time TV programs, on-demand video, and rich-media contents are just several types that can be easily accessible through any video terminal, irrespective of the size of the screen, the processing power of the terminal device, or the type of network connection. In this paradigm shift, peer-to-peer networking, along with many other technologies, is playing an important role. Noticeably, TV is not the first and certainly not the last "target" of peercasting applications.

Popular Peercasting Applications

P2P Internet radio, P2P music streaming, and P2P-based Internet TV (also called P2PTV) are perhaps the most popular peercasting applications we see today.

P2P radio refers to software applications designed to distribute audio streams in real time via a P2P network. P2P radio offers the Internet population the ability to broadcast music and other audio contents to millions of audiences without expensive servers. Any peer with a regular PC or even a low-power handheld device could potentially open up her own radio station and broadcast her own music or audio shows to other peers in the P2P network. At the same time, any peer in the P2P network could listen to audio shows broadcast from millions of other P2P radio stations (other peers). Unlike P2P music file sharing, P2P radio allows peers to listen to streamed music stored on or currently broadcast from other peers without downloading the entire music file to their local devices.

Now let's take another quick look at TV again. With over 1 million aggregated users daily,[293] PPLive, an Internet-based P2PTV service developed by Huazhong University of Science and Technology in Wuhan, China, has gained tremendous popularity since late 2005, and it is not alone. UUSee,[294] SopCast,[295] QQLive,[296] PPStream,[297] Feidian,[298] and TVAnts[299] are among the many popular P2P Video-on-Demand (VoD) and P2P live video-streaming software applications. Without an expensive server, those and other P2PTV systems could potentially make any TV channel and any video content globally available.

Figure 9.1 shows two PPLive screen shots with a bit rate of 350 kbps (see Figure 9.1B). Although the channel change time (CCT) can be seconds to tens of seconds long and the resolution is low, PPLive still has millions of customers who use it to watch movies and TV programs. Why? Obviously, free multimedia is always welcomed by many customers. Additionally, the availability of a wide range of content that is not easily accessible through other means is another important reason that many funs are lured to PPLive and its many competitors.

P2P Internet radio and P2PTV are not the only peercasting applications today. Messaging via peercasting and P2P gaming, for example, also has large potential markets. Other potential applications include distance learning, real-time personal video and audio sharing, workspace collaboration, and so on.

The rest of the chapter is organized as follows: Related terminologies and video streaming are introduced in the next two sections. The two subsequent sections focus on the discussion of technologies and issues for overlay multicast. We'll use P2P video casting as an example, unless otherwise specified. Pros and cons of overlay multicast compared to IP multicast, design considerations, and advanced technologies are addressed. A sample case study is given at the end of the chapter.

TERMINOLOGY

- *Unicast.* A means of point-to-point communication. In unicast, data is delivered from a sender node to one specific receiver node. That is, if a node wants to send the same information to many destinations using a unicast transport service, it must perform a replicated unicast and send *N* copies of the data to each destination in turn. Today unicast is still the predominant form of transmission on the Internet.

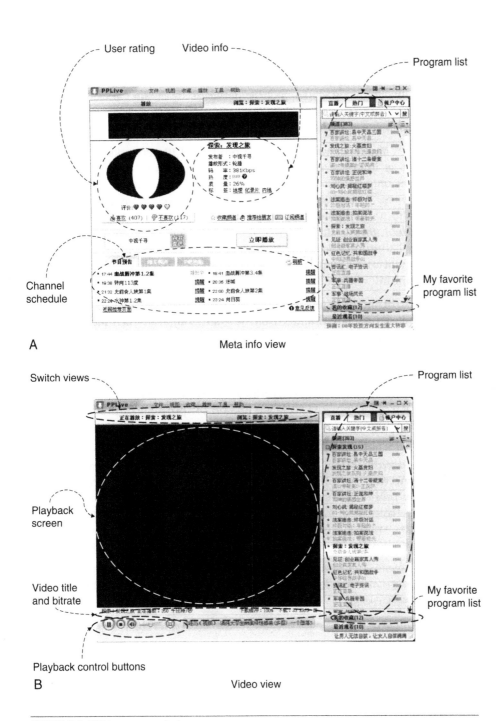

FIGURE 9.1 PPLive screen shots.

- *Broadcast*. An old term that is traditionally associated with radio and television. It generally represents an indiscriminate transmission that can be received by anyone who has the correct equipment. Today broadcast is used in IP networks when data are transmitted from one sender node being "heard" by all other nodes in a specific network, such as within a local area network (LAN). That is, it is a point-to-multipoint transmission, with the information being sent to all connected receivers.

- *Multicast.*[300] Multicast was originally a product of IP networks. Some applications, such as Internet television, Internet gaming, and IP teleconferencing applications, require data to be delivered from one or multiple senders to multiple receivers. A service whereby data are delivered from one or multiple sender nodes to multiple designated receiver nodes is called *multipoint communication* or *multicast*, and applications that involve a multicast delivery service are called *multicast applications*. On the Internet there are two types of addresses: unicast and multicast. A host or node on the Internet normally has only one unicast address but can be a member of many multicast groups.

- *IP multicast.* IP multicast implements multicast service at the IP routing level, with each individual packet transmitted from the source, duplicated at routers, and then delivered to multiple receivers simultaneously. It is also called *native multicast*.

- *Overlay network (ON).*[301] An application layer virtual or logical network in which endpoints are addressable and that provides connectivity, routing, and messaging between endpoints. Overlay networks are frequently used as a substrate for deploying new network services or for providing a routing topology not available from the underlying physical network. Many peer-to-peer systems are overlay networks that run on top of the Internet.

- *Overlay multicast (OM).*[302,303] Overlay multicast implements multicast service at the overlay network layer. Hosts participating in a multicast session form an overlay network and only utilize unicasts among pairs of hosts for data dissemination. The hosts in overlay multicast exclusively handle group management, routing, and tree construction, without any support from Internet routers. This is also commonly known as *application layer multicast* (ALM) or *end system multicast* (ESM).

- *Peercast.* A means of multicasting, broadcasting, or unicasting a data stream via a peer-to-peer network. Peercasting is most often used for P2P broadcasting and P2P multicasting.

Figure 9.2 compares unicast with broadcast and multicast; Figure 9.3 illustrates IP multicast versus overlay multicast.

P2P STREAMING

Streaming refers to a delivery method whereby a content data stream is delivered from a server to a client or clients in a continuous fashion and consumed in real time by client applications. For example, in video-streaming applications, the

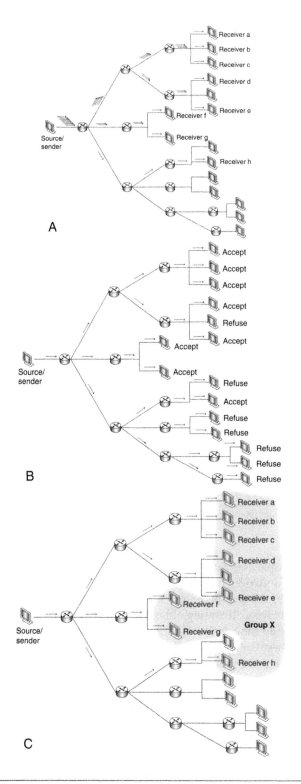

FIGURE 9.2 (A) unicast versus (B) broadcast and (C) multicast.

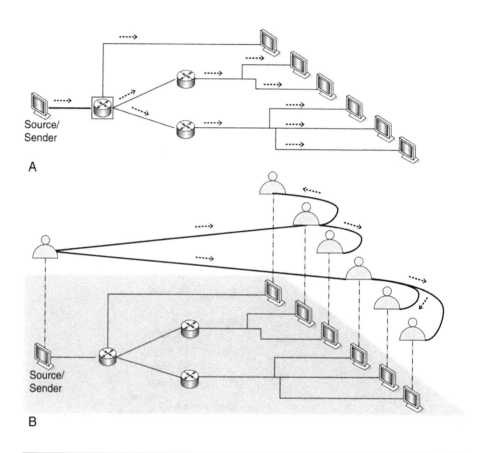

FIGURE 9.3 IP multicast versus overlay multicast.

client can start displaying video as soon as enough data have been received. In a packet-switched network, the server breaks the media into packets and time-stamps them. The timestamped packets are reassembled at the client side while they are being received. Streaming differs from file downloading in that the media are consumed while they arrive. This is indeed one of the most important goals for which a media-streaming system is designed.

Media streaming generally can be classified into live and on-demand categories. On-demand streaming delivers to the clients media content already saved on the server; live streaming sends the media content to the client while it is being captured at the server. One-to-one, one-to-many, and many-to-many are possible configurations in different P2P streaming applications. For instance, a user might stream a recorded video to a single friend (one-to-one) or to multiple friends simultaneously (one-to-many). In a videoconferencing service, many-to-many streaming is likely needed. To facilitate these different kinds of streaming services, unicast, broadcast, and multicast protocols are developed. To offer live and on-demand media-streaming services at low server cost, P2P-based broadcast and multicast mechanisms that take advantage of overlay multicasting are invented and deployed. In the following sections we look at how overlay multicast can facilitate low-cost media-streaming services and potentially offer suitable quality of experience to a large set of audiences.

MULTICAST APPLICATIONS AND P2P OVERLAY MULTICAST

Multicast Applications

To transmit a video, live or stored, from a sender to a receiver, we can use unicast, broadcast, or multicast. The benefit of multicast compared to unicast and broadcast transmission for multimedia applications is network efficiency. According to the Chuang-Sirbu Multicast Scaling Law,[304] the link cost can be significantly reduced with multicast, and the message reduction is proportional to the group size. This efficiency is particularly important for devices connected to limited bandwidth access networks. Consequently, multicast protocols are a key enabler of important applications envisioned in the future networked consumer electronics device world.

Table 9.1 summarizes the characteristics of several emerging applications that can benefit from efficient multicast services. It shows that various group communication applications may require different kinds of support in various dimensions. These applications impose significant technical challenges.

IP Multicast vs. Overlay Multicast

IP multicast and overlay multicast (OM) are the two primary existing multicast approaches (see Figure 9.3). Protocol-Independent Multicast (PIM), Distance Vector Multicast Routing Protocol (DVRMP), and Core-Based Trees (CBT) Multicast Routing are several standardized IP multicast protocols called *host-group multicast protocols* (HGMPs). In a HGMP, one group address per multicast group is created, and each router stores the state for each active group address. In addition, control protocols are implemented to manage group membership. Compared with overlay multicast, IP multicast can realize higher performance and transmission efficiency. However, due to a variety of factors, including cost of deployment, interdomain deployment issues, and the need for pricing models, to date IP multicast has not been deployed by many service providers, especially in wide area networks.

Overlay multicast (OM), on the other hand, is much easier to deploy since it does not rely on router deployment. In OM, an overlay network is built on top of available network services. Peers self-organize into distributed networks that are overlayed on top of the IP networks. The multicast group members

Table 9.1 Characteristics of Several Multicast Applications

Application	Sender	Group Size	Membership Change Rate	Data Rate	Time Bounded	Type
Voiceconferencing	Multiple	Small	Low	High	Highly	Live
Videoconferencing	Multiple	Small	Low	Very high	Highly	Live
Multiparty games	Multiple	Small	Usually low	Low to high	Low delay acceptable but synchronized reception time is important	Live
Personal video/ audio broadcast (small group multicast)	Single/ multiple	Small	Low	High to very high	Some delay acceptable	Live or on-demand
Whiteboard (distance learning/ meeting)	Single/ multiple	Small to medium	Low	Low	Some delay acceptable	Live
News (text and image) broadcasting	Single	Large	High	Low	Some delay acceptable	Live or on-demand
IPTV/Internet TV/ Internet video	Single/ multiple	Large	High	Very high	Some delay acceptable	Live or on-demand
Internet radio	Single/ multiple	Large	High	Low to medium	Some delay acceptable	Live or on-demand
Collaborated/ multiparty real-time document revision in workspace	Single/ multiple	Small	Low	Very low to low	Some delay acceptable	Live
Multicast/ broadcast messaging (stocks, weather, emergency alert)	Single/ multiple	Small to large	Low	Very low to low	Low delay acceptable	Live

(i.e., peers) are connected via the overlay network. Multicast functions, such as group management, multicast routing, and data replication, are performed at the overlay network layer by forming a unicast tree or mesh at the application layer. Figure 9.4A[303] illustrates a basic multicast service architecture using structured

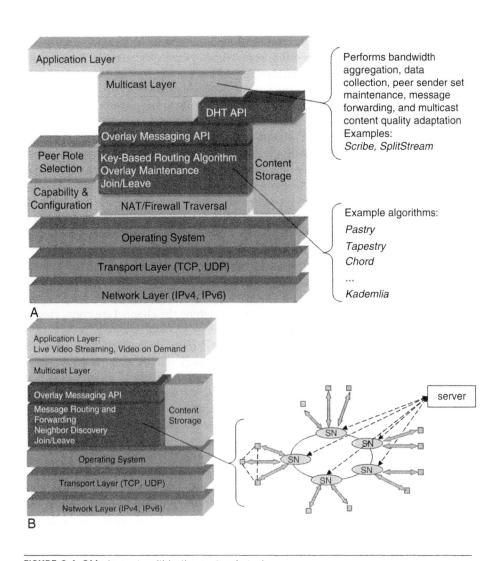

FIGURE 9.4 OM elements within the protocol stack.

overlay networks. In general, the overlay multicast application layer sits on top of a structured or an unstructured overlay network layer that rests on top of the network layer. Multicast groups are formed among the peers in the overlay network, that is, built on top of the overlay infrastructure in the application layer.

Some OM systems form an overlay only among the group members that participate in the multicast session. At the overlay network layer, some basic peer communication functionalities are provided. For instance, peer discovery, message-routing algorithm, overlay network reliability, and overlay security are often implemented at the overlay network layer, whereas multicast is achieved through message forwarding among the members of the multicast groups using unicast across the underlying network or Internet. The generality of the overlay also makes it possible for a single overlay to be shared by many different multicast sessions. This has the advantage of sharing the cost of overlay construction and maintenance among many different applications.

Let's use PPLive as an example again. Figure 9.4B shows an abstract view of the PPLive architecture. The videocasting application sits on top of a hybrid overlay network layer in PPLive. The supernodes form a ring. Each supernode is in charge of one channel in a live streaming application. Peers watching the channel are connected to the superpeer in charge of it in a second P2P layer. In an on-demand application, geographically based space partitioning is done. Each supernode is responsible for a subspace in this case. Peers within a subspace are connected to the supernode in charge of the subspace. Centralized servers take care of peer registration, video listing, and peer bridging services. One P2P group is formed for each video/TV channel. P2P groups may use different overlay multicasting algorithms for content routing as well as group management. Noticeably, although PPLive is popular for its live TV and video streaming services, its platform can be used for the streaming and downloading applications of many types of media content.

One noteworthy moment for PPLive has to do with the most popular show in China, the annual Spring Festival Gala on Chinese New Year. On January 28, 2006, as stated by PPLive,[293] it supported over 200,000 concurrent users at bit rate of 400 to 800 kbps for the four-hour program. This corresponds to an aggregate bit rate of approximately 100 Gbps. This is something not yet achievable with currently available IP multicast-based IPTV systems. According to Hei et al.,[306] PPLive operates as follows: A user launches PPLive client on her computer, which is connected to a channel server via broadband Internet. A set of metadata information that includes a list of several hundred channels is first received. The user can browse through the channel list, look at the rating and information on current popularity, genre, and so on and select the one he's interested in watching. At this time, the PPLive client communicates with a tracker of that channel and gets a list of peers currently watching the channel.

Next, the PPLive client is connected to a set of peers. Data exchange happens thereafter. The retrieved chunks are stored in a buffer and are fed through a local HTTP pipe to the stream player. Several seconds to minutes later, the video stream starts to play, with all viewers of the channel watching the video at approximately the same point. The experience of PPLive at the 2006 Chinese Spring Festival Gala demonstrates that large-scale IPTV service is perhaps achievable through P2P networks, even though today P2P OM is still facing many challenges. The long startup delay and channel change time, the low performance on unpopular channels, the lag between different peers watching the same channel, and the added stress on ISPs are just some of the many issues researchers are investigating. In other words, although P2P OM eliminates the dependency of universal deployment for multicast applications, it comes with a penalty on transmission efficiency and performance degradation.

Easy deployment and a lower server bandwidth requirement are the two most notable advantages of OM. The key drawback is that it is not as efficient as IP-based multicast. It typically requires a large amount of control overhead to maintain group membership to monitor network conditions by sending expensive probing messages. These cause delay and bandwidth penalties. Furthermore, it provides less stability for multicast trees. Thus, when multicast groups are large, efficiently managing the multicast group, propagating messages, and minimizing bandwidth cost pose many challenges. Table 9.2 summarizes the pros and cons of overlay multicast and IP multicast under seven different metrics.

Hybrid Multicast

To reduce the performance penalty of OM, Zhang et al.[307] proposed a hybrid multicast framework called Universal Multicast (UM). The basic idea is to fully utilize native IP multicast wherever available and automatically construct an overall multicast session via unicast tunnels between regions of the network supporting native IP multicast, called *islands*. Isolated IP multicast islands in LANs, especially in enterprise networks and campus networks, exist, even though universal deployment has been slow. To take advantage of the IP

Table 9.2 IP Multicast versus Overlay Multicast

Metric	IP Multicast	Overlay Multicast
Efficiency	High	Low
Stress on ISP	Low	High
Server bandwidth requirement	High	Low
Control overhead	Low	High
Robustness	High	Medium
Lag between customers	Low	Can be high
Deployment cost	High	Low

multicast performance gain, these available IP multicast islands can be utilized to build an UM wherever possible.

To provide ubiquitous multicast delivery services, unicast tunnels between IP multicast islands are built. Multicast messages are transmitted via native IP multicast protocols within the islands and encapsulated in unicast packets to transmit through the tunnels from one island to another. Since native group management protocols don't extend beyond the islands, a mechanism to coordinate the membership across the islands is needed. For hybrid multicast, typically at least two types of protocols are needed: an intra-island and an inter-island group management protocol. P2P OM protocols can be utilized as the inter-island multicast protocol; the Internet Group Management Protocol (IGMP) may be used for the intra-island subgroup multicast. An alternative or even complementary approach to using multicast tunneling is to use an overlay to adaptively combine native multicast regions with overlay multicast.

Peers that are members of a multicast group that are in a common native multicast region can map their multicast paths to the native multicast protocol. He and Ammar[308] have analyzed a hybrid architecture combining host-group multicast with multidestination multicast. Combining these elements, we can see a hybrid multicast architecture that uses native multi-destination routing for small groups for overlay performance enhancement, native host-group routing for larger groups, and overlay multicast to combine native islands into single group sessions.

To leverage performance and cost, today the information technology (IT) industry and the telecommunications industry are also looking into the feasibility of hybrid peer-to-peer system for Internet video and IPTV services. Some popular approaches include content popularity weighted and managed overlay-based approaches. In a content popularity weighted approach, popular content is off-loaded from the server and the low-cost peer-to-peer overlay is used to improve system scalability. The long tail content, on the other hand, is served primarily by the content server to ensure reliability and QoS. Managed overlay takes control of content delivery via server or content delivery networks (CDNs). The servers act like the supernodes in hybrid P2P networks. Consumers (peers) supply bandwidth and storage when needed.

Proxy-Based Overlay Multicast

Another type of multicast approach utilizes infrastructure nodes as proxy nodes to reduce the performance penalty of OM. For example, RMX,[309] Bayeax,[310] Overcast,[311] and RON[312] use this type of multicast. It is sometimes called *fixed nodes-based overlay multicast*[313] as well. In this type of multicast, some strategic nodes are placed around the Internet. These nodes autonomously form overlay multicast trees to provide multicast service. Although it ensures multicast tree stability, this approach offers little flexibility and the fixed nodes can easily become bottlenecks.

OM DESIGN CONSIDERATIONS

Performance Metrics

Yu and Buford[303] summarized some commonly adopted metrics. The three core metrics are:

- *Link stress*. Number of identical packets sent over a link.
- *Stretch (relative delay penalty)*. The ratio of delay between the packet sent over the overlay to that directly sent over the unicast path.
- *Control overhead*. The amount of overhead for control message exchange in terms of number of control messages processed and bandwidth overhead.

Though these three metrics are the most frequently used[303] to characterize OM system performance and impact on the network, other metrics have also been used to further understand an OM system's application value:

- *Startup latency*. Time to start playback of media stream from time of join request.
- *Join latency*. Time to receive first multicast packet from time of join request.
- *Error recovery latency at packet loss*. Time to recover the erroneous packet from the time of error discovery.
- *Reconnection latency at node failure*. Time to be connected to a new parent node from the time of node failure detection.
- *(Average) loss (bit) rate per node*. The ratio of number of packets lost (received) per session to the number of packets that should be received per session.
- *Max number of multicast groups*. Maximum number of multicast groups running simultaneously.
- *Multicast group scalability*. Capability to scale to a group size of *N*.

Different metrics may be used in different applications to characterize an application-specific property or system capability so as to assess an OM system's application value and usability. In voice- and videoconferencing, for instance, low latency and system reliability may be more important than scalability. This is easy to understand. Unlike some other multicast applications, the number of peers in voice- and videoconferencing is often much smaller. However, the time-bounded requirement is much more stringent.

OM Groups and OM Sessions

Many proposed multicast schemes in the literature can be applied on top of different overlay substrates. Scribe,[314] for instance, can be deployed not only on Pastry[315] but also Chord[316] and CAN.[317] It is worth mentioning here that Overlay Weaver,[321] an open-source overlay construction toolkit that provides multiple routing algorithms, Pastry, Tapestry,[318] Chord, Kademlia,[319] and Koorde,[320] with a common API for higher-level services including multicast services, is available for developing P2P-based applications. The Mcast service function in Overlay Weaver allows a user to join and leave a group specified by an ID, and multicast messages to the group. It can also notify an application of topology of a spanning tree on which a multicast message is transferred.

An overlay multicast scheme needs to take group creation, delivery structure, group management, session management, and message dissemination into account. In many multicast applications, such as P2PTV, members of the multicast groups may come and go, causing a high churn rate. Consequently, how to scalably form an efficient multicast delivery structure, manage the dynamic group membership, and maintain the reliability of multicast message dissemination under high churn rates are important issues in OM. In summary, the functionality for each multicast session should at least include:

- Session identification
- Session initiation/creation
- Session subscription/join
- Session leave/graceful departure
- Session message dissemination/data forwarding
- Session fault tolerance/tree reformation at peer failure
- Session termination

Additional useful functions may include:

- Session admission control
- Content access control and security

Group Management

IP multicast groups are normally managed in tree-based structures, but OM groups are constructed and managed in either tree-based or mesh-based structure.[322] The mesh-based strategy provides for more than one path between a pair of nodes. In a single tree-based approach, however, a single path from each nonleaf node to each of its children is established. It is also feasible to apply a mesh first, followed by a tree construction algorithm to implement overlay multicast, where the idea is to take advantage of both strategies.[305]

There are distinct differences in these two strategies that directly impact the control mechanisms as well as the performance of the multicast protocols. A single tree is an acyclic group that leads to loopless routing. This greatly simplifies the routing algorithm. The acyclic nature also brings disadvantages to the system. First, it does not utilize the bandwidth of the leaf nodes, causing a burden of duplicating and forwarding multicast traffic carried by a small subset of peers that are interior nodes of the multicast tree. This violates the fairness in resource and load-sharing requirement in a P2P system. Second, it is sensitive to partitioning. That means that if any nonleaf member of the multicast group leaves the group, voluntarily or by failure, the tree is broken and the children of the failure or departure node need to be reconnected to the multicast to receive messages. In multicast streaming applications, not only is there potential network and end host (peer) heterogeneity, but also the network environment may change dynamically. These entail additional group management costs in single tree-based multicast system.

To cope with the network heterogeneity as well as the active network changes and to enhance the performance of tree-based system, dynamic adaptation approaches are needed. In the meantime, to improve the fairness in resource sharing and thus improve the overall performance of the system, mechanisms that can take advantage of the leaf node bandwidth are indispensable. In response to those requirements, multiple tree-based overlay multicast systems were proposed. CoopNet,[323] SplitStream,[324] and MutualCast[325] are examples of multitree-based systems. In CoopNet and SplitStream, multiple subgroups are formed in such a way that an interior node in one tree is a leaf node in all the remaining trees and bandwidth constraints specified by the nodes are satisfied. It further ensures that the forwarding load is spread across all participating peers. In SplitStream, one video stream is split into k substreams, each distributed along one tree. If all peers want to receive k stripes and they are willing to forward k stripes, SplitStream constructs a forest such that the forwarding load is evenly balanced across all peers while achieving low delay and link stress across the network. This allows a cooperative multicasting environment whereby peers contribute resources in exchange for using the service. A peer that is capable of forwarding more substreams will receive more substreams and hence be able to obtain higher-quality playback. In the case that a peer is unable to contribute enough bandwidth for full stream forwarding, it may receive fewer substreams, giving lower-quality playback.

In their design, the expected amount of state maintained by each node is $O(\log N)$; the expected number of messages to build the forest is $O(N \log N)$ and $O(N^2)$ in the worst case, where N is the number of peers in the multicast group. Figure 9.5 illustrates a simple example of SplitStream with two stripes. An additional advantage of SplitStream is that it offers resilience to node failures and ungraceful departures, even without additional mechanisms, since different substreams to a node come from different peers. When one parent of a subgroup fails, the peer node still may receive other substreams from other parents in other subgroups and may reconstruct the content accordingly, although with lower quality. The detailed multigroup management mechanism of SplitStream over Scribe is described in [324].

MutualCast goes even further. A total number of N trees are used in a multicast group of N nodes. To offer bandwidth adaptation, MutualCast uses TCP buffers to achieve synchronization of the delivered stream.

Mesh-based multicast provides multiple or redundant connections between members of the group with mesh-based construction. This offers the advantage of lower probability of multicast group partitioning by node failure or departure, since alternate paths will already exist without the need for group or subgroup

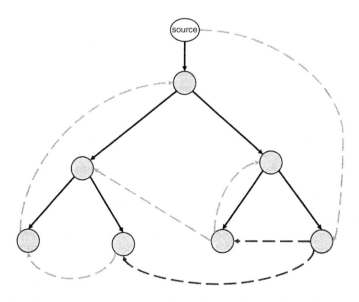

FIGURE 9.5 SplitStream with two stripes.

reconstruction or readjustment. Routing stability and QoS are subsequently improved. PPLive is a good example of a mesh-based multicast system. In PPLive, the delivery path of a message depends on the overlay as well as feedback from neighboring peers. Unlike a tree-based mechanism that relies on overlay adaptation for message dissemination, the status exchange-based message-forwarding strategy is easier to implement and is also helpful in coping with churn and the changing network conditions. The downsides of the mesh-based approach, however, are several-fold. It is inherently more costly, since multiple copies of a message may be forwarded to a link on the routing path, imposing increased link stress. Additionally, a proper routing algorithm is essential in the construction of loop-free forwarding paths between group members.

Message Dissemination

The single tree-based multicast system uses a Rendezvous Point (RP) based message dissemination scheme. That is, a sender of the multicast group sends a message to the root or the RP node of the tree, which then forwards the message along the tree to all receivers. The inefficiency of the approach lies in the fact that all messages must first be routed to the RP before they reach the group members.

In CoopNet and SplitStream, the source stream is "split" into multiple substreams or descriptions. Each substream is distributed along a different single distribution tree via one or more RPs to reach the end hosts. An end host will reconstruct the media stream using the received substreams. With a proper coding scheme such as Multiple Description Coding (MDC),[326] peers in the multi-cast group may join one or more subgroups and are able to decode the content with one or more substreams. The more substreams it receives, the higher the media playback quality. For a network with heterogeneous end host (terminal) devices, this has obvious advantages.

Mesh-based systems can use pull, push, or hybrid push-plus-pull delivery mechanisms for multicast message dissemination. If the sender takes the initiative in moving the message from peer to peer, it is called *push-based message dissemination*. Alternatively, in a *pull-based model*, the receiver takes control of the message delivery path by pulling message blocks from its neighbor. When the sender and receiver manage the message delivery route via negotiation, a hybrid mode is invoked. GridMedia[327] is an example of a hybrid mesh-based multicast system. In GridMedia, media blocks are classified into push blocks and pull blocks. To reduce delay, pull mode is used when nodes first join the multicast group; push mode is adopted otherwise. Since the receiver takes control in a hybrid or pull-based approach, it offers higher probability of on-time delivery of message blocks in a time-bounded multicast application. Meanwhile, active push may benefit from efficient upload bandwidth balancing since the sender can control the delivery path. Readers can reference Chapter 8 on peer-to-peer streaming for more discussion of push versus pull content delivery.

Unlike tree-based systems whereby messages may be immediately forwarded at each intermediate node, messages in mesh-based multicast systems are often forwarded after the neighborhood status information is gathered, causing possible delays in message dissemination. How to take advantage of the reliability and adaptivity of mesh-based schemes while retaining the low latency of tree-based approaches for delay-bounded peercasting applications is being studied by many researchers today.

Categorization of OM Systems

In the past several years, numerous designs for OM have been proposed. Noticeably, designs differ in terms of overlay structure, message routing, tree management, and the like, and each might be suitable for different applications. Obviously, the slow deployment of IP multicast also contributed to the research interests in OM design. In the previous sections, we looked at tree versus mesh at group management and pull versus push at message dissemination, two different ways to categorize OM schemes. In the following we look at some other general means for OM system categorization.

First, depending on whether the group management and data replication are implemented at end hosts (peer nodes) or intermediate overlay proxies, an OM system can be categorized into distributed end systems or proxy-based systems whereby dedicated proxies in the network are deployed to improve performance. Narada[305] and NICE[328] are popular examples of distributed end systems; AMcast,[329] OMNI,[330] Scattercast,[331] and Overcast[311] are some examples of proxy-based ones. Studies[332] show that a well-designed proxy-based overlay multicast may come close to the performance of IP multicast. The tradeoff is that proxied overlay multicast does involve deployment costs and provisioning decisions.

Second,[303] as discussed in Chapters 3 and 4, peer-to-peer overlays supporting multicast protocols can be either structured or unstructured. Unstructured schemes are not constrained by overlay topology. Peers may be organized randomly in a flat or hierarchical graph. Most often, multicast messages are disseminated via flooding or random walk on the graph. Since data and network structure are fully decoupled, unstructured overlays can often support complex search with a sacrifice on query efficiency, network bandwidth consumption, and/or query hit rate. Most of the P2PTV systems we see today use unstructured overlay for video multicasting. PPLive is a typical example of that.

Structured schemes, on the other hand, impose constraints on the topology of the overlay and build multicast trees on top of the structured overlay. A few systems such as Scribe/Pastry and Bayeaux/Tapestry have integrated multicast with structured peer-to-peer overlays. Pastry and Tapestry rely on a DHT to provide the substrate for semantic-free and data-centric references through the assignment of a semantic-free node ID. The DHT performs request routing between peers for operations such as put and get. DHT-based schemes have strong theoretical foundations. There is a guarantee that a key can be found if it exists. On the other hand, most DHT-based systems have a data object lookup latency characterized by $O(\log N)$, where N is the number of peers in the overlay. Furthermore, DHTs assume that all peers equally participate in hosting published data objects or their location information. This leads to a bottleneck at low-capacity peers.

The integration of overlay multicast with DHT-based structured peer-to-peer overlays makes it possible to share routing table management overhead between the DHT and the OM functions. This potentially improves the multicast system performance. Furthermore, the underlying overlay may incorporate techniques to consider and exploit network proximity. This has the benefit of reducing the number of network-level hops an overlay message traverses. From the OM perspective, if the overlay does not consider network proximity, multicast messages may travel substantially long distances in some routing hops. Castro et al.[333] found that incorporating topology awareness into the routing algorithm and proximity into node address selection generally improved tree quality. However, a comparative study of multicast in structured overlays with dedicated OM designs has not been done.

Third, OM systems can also be categorized according to tree construction types:[328]

- Mesh-first, whereby a mesh control topology between peers is computed first, followed by reverse-path forwarding (RPF)[334] construction of the data topology
- Tree-first, whereby the data tree is constructed first, followed by control connections between nodes in the tree
- Implicit, whereby the control and data paths are defined simultaneously

Studies[328] have shown that mesh-first protocols are efficient for small groups, tree-first protocols are more suited to applications requiring high-bandwidth transfers, and implicit protocols can support both latency-sensitive and high-bandwidth applications as well as very large group sizes.

Although OM can overcome some inherent problems of IP multicast, many issues still remain to be explored. Security, privacy, content access control, and billing and accounting are just some of the frequently discussed challenges. Additional challenges also exist for large-scale multicast services such as Internet-scale video broadcasting, IPTV, and large-scale distance learning. How to deal with system heterogeneity, the dynamic network condition, and the host churn rate; handle various security threats and provide application appropriate security measures; provide higher scalability for multicast group management; support various multicast groups simultaneously; and reduce control overhead for low capacity devices are just some examples.

As examples, we compare several popular OM systems in Table 9.3.

IMPROVING OM PERFORMANCE

Quality of Experience (QoE), which indicates user experience and satisfaction, is a popular factor to measure the success of multimedia services. Startup delay and playback jittering are two important factors affecting user experiences. In an overlay multicast system, multicast join latency will impact the startup delay; reconnection latency at node failure and tree reformation latency in a high-churn application (such as a large-scale video-multicasting application) will affect the playback jittering rate.

One popular approach to reduce join and reconnection latencies in overlay multicast services is to use proximity-based routing, which improves arbitrarily long distances in routing hops.[303] In CAN, for example, landmark nodes are used for proximity measurement. Tapestry and Pastry, on the other hand, exploit proximity metric among pairs of nodes. OM schemes based on CAN, Tapestry, and Pastry may use round-trip time (RTT) to approximate network distance between a pair of nodes. As discussed in Chapter 10, to reduce the cost of extensive RTT measurement, various Internet coordinate systems (ICS) have been proposed for proximity measurement.

Another approach utilizes proactive stepparent selection to reduce the reconnection time in tree-based multicast systems. That is, each peer in the multicast group locates its potential stepparent in advance. At tree reformation, a node that is a candidate parent in the multicast tree immediately takes over the role of parenting. This cuts down real-time messaging needed for tree reconstruction, thus reducing the probability of playback jittering at the affected end hosts.

Furthermore, by reducing the message hop counts, not only can the time of a multicast message being delivered from the sender to the receiver be reduced, it

Table 9.3 Selected OM Protocol Comparison

Protocol	Scribe	ESM	CAN	Split Stream	PPLive
Target applications	Large group multicast.	Small group multicast.	Large group multicast.	Large group multicast.	Large multigroup multicast.
Approach	Multicast tree is built on top of Pastry. Uses reverse path forwarding to build a multicast tree per group. Each group is identified by the groupId. Multicast message propagates through the multicast spanning three.	Multicast group members self-organize into an overlay structure. End hosts (peers) periodically exchange group membership and routing information, build a mesh based on end-to-end measurements, and run a distributed distance vector protocol to construct a multicast delivery tree.	CAN-based multicast has two steps: (1) the members of the group first form a group specific overlay; (2) multicasting is achieved by flooding over the overlay, creating a separate overlay per multicast group. Multicast message is broadcast within each overlay.	Multiple trees per multicast group are established with the video stream split into multiple stripes and each video stripe delivered via one tree.	Mesh-based system that utilizes a tracker to identify neighborhood peers for data exchanging. Buffer map is employed to decide on the chunks of media stream to retrieve at each peer.

Fault detection and tolerance	Uses heartbeat messages from each nonleaf node to its children to detect node failure.	Each member needs to refresh the membership to other members along the mesh, needs to probe other members periodically, and maintains the path that leads to each destination.	Uses periodical message probing to detect faulty nodes.	Offers resilience to node failures and ungraceful departures, since different substreams to a node come from different peers. When one parent of a subgroup fails, the peer node may still receive other substreams from other parents in other subgroups and may reconstruct the content accordingly, although with lower quality.	Using mesh to offer inherent fault-tolerant capability.
Scalability	Supports large group.	Supports small group.	Scalability is not as good as Scribe.	Supports large group.	Supports multiple very large groups.
Advantages	Lower delay and overhead than flood-based approach.	Optimizes the efficiency of the overlay routing tree based on end-to-end measurement.	Low cost when all or most nodes in the overlay are members of the multicast group.	Better resource sharing and load balance than single tree-based system; better reliability at node failure.	High scalability and low multicast group management overhead.

also potentially increases the reliability of message forwarding and hence reduces playback jittering rate in videocasting applications.

It is also observed that the stream-splitting approach of SplitStream and the hybrid multicast approach of UM also effectively improve multicast performance by improving the probability of a message being successfully delivered to the receiver nodes.

CASE STUDY: SCRIBE

Castro et al.[333] compared flooding-based with tree-based multicast approaches and found that tree-based construction in a single overlay outperformed the flooding-based approach[317] using separate overlays for each multicast session. One generic P2P overlay multicast system using the tree-based approach is Scribe.[314] In the following we use Scribe as an example to look more closely at the minimum requirements for building an overlay multicast system.

Scribe is a large-scale overlay multicast scheme built on top of Pastry,[315] a structured peer-to-peer object location and routing overlay substrate. A Scribe system consists of a network of Pastry nodes with each node running the Scribe application software. To create a multicast group, a unique groupId is first generated, for example, using the hash of the group's textual name. A group with this groupId is created by a CREATE message sent toward the peer node with the ID closest to the groupId. That peer node subsequently becomes the RP that is the root of the multicast tree. The group with this groupId is then added to the list of multicast groups. Scribe uses a scheme similar to reverse-path forwarding (RPF)[334] for multicast tree formation.

To join a group, a node X sends a JOIN message routed toward the RP through Pastry, with the group's groupId as the key. Each node along the path from the subscriber to the root (RP) checks to see whether it is already within the multicast tree. If it is not, it creates a children's table that is used for multicast message routing for the group, adds X to its children's table, forwards a join message toward RP, and becomes a forwarder of the group (see Figure 9.6A). Otherwise, it simply registers X as a child and stops forwarding the JOIN message (see Figure 9.6B). Notice that a forwarder is a member of the multicast tree but might not be a member of the multicast group. Any source node in the multicast group can multicast a message to the group by sending the message to the RP, and the RP then disseminates the message to all group members along the multicast tree.

Scribe employs heartbeat messages from each nonleaf node to its children to detect node failure. Multicast messages may be used as implicit heartbeat messages. On detection of the failure of its parent, a node rejoins the multicast group by calling Pastry to route a JOIN message to the RP with the groupId (see Figure 9.6C). Pastry will route the message to a new parent, thus repairing the multicast tree. If a node finds itself to be overloaded, it passes some of its children to its other children and making those its grandchildren. This mechanism effectively minimizes the probability of a node becoming a bottleneck. Scribe can also tolerate RP (multicast tree root) failure. This is realized via replication. The state associated with the RP is replicated across the k closest leaf set nodes to the root

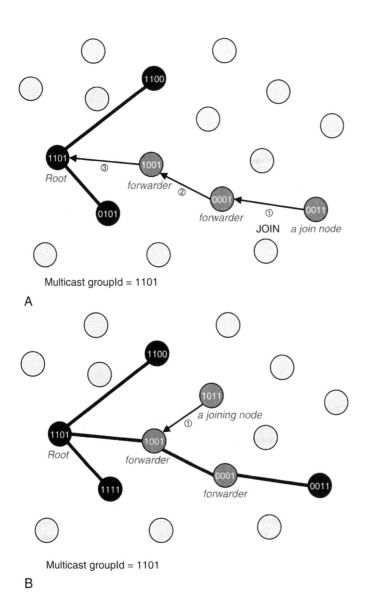

Multicast groupId = 1101

A

Multicast groupId = 1101

B

FIGURE 9.6 Scribe membership management.

(Continued)

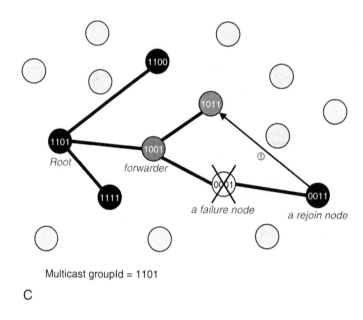

Multicast groupId = 1101

C

FIGURE 9.6–Cont'd

node in the nodeId space. If the root fails, its immediate child or children detect the failure and join the multicast group again through Pastry. Pastry routes the join messages to a new root with the closest `nodeId` to the `groupId`, making it the new RP. Multicast senders likewise discover the new RP by routing via Pastry.

Because in Scribe tree formation is completely decentralized, membership change is also handled in a distributed fashion. Scribe has mechanisms to handle node failure as well as overloaded nodes. Since its underlying overlay, Pastry, uses randomized overlay addresses, well-balanced trees and fairness in multicast message forwarding can be achieved. These lead to a scalable overlay multicast system.

Scribe offers best effort message dissemination using TCP. However, it also provides a simple framework to allow implementation with stronger reliability guarantees for streaming media and other time-bounded applications. This is done through buffering and assigning a sequence number to each message. All recently multicast messages are buffered by the root and by each node in the multicast tree. Messages are retransmitted after the multicast tree is repaired. To ensure reliable delivery, the messages must be buffered for an amount of time that exceeds the maximal time to repair the multicast tree after a TCP connection breaks.

Noticeably, when most nodes in an overlay network are members of a multicast group, a flooding-based mechanism offers a cheaper way for message propagation by eliminating the control overhead.

SUMMARY

Many challenges still exist in building an appropriate peercasting system for various applications. We discussed some of the challenges throughout this chapter. For example, challenges for large-scale overlay multicast systems and some frequently mentioned P2P system challenges were briefly described. Some performance-related challenges were discussed. Here we summarize them into several categories:[303]

- *Performance.* Today some of the most popular peercasting applications still have many problems in terms of performance and end-user quality of experience. This is especially true for the large-scale videocasting services. For instance, many P2PTVs have a startup delay of seconds to minutes. We believe an OM scheme should be tuned to the specific real-life application the scheme is designed for, to maximize system performance.

- *Scalability for large-scale P2P applications.* An OM solution may be unscalable for many reasons, including control message overhead, network heterogeneity, imbalanced tree, high link stress, and long delay in message dissemination. Today's commercial IPTV systems have not adopted peercasting approaches. Can overlay multicast or hybrid multicast improve commercial IPTV systems' scalability without sacrificing system performance? In this chapter we discussed approaches that provide ways to deal with some of the problems of conventional OM schemes. Although these schemes together may offer better scalability for a large-scale system, extensive real-life tests are needed to better understand their properties, strengths, and weaknesses.

- *Reliability.* Streaming multicast applications requires a guarantee of on-time packet delivery. How to provide quality of service, ensure system recoverability, and assure fast recovery from failure all are issues that need to be considered in designing a successful real-life system. UM and low overhead proximity-aware routing schemes offer a certain level of benefit for streaming multicast applications. Many other approaches also exist in the literature. A comprehensive real system test can help to further quantify the benefit of these schemes.

- *Security and trust.* Most existing solutions do not yet consider the security aspects of a peercasting system. Distributed mechanisms for group membership control, secure message forwarding, distributed secure key distribution schemes, and distributed trust mechanisms are some of the important security issues that arise in peercasting.

- *Cost.* A peercasting scheme should be easy to deploy to offer a practical solution over native IP multicast. Furthermore, it should incur high deployment cost at the network, service provider, or the end-user side.

FOR FURTHER READING

Scribe[314] is one of the first and one of the most classical OM systems in the literature. Those interested in building a test overlay multicast system can try out Overlay Weaver.[320] Several survey and tutorial papers on overlay multicast[322,332,335,336,337] can also serve as good starting points. Meanwhile, the Scalable Adaptive Multicast (SAM) Research Group of the Internet Research Task Force (IRTF) homepage (www.samrg.org) is a place to get information on the latest advances in the field.

Measurement for P2P Overlays

The P2P overlay depends on the service characteristics of the underlying network, but in today's Internet the state of links and routers is not easily available to applications. Thus many overlay networks use periodic probing of the underlying network to measure network conditions. Since such measurements on the scale of a P2P overlay can significantly load the network, techniques for reducing the probing are of interest. P2P overlays frequently need to exploit network latency for decisions regarding locality, proximity, and topology. This chapter discusses the use of Internet coordinate systems and other techniques for estimating latency-related measurements in P2P overlays.

MOTIVATION

As discussed in previous chapters, peers have the flexibility to choose their communication peers for their P2P overlay networks, overlay routing, and overlay-based multicast applications. This flexibility can significantly improve P2P overlay system performance by exploiting the localized properties of the underlying networks. This is because most requests in peer selection are able to be fulfilled by peers in the nearby area of the requester and thus do not incur the high cost associated with the massive scale of the entire Internet. Furthermore, selecting network peers based on their proximity and topology locations in the network is a basic building block for many P2P systems.

For example, in an overlay-based multicast application, there exists the problem of low-latency server selection. A client ideally wants to know the latency or available bandwidth between itself and all the peers to construct latency-sensitive multicast topology that can scale the Internet and is able to give the best possible end-to-end multicast path in terms of the minimum delay penalty, minimized response time to the user, and so on. Although dynamic network performance metrics such as latency or available bandwidth are the most relevant to such applications and can be accurately measured on demand, the huge possible number of end-to-end paths that need to be considered makes performing on-demand network measurements impractical due to high cost and time consumption.

Similarly, in an online multiuser gaming application, some ideas for distributed game server discovery mechanisms have been put forward in [338]. A player can simply measure its latency to all game servers and bind to the closest one for optimal gaming experience. The discovery mechanism must be scalable in terms of returning a set of servers that is mostly closer to a player (e.g., k-Nearest Neighbors query). In such, the proximity information about the servers and players and the efficient and scalable discovery of closest server mechanism are important distributed system design commitments. Online multiuser gaming applications can benefit substantially from selecting nodes based on their location in the network.

In small distributed systems, it is possible to perform extensive measurements and make decisions based on the global information of network metrics such as Internet latencies between nodes. Unfortunately, knowledge of such global information is not available without cost, even in small distributed systems. On-demand network latency measurements for large-scale distributed Internet applications such as P2P applications are expensive and time consuming, especially so when the number of possible communication nodes is massive at Internet scale, global information is unwieldy, and lack of centralized servers makes it difficult to find nodes that fit the selection criteria.

As shown in Figure 10.1, the geographical distances between a node in Brazil (Brazil Node) to other Internet nodes such as Node1 and Node2 are not

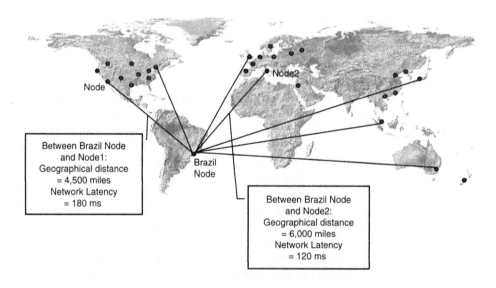

FIGURE 10.1 How far is the Brazil Node to Node1 and to Node2 in terms of geographical distances? Which one is closest to the Brazil Node in terms of network latency?

proportional to the Internet latencies between the nodes. In the figure, Node1 is geographically close to the Brazil Node, but the network path between them might not have the network connectivity and resources to route data packets with the lowest possible latency. The route between the Brazil Node and Node1 has a higher latency than the one between the Brazil Node and Node2. Internet latency depends on the underlying international network links provisioned as well as the Internet routing policies that are implemented. Internet routing policies also do not guarantee symmetric shortest paths.[339]

A highly promising and scalable approach is to construct an Internet geometry that can estimate unknown network distances such as Internet latencies (or available bandwidth) for a given pair of nodes in a network from a set of partially observed measurements—network embeddings for Internet coordinate systems. Such a mapping is called a *network embedding,* and ideally network distances between node pairs are exactly embedded into the geometric space as their geometric distances. The latencies on links are usually used as the network distances for the network embedding because they are a fundamental property in distributed systems and arise from the propagation delay, queuing at routers, and computational load on end hosts.

Recent Internet coordinate systems[340,341,342,343,344,345,346,347,348,349,350,351] have widely been used to embed the measured underlying end-to-end Internet latencies in terms of roundtrip times (RTTs) between *some* node pairs in a network of N nodes into some geometric space and to assign node coordinates to *every* node to predict the unmeasured latencies between the nodes as their computed geometric distances. The network embedding is scalable because the procedure is carried out with much fewer latency measurements without a full mesh of N^2 extensive measurement. Thus, Internet coordinate systems could be used to make latency-conscious decisions in large-scale distributed applications, without the overhead of directly probing the network with all pairs RTT measurements.

Coming back to the earlier example and as shown in Figure 10.2, node coordinates and geometric distances between all node pairs can be computed after probing and embedding the RTTs to only a small set of nodes, usually referred to as *landmarks*. In the figure, node coordinates are assigned to the Brazil Node and Node1, and their computed geometric distance approximates the Internet latencies between them.

An example illustrating a three-dimensional Euclidean coordinate space for 226 PlanetLab nodes is shown in Figure 10.3.

A distributed hash table (DHT) is network-oblivious by design because nodes pick logical identifiers at random and data objects are replicated on neighbors in the identifier space. Structured DHT-based P2P overlays are examples of network-oblivious overlays; each overlay node creates connectivity to its immediate neighbors in the logical identifier space. A short distance in the identifier space in overlay routing may cause a long distance in the underlying network routing.

http://www.planet-lab.org/

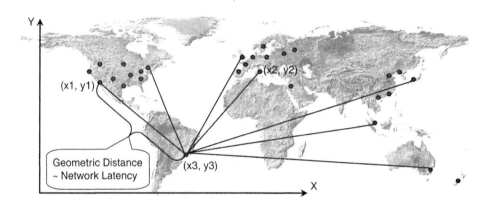

FIGURE 10.2 Internet coordinates and geometric distances between Brazil Node and other Internet nodes.

Network Coordinates of 226 PlanetLab Nodes

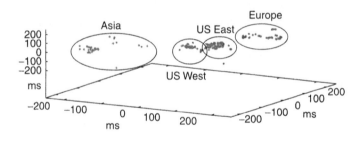

FIGURE 10.3 Network coordinates for 226 PlanetLab nodes (Used by permission from Peter Pietzuch).

Proximity-aware DHT-based P2P overlays exploit the freedom to select physically close nodes for inclusion in the overlay routing tables. Many existing Structured DHT-based P2P overlays such as Pastry,[352] Chord,[353] and DHash[354] use such network coordinate systems to determine nearby nodes for efficient construction and scalable routing lookup operation. Besides routing lookup operation, Chord and DHash (which is built on top of Chord) also use the Internet coordinate system Vivaldi[347] in their remote procedure call (RPC) system to predict end-to-end latency for a given pair of nodes, because Chord often contacts other nodes just once and it cannot measure the latencies to set the RPC retransmission timer inexpensively. So, the node coordinate information makes the search for nearby nodes more efficient and scalable by saving probe bandwidth and reducing the time spent in searching for neighbors.

Network-aware P2P overlays such as Lightweight SuperPeers Topology (LST)[355] and network-aware SuperPeers-Peers overlay multicast streaming application

(Bos)[356,357] are examples of P2P overlays that do not use logical identifier space. Instead they create an overlay topology that is based purely on internode physical latencies derived from scalable Internet coordinate systems and that exploits network locality properties for their overlay routing strategy. A network-aware P2P overlay content multicast application constructs streaming trees that benefit from the smaller number of network routing hops and localized quality of service (QoS) characteristics such as latency, bandwidth, and reliability.

Another overlay application example that uses an Internet coordinate system is the recently proposed distributed stream-processing system (DSPS) called a *stream-based overlay network* (SBON)[358] that streams data from multiple producers to multiple consumers via network processing operators. As illustrated in Figure 10.4, the SBON collects, processes, and aggregates data across massive numbers of real-time streams and uses a modified stable and adaptive version of Vivaldi[359] to predict latencies between nodes in their operator placement algorithm. The key challenge for an operator placement algorithm is the potentially large number of nodes that need to be considered for placement in the overlay network. No network entity has complete information about the current network and node conditions to make an optimal decision. So, using the Internet coordinate system, the operator placement algorithm can be designed to satisfy the three basic requirements of scalability, efficiency, and adaptivity.

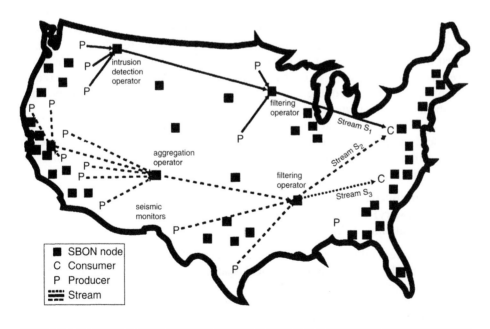

FIGURE 10.4 Network-aware operator placement for stream-processing systems[358]
© 2006 IEEE.

NETWORK EMBEDDING

This section begins with an overview of the basic properties of network embedding for Internet coordinate systems. Two main categories of network embedding techniques are described: numerical optimization of some defined objective function and Lipschitz embedding[360,361] with matrix factorization for dimensionality reduction. A survey of the existing proposed Internet coordinate systems is provided.

Basic Properties of Network Embedding

Given a network X consisting of a set of N nodes and a network distance metric function d indicating the network distances between them, we are able to embed these networked nodes into low-dimensional vector space with the aim of preserving network distances between the nodes in the metric space. At times this distance function is represented by an $N \times N$ distance matrix containing the distance between every pair of nodes. The justification for applying embedding is that for any finite metric space (X, d), we can usually find a one-to-one mapping $\emptyset$ that maps the N nodes into a vector space of dimensionality k. By doing so, the distances between the points are approximately preserved using a distance function d. Such a mapping is called a *network embedding*.

As illustrated in Figure 10.5, the network embedding is *scalable* because it is done with many fewer network distance measurements between nodes than the $O(N^2)$ required on a full mesh of N nodes. Ideally network distances between nodes are exactly embedded as their geometric distances in the geometric space. That is, the geometric distances between the node coordinates allow the unmeasured network distances of all pairs of nodes to be estimated *accurately*. However, as shown in Figure 10.6, even if the full mesh of N nodes is measured in the full network embedding, some levels of embedding accuracy can be lost; we show this effect later in the chapter.

Formally, a metric space is a pair $M = (X, d)$ where X is a finite set of size N nodes, equipped with the distance metric function $d: X \times X \rightarrow \mathbf{R}^+$; for each $a, b \in X$ the *distance between a and b* is given by the function $d(a, b)$. We require that for all $a, b, c \in X$,

- (Antireflexivity) $d(a, b) = 0$ if and only if $a = b$
- (Symmetry) $d(a, b) = d(b, a)$
- (Triangle inequality) $d(a, b) \leq d(a, c) + d(c, b)$

A norm in a real valued vector space is a measure of the length of a vector, which serves as the basis of a distance metric. Usually, the norm is one of the L_p norms, $\|x\|_p = (\Sigma |x_i|^p)^{1/p}$.

Distance metrics based on such a norm are often termed *Minkowski metrics*.[453] The most common Minkowski metrics are the Euclidean distance metric (L_2), the City Block distance metric (L_1), and the Chessboard distance metric (L_∞).

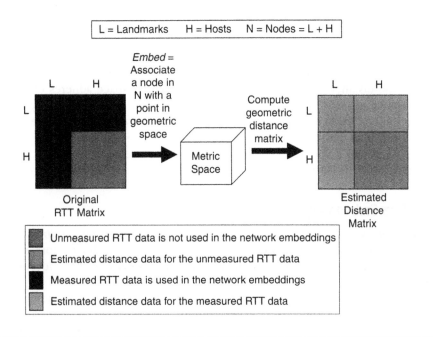

FIGURE 10.5 Overview of network embedding.

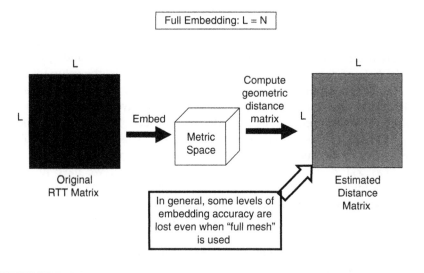

FIGURE 10.6 Full network embedding.

An embedding of a finite metric space (X, d) into $(\mathbf{R}^k, \delta)$ is a mapping $\emptyset$: $X \to \mathbf{R}^k$, where k is the dimensionality of the embedding space and δ: $\mathbf{R}^k \times \mathbf{R}^k \to \mathbf{R}^+$ is the distance metric function of the embedding space. If we denote the norm in $\mathbf{R}^k$ with $\|.\|$, the distance metric δ is defined as $\delta(x, y) = \|x - y\|$. Ideally, the distance $\delta(\emptyset(a), \emptyset(b))$ in the embedding space adheres closely to the distance $d(a, b)$ in the original space. However, it is often not possible and/or impractical to achieve exact correspondence between the distances based on d and δ. If an embedding mapping function $\emptyset$ exists such that $\delta(\emptyset(a), \emptyset(b)) = d(a, b)$, for all $a, b \in X$, then (X, d) and $(\mathbf{R}^k, \delta)$ are said to be isometric. Strictly speaking, (X, d) is isometric to $(\emptyset(X), \delta)$, where $\emptyset(X) \in \mathbf{R}^k$ is the range of X.

Lipschitz Embedding

A powerful class of embedding methods is known as *Lipschitz embeddings*.[360,361] These are based on defining a coordinate space whereby each axis corresponds to a reference set (or a set of landmarks) that is a subset of the nodes in the network.

A Lipschitz embedding is defined in terms of a set L of subsets of the network X, where $L = \{l_1, l_2, l_i, \ldots, l_k\}$. The subsets l_i are termed the *reference sets* of the network embedding. Let $d(a, l)$ be an extension of the distance function d of node $a \in X$ to a subset $l \subset X$, such that $d(a, l) = \min_{x \in l}\{d(a, x)\}$. An embedding with respect to L is defined as coordinate mapping $\emptyset$ such that $\emptyset(a) = (d(a, l_1), d(a, l_2), \ldots, d(a, l_k))$. In other words, we are defining a coordinate space in which each axis corresponds to a subset $l_i \subset X$ of the nodes, and the coordinate values of node a are the distances from node a to the closest element in each of l_i. Note that the distance preserving l_∞ embedding is a special case of a Lipschitz embedding, where L consists of all singleton subsets of X (i.e., $L = \{\{a_1\}, \{a_i\}, \ldots, \{a_N\}\}$).

The intuition behind the embedding is that at an arbitrary node $x \in X$, some information about the distance between two arbitrary nodes a_1 and a_2 is obtained with the help of comparing $d(a_1, x)$ and $d(a_2, x)$, that is, the value $|d(a_1, x) - d(a_2, x)|$. This is especially true if one of the distances $d(a_1, x)$ and $d(a_2, x)$ is small. Observe that due to the triangle inequality, we have $|d(a_1, x) - d(a_2, x)| \leq d(a_1, a_2)$. This argument can be extended to a subset l. In other words, the value $|d(a_1, l) - d(a_2, l)|$ is a lower bound on $d(a_1, a_2)$. This can be seen as follows.

Let $x_1, x_2 \in l$ be such that $d(a_1, l) = d(a_1, x_1)$ and $d(a_2, l) = d(a_2, x_2)$. Since $d(a_1, x_1) \leq d(a_1, x_2)$ and $d(a_2, x_2) \leq d(a_2, x_1)$, we have $|d(a_1, l) - d(a_2, l)| = |d(a_1, x_1) - d(a_2, x_2)|$. For the case that $d(a_1, x_1) - d(a_2, x_2)$ is positive or negative, we have $|d(a_1, x_1) - d(a_2, x_2)| \leq \max\{|d(a_1, x_1) - d(a_2, x_1)|, |d(a_1, x_2) - d(a_2, x_2)|\}$. From triangle inequality, we have $\max\{|d(a_1, x_1) - d(a_2, x_1)|, |d(a_1, x_2) - d(a_2, x_2)|\} \leq d(a_1, a_2)$. Thus, $|d(a_1, l) - d(a_2, l)|$ is a lower bound on $d(a_1, a_2)$. Using a set L of subsets, we increase the likelihood that the measured distance $d(a_1, a_2)$ between two nodes a_1 and a_2 (as measured relative to other distances) is captured adequately by the embedded distance δ in the embedding space between coordinates $\emptyset(a_1)$ and $\emptyset(a_2)$, that is, $\delta(\emptyset(a_1), \emptyset(a_2))$.

Numerical Optimization Embedding

One method is to construct an embedding $\varnothing$ that works for an arbitrary metric space by treating the embedding as an error objective function minimization problem; this can be solved by any numerical optimization method. The purpose of the numerical optimization algorithm is to detect the minimum of the objective function in the k-dimensional parameter space. Starting from an initial parameter set, the minimum has to be found iteratively by evaluating the value and/or gradient of the objective function, and performing small steps toward the minimum. There are many different minimization algorithms, and the choice depends on the characteristics of the objective function, the number of parameters to be estimated, and the efficiency with which the forward problem can be solved.

One of the more common variants of objective functions seeks to minimize stress, as defined as:

$$\frac{\sum_{a,b \in X}(\delta(\phi(a),\phi(b)) - d(a,b))^2}{\sum_{a,b \in X}d(a,b)^2}$$

Minimizing stress is essentially a nonlinear optimization problem, whereby the vector variables are the $N \times k$ coordinate values corresponding to the embedding, that is, k coordinate values for each of the N variables (nodes), and then trying to improve the stress in an iterative manner using any of the numerical optimization methods. The result of the optimization is not always the embedding that obtains the absolute minimum stress, but instead it is one that achieves a local minimum. That is, the minimization can be depicted as finding the deepest valley in a landscape by always walking in a direction that leads downhill; the process can thus get stuck in a deep valley that is not necessarily the deepest.

INTERNET COORDINATE SYSTEMS

Internet coordinate systems use network embedding techniques to embed the underlying network distances such as RTTs between some Internet nodes into a geometric space and assign geometric coordinates to all Internet nodes in such a way that the computed geometric distances between the nodes closely approximate their network distances. That is, an Internet coordinate system starts with a collection of some nodes and measured network distances between these node pairs. It then embeds all the nodes into a geometric space by associating each node with a point in that geometric space.

Among the existing Internet coordinate systems described in the literature are Global Network Positioning (GNP),[341] Lighthouses,[342] Virtual Landmarks,[343] Internet Coordinate System (ICS),[344] Internet Distance Estimation Service (IDES),[345] Practical Internet Coordinates (PIC),[346] Vivaldi,[347] Big Bang Simulation (BBS) in Euclidean space,[348] and BBS in Hyperbolic space.[349,350]

The challenges of constructing such an embedding into node coordinates are twofold. First, the method must be scalable and done with many fewer measurements than the $O(N^2)$ required on a full mesh of N nodes. It should also remain accurate even when the input is a small subset of all possible network metric measurements. That is, the nodes' coordinates being assigned should allow the unmeasured network distances between nodes to be estimated accurately. If an Internet coordinate system required $O(N^2)$ measurements, it saves nothing compared with exhaustive measurements and search! Second, this must be done so that the resulting system is accurate for all pairs of nodes, in the sense that the geometric distances between embedded nodes should, in some way, closely approximate their network distances. If accurate, such embedding techniques would allow us to predict unmeasured network distances without costly extensive measurements.

In all the Internet coordinate systems, there are two general methods for embedding a finite metric space into low dimensional geometric space:

- Lipschitz embedding is done with matrix factorization of measured distance matrix for dimensionality reduction of the geometric space. Matrix factorization is a form of mathematical optimization and error function minimization. This idea is illustrated in Figure 10.7. It is important to look at the Lipschitz embedding step because inherent loss of accuracy may occur here.
- Numerical optimization of some defined objective distance error functions based on accuracy metrics for node-to-landmark distances. This concept is illustrated in Figure 10.8.

Table 10.1 enumerates the embedding schemes for constructing Internet coordinate systems. The table presents their differences in terms of the fundamental embedding techniques and the metrics that determine the accuracy of the distance estimation.

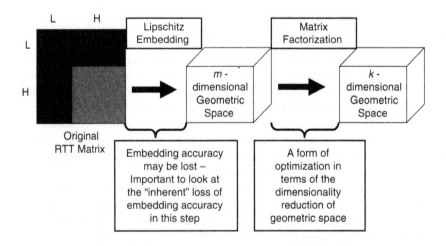

FIGURE 10.7 Systems using Lipschitz embedding with matrix factorization algorithms.

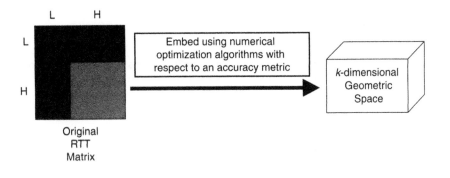

FIGURE 10.8 Systems using numerical optimization embedding algorithms.

Table 10.1 Network Embeddings for Internet Coordinate Systems

Internet Coordinate Systems	Fundamental Network Embedding Techniques	Accuracy Metrics
ICS	Lipschitz embedding and Principal Component Analysis (PCA)/Singular Value Decomposition (SVD) is performed for dimensionality reduction in Euclidean space. Scaling from original distance is done.	Average Relative Error
Virtual Landmarks	Lipschitz embedding with scaling done on the Lipschitz coordinates in Euclidean space. PCA/SVD is performed for dimensionality reduction.	Relative Error
IDES using Matrix Factorization	Distance computation based on matrix factorization using SVD and Nonnegative Matrix Factorization (NMF) on $N \times N$ distance matrix into smaller sub-matrices X and Y in Euclidean space. Such an embedding is a form of dimensionality reduction.	Relative Error
Lighthouses	Makes use of multiple local bases C together with a transition matrix in vector space, allows flexibility for any node to determine coordinates relative to any set of pivot nodes provided it maintains a transition matrix for global basis G. It uses linear matrix factorization such as the QR decomposition (Gram-Schmidt orthogonalization).	Relative Error

(*Continued*)

Table 10.1 Network Embeddings for Internet Coordinate Systems—Cont'd

Internet Coordinate Systems	Fundamental Network Embedding Techniques	Accuracy Metrics
GNP	Landmark nodes compute coordinates and location in Euclidean space based on minimization of objective squared error function using Downhill Simplex algorithm. The nodes also adopt minimization of the same objective error function between measured and computed Node-to-Landmark distances.	Squared Relative Error
PIC	Nodes compute coordinates in Euclidean space using Downhill Simplex method for minimization algorithm based on objective squared error function. The nodes join the system does not rely on infrastructure nodes. This is done by having any secured nodes with coordinates to act as the selected landmarks. The landmarks are chosen with closest, random and hybrid (closest and random) strategies.	Squared Relative Error
Vivaldi	Distributed minimization algorithm based on objective squared-error function (equivalent to Spring Energy/Force). The distributed distance computation involves nodes to compute coordinates based only on measured RTTs from node to a handful of other nodes, and from current coordinates of those nodes.	Squared Relative Error
Big Bang Simulation (BBS)	Derivation of coordinates and location of nodes in Euclidean space by minimization involving: First phase – difference between Euclidean and network pair distances based on objective squared error function; simulating spring and rest length of the spring in each pair is equivalent to network pair distance; Second phase – reduce the distortion of large relative error edges at the price of slightly increasing average relative error; Subsequent phases – involves the combined functions of the second phase's error minimization. Embedding in hyperbolic space uses 'Loid model (Hyperboloid) of hyperbolic space which averts the distance singularity on the boundary of the poincaré.	Directional Relative Error and Distortion

Systems Using Lipschitz Embedding and Matrix Factorization

Numerical optimization embeddings are done using iterative algorithms for non-linear optimization, which is computationally expensive, especially working with large network latency datasets. In addition, each node determines its coordinates from measurements to a set of landmarks. Thus the measurement traffic arriving at the landmarks increases in proportion to the number of nodes in the system. Both ICS and Virtual Landmarks are proposed to solve numerical optimization problem of computational complexity and computation of node coordinates and the scalability of the associated measurement process.

ICS and Virtual Landmarks are based on Lipschitz embedding of an assumed finite metric space into Euclidean space. Two nearby nodes in the original metric space may have very similar coordinate vectors and so may map to nearby points under the Lipschitz embedding. They use Singular Value Decomposition (SVD) with Principal Component Analysis (PCA) to reduce dimensionality of the Euclidean space. Matrix factorization based on SVD is of the form $D = UWV^T$, where D is the measured RTT distance matrix, U and V are orthogonal matrices, and W is a diagonal matrix with nonnegative elements arranged in decreasing order and that measure the significance of the contribution from each principal component. This is related to PCA on the distance matrix row vectors in ICS and Virtual Landmarks, where the first k rows of the matrix $U(U_k)$ or k column of matrix $V(V_k)$ are used to compute the k-dimensional coordinates for the network nodes.

ICS employs this method to create a vector basis using a set of landmarks by taking the full measured latency distance matrix of this set of landmarks. Then SVD and PCA are performed with optimal scaling, and node k-dimensional coordinates are computed from their Lipschitz coordinates. Virtual Landmarks directly uses the node's Lipschitz coordinates and performs SVD and PCA without scaling to reduce the dimensions of the node coordinates. Thus, in Virtual Landmarks, no knowledge is required of the inter-landmark latency distance matrix.

IDES uses the measured network distance matrix D, the rows of which are not linearly independent, that is, it has rank strictly less than N number of nodes and uses matrix factorization to approximate D, the elements of which represent pairwise distances by the product of two smaller matrices. The nodes measure their network distances to random sets of landmarks to build the measured network distance matrix D. The model is based on matrix factorization of the measured network distance matrix D to give embedded distance matrix for representing and estimating the network distances. Such an embedding can be viewed as a form of dimensionality reduction.

The pairwise measured distance matrix D is expressed as the product of two smaller matrices of X and Y through SVD or Nonnegative Matrix Factorization (NMF) algorithms. It contains the outgoing X vector and incoming Y vector in k dimensions, respectively, for each node. Estimated distances between nodes are derived from the dot product of these *two* vectors, that is, the estimated distance is computed from the dot product between the outgoing vector of one node and the incoming vector of the other node. Thus, the distance between two nodes is estimated as the inner product of the source's outgoing vector and the destination's incoming vector.

The embedding technique in Lighthouses uses linear matrix factorization of the measured distance matrix such as the QR decomposition (Gram-Schmidt orthogonalization). It also allows the flexibility for any node to determine local coordinates relative to any arbitrary set of $k + 1$ local landmarks that spans the local vector basis C as long as it maintains a transition matrix for transforming the local coordinates to global coordinates in global vector basis G. The Lighthouses technique uses multiple local bases together with a transition matrix to overcome the issue of using a fixed set of well-known landmarks to form the vector basis to compute node coordinates when the landmarks become unavailable. This fixed set of well-known landmarks can limit scalability of the system if they become communication bottlenecks and the accuracy is sensitive to their placement. The Lighthouses technique relies on a set of nodes from which different joining nodes may select differently. A node that joins the Lighthouses system does not have to query those global landmarks. Instead, the new node can query any existing set of nodes to find its coordinates relative to that set and then optionally transform those coordinates into coordinates relative to the global landmarks.

The number of landmarks is $k+1$, where k is the number of dimensions in the target vector space. This is to solve the possible problem that coordinate vectors of the landmarks could be linearly dependent in the geometric space, which may cause the nodes to be unable to differentiate their distinct geometric locations from these landmarks and could hinder the computation of the node coordinates. That is, if the landmarks have their coordinate vectors as a multiple of the other (in other words, the landmarks are in a straight vector line), the nodes would not be able to compute their distinct geometric locations from these landmarks. Only when the vectors of the landmarks are linearly independent is a basis of the vector space formed.

Systems Using Numerical Optimization

For techniques involving minimization of some defined objective distance error function, many algorithms are proposed to compute the coordinates of the network nodes.

Both GNP and PIC systems use the Downhill Simplex algorithm[362] to minimize the objective distance error function: sum of relative errors. The problems with the Downhill Simplex method are slow convergence, sensitivity to the *initial* coordinates or positioning of the network nodes, and the potential chance of getting stuck in the local minima. This leads to the eventual assignment of different coordinates for the same node depending on the minimization process (e.g., selection of the initial position). So, methods that are clever to converge to the global minimum are required.

GNP is an architecture for network distance prediction that is based on a kind of absolute coordinate. The key idea of GNP is to model the Internet as a geometric space (e.g., a three-dimensional Euclidean space) and characterize the position of any node in the Internet by a point in this space. The network distance between any two nodes is then predicted by the modeled geometric distance between them. The first part of their architecture is to use a small distributed set of nodes known as *landmarks* to provide a set of reference coordinates necessary to orient other nodes. These landmarks first compute their coordinates in a chosen geometric space. The goal is to find a set of coordinates for the landmarks such that the overall error between the measured distances and the computed distances in that geometric space is minimized in an objective function F that measured the errors. The way error is measured in F will affect the eventual distance prediction accuracy. For a geometric space of dimensionality k, this should have at least $k+1$ landmarks. If the number of landmarks is not greater than k, the landmark coordinates will lie on a hyperplane of at most $k-1$ dimensions. Consequently, a point in the k-dimensional space and its reflection across the landmarks' hyperplane cannot be distinguished by the objective function.

The computation of coordinates is considered as a generic multidimensional global optimization problem that can be approximately solved by many available methods. GNP uses the Downhill Simplex algorithm as the error minimization method, which is used to first construct a basis and then using that basis to find the coordinates of the nodes relative to that basis. The landmarks simply measure the interlandmark RTTs using Internet Control Management Protocol (ICMP) ping messages and take the minimum of several measurements for each path. In the second part, equipped with the landmark coordinates, any end node can compute its own coordinates relative to those of the landmarks and perform the similar computation of a generic multidimensional global minimization problem. Similarly, the node measures its RTT to the $k+1$ landmarks using ICMP ping messages and takes the minimum of several measurements for each path as the distance. This embedding technique sought a minimum of total square embedding errors over all node pairs, which is proportional to the average pair distortion.

PIC attempts to solve the problems that limit the system practicality of relying on a fixed set of well-known landmarks that are a single point of failure and can limit scalability if they become communication bottlenecks. Any node whose coordinates have already been computed can act as a selected landmark for other nodes. Therefore, it can distribute communication and computation load evenly over all the nodes in a system. PIC experimented with three strategies to choose the arbitrary set of landmarks:

- Pick the landmarks randomly with uniform probability.
- Pick the landmarks closest to the node.
- Pick some random and closest landmarks (hybrid).

The closest and hybrid strategies require a mechanism to find the closest nodes to a node in the network. This can be done in using expanding ring search using a multicast mechanism[363] or other algorithms.[364,365]

PIC is able to compute node coordinates even when some nodes are malicious by devising a security test to eliminate these malicious nodes. The test relies on the observation that the triangle inequality holds for nodes in the Internet. But in actual fact, triangle inequality does not hold for most nodes in the Internet due to the problems of Internet routing policies such as Border Gateway Protocol (BGP)[366] and some structural network planning situations.

Both Vivaldi and BBS systems are based on the numerical minimization of sum of distance error functions that are related to the problem of minimizing the potential energy of Newtonian mechanics principles. The use of physical springs to tabulate relative network positions with the rest length of the springs being the observed latency was first used by BBS. The BBS algorithm models the network nodes as a set of particles having a geometric position in Euclidean space. Each particle or node is the geometric image of a vertex. The nodes are traveling in that space under the effect of the potential force field that reduces the potential energy of the nodes. This is related to the total embedding distance error of all node pairs in Euclidean space:

$$\epsilon_T\left(v_1,\ldots,v_N\right) = \sum_{\substack{i,j=1 \\ i>j}}^{N} \epsilon_{ij}(v_i,v_j)$$

where v_d, $d = 1,\ldots,N$ are vectors designating the coordinates of the N network nodes in the target k-dimensional Euclidean space, $\mathbf{R^k}$. The embedding distance error of a pair of nodes, called the *pair embedding error*, is denoted by ϵ_{ij}.

Each pair of nodes is pulled by the field force induced between them, depending on their pair embedding distance error, that is, the embedding error of the distance between them. The nodes accelerate under the effect of the force field, attenuated by simulated friction force. The induced pair field force is equal to the difference between the Euclidean and network pair distances. The resulting field force can be realized by attaching an ideal spring with fixed elastic coefficient to each pair of particles. The rest length of the spring in each pair is equal to the network pair distance. Then a calculation phase consists of several iterations that move the particles or nodes in discrete time intervals by applying Newton's movement equations to calculate the positions and velocities.

BBS has an advantage over conventional gradient minimization schemes, such as steepest descent[367] and Downhill Simplex algorithms, due to the kinetic energy accumulated by the moving nodes, which enables them to escape the local minima. The Downhill Simplex algorithm is sensitive to the nodes' initial coordinates. There are three embedding methods in the BBSs:

- *All-pairs (AP) embedding.* Embedding is done for the *full* mesh of the N nodes of the network topology, with all N nodes selected as the landmarks.

- *Two-phases (TP) embedding.* Embedding is done using landmarks similar to GNP, where the landmarks are embedded first and the coordinates of the other nodes are calculated from the distance to *several* chosen *closest* landmarks through minimization of the symmetric distortion in these node-to-landmark pairs. Specifically, the TP embedding requires k+1 landmark measurements for *k*-dimensional coordinate vectors.

- *Log-random and neighbors (LRN) embedding.* This method aims to increase neighbor distance accuracy. The LRN embedding concurrently embed nodes through minimization of objective error function of *N* nodes and the LRN subset, which comprises the node pairs for which distance is below a certain threshold, that is, the threshold is selected so that the number of distance pairs that are below the threshold is $O(N \times \log N)$ and together with a set of randomly sampled distance pairs that are selected uniformly with probability $(\log N)/N$.

The number of randomly sampled distance pairs is equivalent to $N \times \log N$. The LRN algorithm embeds all the *N* nodes concurrently. The objective function is the sum of embedding errors for all *N* nodes in the system, and the embedding error of one node is the error of distance from that node to the LRN subset of nodes.

In hyperbolic geometric space[368,369,370], a distance decreases as it moves away from the origin. Similar to Euclidean line distance, the hyperbolic distance line between two nodes is defined as the parametric curve, connecting between the nodes, over which the integral of the arc length is minimized. Unlike Euclidean line distance, a hyperbolic line distance bends toward the origin point. The extent of the bend depends on the curvature of the hyperbolic space. The bending enlarges when space curvature increases; thus, the hyperbolic distance between two nodes increases.

BBS in hyperbolic space uses the 'Loid model that is embedded in the upper sheet of the hyperboloid with hyperbolic distance in the Minkowski model. The movement of the nodes is adjusted using the hyperbolic distance function. The *metric curvature* is defined as the Gaussian curvature of the hyperbolic space in which this metric is embedded with optimal accuracy and with minimal distortion. By embedding into the *k*-dimensional hyperbolic space with various metric curvature values, we are able to deduce and select the optimal metric curvature by comparing the distance estimation errors.

In [350], they have shown that the embedding in hyperbolic space with curvature κ is equivalent to embedding the $\sqrt{\kappa}$, which is the stretched metric in canonical hyperbolic space. The curvature κ is used for BBS-LRN embedding of $N \times \log N$ randomly sampled pairs, BBS-TP embedding of first *t* nodes as the selected landmarks, and BBS-AP embedding with all nodes as the selected landmarks. Before the stretching with κ is done (i.e., multiply with κ), the measured distances are divided by the following normalizing factors, depending on the types of BBS embedding methods:

- The mean node-to-node network distance is used as the normalizing factor (η). BBS-AP embedding uses this normalizing factor together with κ. Note that for the case of BBS-AP embedding, it is *full* embedding whereby *all* nodes are selected as landmarks.

- The maximum node-to-node network distance is used as the normalizing factor (η). Both BBS-TP and BBS-LRN embeddings use this normalizing factor together with κ.

The hyperbolic distance function δ_H between two nodes with k-dimensional coordinate vectors $X = (x_1, \ldots, x_k)$ and $Y = (y_1, \ldots, y_k)$ together with shrinking factor (η/κ) is computed as follows:

$$\delta_H = arc \cosh \left[\sqrt{(1 + \| X \|^2) \times (1 + \| Y \|^2)} - \sum_{i=1}^{k} x_i y_i \right] \times \frac{\eta}{\kappa}$$

Vivaldi constantly adjusts the node coordinates to minimize the error between the predicted Euclidean distance in Euclidean space and the network latencies, because each node contacts a random set of nodes in a decentralized manner. Vivaldi uses each RTT sample to update its node coordinates. The weight w of a sample is based on the ratio between the local and the remote error estimates. The algorithm tracks the local relative error using a weighted moving average. The node coordinates are updated by moving a small step toward the position that best reflects the measured RTT. The size of the modification depends on the weight of the sample and on the difference between the measured RTTs and the estimated distances.

The work in Vivaldi has concluded that spherical coordinates do not model the Internet well because the paths through the Internet do not wrap around the Earth. A *height vector* model was proposed to model the time it takes packets to travel the access link from he node to the core, and this is included in the two-dimensional Euclidean coordinates. The distance between two nodes with coordinates ((x_1, y_1) and (x_2, y_2)) is the sum of their *heights* (h_1 and h_2) and the usual Euclidean distance as follows:

$$\sqrt{(x_1 - x_2)^2 + (y_1 - y_2)^2 + h_1 + h_2}$$

MERIDIAN

Meridian[371] is a lightweight and scalable network positioning and measurement overlay that makes use of a loose routing system based on multiresolution rings on each node; an adaptive ring membership replacement scheme that maximizes the usefulness of the nodes populating each ring; and a gossip protocol for node discovery and dissemination. The system can efficiently find the closest node to a target that is required as the building block operation in many location-sensitive distributed systems.

Multiresolution Rings

Each Meridian node organizes a small and fixed number of other nodes in the system into concentric and nonoverlapping rings of exponentially increasing radii, as shown in Figure 10.9. The reason for exponentially increasing ring radii is

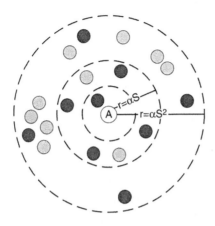

FIGURE 10.9 Meridian rings[371] © 2005 ACM, Inc. Reprinted by permission.

for the need of a node to have a representative set of pointers to the rest of the network. Within a given ring, a set of nodes that span a large amount of space (dark) are more desirable than a more limited subset (light).

The process of sorting neighbors into concentric rings does not require fixed landmarks or distributed coordination; this is done independently. There is an upper bound in terms of the number of k nodes maintained in each ring. The overpopulated ring will drop nodes in such a way that the space requirement per node is proportional to k.

Ring Membership Management

A large number of k nodes increases a node's information about its neighbors and helps make accurate choices when routing queries. On the other hand, a large k represents more state, memory, and bandwidth overhead at each node. Within each ring, a Meridian node keeps track of the k primary ring members and a constant number l of secondary ring members. Each node defines a local coordinate space using Lipschitz embedding. That is, a node i will periodically measure its latency $d(i,j)$ to another node j in its ring for all $0 \leq i, j \leq k+1$. The coordinates of node i are $\{d(i,1), d(i,2), \ldots, d(i,k+1)\}$, where $d(i,i) = 0$.

Having computed the node coordinates for all the members of a ring, a Meridian node can determine the subset of k nodes that provide the polytope with the largest hypervolume. A simple and greedy approach to ring membership management is adopted and occurs in the background: A node starts out with $k+1$ polytope and iteratively drops the vertex, the absence of which leads to the smallest reduction in hypervolume until k vertices remain.

Gossip-Based Node Discovery

Meridian's gossip protocol is not for each node to discover every node in the system but for each node to discover a sufficiently diverse set of other nodes:

1. Each node A randomly picks a node B from each of its rings and sends a gossip packet to node B containing a randomly chosen node from each of its rings.
2. On receiving the packet, node B determines through direct probes its latency to node A and to each of the nodes contained in the gossip packet from node A. Node B sends probes to node A and to the nodes in the gossip packet from node A regardless of whether node B has already discovered these nodes.
3. After sending a gossip packet to a node in each of its ring, node A waits for the start of its next gossip period and then begins from Step 1.

When a node initially joins the system, it needs to know the IP address of one of the nodes in the Meridian overlay. The newly joining node contacts the Meridian node and acquires the whole list of ring members, then it measures its latency to these nodes and places them on its own rings. After that, the new node participates in the gossip protocol as described.

During node churn, when an unreachable node is discovered during the replacement process, it is dropped from the ring and removed as a secondary candidate node; when an unreachable node is discovered during gossip or actual query routing, it is removed from the ring and replaced with a random secondary candidate node.

Closest-Node Discovery

The system discovers the closest node by performing a multihop search where each hop exponentially reduces the distance to the target, where each hop brings the query exponentially closer to the destination, similar to searching in Structured P2P overlay networks such as Chord, Pastry, and Tapestry. The differences are that Meridian's routing is performed using physical latencies and the target nodes need not be part of the Meridian overlay.

When a closest-node query is received, the Meridian node determines the latency between itself and the target, d. It then locates its corresponding ring, j, and queries all nodes in this ring and the nodes in the adjacent rings, $j - 1$ and $j+1$, such that the distance to the origin is within $d/2$ to $3d/2$. These nodes report back to the source of their distance to the target. Those nodes that have distances more than $2d$ are ignored because they are farther to the target than the source. A route acceptance threshold β is used to determine the reduction in distance at each hop.

As shown in the Figure 10.10, which illustrates the process, a client node makes a closest-node query to target node T, to a Meridian node A. This node A determines its latency d to target node T and probes its ring members between $(1 - \beta) \times d$ and $(1+\beta) \times d$, to determine their distances to the target node T.

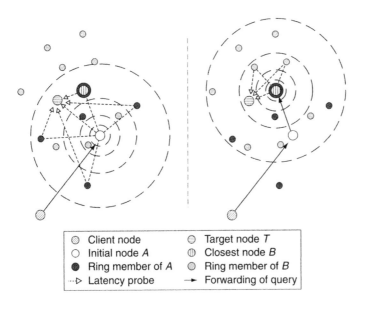

⊘ Client node	⊖ Target node T
○ Initial node A	⦶ Closest node B
● Ring member of A	◉ Ring member of B
⋯▷ Latency probe	→ Forwarding of query

FIGURE 10.10 Closest-node discovery to target T^{371} © 2005 ACM, Inc. Reprinted by permission.

The client request is forwarded to the closest node. If no closer nodes meet the acceptance threshold, routing stops and the closest node currently discovered is chosen.

ACCURACY AND OVERHEAD

The work in [372] and [373] experienced and experimented with Internet coordinate systems and found their accuracy to be disappointing in several respects. First, distance estimation results are often unpredictable in the sense that many nodes obtain good estimates whereas a few obtain extremely bad results. In a real-world setting it seems that nodes cannot determine the *quality* of their estimates without performing exactly the full probing that coordinate systems are intended to eliminate. Second, the quality of an embedding often varied considerably with small changes to the topology of the underlying network, something that would be beyond the control of most users of a coordinate system. Third, the quality of embeddings often varied considerably as the number of participating nodes changed, even when the underlying topology remained fixed. In short, these observations suggest that it is very hard to predict when a coordinate system will work well at any given node.

Highly aggregated accuracy metrics, such as absolute relative error, seem to give little indication of these types of quality problems. The work presents *three* new accuracy metrics that attempt to capture more application-centric notions of quality. The first is called *relative rank loss at node A* and is intended to be useful for applications that need to know only their *relative* distance to other nodes. That is, node *A* needs to answer the question: Which node is closer to me, B or C? Which is *A*'s proximity query for nodes *B* and *C*? The other new metric we define is *closest neighbor loss at node A*. This metric is intended to be useful to nodes using applications that are interested only in determining which nodes are *closest*. The last scalability meta-metric attempts to answer this question: Would it be better to use a coordinate system generated from a topology consisting of all sites, or one generated just from intersite RTTs restricted to smaller clusters consisting of closer sites? The answer to this question will determine how the Internet coordinate services could be designed for better embedding accuracy in a scalable manner.

Both Figures 10.11 and 10.12 illustrate the latency data from the PlanetLab site planetlab1.pop-mg.rnp.br for Lipschitz embedding and the Vivaldi system. The X axis enumerates sites and the Y axis shows the latency distance of each site

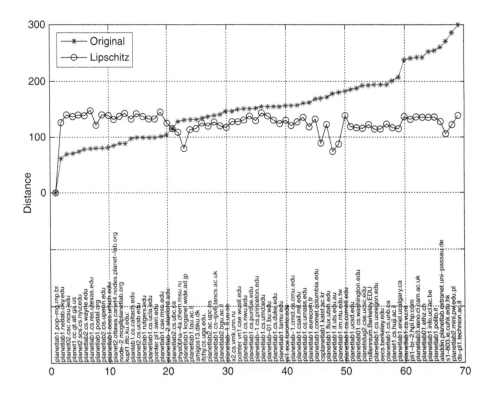

FIGURE 10.11 Distance order ranking for PlanetLab site `planetlab1.pop-mg.rnp.br` using Lipschitz embedding[362] © 2005 ACM, Inc. Reprinted by permission.

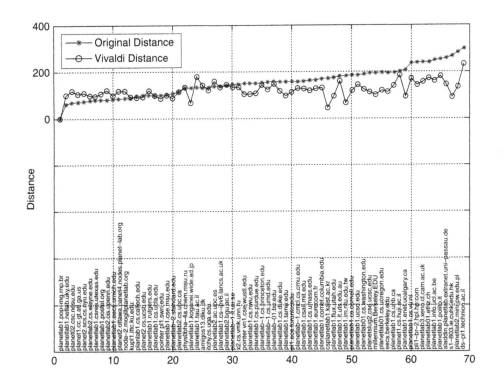

FIGURE 10.12 Distance order ranking for PlanetLab site `planetlab1.pop-mg.rnp.br` using Vivaldi.

from planetlab1.pop-mg.rnp.br (in milliseconds). The signature plot marked with *
indicates latencies in the original distance matrix, and the PlanetLab sites on the
X axis have been sorted to ensure that this plot is in ascending order of latencies. The signature plot marked with **o** is the embedded distance between the
same sites in the embedded Euclidean space. The results shown here are not
very impressive. It would appear from these two plots that using Lipschitz
embedding and Vivaldi algorithms on PlanetLab site planetlab1.pop-mg.rnp.br
would give very poor results in terms of accurately identifying the list of closest
nodes' rankings.

The work in [374] investigates the tradeoff in overhead between Vivaldi and
Meridian in terms of a node's overhead over a range of query frequencies. The
experiment was done with the same parameters as in the evaluation of Meridian
(2048 nodes, 16 nodes per ring), and Vivaldi uses Content Addressable Network
(CAN) to find the closest neighbor. Figure 10.13 illustrates the ratio of the number of messages a node needs to route using Vivaldi and Meridian with varying
query rates. The results indicate that when the system query frequency is greater
than once per minute, maintaining Vivaldi has better scalability and is cheaper in

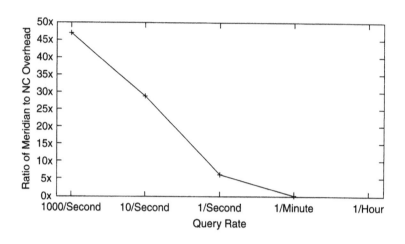

FIGURE 10.13 Overhead comparison: Meridian and Vivaldi[374] © 2006 IEEE.

terms of overhead than Meridian when a system often performs network-aware (proximity-aware) measurements. This means that each query for closest node in Meridian may have a large measurement overhead when a node's ring membership changes.

SUMMARY

Network latency is the key network metric commonly used to allow P2P overlays to make decisions to optimize application performance by exploiting the locality, proximity, and topological information of nodes in the underlying network performance. It is found that the decisions made in terms of network awareness based on the structure of the Internet latency result in good bandwidth characteristics, too.[375,376] Raw measurement of such metrics in massive-scale Internet can be extensively demanding and impractical. Internet coordinate systems solve such measurement problems using primitives from computational geometry. Although Internet coordinate systems exploit scalable geometric techniques, there exist serious accuracy problems in latency estimation due to the persistent and structural triangle inequality violations (TIVs) of Internet latencies in metric space, arising from complex Internet routing policies.[373] Other techniques, such as Meridian, attempt to implement measurement overlay without subjecting to the TIV conditions of the metric space; however, they suffer from large measurement overhead due to the dynamism and node churn characteristics of the P2P membership.[374] Though developing measurement systems for overlay network design is important, there is still a long-term research challenge to create systems that are scalable, accurate, and stable for dynamic P2P overlay under node churn.

FOR FURTHER READING

As this chapter was being written, a new implementation of a large-scale latency estimation system based on GNP[377] has been incorporated into the Google content delivery network. Google's implementation employs standard features of conventional Web clients and carefully controls the overhead incurred by latency measurements using a scalable centralized scheduler.

Service Overlays

An overlay designed to provide a network service such as selecting an alternate routing path, multicast delivery, or session establishment is referred to as a *service overlay*. In addition, the application of principles of service-oriented architectures to P2P overlays is of growing interest. Three concepts—resource virtualization, service orientation, and devices as peers—unify these two categories of service overlay and are described here. For network services we look at examples such as delivering DNS records from a DHT, resilient overlay networks, and QoS-aware overlays. Then we discuss service discovery, replication, and load balancing in the context of service-oriented service overlays. The chapter concludes with some examples of service composition.

SERVICE ORIENTATION AND P2P NETWORKING

Service orientation is growing in importance as a fundamental architecture in distributed enterprise computing. In the P2P context, an overlay could be used by multiple applications, as opposed to a dedicated overlay for each type of P2P application. The advantage is that common mechanisms such as routing, naming, search, and security can be shared across multiple applications. Using the P2P overlay as a service delivery platform could also accelerate the delivery of new services. To enable this requires that the service-oriented architecture be used for organizing the resources of the peer platform. Key elements of service orientation, such as service discovery and service invocation, need to be integrated with the P2P overlay.

Overlays have also been used to deliver services traditionally built into the network layer. One reason for this is that wide-scale deployment of network layer services can require changes to routers throughout the Internet. This is expensive and is one reason that adoption of protocols such as IPv6 and multicast has been slow. Many network services can be more easily deployed at the overlay level, since infrastructure changes are not required. Although efficiency may be lost, the ability to quickly deploy and experiment with potential services is an advantage of an overlay deployment.

Service overlay networks (SONs)[392] have been proposed to address the difficulties of deploying end-to-end network services that span multiple network service provider domains. In this model, a SON operator purchases native network services from service providers and provides an overlay that integrates these services into an end-to-end service model for SON customers. There has also been growing interest in using service overlays in the evolution of the Internet. Current research projects include SpovNet[407] and Ambient Networks Service-Aware Transport Overlay (SATO).[408] Clark et al.[8,510] have examined the impact on overlays on the technology and business of the Internet.

This chapter examines service overlays from these two perspectives: as a means to deploy network services and as platform for deploying applications packaged as services. We first discuss key concepts of services overlays, including virtualization and service orientation. The discussion of service overlays in the remainder of the chapter follows the taxonomy shown in Figure 11.1. Several of the network service categories (ALM, P2P-SIP, and telephony services) are described in other chapters.

Service Overlays

Network Service	Overlay Example
Routing	Resilient Overlay Network Routing Overlay
Domain Name Service (DNS)	DNS via DHT
Multicast	Application Layer Multicast
Content Delivery	Stream Based Overlay Network (SBON)
AAA	Peering of RADIUS Domains
QoS	QoS Aware Overlay
Session Establishment	IETF P2P-SIP
Telephony Services	Relays Feature Servers

Service Oriented Architecture	Overlay Example
Service Discovery & Advertisement	INS/Twine
Service Composition	SpiderNet
Middleware	NEMO
Service Models	
Load Balancing	Beehive

FIGURE 11.1 Taxonomy of service overlays, divided into network services and application services.

SERVICE OVERLAY CONCEPTS
Resource Virtualization

So far we have presented the P2P overlay as a virtualization of network transport, providing transparent end-to-end connectivity across multiple internets. The features of virtualization include indirect and dynamic mapping to the associated physical resources. Virtualization of computing resources has been used in computing, starting with early multitasking operating systems. It has proven to be a powerful technique to manage physical resources to achieve scalability and specific resource-sharing policies. Virtualization comes with a cost. The resource is accessed indirectly, meaning that virtual-to-physical mappings have to be created, assigned, and applied to resource requests.

A key idea of service overlays is to extend the virtualization offered by the basic overlay concept to other network and system resources. At the network layer, services that can be virtualized include multicasting, content delivery, and end-to-end quality-of-service guarantees. Although these services are efficiently offered directly by network service providers, overlay service providers can provide value-add by tying the services of multiple NSPs together.

At the system layer, resources include storage and computation. Storage includes replicated and distributed file systems, media servers, and caches. Virtualized distributed computation is the focus of grid computing, including methods to locate, distribute, coordinate, and schedule complex computations across large grids of computers connected in an overlay network. As in the network layer, virtualization means that the details of the physical resources can be hidden from the application, can be selected dynamically, and application use can be reassigned dynamically.

Service Orientation

A second trend fueling service overlays is the growing importance of *service orientation* as a fundamental architecture in distributed enterprise computing. In the P2P context, this offers the possibility that an overlay could be used for multiple applications, as opposed to a dedicated overlay for each type of P2P application. The advantage is that common mechanisms such as routing, naming, search, and security can be shared across multiple applications. To enable this sharing requires that the service-oriented architecture be used for organizing the resources of the peer platform.

Service orientation in peer-to-peer architecture means that peers can offer and use services from any peer without relying on centralized resources. Other elements of SOAs, including service discovery and service description, are also incorporated into the peer-to-peer architecture. By constructing the service-oriented middleware on a peer-to-peer overlay network, a highly scalable service discovery mechanism is possible, addressing a critical requirement in achieving wide area service advertisement and lookup.

Devices as Peers

The third driver for service overlays is the goal of connecting networked mobile devices and sensors into the P2P overlay as peers. Although such devices are not general-purpose computing platforms—for example, they run special-purpose operating systems, have relatively limited system resources, and typically cannot be easily extended with new applications—their participation in the overlay is a vehicle for sharing device resources, as described in Chapter 2, and collecting real-time information from widely deployed sensors. Such resource sharing is feasible today for devices connected in ad hoc, personal area, or home networks. The use of an overlay means that such sharing can be extended to Internet scale.

To enable this functionality means that service advertisement and service discovery mechanisms used by devices must be enveloped in the overlay.

The next several sections examine supporting specific network services using an overlay. These services include DNS, routing, quality of service, and real-time stream processing. We then return to examining P2P service orientation.

SERVING DNS RECORDS FROM AN OVERLAY
Domain Name Service

The Domain Name Service (DNS) has been an essential part of the operation of the Internet since the 1980s. DNS is used by clients to resolve human-readable domain names such as example.com into their corresponding routable IP addresses. It is also used to look up mail servers and other network services. DNS makes it possible for applications and clients to refer to hosts and services using symbolic names that are mapped to their IP addresses prior to making a connection to the host or service. IP addresses can be changed without impact on applications and clients.

To manage the huge volume of name resolution requests, DNS is organized as a hierarchy of servers, each of which is responsible for one or more namespaces or zones. A server responsible for a specific zone is called the *authoritative* DNS name server for that zone. There may be more than one authoritative DNS server for a zone. Each root server is responsible for a top-level domain. For example, *com* is the top-level domain for example.com. A DNS server may delegate responsibility for portions of its zone to other servers. Thus, the root server for *com* may delegate management of names in the domain example.com to a subsidiary server. This subsidiary server can then handle all lookups for example.com, such as www.example.com and ftp.north.example.com.

Each client needing to resolve a domain name sends a request to its local DNS server if it hasn't previously cached the resolution locally. The server may be responsible for that zone, in which case it resolves the domain name using its local configuration. Alternately, the server may have cached the resolution of the domain from a previous response. In this case it resolves the domain name using its cache. In either case, the response is performed immediately by the local server without consulting other servers in the hierarchy. If the server can't resolve the domain name using one of these two methods, it needs to locate the authoritative DNS server for that domain. First it requests the root name server for the top-level domain for the name server for the next level. Thus the root server for *com* will be consulted to find the server for example.com. Likewise, the authoritative server for example.com will be consulted to find the server for north.example.com, and so on.

The hierarchical organization of DNS is one of its strengths, since it distributes the load of name resolution to the associated subsidiary servers. If a particular zone becomes overloaded, new servers serving popular subsidiary zones can be added. In addition, the DNS caching mechanism further reduces the lookup load on the top-level servers in the hierarchy.

The characteristics of DNS make it an interesting application for a DHT. It requires a global scale lookup mechanism, tens of millions of index entries, and the ability to handle a large volume of lookups. It also creates some important challenges:

- The distribution of index entries in the DHT may not be uniform across the population of peers, skewing the load.
- The lookup load itself is not uniformly distributed. Without some means to distribute the load according to entry popularity, some peers will be heavily loaded and others lightly loaded.
- Caching may be more difficult to implement since the lookup path is more diverse in most overlays compared to DNS lookup. This fact affects whether a subsequent lookup is likely to find an entry at an intermediate peer along the lookup path.
- Indexing DNS records in a DHT requires that the DHT implement an authorization mechanism so that only authorized peers can create or modify an address binding for a domain or service. Otherwise the lookup is vulnerable to corrupted entries or host spoofing attacks.

DDNS

Cox and Morris[379] evaluated the use of a DHT to serve DNS record lookups, simulated using a DNS dataset from previous work.[380] DDNS uses a DHT called DHash, a Chord DHT that implements six-way replication and caching along the lookup path. That is, the response to a DHT lookup is sent back over the path the request followed and stored at each peer. Subsequent requests that are routed over a portion of the path will be served from the peer's cache instead of being forwarded to the destination peer. Note that reverse path caching means that responses are sent back over up to log N hops rather than directly to the sender of the lookup request.

In their simulation of DDNS, they used a 1000-node overlay with replication disabled and no node failures. DNS records are inserted and digitally signed by the owner. An example key for a domain's address record is www.example.com, A;

120,000 records were inserted. The dataset includes 280,000 successful queries and 220,000 unresolved queries. Each lookup is sent from a random peer in the overlay.

Figure 11.2 shows the record distribution in the DHT (top) and the query distribution (bottom). For record storage, a small percentage of peers have up to seven times the index entries as the median of 120 records. Caching works well for successful queries but doesn't improve the load distribution for unsuccessful queries that result

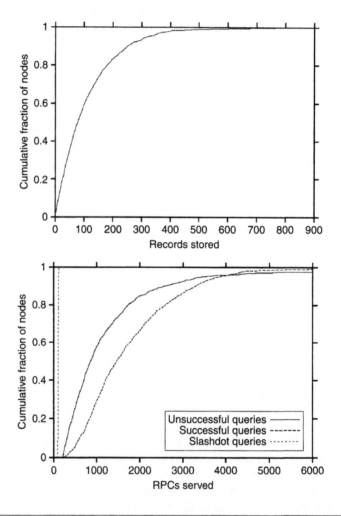

FIGURE 11.2 (Top) Cumulative distribution of records in the DHT. The median is about 120 records per peer. (Bottom) Cumulative distribution of queries in the DHT by query type. The median is about 220 per peer for successful queries and 260 per peer for unsuccessful queries.[379] © 2002 Springer-Verlag, with kind permission of Springer Science and Business Media.

from domains that don't exist. This is shown by the long tail in the figure. The slashdot query is 100,000 lookups against one record, which evaluates lookup behavior for very popular domains. As shown in Figure 11.2 (bottom), the slashdot record rapidly propagates to the other peers in the overlay as a result of the caching mechanism. After that point is reached, queries no longer propagate to the index peer.

Another important performance metric for DNS is the lookup latency distribution. As shown in Figure 11.3 (top), the majority of successful DNS lookups in the dataset are less than 200 ms in duration, but a small percentage can have lookups

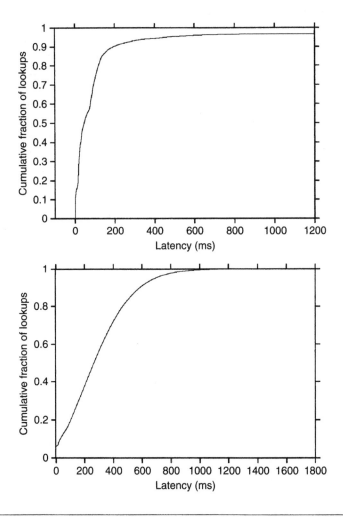

FIGURE 11.3 (Top) measured DNS latency. (Bottom) DDNS estimated latency.[379] © 2002 Springer-Verlag, with kind permission of Springer Science and Business Media.

in the tens of seconds. To estimate DDNS latencies, the RTT between pairs of peers in DDNS is estimated using the times from the DNS dataset. This gives the latency distribution shown in Figure 11.3 (bottom) for the same set of DNS lookups. Though most responses aren't handled in 200 ms, no queries exceed 1 second. So DDNS increases the average lookup time while removing the long tail for a small percentage of lookups.

RESILIENT OVERLAY NETWORKS
Internet Routing and ISP Peering

The Internet is a collection of many different physical networks that use common protocols and services to create a universal routing and transport fabric for applications. Generally, the different networks are operated as separate autonomous systems (ASs) by their network service providers (NSPs). Inside an AS, an NSP will use routing protocols that maintain detailed connectivity information for all routers in the AS. At the boundaries of the AS are connections to other NSPs' networks at connection points called *peering points*. The routers at these peering points use the Border Gateway Protocol (BGP), which maintains information about BGP topology in the Internet and typically has limited details about routing within a given AS. A consequence is that network traffic that is routed through an AS will have a restricted path. Such transit paths are determined by each NSP according to its peering relationships with other NSPs. Each NSP manages transit traffic to balance its customer traffic with reciprocal sharing of network capacity with peer NSPs.

As discussed in Chapter 10, one consequence of BGP routing policies is that some routes cause violations in the triangle inequality property. That is, the direct path from A to B may be longer in terms of latency than the indirect path A-C-B. Another consequence is that route outages due to router failures may not be automatically rerouted since the necessary routing table information may be missing from the BGP tables.

Resilient Overlay Network

A Resilient Overlay Network (RON)[383,384] is an overlay network that routes application traffic over the network by finding low-latency and available paths that might not be identified by the usual routing protocols. A RON requires peers placed in different ASs, and these peers determine the latency and connectivity state with their neighbor peers. When an application wants to send packets to another application via the RON, the sender connects to the nearest RON peer, called the *ingress peer*, and issues the packet. The ingress peer determines whether the usual routing path is preferred over the overlay path. If it is, the packet will be sent directly to the endpoint. If not, the packet is then routed at the overlay level using the lowest latency path as determined by the cooperating peers. After reaching the egress peer to which the destination is attached, it is forwarded by the egress peer to that application.

RONs are typically small, fewer than 50 nodes, and may be dedicated for specific applications. New peers join the RON by locating an existing member peer, and the RON dedicates a well-known peer for bootstrap purposes. It then notifies all other peers in the RON by flooding an announcement of its existence. Periodically each peer in the RON floods its list of member peer to all other peers. The RON is a full-mesh network, and a peer maintains performance metrics for its links to all other peers in the RON. It does this by a combination of active probing and observation of existing flows. These metrics are for latency, reliability, and throughput. Depending on the application, the peer computes scores for selecting the best link for a given type of traffic.

Using a RON of between 12 and 16 peers distributed across the United States and Europe, experimental measurements show that the RON is able to find alternate routes in at least 60% of link outages. The time to detect and find an alternate path averaged 18 seconds. BGP can take on the order of several minutes to converge to a new route. An example of link outage avoidance for the 12-node RON is shown in Figure 11.4. An outage (t,p) occurs when the packet loss rate is greater than p for some interval t. In Figure 11.4, $t = 1800$ seconds and $p = 30\%$. The plot shows that the RON successfully found alternate routes for all Internet outages. Points to the right of the $x = y$ line indicate RON loss rates that exceeded the Internet loss rate, but none of these points exceeded the 30% loss rate threshold.

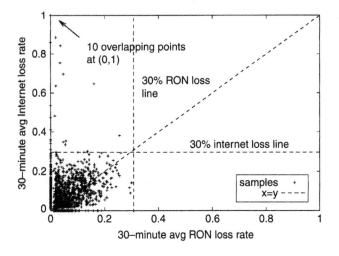

FIGURE 11.4 RON impact on loss rates by finding an alternate path in the overlay.[383]
© 2001 ACM, Inc. Reprinted by permission.

In these experiments, about 5% of the time two RON peers found a better route via each other than via the normal path provided by the Internet. RONs avoided around 50% of Internet outages.

DG-RON[385] is a proposal for increasing the scalability of RON by eliminating the need for the RON to construct a full mesh between all peers in the overlay. It uses topology awareness based on a small set of landmark nodes to organize peers into regions and performs direct probing of links only when a link failure is detected. When an alternate path is needed, it uses the landmarks and heuristics to select an alternate destination peer. In simulations, DG-RON performed comparably to RON for alternate route selection in the face of path failures. However, DG-RON does not provide metrics for best-path selection. Topology awareness techniques for overlays are discussed in Chapter 10.

Bandwidth-Aware RON

For applications that deliver streaming media over the network, available bandwidth along the path can be more important than latency for selecting the path dynamically. As discussed in Chapter 6, there are a number of techniques for an endpoint to measure the available bandwidth along a path to another endpoint. Available bandwidth depends not only on the minimum link capacity for all hops along the path. Other applications typically share the link capacity. Available bandwidth for a link is then the difference between the link capacity and the average traffic load by other applications on that link. The available bandwidth for a path is the minimum available bandwidth for links for the set of network hops the path traverses. Since this varies over time due to changes in traffic from other applications, it must be periodically measured for each path to have an accurate picture for path selection. As in the RON, each peer in the bandwidth-aware RON periodically disseminates the available bandwidth measurements to all other peers in the RON.

Given the available bandwidth state of the overlay, when a new flow enters, the RON determines whether there is a better path available in the overlay than the native path provides. If there is, the flow will be routed via the overlay path. Over the lifetime of the flow, available bandwidth can change, both for the active path and for alternate paths. Thus the RON can periodically try to switch the flow to an alternate path with more capacity. Even if the existing path has sufficient capacity, a path with more available bandwidth can make the flow more immune to bursts in flows sharing links along the path. This aggressive use of alternate paths is a proactive strategy. The RON could instead wait until a flow experiences bandwidth loss on an existing path and then switch to an alternate path, a reactive strategy.

Zhu et al.[386] compared the proactive and reactive strategies using a simulation involving 275 native nodes and 18 overlay nodes using a network topology modeled after that of the four largest U.S. ISPs. They found (Figure 11.5, top) that reactive overlay routing performs better than proactive overlay routing. Further, as the

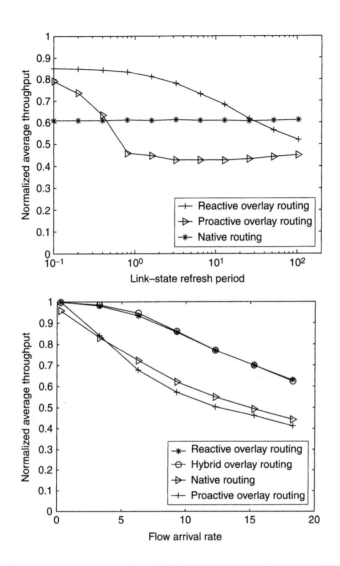

FIGURE 11.5 For a bandwidth-aware RON: (top) reactive overlay routing generally outperforms native routing, and (bottom) reactive and hybrid overlay routing outperform native routing.[385] Reprinted from [386], © 2006, with permission from Elsevier.

frequency of path measurements increases, reactive overlay routing gives a substantial improvement in throughput compared to native routing. They also studied a hybrid scheme that probabilistically combines reactive and proactive routing. Both reactive overlay routing and the hybrid scheme outperform proactive overlay routing and native routing over a range of flow arrival rates (Figure 11.5, bottom). An important result is that overlay paths with at most one intermediate peer perform best.

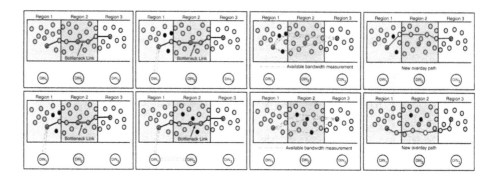

FIGURE 11.6 (Top) A BARON ingress peer consults a DIN in its region for bandwidth measurements to peer Y. (Bottom) The region DIN consults a DIN in a neighboring region.[387] © 2008 IEEE.

Lee et al.[387] implemented Bandwidth-Aware Routing in Overlay Networks (BARON) using 174 PlanetLab nodes in the United States, Europe, and Asia. Their proactive strategy defines a bandwidth threshold that must be satisfied before a new path is chosen. In addition, to increase scalability, a small number of distributed infrastructure nodes (DINs) in different regions of the network act as a repository of bandwidth measurements for each peer in their region. An ingress peer consults with its local DIN to obtain information about better paths from its region of the network (Figure 11.6, top). If the DIN doesn't have a good path, it can consult with DINs in adjacent regions for path candidates (Figure 11.6, bottom). Because the peers don't need to share measurements with all other nodes in the overlay, this design increases scalability while requiring that additional infrastructure nodes be deployed.

Increasing the bandwidth threshold in BARON's control algorithm generally reduces the number of times a given session switches to a different path. However, it doesn't increase bandwidth availability. An example six-hour session between endpoints in New York and Colorado is shown in Figure 11.7. The maximum bandwidth overlay path shown in this figure is determined from five different overlay paths that could be used in this session. In most cases the overlay path provides more available bandwidth.

QoS AWARE OVERLAYS

Overview

In the quality-of-service (QoS) networking model, an application requires some level of service guarantee for end-to-end delivery of packets. The alternatives to the QoS model include best-effort service and priority service. In best-effort service,

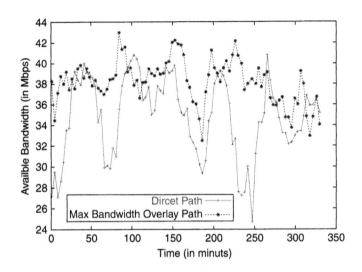

FIGURE 11.7 Available bandwidth in the native network versus the maximum available across five different overlay paths, from New York to Colorado for a BARON deployment.[387] © 2008 IEEE.

the network provides a variable and unspecified bit rate and service time. In priority service, packets are classified into different priority levels, and the router forwarding function delivers higher-priority packets before lower-priority ones.

In practice an organization establishes a service-level agreement (SLA) with its network service provider. The SLA is implemented by the service provider by provisioning the necessary network resources, allocating resources as application requests arrive, enforcing service guarantees, and policing traffic.

The Internet today is primarily a best-effort network. Efforts to extend the Internet service model to support QoS date back to the early 1990s. The leading techniques are the integrated services model (IntServ)[388] and the Differentiated Services model (DiffServ).[389] The general deployment of these architectures has met obstacles, including scalability and peering incompatibilities between different service providers. Consequently there have been proposals to use overlay networks to implement end-to-end QoS.

Since an overlay network is implemented at the application layer in the network protocol stack, it is not possible for an overlay to provide complete QoS guarantees without network support. A QoS-aware overlay could be implemented on top of preprovisioned dedicated network links. In this case, it provides an end-to-end view of the collection of links and performs admission control to ensure that applications don't exceed the available network resources. This works if the application topology can be reliably anticipated. If the underlying network doesn't provide QoS support or if the application topology varies frequently, the ability of an overlay mechanism to enforce service guarantees is significantly limited. It is also possible for a QoS overlay to use a combination of provisioned network resources and best-effort links.

For the portions of the network where only best-effort service is available, a QoS-aware overlay can nevertheless provide some service benefits to applications. Using techniques described in bandwidth-aware RONs, it can adapt to network changes and provide better service quality than might be otherwise realized. It can also distribute the traffic over different overlay links and monitor overlay traffic. It can also trade off bandwidth use for lower packet loss rates.

In the next sections we describe two QoS-aware overlays: OverQoS and QRON. Table 11.1 briefly compares them to the native layer QoS mechanisms.

OverQoS

OverQoS[390] introduces a controlled-loss virtual link (CLVL) abstraction into a RON-like overlay. The CLVL uses a combination of forward error correction (FEC) and packet retransmissions to ensure that the collection of flows over an overlay link are always within the statistical guarantee for the loss rate for those flows. The use of FEC and packet retransmission requires that sufficient bandwidth in the link be reserved for redundant packets. The incoming packet rate is constrained to a certain level, above which packets are dropped.

Table 11.1 Comparison of Native Layer QoS Architectures with QoS-Aware Overlays

	IntServ [482]	DiffServ [483]	OverQoS [484]	QRON [485]
Layer	Native	Native	Overlay	Overlay
Resource Control Mechanism	Flow based	Class based	FEC and retransmission to provide statistical loss rate guarantee	Adapts to changes in available bandwidth
Parameters / classes	Traffic rate Traffic burst Best effort/ soft QoS/ guaranteed	Best effort Low loss, low latency Rate limited with drop priority	Maximum flow rate Statistical guarantee for loss rate	Available bandwidth Shortest distance
Network support	Routers implement soft state for flow reservations	Routers in a DiffServ domain implement common policies for traffic classes	RON-like overlay Underlay is best effort	Overlay Broker nodes are deployed in each domain of the network Underlay is best effort

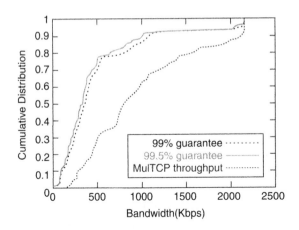

FIGURE 11.8 Distribution of guaranteed bandwidth for 83 different overlay links.[390] © 2004 L. Subramanian, I. Stoica, H. Balakrishnan, and R. H. Katz, used by permission.

OverQoS was tested using the RON test bed and in PlanetLab using known lossy network links. Figure 11.8 shows the cumulative distribution of bandwidth for flows over 83 different overlay links, comparing 99% guarantee, 99.5% guarantee, and best effort. The difference in available bandwidth between best-effort and statistically guaranteed flows is due to the additional redundancy in the CLVL, specifically the FEC and packet retransmissions.

The impact of these guarantees on packets' delivery latency depends on the whether a packet-ordering requirement is applied to the flows. For unordered flows, an increase in latency of less than 50 msec was observed.

QRON

QRON[391] assumes a best-effort native network and places Overlay Broker (OB) nodes in different regions of the network to coordinate traffic routing and maintain network measurement information. The OBs connect to each other to form the overlay over which application traffic is sent. A key feature of QRON is the hierarchical arrangement of OBs. Each OB is a member of a cluster that includes a number of nodes in a given region of the network. These clusters are further grouped into larger clusters. Each OB periodically measures the available bandwidth of the overlay links to which it is connected and propagates these measurements to other OBs in its cluster. Only gateway OBs with links to adjacent clusters share their measurements to form aggregated views. When a new overlay path is needed, QRON divides the path into cluster-by-cluster segments and, in parallel, searches for suitable segments by propagating requests through the hierarchy. QRON path selection is based on least-cost path routing that considers the costs of link capacity and OB capacity.

SERVICE ORIENTATION

Overview

Service orientation is a paradigm for organizing distributed systems such that the functions and resources of those systems are available to clients as modules with well-defined programming interfaces called *services*. Services are described using a document format suitable for run-time interpretation by other software applications. The documents, referred to as *service descriptions*, can be considered as contracts between the client and the service. Service orientation hides the implementation from the client and leverages software technology trends, including XML and Web protocols. The most popular instance of a service-oriented architecture is Web services.

As discussed in Chapter 2, devices and applications need to discover services that are available on other devices. A key part of service-oriented architectures is the protocol to discover and advertise services. Well-known service discovery protocols include Simple Service Discovery Protocol (SSDP) for UPnP and Service Discovery Protocol (SDP) for Bluetooth. Once a service is discovered, a client can invoke it using a service invocation protocol. The service invocation protocol used in Web services is called Simple Object Access Protocol (SOAP).

A large number of protocols have been developed for service discovery, but most of these are designed for local area networks. The need to locate services in wide area networks is a good fit for P2P search mechanisms and is a prerequisite for using P2P as a service platform. In the following discussion we use the following terminology:

- *Service description.* Information about a networked service such as type of service, name of service, attributes of service, location of service, and invocation of service. The service description may be stored in a document, at a service repository, or at the node offering the service. It may be broadcast or multicast by the node offering the service. It may be machine readable, human readable, or both. For example, in Web services, service descriptions are encoded in an XML format called Web Services Description Language (WSDL).

- *Service advertisement.* The publication of a service description, in whole or part, by or on behalf of the service offerer, for access by other nodes.

- *Service composition.* The definition of a new service using two or more existing services.

- *Service discovery.* Retrieval or access of a service description by nodes other than the service offerer, including browsing and search by name, class, type, and/or service attribute.

- *Service invocation.* Remote execution of a service over a computer network.

Wide Area Service Discovery

Consider a device that connects to the Internet and discovers services offered by any other device on the Internet. This is wide area service discovery, to distinguish it from protocols that work in home networks, personal area networks, and so on.

Many commercial services are already offered to devices as Web services. Using wide area service discovery, location-specific discovery can be performed outside the immediate area to access these Web services. For example, a roaming device might discover services along a planned route. Wide area service discovery does not require devices to offer services to other devices on the Internet.

Next consider devices that connect to the Internet, offer services, and discover services offered by other devices connected to the Internet. This usage is wide area peer-to-peer service discovery. Compared to wide area service discovery, it means that all participants can act as both service providers and service users. There are several advantages to this strategy. Users can be content publishers as well as consumers. Collections of home networks and PANs can interoperate, as illustrated in Chapter 2. Multiple users in a social network can share device resources regardless of geographic proximity.

Wide area P2P service discovery requires a global-scale service discovery mechanism with the following capabilities:

- Internetwide service advertisement and discovery of services such that any service on the Internet can be discovered by any peer on the Internet
- The ability to index service descriptions by geographic location and Internet domain in which the services are available
- The ability to index service descriptions by arbitrary metadata describing the service; metadata might be the owner of the service, implementation compatibility, or some classification scheme

Since service descriptions are complex documents that include information such as service name, type, unique identifier, offerer, and interfaces, lookup of a service by direct hashing of the service description is likely to fail. In addition, it is convenient to search for services by partial match, such as the service name. One approach to achieve this goal is to index fragments of the service description. Then at lookup time, partial matches can be found, provided that the fragments have been previously indexed.

INS/Twine

INS/Twine[394] is the first system to use a peer-to-peer overlay for indexing and retrieving resource descriptions. INS/Twine is built on Chord. It indexes description fragments and limits the number of identical strands that can be stored at any peer. Each fragment is replicated at a fixed number of peers for reliability and load distribution.

Location-Based Service Discovery

Some services such as media players might be widely implemented. Directly indexing the service descriptions using the service name as the key would lead to an enormous number of entries at one peer. To avoid this, we need some means to distribute the entries across the index. One approach is to combine the service name with other values in a multipart key. The other fields in the key should have a distribution of values that is preferably random but that is easily generated by the peer doing the lookup. An example is the location of the service expressed in some coordinate system. For example, service indexing using latitude-longitude (LL) is described in [397], and service indexing using position in a network coordinate system is described in [409]. An advantage of service indexing using LL is that it can be used to support location-based services. A disadvantage is that it might not be suitable for services delivered from mobile devices or other positions where location privacy is important.

Assume that each service is associated with a location, such as a retail store's address. The position can be represented as LL and can be normalized to decimal format and aligned to the nearest grid point. The resulting grid point can be directly indexed or can be combined in a multipart key with other information about the service. For example, the key could be `media-player:grid-position:media-format`.

To illustrate index sizing and key distribution, [397] assumed that locations would correspond to population densities. In this experiment, two datasets were used, one containing the LL position for the 2555 largest cities and another containing the square area for the 40 largest cities. Both are worldwide datasets. For the 40 largest cities, assuming a grid spacing of 1 city block (about 200 meters), there are about 3.5 million grid points in the largest 40 cities. Randomly distributing points in this grid produced a key distribution shown in Figure 11.9 (top). A separate experiment indexing over 400,000 Internet domains registered in 1997 is shown in Figure 11.9 (bottom). These distributions are similar to those of randomly generated keys performed in [410].

Other P2P Approaches to Service Discovery

Other examples of peer-to-peer service discovery using Web services descriptions include the Space Filling Curve system[401] and the NEMO service orchestration framework.[396] Gu et al.[405] propose a service-oriented P2P system called *P2P service overlay* whereby peers can provide not only media files but also a number of application service components.

REPLICATION AND LOAD BALANCING
Churn and Index Availability

When a peer in a DHT shares an object with other peers, it inserts an index entry that can be stored at any peer in the DHT. The owner of the object has no control over the peer storing its index entry. If the peer responsible for that portion of the DHT index subsequently leaves the DHT, the availability of each entry for which that peer is responsible depends on whether the peer has transferred its DHT elements to the next peer that is assuming the responsibility for these entries. If the peer's departure from the index occurs without transferring these

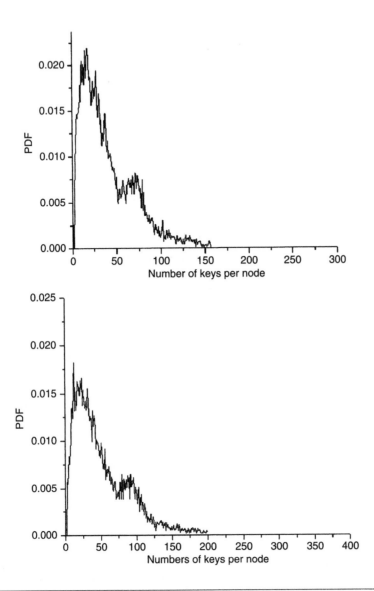

FIGURE 11.9 (Top) Key distribution of 500,000 location index service keys in a 10,000-node DHT. (Bottom) Key distribution of 400,000 real domain names in a 10,000-node DHT.[397] © 2006 IEEE.

entries, subsequent lookups for these entries will fail. Further, some peers might be disconnected from the overlay due to a network failure.

To avoid the loss of access to index entries, copies of the index entries can be stored at other peers in the overlay. Index entry replication involves selecting a replication level and determining which peers would be the owners of these entries if the primary peer fails. If the secondary peers holding the replicas are on a path to the primary peer for lookups, replication can also distribute load.

Replication increases index availability at the cost of additional storage at each peer.

Index Load and Object Popularity

We refer to the distribution of keys across the set of peers in the DHT as the *index load*. Assuming that each key is equally likely to be accessed, any nonuniformity in the index load will lead to nonuniformity in the lookup load on the peers. One factor in the index load is the assignment of overlay addresses to peers. Byers et al.[411] show that random assignment of overlay addresses to peers produces an imbalance so that, with high probability, a highly loaded peer stores a factor of $\Theta(\log n)$ more keys than a peer with average load. Additionally, the arrival and departure of peers change the index load balance. Several techniques have been proposed for reducing this imbalance.[411,412,413]

Other factors that determine the index load are the design of the key space and the selection of keys from the key space that are actually used by the applications. For example, suppose service names of 20 symbols in length are the key space, with 50 unique symbols in the alphabet. Thus 20^{50} possible keys can be generated for the key space, but in practice only a small fraction of these keys are likely to be used, since keys are also generally expected to be human readable or have application semantics.

In addition to imbalances in key distribution and peer ID assignment, the load at peers is likely to be skewed due to different popularity of the objects being indexed. Key distribution might be reasonably known ahead of time, but object popularity is highly variable.

Two techniques have been proposed to adapt the DHT to nonuniform object lookup: replication and load balancing. In replication schemes, the replication factor for a given object is determined dynamically based on the popularity of the object. Replicas are placed at other peers that are along the path to the primary peer responsible for that object. As the popularity increases, additional replicas are added at the leaves of the tree formed by the lookups routed in the overlay. As the popularity decreases, replicas are gradually removed, for example, by expiration of the replica.

In load-balancing schemes, objects are moved from heavily loaded peers to lightly loaded peers. Load balancing using virtual servers is described in [413].

Beehive

Beehive[404] is a replication mechanism for prefix-based multihop overlays such as Tapestry and Pastry. Assuming that object popularity follows Zipf distribution, Beehive uses object access statistics to proactively push objects to sufficient levels in the overlay to meet the required number of hops per query.

In Beehive, object access statistics are aggregated at each object's home node and propagated to nodes along the access path (Figure 11.10, top). Each peer

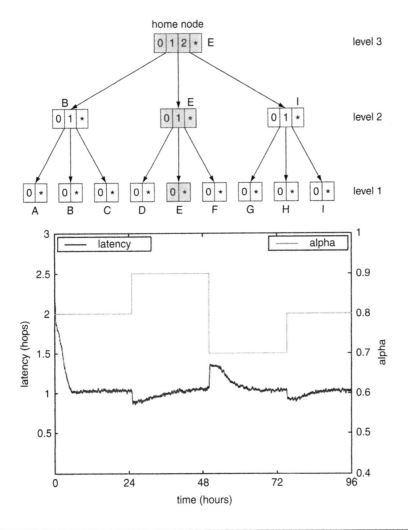

FIGURE 11.10 (Top) Beehive proactively pushes objects along the prefix path and (bottom) holds the lookup hop count to 1 as the object popularity changes.[404] © 2004 R. Ramasubramanian, E. Sirer, used by permission.

locally determines for objects that it currently stores, whether the access level for each object requires increased replication and will push the object to other peers that precede it in the prefix-based routing path. Because of these local decisions and propagation of access statistics along the prefix tree, Beehive is able to respond to both increases and decreases in object popularity (Figure 11.10, bottom).

Service Composition

Another potential benefit of service orientation is to dynamically create new services by composing them from existing services. This requires that the service descriptions provide sufficient semantics about the interfaces and operations so that correct bindings can be made. This is difficult to implement in general, but it is possible to envision composition of device functions such as displays, user input interfaces, and media processing components that can be configured for predefined composition.

The basic idea of service composition using the service discovery and advertisement (SDA) capability of the P2P overlay is illustrated in the following example.

A media-storing peer (Peer-9095 in Figure 11.11A) advertises a search service that provides content-based retrieval (CBR). Another peer (Peer-3321) discovers this service using the service discovery method in the SDA layer. The SDA layer connects to the DHT to search for the service description. After Peer-3321 has discovered a peer offering the service of interest (Step 1), it then uses the service invocation protocol (SI_3) required by the service description for service `search-cbr-intf-v3` (Step 2). To implement this service, two subinterfaces have been defined: preprocess and query process, which may be provided either locally or by other peers. Peer-9095 discovers peers implementing these subinterfaces and uses these peers' services when it receives the incoming search request from Peer-3321. Such service composition (Step 3) is mediated by the SDA layer.

Next, a camcorder (Figure 11.11B) used to capture media immediately encrypts the media using a DRM service, applies the owner's rights management policy, and prepares it for publication to a wide area peer-to-peer index. Once the content is published in the P2P index, any peer may retrieve it. In Figure 11.11B, Peer-4593 has retrieved the media file `tom-movie-20050630-081003` from the P2P index. Peer-4593 uses a local service (`media-player-intf-v3`) to play the content, assuming that the peer also has the appropriate license. In addition, this media player service uses two components that may be either local or provided by other peers. In this simplified example, the components provide two key functions of the media player: media decryption and media rendering. Peer-7239 and Peer-1782 have previously registered services in the P2P index which correspond to these interfaces. Peer-4593 can discover these services and use them to perform the necessary function.

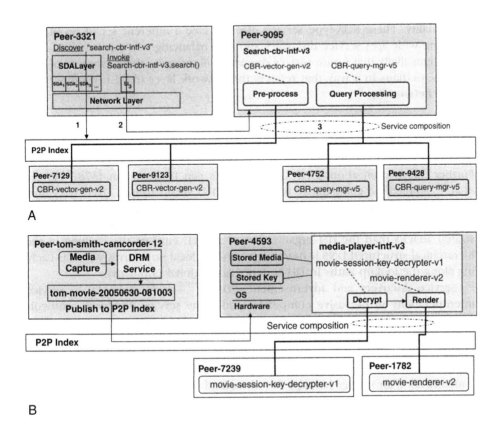

FIGURE 11.11 (A) A peer discovers and invokes a content-based retrieval service, which is in turn implemented using services from other peers, combined using service composition. (B) A peer publishes protected content to the index using a local DRM service.

SUMMARY

The concept of service overlays has developed in parallel for network services and application services. In overlays for network services such as resilient overlay networks, the overlays are small, for example, less than 100 nodes, and may be integrated with each application instance. The focus of these service overlays is often efficient integration of network measurement mechanisms, resource allocation, and dynamic decision making based on a common set of measurements. The success of these efforts has generated growing interest in using such service overlays systematically in the evolution of the Internet. In May 2008 the IEEE Standards Association approved a work plan for a new standard on service overlays.[393]

Meanwhile, the adaptation of service-oriented architectures to P2P overlays also sparked interest as a means of generalizing the sharing of resources and functionality. These SOA-type service overlays face a different set of problems, including wide area service discovery and load balancing.

It seems likely that future service overlays will integrate these two sets of capabilities, perhaps in a way that reflects the network layer trend toward service-centric networking.

FOR FURTHER READING

Further information about DNS characteristics can be found in [378]. Pappas et al.[381] studied the comparative reliability of DNS versus using a DHT. They conclude that the DNS hierarchical structure with greater redundancy at key servers is more resilient to random failures than a DHT but is more vulnerable to orchestrated attacks than the flat organization of a DHT. Further, the caching in the hierarchical structured DNS is more responsive to local popularity, whereas caching along the lookup paths in DHTs depends on global popularity.

Service discovery and advertisement (SDA)[399,400] is fundamental to service interoperability in pervasive computing, and many service discovery protocols have been developed. Surveys of existing methods of SDA protocols include [402], [398], and [395]. The Secure Service Discovery System (SSDS)[403] is a client/server architecture that provides for wide area service discovery using a hierarchy of servers to provide scalability. Centralized authentication servers provide authentication for service lookup. To reduce load at the top of the hierarchy, SSDS uses Bloom filters to create service description summaries.

Voice Over Peer-to-Peer

Voice over Peer-to-Peer (VoP2P) is another compelling application of P2P technology. In VoP2P, peers take on roles that were previously reserved to servers in call processing architectures. In this chapter we look at VoIP elements for session establishment, feature servers, and gateways and discuss how these can be mapped to P2P overlays. In addition, we describe the use of application relays, an important technique for reducing latency and increasing bandwidth for stream delivery. The chapter concludes with case studies on Skype and the proposed IETF P2P-SIP design.

FROM VoIP TO VoP2P

The delivery of communication services via the Internet has become a widespread reality. Enterprises use SIP phones, service providers transport VoIP traffic over their backbone networks, broadband access providers offer VoIP bundles to consumers, and mobile operators are developing IP-based architectures. In addition to voice calls, the Internet is widely used for instant messaging, email, and other communications services.

To achieve the goal of enabling VoIP to compete with PSTN required designing a new scalable signaling and media transport architecture and set of protocols that could be extensible and media independent. A key requirement was to be able to address the service quality requirements needed in voice communications in a packet-switching environment. Two important architectures emerged from international standards communities: SIP from IETF[414,415] and H.323 from ITU-T.[416] As of 2006, about 20% of international calls were made using VoIP.

Given the success of VoIP, then, what have been the drivers for using peer-to-peer technology for communication services? Certainly the rate of adoption of VoIP has left room for other approaches. Millions of instant-messaging users were lacking integrated VoIP capability. Moreover, the leading VoIP models are designed for deployment by service providers. In the past many observers have argued that communication services could be delivered more economically and with richer features if the service provider model could be opened up to third-party vendors. This is one motivation for the proposed IP Multimedia Subsystem (IMS) being developed by 3GPP.[417,418]

Proponents of VoP2P have then similar goals: to accelerate delivery, increase availability, and reduce costs of IP communication services. Several characteristics of P2P enable high scalability, easy upgrade, and minimal infrastructure dependence. The VoP2P approach doesn't require a traditional service provider. It goes beyond the idea of opening up the service provider model to a new model whereby overlay operators use end-system resources and third-party services to deliver these capabilities. The overlay operator role is discussed in Chapter 15, "Managed Overlays."

Voice calls have important real-time quality requirements that must be satisfied, whether the fabric is PSTN, VoIP, or VoP2P. These include time to set up a call, end-to-end delay between the call endpoints, and variation in the delivery of voice packets during the call, also called *jitter*. It is equally important that session setup and session connections be highly reliable. Users expect to be able to reach other parties when they are available and to not lose connections during calls. Finally, PSTN users enjoy the ability to place calls worldwide using a uniform dialing plan from both wireline and wireless handsets.

In this chapter, we discuss the key issues for implementing VoP2P. How suitable is the overlay routing for meeting the real-time transport requirements for voice? How does churn in the overlay impact call reliability? How do VoIP signaling and transport elements such as proxies, media servers, gateways, and feature services map to the peer-to-peer architecture?

In the next section we give an overview of mapping VoIP architectural elements to VoP2P. This is followed by sections discussing specific VoP2P issues media relays and P2P call feature processing. At the end of the chapter we present two case studies, Skype and P2P-SIP.

VoP2P

VoIP Elements

Before discussing VoP2P, it is important to relate it to the VoIP architecture, from which it derives many of its elements. VoIP signaling can be broadly divided into three layers (Figure 12.1): access, connectivity, and application. Access relates to the handsets, network elements, and protocols by which endpoints connect to the VoIP network. Due to the variety of media and protocols used by endpoints and for security, scalability, and configuration purposes, endpoint connectivity into the core signaling area is usually mediated by gateways. Session setup, call routing, and media handling are performed in the connectivity layer. Connectivity to other networks such as Signaling System 7 (SS7) is also handled in the connectivity layer. Finally, call-processing features beyond those performed by endpoints are provided by the application layer through feature servers or application servers.

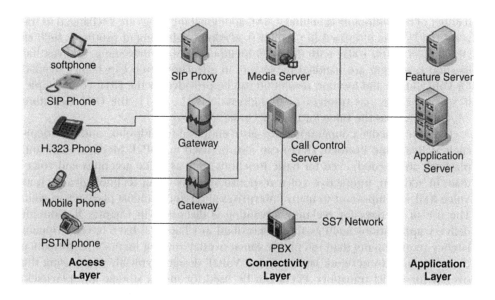

FIGURE 12.1 Simplified VoIP architecture.

The term *session* is widely used to refer to the application of VoIP-type signaling to other media, including video, text messaging, whiteboarding, and application conferencing. *Session establishment* is the creation of one or more media paths between endpoints, feature servers, and media servers. Media servers perform a range of functions, from DTMF processing, playback of greetings, voicemail, and conference call mixing. *Feature processing* refers to a variety of call operations such as call blocking, call forwarding, call parking, and so forth.

Mapping VoIP Elements to a VoP2P Overlay

The P2P design principles discussed in Chapter 2 include self-organization, role symmetry, and distribution of functions. The VoIP functions illustrated in Figure 12.1 need to be distributed and widely replicated across the peer population. Later in this chapter we'll look at two approaches to this distribution: the Skype P2P telephony application and the P2P-SIP standardization activity in the IETF. In general, the functions that need to be distributed in VoP2P include session establishment, media servers, and feature processing.

IP telephony involves two-way real-time media streaming, and the transition to VoP2P must continue to satisfy call-quality constraints such as call setup time, end-to-end delay and jitter, and sufficient bandwidth. Call setup time includes time to resolve the callee's address to one or more network addresses, locate the preferred network address, send a message to the callee to initiate the session, and exchange further messages to negotiate session parameters and create the media connections.

If either of the endpoints is behind a NAT, additional messages are exchanged to traverse the NAT, as discussed in Chapter 6. Session establishment protocols such as SIP do most of this today with direct endpoint-to-endpoint messaging. Address and location resolution are handled by servers in SIP. The search capabilities needed for VoIP address and location resolution can be provided by the DHT. For example, if `tom@example.com` resolves to IP address `24.255.10.11`, the DHT can store `24.255.10.11` as the value for the key `tom@example.com`.

Likewise, media connections are also endpoint-to-endpoint, and protocols such as Real-Time Protocol (RTP) can also be used in VoP2P. Media storage and playback are needed, even for basic functions such as voice greetings and voicemail. In addition, interactive voice response systems using technologies such as Voice XML are important to many enterprises and require media playback as well. The use of overlays for real-time streaming is discussed in Chapter 8. Content delivery applications such as those described in Chapter 8 have fewer stringent latency requirements than telephony. Since overlay routing incurs a performance cost compared to network layer routing, VoP2P designs typically avoid using the overlay for media transport. Peers can be used for media storage and playback, provided that reliability and security requirements are met, as discussed in Chapter 8. Later in this chapter we discuss an important performance technique called *application relays* in P2P streaming applications.

In addition to call establishment, many additional features are desired in telephony. Examples include call waiting, call forwarding, call parking, and call bridging. Enterprise PBXs have hundreds of such features, and the implementation of these features involves both endpoints and feature services. To date, VoP2P designs have incorporated only a few elementary call features. Later in this chapter we describe some of the issues in distributing feature processing in VoP2P.

In large-scale VoIP systems, many types of gateways are needed for compatibility with legacy communication systems and to support the plethora of handsets and access technologies that are used. Many gateways have special hardware to support specialized equipment interfaces. It might not be practical to distribute gateway functions to peers if either hardware or physical location are important attributes of the gateway.

APPLICATION RELAYS
Types of Relays

Application relays can reduce end-to-end delays and increase throughput for TCP connections. To improve the performance of streaming between peers in the overlay, additional capabilities can be added, such as application relays, media transcoding, and mixers. Peers that provide these functions can be dynamically integrated into streaming sessions. This provides more flexibility in meeting QoS, fair load distribution, reliability, and performance goals.

Table 12.1 Inband Streaming Services[419]

	Relay	Mixer	Transcoder
Summary	Protocol endpoint to reduce end-to-end delay	Adds two or more streams of the same format in a multipoint session	Translates a stream from one format to another
Media handling	No	Yes	Yes
Admission criteria	Available bandwidth	Available bandwidth Media formats CPU utilization	Available bandwidth Media formats CPU utilization
Advertisement attributes	Current bandwidth capacity Availability Network position and address Max/avg delay and jitter	Media format(s) Current bandwidth capacity Max # of streams per mixer Availability Network position and address Max/avg delay and jitter	Media formats Current bandwidth capacity Max number of streams per mixer Availability Network position and address Max/avg delay and jitter

Such streaming services (Table 12.1) are typically selected in band during session initiation. These services operate continuously on the media streams during the session. Session characteristics might change, requiring renegotiation or reselection.

Relay Selection and Discovery

Application relay discovery and selection are important for streaming media applications and are representative of other inband streaming services. Liu et al.[420] analyzed application relays and showed optimal relay selection algorithms for multirelay paths in a connected overlay graph. TCP throughput B over a link is $B \sim 1/d \cdot p^{1/2}$, where d is the link delay and p is the packet-loss probability. Assuming homogenous packet loss probability on all links, the effectiveness of the relay for increasing throughput and reducing end-to-end delay depends on its proximity to the midpoint position in the end-to-end delay between the endpoints.

Using RTT measurement as an estimator of packet delay over a path, a direct way to find a relay located closest to the midpoint position is to measure the RTT between candidate relays and each of the endpoints to obtain RTT_1 and RTT_2. Since the end-to-end throughput is constrained by the segment with the largest value of d, choose the relay that produces the minimum of $RTT_1 + RTT_2 + ABS (RTT_1 - RTT_2)$. This requires at least two probes per relay candidate, one for each segment.

In a large overlay there are many thousands, perhaps millions, of possible candidates. The population of relay candidates should be a significant portion of the overlay population for there to be fair load distribution and sufficient capacity for many concurrent streaming sessions. Because of the large number of peers, it is impractical to probe all the candidates. It might be possible for a peer to cache RTT measurements for a large number of other peers. However, the other endpoint must also cache RTT measurements and the set of cached measurements must be for common peers; otherwise additional measurement is needed, reducing the utility of the cache. Next we discuss how use of measurement techniques described in Chapter 10 can be incorporated in to the overlay for aiding relay selection.

Suppose a peer p_1 initiates a relayed session with a remote peer p_2. Peers p_1 and p_2 must agree on an intermediate peer to act as a relay. Peers that are prospective relays are called *candidate relays*. Identifying peers that are candidate relays is the process of *candidate discovery*. Choosing a relay from a set of candidates is the process of *relay selection*. Assuming that peers engage in many sessions with different peers in the overlay, having a large set of candidate relays is a prerequisite condition for selecting a high-quality relay for a session. This is because of the arbitrary distribution of session endpoints in the overlay and the Internet-scale overlay topology.

In general both peers and relays are part of the overlay network. To be a relay candidate, a peer must have a public Internet address and have sufficient capacity.

There are several ways for a peer to obtain relay candidates, including configuration, using entries in the peer's overlay routing table, sharing relay selection history between proximal peers, and explicit advertisement and lookup. If the peers in the overlay register with a bootstrap server, then when a peer joins the overlay it can receive a configured list of relay candidates. Peers can remember relay selection history for future sessions, and proximal peers can share such history. As discussed in Chapter 4, peers that participate in the overlay have a routing layer that maintains address information about other peers in the overlay, and this information is updated as peers join and leave the overlay. Routing table entries could be used as relay candidates.

Selection of peers to perform inband stream services is important for providing good session quality for streaming overlay applications. Systems today typically use configuration to discover relay candidates and use RTT probing to select the relay. To improve on these approaches, relays can advertise and be discovered by peers using the DHT to store the advertisements, as discussed in Chapter 11. Since selection of a suitable relay depends on the position of the relay in the network in relation to the position of the peers, the advertisement can be indexed in the DHT by network location. Methods for determining network position in a global coordinate system are referred to as *Internet coordinate systems* (ICS) and are discussed in Chapter 10. Since there could be a large number of relays in the overlay, using network location has the advantage of distributing the advertisement load over the DHT.

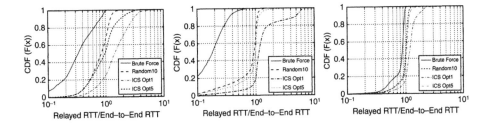

FIGURE 12.2 For three different P2P datasets, the ICS with about 5 probes performs as well as random probing with 10 probes. The x axis is the ratio of the RTT via the relay versus direct.[419] © 2007 IEEE.

Figure 12.2 compares the performance of relay selection using an ICS versus direct probing of RTT. For the same quality of relay performance, the ICS index reduces the message overhead by about 50%. These experimental measurements used the Vivaldi ICS.

Dynamic Path Switching

The above relay selection mechanism finds relays which are close to the mid-point of the path between the two endpoints. This reduces end-to-end delay and increases throughput. If call quality subsequently deteriorates during a call, an alternate path can be located. This is referred to as dynamic path switching, and is a key capability of RONs discussed in Chapter 11. Mid-call switching to an alternate path involves real-time detection of call quality degradation, measurement of call quality parameters over alternate paths, and session signaling to redirect the call path.

Orbit[442] is a relay overlay which focuses on real-time measurement techniques suitable for large-scale VoIP deployments such as found in global enterprises. Call quality is passively monitored in real-time and scored using the ITU-T R factor. When the score falls below a certain threshold, the receiver signals the sender to select a better path. Orbit is used to perform measurements on alternate paths. If a better path is found, the call is re-routed through that relay. Simulations indicate that recovery can be performed in less than one second.

CALL PROCESSING

Overview

Apart from basic call-processing features, such as dialing in and dialing out, selecting gateways, and some conferencing capabilities, little work has been done to map call features to VoP2P overlays. Consequently, the degree of feature granularity that could be provided in a VoP2P overlay is an open question. Here we discuss some scenarios: per-call feature selection, selection of feature bundles, and individual feature selection.

Then we present detailed message flows for several representative widely used features, showing signaling between both the endpoints and the feature peers and between the endpoints and the overlay. The purpose of these examples is to provide concrete illustration of how call processing could be achieved and how service discovery is incorporated into the overall model.

Assumptions

Hybrid architectures that combine call-processing servers and gateways with the P2P overlay are important, but here we take the general approach of permitting any server-based feature in conventional VoIP systems to be implemented by an arbitrary peer in the overlay. In practice, factors such as details of the feature, its usage, its interaction with other features, and scalability of the feature will influence the implementation decision. Example call features are taken from [425]. If a call involves multiple features, we consider both bundled and unbundled service offerings. In the unbundled case, separate peers implement each feature, and different peers may be used for the same feature on separate calls for the same endpoint. In the bundled case, feature sets might be offered as bundles, such as an origination bundle or a media-processing bundle, by a single peer.

Any feature including call routing can be mapped to an arbitrary peer in the overlay. This dynamic mapping is suitable for VoP2P overlays, which are characterized by limited resource peers and a highly volatile peer population. It is also highly scalable in terms of processing resources, at the possible cost of increased P2P message overhead and signaling time.

Consider an overlay in which peers referred to as *proxy peers* offer a call-routing service for the P2P overlay. When user Jane calls user Bob, Bob's proxy service may be handled by proxy peer A. But when another user, David, calls Bob, Bob's proxy service may be handled by proxy peer B. Proxy peer A and proxy peer B are two independent peers. They can both acquire Bob's user profile and state information from the overlay and route Bob's calls. Without appropriate coordination mechanisms between proxy peer A and proxy peer B, they may perform conflicting actions. Suppose Bob has a presence-based call-handling feature that rejects calls when Bob is on a call. If Jane and David call Bob at the same time, both proxy peer A and proxy peer B independently conclude that Bob is not on a call and they route calls to Bob. This situation is avoided if Bob uses a single proxy peer to handle his calls or if some coordination mechanism is introduced.

Dimensionality

There are several dimensions to realizing call-processing features in P2P overlays:

- *Feature peer selection.* For a call with feature sequence $F1 \Rightarrow F2 \Rightarrow \ldots \Rightarrow Fn$, the endpoints may recursively select peers for each Fi, the predecessor peer in the path may iteratively select the next peer, or some other distributed control may be used.

- *Feature granularity.* One peer can provide for an endpoint a complete set of features, a bundle, or only an individual feature.
- *Call granularity.* An endpoint may select feature peers for a single call or for an extended set of calls.
- *Feature atomicity.* A feature is indivisible or could be composed of subservices that are each implemented by other peers.
- *Overlay coupling.* Some features may be intrinsic to the overlay, such as a relay or NAT traversal. Others may be layered on the overlay. Features might be implemented as a specialized overlay, such as group overlay, which only contains group information and handles call routing among various group members.
- *Peer autonomy.* The peers in the overlay may belong to the same administrative domain or different domains without prior trust relationships.
- *Peer addressing.* All peers in a given call may belong to a single overlay (flat address space) or may be members of different overlays (hierarchical address space). Federated overlays introduce additional complexity on call routing and trust relationship handling.

For simplicity in this discussion, let's assume that a single endpoint discovers and selects feature peers on a per-call and per-feature basis. Features are atomic. Peers are autonomous, but the overlay provides a trust mechanism. All peers belong to the same overlay, and the overlay provides generic services, including a DHT, secure routing, NAT traversal, and group membership management.

Example Peer Features

In this section, we describe some call features and discuss ways of implementing them in a P2P overlay. A basic set of call features are documented in [425]. Some of these features (call hold, three-way calling, call transfer, call screening, and automatic redial) are best implemented at endpoints. Call hold, three-way calling, and call transfer are for an existing call on an endpoint, since the endpoint maintains the call states and can manipulate the media streams. Call screening and automatic redial require the target endpoint to be online and to maintain a screen list and a call number. Therefore, they should also be implemented on endpoints.

Call coverage features such as call forwarding, find-me, and group features such as call park and call pickup can be implemented in a P2P overlay because those features should still be available even when the called endpoint is offline. Features that require specific resources, such as music on hold and click to dial, can be better implemented in a VoP2P overlay.

In addition to the features in [425], there are many other features that can be implemented in VoP2P overlays, such as anonymous call, voicemail, call bridging, call hunting, and conferencing. Next, consider voicemail and call park as examples of ways to implement features in a VoP2P overlay.

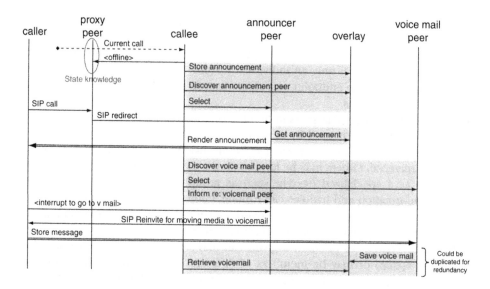

FIGURE 12.3 Voicemail service message flow using separate peers for announcement, proxying, and recording.[424]

Figure 12.3 shows a call-signaling flow for a voicemail feature in a P2P overlay. The callee is active on a call, so it stores its cover announcement media in the overlay and discovers an announcement peer in the overlay that will render the announcement. When a second incoming call arrives, the callee's proxy peer redirects the call to the announcement peer. The callee discovers and selects a recording peer in the overlay. When the announcement is completed or interrupted, the call is routed to the recording peer, which captures the media and stores it in the overlay for later retrieval by the callee. Media objects such as voicemail can be replicated in the overlay for reliability.

Figure 12.4 shows the call flow for a call park/pickup service. Call park and call pickup are group services that require group membership management. The group for this example is handled by peer Group G, which maintains group membership for all the member callees. Peers join the group using a join operation, which validates the peers against the membership criteria. The group service subscribes to service notifications and propagates these to the group members.

Group G is notified by the park peer when a member in the group parks a call. In turn, it notifies other members to pick up the parked call. Note that the state information is handled by the group overlay and in this case proxy peers do not require state information.

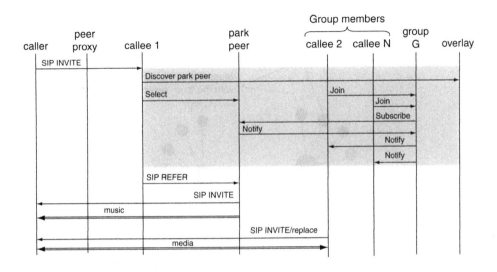

FIGURE 12.4 Call park/pickup service in which two callees are in the same group.[424]

CASE STUDY: SKYPE

Skype is a popular freely downloadable software application that supports free computer-to-computer voice calls worldwide. Since its launch in August 2003, Skype has grown to several hundred million registered users. In January 2007, Skype reached 9 million concurrent online users. At the end of 2006, Skype usage accounted for 4.4% of 313 billion international call minutes, VoIP services were 19.8%, and the remaining usage was traditional switched telephony.[421] The user view of Skype is described in Chapter 1. A general overview of Skype is found in [422]. In the remainder of this section we are primarily interested in the operation of the P2P Skype network.

A Skype network is a peer-to-peer network implemented using a proprietary and encrypted protocol. Details of this protocol have not been released, and various efforts by researchers have been made to infer the architecture and operation of the P2P protocols used in Skype.

Peers are supernodes if they have sufficient resources and have a public IP address; otherwise, a peer is an ordinary node.[426] Skype uses a central login server to authenticate peers when they connect to the network. At login time, the client receives a list of IP addresses that help bootstrap the node into the network and act as supernodes if the client is an ordinary node. It is conjectured that Skype uses a variant of STUN and TURN protocols to perform NAT traversal.[426] Over time the client collects additional supernodes until its host cache is full. An example of the key architectural elements of the Skype network is shown in

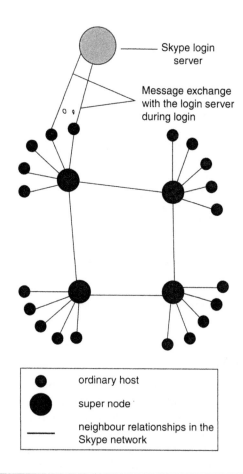

FIGURE 12.5 Skype network entities.[426] © 2006 S. Baset and H. Schulzrinne.

Figure 12.5. This figure does not show other key elements needed to support other features of Skype, such as Skype-to-PSTN calls and voicemail.

Calls involving one or more ordinary nodes are relayed through supernodes. Then the network and computing resources used by supernodes can be considerably higher than ordinary nodes. Some limited study has been made of Skype selection of supernodes. Experimental evidence seems to indicate that supernodes may be used that are remote from the actual call path.[423] For example, on a set of international calls, the RTT on the call path sometimes exceeded 300 msec, which crosses the acceptable perceptual threshold of delay for voice calls (Figure 12.6A).

Further, the time to select a relay sometimes exceeded several hundred seconds (Figure 12.6B). Xie and Yang[430] show that Skype call quality would decrease significantly if supernodes in edge networks (called *AS stubs*) adopted a policy of blocking relay traffic. Zhou et al.[424] show that if the relay population dropped

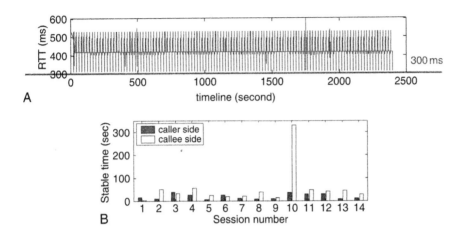

FIGURE 12.6 (a) Skype session path length and (b) relay selection time.[423] © 2007 IEEE.

below 15% of the total peer population, relay selection rates would drop significantly.

Each client stores a buddy list and displays presence information about the user's buddies. This buddy list appears to be stored in the Skype network. When a client login is performed, the buddy presence information is collected for the client. As buddy state changes occur, such as when a buddy becomes unavailable, these are propagated to each client. The protocol by which Skype manages buddy state and how distributed search for buddies is performed are not known.

Peers on the Skype network exhibit signficantly longer lifetimes than those measured for peers in P2P file-sharing systems.[29] In P2P telephony, users are motivated to stay connected, both to be able to receive calls and to view the current status of their buddies. Long application lifetimes mean a low churn rate. These factors are not present in the file-sharing applications.

Part of Skype's success has been due to the perceived high call quality. This has been attributed to the audio codecs Skype uses.[426] Skype's key innovations include integration of a successful NAT traversal mechanism, leveraging of resources on user machines in a sufficiently benign way so as to not deter users, a scalable system architecture that integrates P2P routing, centralized authentication, and access to PSTN gateways to enable low-cost PSTN calling.

CASE STUDY: PEER-TO-PEER SIP

Overview

P2P-SIP is a standardization effort chartered in the IETF in 2007 to develop new protocols that will permit a DHT to be used in place of the SIP location server.

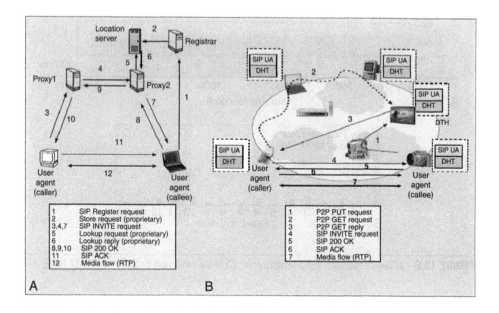

FIGURE 12.7 (a) SIP messaging versus (b) P2P SIP messaging. *UA* = user agent.[18] © 2007 IEEE.

In SIP, a location server is used to resolve a SIP address such as john@example.com to the IP address of John's device. SIP[414] uses various servers to establish sessions between two endpoints. P2P-SIP is intended to eliminate the need for servers by using the DHT to perform address and location resolution. In the remaining steps of session establishment, a peer uses the existing SIP protocol.

Figure 12.7 compares (a) SIP signaling with (b) the proposed P2P-SIP signaling. In both cases, endpoints called *user agents* (UA) issue a SIP INVITE request from the caller to the callee. The address of the callee, for example, john@example.com, must be resolved to its IP address. In SIP, as shown in Steps 5 and 6, a location server is used. In P2P-SIP, as shown in Steps 2 and 3, a DHT lookup is performed. In both cases, after the address is resolved, the request is forwarded to callee UA and the usual SIP message exchange follows.

As described earlier, NAT traversal is a key issue for VoP2P. The P2P-SIP work plan will leverage the ICE protocol described earlier. Since P2P-SIP is concerned with the practical issues of building a reliable and secure overlay, some of the P2P-SIP specifications are relevant to any application overlay.

Hip-Hop

Hip-Hop[431] was an early proposal for a P2P-SIP overlay architecture based on the Host Identity Protocol (HIP).[532,533,534] HIP is an experimental protocol being defined by a separate IETF working group. The idea of HIP is for each host to have a unique cryptographically secure host identifier (HI) separate from its IP address. The HI (or a hash of it) is used to create a secure association between communicating hosts. Once a secure association is established, using a four-step handshake, subsequent exchanges are encrypted and the endpoints can be protected against various security attacks, including replay, man in the middle, and denial of service.

The introduction of a new namespace to the Internet would mean that host identities would be decoupled from routing and locating operations. For that reason, there are important potential benefits for overlays for problems such as NAT and peer mobility. In these cases, a HIP host has a unique identifier for application-level addressing that is independent of whether the host is changing its IP address due to roaming or having its address translated by one or more intervening NATs. Further, the large HI address space with randomly selected addresses fits well with the addressing requirements of P2P overlays, and a HI could be used directly as an overlay identifier.

HIP defines a rendezvous server to store and resolve the association between host identifier and IP address. This is similar to a DNS server, which resolves hostnames to IP addresses. A mobile host updates its IP address at the rendezvous server when its address changes after a roaming transition. Other peer hosts that want to connect with the mobile host consult the rendezvous server to determine the current IP address for the specified HI.

Using HIP means a new HIP layer is inserted into the network stack between the IP layer and upper layers such as TCP and UDP (Figure 12.8). Each host self-generates its own cryptographic identifiers using a public key and private key pair. A host can have many such pairs. Additional pairs can be used for anonymized communication or to make it more difficult for traffic analysis. The host

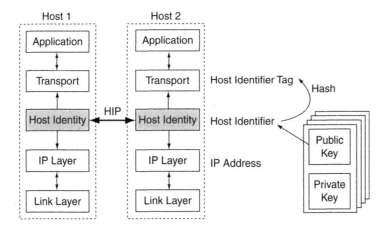

FIGURE 12.8 Network stack with new HIP layer.

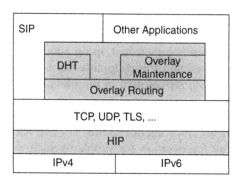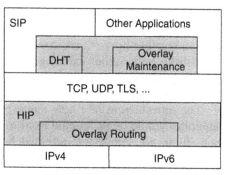

FIGURE 12.9 (Left) Overlay functions layered on top of transport layer and (right) a HIP-HOP model in which overlay routing is integrated into HIP layer.

identity layer uses its public key as its HI to establish a secure association with another host. Applications use an abbreviated version of the HI, called a *host identifier tag* (HIT), which is a fixed-length hash of the HI. HITs are used because they can be interchanged with IPv6 addresses at the API layer without requiring the existing network APIs to be modified.

Given HIP support throughout the peer population (Figure 12.9, left), the overlay functions of routing and maintenance could be placed above the transport layer. Then the overlay layer uses HITs as peer identifiers. Overlay messaging requires the corresponding peers have a HIP association. Although having a peer's address in the routing table doesn't require the HIP association to be created, any message exchange with that peer does. As described earlier, creating a HIP association requires a 4-packet message exchange between the two peers.

The HIP-HOP stack (Figure 12.9, right) proposes a further optimization, which is to integrate the overlay routing function with the HIP layer. Then overlay forwarding decisions remain in the HIP layer, invisible to the application layer and avoiding transport layer conversion overhead. In either case, the use of HIP to support the overlay does not require a particular overlay routing algorithm.

Address Settlement by Peer-to-Peer

Address Settlement by Peer-to-Peer (ASP)[435] is another early proposed design for P2P-SIP that includes support for multiple overlay networks, digital certificate-based security mechanisms for both routing and data storage, and an interesting mechanism for upgrading overlay routing algorithms while the overlay is running. It is intended to work with different overlay routing algorithms.

ASP incorporates the ICE protocol for NAT traversal but uses peers instead of STUN and TURN servers. When first joining the overlay, each peer uses a central STUN server to determine whether it is NATed or not. If it's not, the peer is able to act as a STUN or TURN server for other peers. Each peer stores its availability as a STUN or TURN server in the DHT at one of N predetermined positions in the DHT space, where N is determined by an estimate of the overlay's size. The use of N positions distributes the lookup load in the DHT for these entries. After a peer connects to the overlay using the central STUN server to mediate its NAT traversal, it retrieves the peers to use as subsequent STUN or TURN request servers for further overlay operations.

An important practical problem is how an overlay running one routing algorithm might be dynamically upgraded to a new routing algorithm without causing a service interruption for the existing clients. In ASP, peers that support the new routing algorithm form a new overlay, which runs in parallel with the existing overlay. This could continue for a period of months until the switchover is completed. In the interim period, peers would be connecting to two overlays.

Reload

REsource LOcation And Discovery (RELOAD) [443] has been adopted by the P2P SIP working group as its starting point for the primary P2P-SIP protocols. RELOAD incorporates aspects of the ASP design, the P2PP proposal described in Chapter 6, and other proposals related to security and the use of Chord. It is described here as a snapshot of the current direction of the working group and is likely to change.

The core components of the RELOAD architecture involve the overlay functions which are divided into a generic routing layer, a forwarding layer, and a pluggable topology module which implements specific overlay algorithms. The routing layer uses a routing table in the topology module to determine next hop decisions. The topology layer implements algorithm specific maintenance and measurement mechanisms. The forwarding layer handles algorithm independent message transit decisions and interfaces with NAT traversal and secure transport protocols. The purpose of the pluggable topology module is to support a variety of different overlay algorithms without changing the basic protocol or peer software. The forwarding layer performs packet header processing in an efficient manner.

Key aspects of the RELOAD design include:

- A central registration server which is the basis for securing the overlay. Each peer receives digital credentials from the registration server prior to joining the overlay. Each message in the overlay is signed by the peer which is the source of the message. Each object stored in the overlay is signed by the peer which is the source of the object.
- NAT traversal is integrated into the overlay using the ICE protocol described in Chapter 6. Peers behind firewalls use ICE and the TURN server capabilities in each peer to make new connections with other peers in the overlay.
- Nodes self-organize in to peers or clients, depending on their capability. Clients do not perform overlay routing and store no objects.

Table 12.2 Peer Statistics

Parameter	Meaning
ROUTING_TABLE_SIZE	Number of peers in the routing table
SOFTWARE_VERSION	Manufacturer, model and version of the peer's software
MACHINE_UPTIME	Time the node has been up, in seconds
APP_UPTIME	Time the peer's software has been running, in seconds
MEMORY_FOOTPRINT	Memory used by the peer's application software
DATASIZE_STORED	Disk storage used by the peer
INSTANCES_STORED	An array of bytes stored by data type
MESSAGES_SENT_RCVD	An array of number of messages sent and received by message type
EMWA_BYTES_SENT	Average number of bytes sent, using a weighted average with previous estimate
EMWA_BYTES_RCVD	Average number of bytes sent, using a weighted average with previous estimate

- Each object stored in the overlay has an associated data type. The data type constrains how the object can be used, the keys that can be used to index it, and which types of peers can access it.
- Messages are routed recursively and the response is sent back in the reverse path that the request came. This is to avoid the overhead of creating new connections between the destination peer and the requesting peer, which incurs delay both because of the secure handshake and, in general, NAT traversal for either or both of the endpoints.

Peers can collect operational statistics and status for the parameters shown in Table 12.2. This information can be shared with other peers.

SUMMARY

At the beginning of this chapter we posed several questions that we recap now. How suitable is the overlay routing for meeting the real-time transport requirements for voice? Application-layer routing can pay a substantial performance penalty, so once the endpoint peer is contacted, direct network layer connections are made between endpoints, avoiding the overlay routing layer. However, peers may be behind NATs or may benefit from use of an application relay because of their distance from each other in the network.

How does churn in the overlay impact call reliability? Once the call is established, the peers connect directly except when using NAT traversal or media relays. In these latter cases, the impact of churn can be avoided but not fully eliminated without additional redundancy in the media transport. However, node lifetimes are longer for communication applications than for file-sharing applications.

How do VoIP signaling and transport elements such as proxies, media servers, gateways, and feature services map to the peer-to-peer architecture? Such mapping is an ongoing issue, so that existing VoP2P overlays have focused primarily on functions which are basic and can be easily distributed.

How do NATs effect connections? Due to their widespread use and the variety of NATs, P2P overlays particularly including VoP2P overlays need mechanisms to automate NAT traversal. These mechanisms involve some intermediate peer or server mediating the NAT traversal, and there are both proprietary solutions and open protocols such as ICE to perform this task.

FOR FURTHER READING

There are many resources for gaining an introduction to VoIP technology, one starting point is available online at the IEC Website.[436] The two most widely used VoIP protocols, SIP and H.323, are discussed in several books, including Seinreich and Johnston[415] and Kumar, Korpi, and Sengodan.[439] A proposal for integrating P2P technology with IMS is found in [440]. The issues caused by NATs in peer-to-peer communication and various techniques to solve them are described in [437] and [438]. The latest information on P2P-SIP can be found at the P2P-SIP Website.[441]

Mobility and Heterogeneity 13

Using mobile devices as peers in an overlay introduces the possibility of increased churn due to frequent roaming transitions that such devices experience. Possible solutions discussed in this chapter include using mobility support in the native layer, virtualizing such support in the overlay itself, or restricting the role of mobile devices as peers. In addition, mobile devices and other networked consumer electronics introduce a degree of resource heterogeneity into the peer population. Adaptability to heterogeneous peer conditions is the scope of another category of P2P overlays called *variable-hop overlays*, which are discussed here. As mobile ad hoc networks (MANETs) and sensor networks proliferate, there is likely to be significant value in integrating such networks into P2P overlays; proposals for doing so are discussed at the end of the chapter.

IMPACT OF MOBILE DEVICES ON P2P OVERLAYS

Increasingly portable electronic devices are providing functionality previously restricted to desktop computers. Such devices can connect to the Internet using broadband wireless network interfaces. Local storage and compute capacity are sufficient for storing and playing high-quality audio and movie files. Due to their low cost, such devices are growing in popularity and may at some time become the dominant mode by which users reach the Internet. Consequently, such mobile devices will have an important role in future P2P overlays.

Mobile devices have four important characteristics that differentiate them from desktop computers and that affect their interaction with the overlay. First, due to their mobility, a device may move from one access network to another, a behavior referred to as *roaming*. When a device roams, its IP address will change. After its IP address changes, it can still connect to the Internet, but depending on how the transition from the old IP address to the new IP address is managed, networked applications that were running prior to the roaming transition may be interrupted. P2P overlays are one type of such application. In addition, any peers that were neighbors of the roaming peer may now have the wrong network address for the roaming peer. Thus roaming peers can cause the same kind of churn behavior that was discussed in Chapter 5 but as a result of roaming transitions instead of nodes leaving the overlay. Since roaming transitions can happen frequently, the churn rate can increase for the overlay due to the presence of mobile peers.

The second characteristic is *node heterogeneity*, which refers to the variation in network capacity and compute resources available across the set of nodes in the overlay. The overlay design can address heterogeneity by distinguishing between more capable and less capable nodes, such as superpeers and regular peers. It can also adapt the overlay maintenance algorithm so that, depending on the available bandwidth, nodes with more bandwidth can maintain more routing state. This approach, called a *variable-hop overlay*, differs from most overlay algorithms in which maintenance traffic is the same for all nodes.

The third characteristic is the need to preserve energy[445] in mobile devices. Power consumption by personal computers and consumer electronics devices is an economic and energy conservation issue, accounting for an estimated 2% of energy use in the United States.[446] Power management involves a combination of techniques, including network adapters that can trigger power resume of the host while offloading certain network activity and network protocols that reduce power consumption. In current overlay design, a mobile peer that goes into power-saving mode would be treated as a node that has left the overlay.

The final characteristic is that future portable devices will most likely be *multihomed*, that is, a device supports multiple network interfaces such as IEEE 802.11, WiMax, and UWB. These networks differ in range and bandwidth capacity. A roaming device might not only be changing its IP address during roaming but also switching to a different type of access network. Changing the access network could change the available network bandwidth. The available network bandwidth affects the ability of a node to act as a superpeer or relay. It also affects the capacity of the parent nodes in *Application Layer Multicast* (ALM) trees and in streaming applications. Further, there is tradeoff between peer routing state and overlay diameter, as discussed in Chapter 2. In general, excess bandwidth capacity can be used for improving overlay maintenance, potentially improving performance.

P2P OVERLAY ISSUES CAUSED BY MOBILITY
Roaming and Node Lifetime

Several issues caused by the mobility of the peers in the overlay affect overlay performance. These issues lead to higher churn rates compared to desktop peers, which means either higher bandwidth usage for structured overlay maintenance or increased hop counts for overlay operations. These issues affect the average node lifetime and changes to the native address associated with a peer:

- Energy limitations, device usage patterns, and network connection costs can all shorten the node lifetime.
- Roaming scenarios cause native layer address changes, which are effectively leave-join sequences.

In this chapter we use *mobile peer* to represent a peer that has active roaming behavior and limited node lifetime compared to a peer running on a desktop computer with a wired network connection.

Assuming that a device moves through an access network, we illustrate the transition rates for driving and walking movement in Table 13.1. In most cases, these transition rates exceed the churn rates reported in existing P2P file-sharing systems. High churn rates mean that more overlay maintenance overhead is needed to stabilize the overlay.

In addition, variation in the available bandwidth affects the rate at which a mobile peer can send and receive packets to maintain and use the overlay. Wired networks encounter bandwidth variation due to network congestion. In addition, wireless networks face bandwidth variation due to a variety of media-related factors. These include signal-strength issues such as the distance between the device and the access point, obstacles in the transmission path, and signal reflections. Depending on the media access protocol, there may also be capacity loss due to competition for the media with other devices sharing the network.

For example, Figure 13.1 illustrates throughput variation within a single access network according to the distance of the device from the access point. As a device's distance from an access point increases, the available throughput capacity decreases. Thus, even if a device doesn't roam to a different network, its position and other factors mean that significant variation in the node's capacity could occur.

Table 13.1 Example Transition Rates for Device Movement Across Various Access Networks

Access Network	WiMax	802.11n	UWB
Range	5 km	50 m	10 m
Driving at 20 km/hour	4 transitions/hour	400 transitions/hour = 6.7 transitions/min	2000 transitions/hour or 0.55 transitions/sec
Walking at 1 km/hour	0.2 transitions/hour	20 transitions/hour	100 transitions/hour

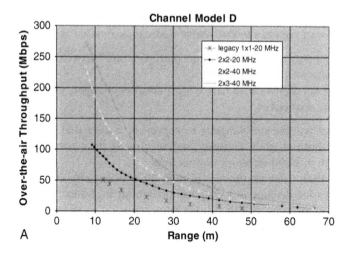

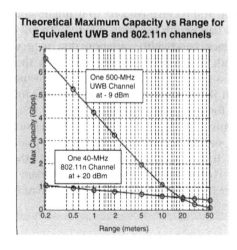

FIGURE 13.1 Throughput versus range for (A) 802.11n,[466] used by permission and (B) UWB.[467]

Growing Mobile Peer Frequency

Most studies of mobility in P2P overlays assume that the peer population consists primarily of nonmobile nodes. Trends in consumer electronics and cell phone usage suggest that in the future the majority of Internet-connected devices could be operating on mobile nodes. If a large percentage of peers are mobile, overlay-based techniques that accommodate mobility using the resources of stationary peers may degrade in performance.

A study of *mobility churn*[447] shows the effects of increasing numbers of mobile peers in an overlay. Stationary peers in the simulated overlay are given infinite lifetime and do not contribute to churn, thus allowing the identification of delay and bandwidth induced due to node mobility. When the number of mobile peers is small, an overlay with conventional failure detection and recovery algorithms experiences fewer lookup timeouts and routing latency is not as impacted. In addition, maintenance requires fewer messages to detect and correct the changed state of mobile peers. As the population of the mobile peers in the overlay increases to a substantial proportion, timeouts due to lookups increase substantially, and the amount of maintenance traffic needed to stabilize the overlay also grows.

To shield the overlay from native address changes as much as possible, messages to a mobile peer can be routed via an intermediate agent with a fixed network address. When the address of the mobile peer changes, the intermediate agent is notified. However, the change is invisible to other peers in the overlay. This indirection can be done either at the native layer, via Mobile IP, or at the overlay. Mobile IP is a native layer protocol that has been developed to mitigate the impact of network address changes on applications. In Mobile IP, a mobile node can use a *home address* (HoA) as its intermediate point for message and connection routing. In the overlay, a mobile node uses its HoA instead of its mobile address. Then when the mobile node roams, only the home agent sees the address change. If Mobile IP is not available, an alternative is to designate a stationary and stable peer in the overlay as a virtual home agent.

To compensate for an increasing number of mobile peers in the overlay, a P2P overlay operator could provide superpeers to act as home peers for mobile peers.

MITIGATING MOBILITY CHURN

In a typical structured overlay, a mobile peer migrating between mobile networks has to rejoin the overlay due to the invalidation of both its own state about other peers and their state about it. Following [447], we refer to this churn due to roaming mobile devices as *mobility churn*. The effects of mobility churn include more traffic in the structured overlay due to increased overlay maintenance, degradation of overlay routing efficiency, and an increase in average lookup latency. As the number of mobile peers grows, many structured overlays may simply break down under such high levels of churn.[448,449] Consequently, techniques to mitigate the impact of mobility churn on the performance of the overlay are needed.

Mobile IP Support

When a mobile peer moves, it may receive a new network address on connection to a new network access point. The peer then informs its neighboring peers of its address change, which leads to routing table updates at those peers and potential propagation of the new information to other peers in the overlay. As discussed earlier, the mobile peer may use an available Mobile IP infrastructure to use its HoA IP address[451] in the overlay. A drawback of using HoA is that it makes topology and proximity information for a mobile peer and its neighboring peers incorrect, since the mobile peer could be quite far from the HoA location.

A peer is assumed to have no prior knowledge of its mobility behavior and therefore cannot inform other peers of any predictions of its mobility pattern. Mobile IP infrastructure consists of home and foreign agents that may introduce critical points of failure and performance bottlenecks. Therefore, configuring and managing the mobile IP support requires additional administrative support. In addition, Mobile IP as a network layer protocol cannot exploit the semantics of the applications. It also needs the assistance of a reliable home agent to resolve the validity of the network address of mobile nodes. The use of any indirection increases latency in the overlay.

There are several proposals for fast handoff mechanisms in roaming transitions in Mobile IP. However, the network layer delay is a small part of the overlay maintenance time in propagating a new native address for a peer in the overlay (Figure 13.2).

Stealth Nodes

The use of stealth nodes[450] is a strategy in which mobile peers are used only as clients of the overlay. The structured overlay has two distinct sets of nodes: *stealth nodes,* which do not route data or store keys and are transparent to all routing operations, and *service nodes,* which execute all overlay operations supported by a generic DHT. The selection of a peer as a service node depends on stability of its network connection and its peer capacity.

Stealth nodes use a lightweight join mechanism and do not participate in sending join announcement messages, which keeps them from appearing in service nodes' routing tables. When a stealth node joins or leaves the network, no updates to the routing state are required. The stealth nodes also do not receive routing table updates. Over time, a stealth node's routing table becomes stale. To solve this problem, a stealth node may periodically obtain additional state from service nodes in the overlay, in either an active or passive manner.

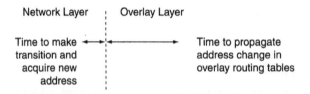

FIGURE 13.2 Fast network handoff vs. overlay maintenance.

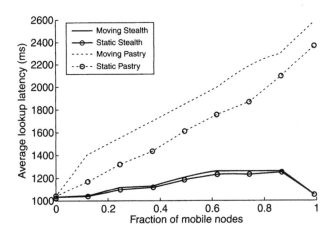

FIGURE 13.3 Comparison of the average lookup latency[450] © 2006 IEEE.

Figure 13.3 shows the impact of mobility as the percentage of mobile peers increases in the overlay, using the Pastry structured overlay for comparison. Pastry is a multihop overlay and is described in Chapters 4 and 5. In this graph, average lookup latency is the average time elapsed from when a node sends a get request to when the response is received. The measurement of average lookup latency is made for when the overlay treats the mobile nodes as stealth nodes (labeled *stealth*) as well as when mobile nodes are included as regular peers (labeled *Pastry*). For each case, there are two subcases, labeled *static* and *moving*.

The static and moving stealth nodes have similar end-to-end performance, which confirms that the use of the stealth node role maintains efficient overlay performance over a large range of the number of mobile nodes in the overlay. The simulation model used in Figure 13.3 assumes that the mobile node's access links have high delay (about 200 ms) compared to conventional access networks. By incorporating mobile nodes into the overlay routing mechanism, the latency is increased. Thus, in this simulation Pastry's average latency without stealth nodes is larger than Pastry with stealth nodes. Stealth nodes hide the impact of mobility churn and also can reduce the impact of high-latency access links for mobile nodes.

Bristle

Bristle[452] routes to a mobile node using a stationary node, the address of which is closest in the overlay address space, to shield the overlay from mobile churn. Bristle is based on the Tornado overlay[453] and consists of *stationary* and *mobile* nodes. A stationary node stores the current IP address of those mobile nodes for which the overlay addresses are close to that of the stationary node. Each stationary node maintains a location information repository for its set of mobile nodes.

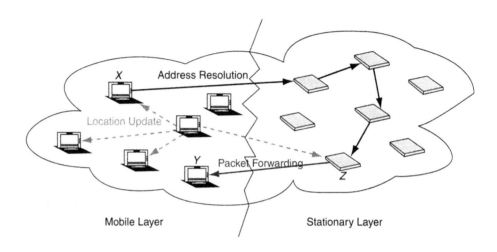

FIGURE 13.4 Bristle architecture[452] © 2003 IEEE.

Figure 13.4 depicts the Bristle architecture, which separates the stationary and mobile peers into separate structured overlays that share some number of stationary nodes. These shared stationary nodes are used to forward routing requests between the two overlays. For example, say that node X is forwarding a message to node Y, and node X does not have the current IP address of node Y. To resolve node Y's address, node X sends the request to its associated peer in the stationary overlay. The request is routed in the stationary overlay to a node Z, where Z's overlay address is closest to node Y's overlay address. Z then forwards the request to mobile node Y.

In addition, mobile nodes in Bristle maintain connections to small sets of other mobile nodes of interest, using a location update tree. When a mobile node changes its IP address, it forwards the update to other members of the location update tree.

Warp

Warp[454] addresses mobility transitions both for individual mobile peers and for crowds of mobile peers, such as might occur when a group of mobile peers on a passenger train change networks at the same time. The transition of a mobile crowd creates a burst of address changes. Warp allows a group of collocated mobile peers to share a single overlay state update rather than having each mobile peer separately perform the update.

As in Bristle, a mobile node in Warp is not part of the overlay. Instead it stores its location in the DHT via a proxy node in the overlay, which performs the insertion using the node's mobile name as the key. This is referred to as *type indirection* in Warp. Figure 13.5 illustrates the registration step using the Tapestry structured overlay, which is discussed in Chapters 4 and 5. The mobile node (MN) first registers its address information via the proxy node (P), which in turn inserts it along the path to the root node (R), per the Tapestry insertion algorithm.

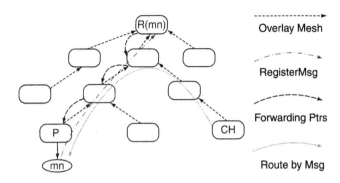

FIGURE 13.5 Warp communication with mobile nodes[454] © 2004 Springer-Verlag, with kind permission of Springer Science and Business Media.

The mobile node's unique name is used to choose the members of a virtual hierarchy of indirection nodes; these nodes in the overlay act as foreign agents for the mobile nodes to support fast handover operations. The mobile crowds can redirect traffic through a single indirection point and aggregate handoffs as a single entity. Later, a peer that wants to send a message to MN, called the *correspondent host* (CH), uses the hash of the mobile node's name as the key. This message is routed indirectly to MN using the previously stored values for MN's location information, implementing the type indirection.

When mobile nodes move in Warp, proxy handover messages modify the forwarding path between proxies. Similar to Mobile IP discovery techniques, mobile nodes listen for periodic broadcasts from nearby proxies

Figure 13.6 summarizes the two types of mobility achieved by type indirection. The type indirection for a group of mobile nodes reduces handoff messages

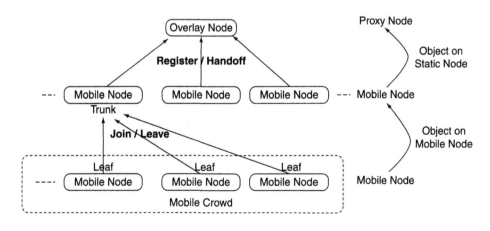

FIGURE 13.6 A summary of levels of type indirection[454] © 2004 Springer-Verlag, with kind permission of Springer Science and Business Media.

from one message per node to one message per mobile crowd with a unique crowd identifier. Using the crowd identifier, any mobile trunk registers with the proxy. When the trunk changes its position, it uses the same mechanism used by mobile nodes. This allows the group of mobile nodes to relocate to a different proxy in one step. In addition, for a corresponding host to address a mobile node in a mobile crowd, it must be able to resolve the mobile node's identifier to the crowd identifier and in turn to the associated mobile node, which proxies the crowd. In addition, each mobile node uses a join/leave mechanism to attach to and detach from the crowd.

MULTIHOMED PEERS

Improvements in wireless networking and technologies such as cognitive radio mean that it is practical to package multiple network interfaces in a mobile device. The currently emerging wireless technologies important for mobile devices are WiMax, 802.11n, Ultra Wide Band (UWB), and 3G/4G. These have different ranges versus throughput characteristics (Figure 13.7).

For example, consider a device that connects to both WiMax and 802.11n networks simultaneously. As a result, it has two IP addresses and could be connected to a P2P overlay with both IP addresses. In this case, WiMax offers a larger range but a smaller peak data rate than the 802.11n network. For example, the multihomed peer can register in the overlay using its WiMax IP address and provide its 802.11n IP address as a secondary alternative path.

The availability of both addresses provides redundancy and potential performance advantages. For example, a mobility transition on a single interface is less

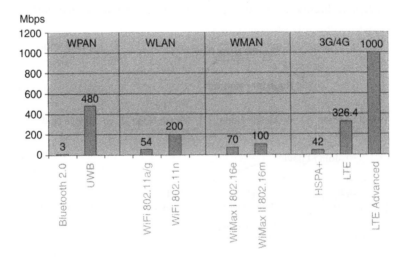

FIGURE 13.7 Throughput versus wireless network technology.

likely to lead to a leave/join sequence since the device will still be connected on the other network interface. Redundancy can be used in several ways. Packets that aren't acknowledged on the primary path can be resent on a wide area interface. Alternately, packets can be sent simultaneously on all available interfaces.

VARIABLE-HOP OVERLAYS
Overview

The concept of a *variable-hop overlay* is anticipated in the evaluation of multihop structured overlays performed in [455] and discussed in Chapter 4. Important insights developed in this work include the ability of a protocol to adapt its bandwidth utilization through changing configuration parameters and the trade-off between overlay latency and routing state evidenced in multihop versus one-hop overlays.

In a variable-hop overlay, the key to efficiently using additional bandwidth under overlay churn is for the protocol to adjust its routing table size. A peer limits its routing table size and its update message level based on its available bandwidth. The routing table stabilization can be replaced with opportunistic learning through normal overlay lookup traffic. That is, as in EpiChord, peers can use lookup traffic to improve their routing table accuracy for certain regions of the overlay address space and can also transmit maintenance information with lookup requests. During the periods where the nodes have low bandwidth capabilities, overlay routing performance may reach that of multihop overlays, whereas for higher bandwidth, routing performance reaches one hop.

Each peer has a bandwidth budget that is allocated to routing table maintenance. A higher bandwidth budget means that more routing table updates can be exchanged, thus leading to higher routing table accuracy. Each peer manages its bandwidth budget independently. This requires that the peer be able to determine its overall bandwidth capacity (both inbound and outbound) and measure bandwidth utilization.

By explicitly accounting for the network bandwidth that each peer consumes, lookup latency performance can be better adapted for devices with heterogeneous resources and access network capacity. Additional goals of variable hop overlay design are to accommodate low-bandwidth nodes while minimizing the impact on high-bandwidth nodes.

Accordion

Accordion[456] is a variable-hop overlay that uses consistent hashing in a circular identifier space to assign keys to nodes. A primary goal of Accordion is to adapt the routing table size to achieve the lowest latency, depending on bandwidth budget and churn. Accordion provides a single bandwidth budget as a parameter to adapt during the operation of a peer. Latency depends on both the average number of timeouts incurred during a lookup and the average number of hops in that lookup. There are two processes that help Accordion maintain its best routing table size in terms of the overlay churn rate and given bandwidth budget:

- The state acquisition process involves the learning of new neighbors.
- The state eviction process removes stale routing table entries depending on the churn rate.

Unlike Kademlia and EpiChord, Accordion uses recursive parallel lookups to maintain fresh routing table entries in its neighborhood of the overlay and reduce the probability of timeouts. A peer gathers routing table entries during recursive parallel lookups. The peer requesting the lookup selects destinations based on the key as well as gaps in its routing table. Responses to forwarded lookups contain entries for these routing tables' gaps. Note that the recursive parallel lookups create more load on the target peer than iterative parallel lookups, since the target node receives p messages for each request. Excess bandwidth is used for parallel exploratory lookups to obtain routing table entries for the largest scaled gaps in the peer's routing table. The degree of parallelism is dynamically adjusted based on level of lookup traffic and bandwidth budget, up to some maximum value based on the maximum burst size of the parallelism window.

Accordion's parallel lookup protocol improves lookup latency, since one lookup can proceed while other lookups wait in timeout. Each response to a lookup contains routing table information from the responding peer, which generally has more accurate information about its portion of the overlay address space than does the requesting peer. This routing table information may contain the identity of new nodes the requesting peer does not have in its own routing table. By issuing parallel lookup requests, the peer can simultaneously explore regions of the overlay for which its own table is sparse and obtain the needed application data. As shown in Figure 13.8, Accordion's average lookup latency matches or improves on OneHop[457] when bandwidth is in abundance. The results are generated from a 3000-node overlay network with an extensive churn workload. Each point in the figure represents a certain combination of parameter settings for the protocol.

Using the same simulated 3000-node overlay network, Figure 13.9 compares the adaptability of Accordion, Chord, and OneHop in terms of various levels of overlay churn, where a lower node lifetime means higher churn. The results are generated by setting Accordion's bandwidth budget constant at 24 bytes per second per node, whereas Chord and OneHop consume at fixed 17 and 23 bytes per second, respectively, that minimize lookup latency, for a median node lifetime of one hour. The average lookup latency of Chord and OneHop increases during high node churn rate due to large number of lookup timeouts. Accordion's average lookup latency decreases slightly and is lower than both Chord and OneHop when the network becomes more stable.

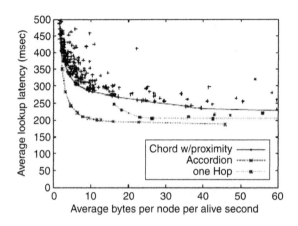

FIGURE 13.8 Average lookup latency performance versus bandwidth: Accordion, Chord, and OneHop[456] © 2005 J. Li, J. Stribling, R. Morris and M. F. Kaashoek, used by permission.

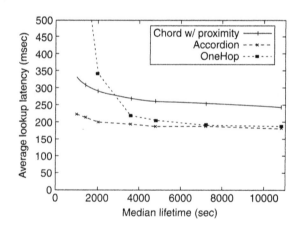

FIGURE 13.9 Average lookup latency versus median node lifetime for three structured overlays[456] © 2005 J. Li, J. Stribling, R. Morris and M. F. Kaashoek, used by permission.

P2P AND MANETS

Overview

A *mobile ad hoc network* (MANET) is a collection of mobile nodes that act as both routers and hosts in an ad hoc wireless network and that dynamically self-organize in a wireless network without using any pre-established infrastructure.

Nodes typically transmit in broadcast messages that reach only nearby nodes. Since routers may move randomly, the topology may change rapidly and in unpredictable ways. Energy efficiency is also an important criterion for MANET routing protocols. Like P2P overlays, MANETs are self-configuring. Uses of MANETs include sensor networks and vehicular ad hoc networks (VANETs).

MANET applications are typically peer-to-peer and are reflected in application-driven protocol behavior and networking operation.[458] The benefits of P2P overlay networking in a MANET include:

- Extending the MANET routing layer to support more sophisticated mobile applications and services
- Adding higher-layer mechanisms to address the unpredictability of the radio channel and challenges caused by node mobility

In addition, since MANETs may be connected to infrastructure-based networks and the Internet, supporting a P2P overlay on a MANET can be used to provide end-to-end interoperability for search and data movement between nodes in the MANET and peers in the Internet.

However, the underlying design assumptions for most P2P overlays are quite dissimilar from the routing architectures developed for MANETs. MANETs are characterized by low-bandwidth, higher-error rates of the wireless medium and low computation power of each node. Energy preservation is also an important consideration in the protocol design.

Node mobility and the continually changing network topology pose challenges to scalability and the design of a structured overlay for MANETs. A key design strategy is to keep the MANET routing and transport protocols simple and to complement them where possible with upper-layer functions via a P2P overlays. If the MANET is small, flooding and broadcast can be used as an alternative to the usual DHT overlay routing.

Mobile Hash Table

Since the assumptions of the underlying network used in most P2P overlays are quite dissimilar to MANETs, one approach is to adapt the overlay design to the underlying MANET routing algorithm rather than apply an existing structured overlay algorithm to a MANET. An example of this approach is the *mobile hash table* (MHT).[459] MHT maps data onto mobile nodes by storing the data on the node that moves along the most similar path to that associated with the data item. The path of each data item is constructed as a loop and is derived from its key. The location of a data item at any point in time can be calculated. To query for a data item, a MHT node first calculates the data item's location and then routes the query to that position in the MANET.

A path consists of two points, and the x–y coordinates of these two points are derived from the key. Using node information such as location, direction, and speed, the node carrying a data item is determined. The larger the number of nodes in the overlay environment, the higher the probability that a node with the path and speed similar to the path of the data item exists. So, as the number of nodes increases, better matches can be achieved. Further, the data needs to be moved between the associated nodes less frequently.

Routing in MHT is built on top of Greedy Perimeter Stateless Routing (GPSR).[460] In GPSR, each node knows the location of its neighbors to one-hop distance through periodic exchange of announcements. Each announcement consists of the node's current speed and the direction of the node in which it is moving. MHT nodes cache these announcements and use the information to find a node that has the location, speed, and direction similar to the path of a data item of interest. All the nodes frequently announce their locations, directions, and speeds to their neighbors but with no explicit communication required.

In MHT, a joining node starts the normal local broadcast of its location, speed, and direction. The neighboring nodes acknowledge its existence and consider this new node for routing and storage. To leave the system, the departing node stops sending regular local broadcasts. In turn, the neighboring nodes stop using the departing node for routing and storage. The neighboring nodes' routing tables stay consistent after the departure of the leaving node and all updates are based on local knowledge. So, no repair algorithm is necessary compared to conventional maintenance algorithms such as Chord, which requires fixing the finger tables. Data stored on the leaving node could be lost. To avoid this, a leaving node announces its departure to its neighbors. This removes the leaving node from being considered for routing and storage. The departing node forwards all pending data messages to the next hop and stores all data on the current best-matching peer.

Figure 13.10 shows a typical data placement in the MHT. Data item d is stored on a node n_d, which is moved to another node n_{next}. Let r be the communication range of a node. The data item d should be stored on a node n_d, which is not further away than $r/2$ from the data item's position p_d. This is determined by the key that describes the data item d. As long as the data item d is stored not further away from its position of $r/2$, for instance, a node n_d in Figure 13.10, another node

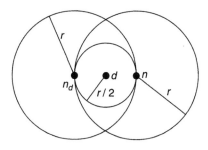

FIGURE 13.10 Example data placement in MHT[459] © 2006 IEEE.

can reach it when it comes within *r/2* range of the data *d*. The current speed and direction of data and nodes predict future locations. It may be temporarily not reachable when this node is farther away than *r/2* from the data item's position. This is evaluated by the node that determines in which node to store the data item.

MADPastry

MADPastry[461,474,476] is an adaptation of the Pastry structured overlay to MANETs using *ad hoc on-demand distance vector* (AODV) routing. MADPastry uses a small set of the mobile nodes to subdivide the overlay address space. These nodes are called *landmark* nodes. Landmark nodes self-select by comparing their identifier values against the predefined set of landmark keys. The node numerically closest to a landmark serves as a landmark node.

Nodes in the vicinity of a landmark node use the prefix of that landmark node's address to select their own address. Nodes with a common prefix form a spatial cluster in the mobile space. Figure 13.11 shows an example of spatial clustering in which different icon types represent different prefixes in the region.

Like Pastry, MADPastry uses prefix routing and organizes its routing table to easily match prefixes of different lengths. In addition, both use leaf sets to route to peers with the same prefix. MADPastry uses its clustering organization to support key-based routing in two steps. In the first step, assuming that the destination is in a different cluster from the source peer, the message is routed toward the landmark matching the initial prefix. After the message reaches the cluster

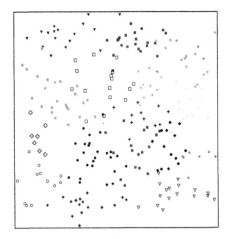

FIGURE 13.11 Spatial distribution of node address prefixes using random landmark clustering in MADPastry. Reprinted from [461], © 2008, with permission from Elsevier.

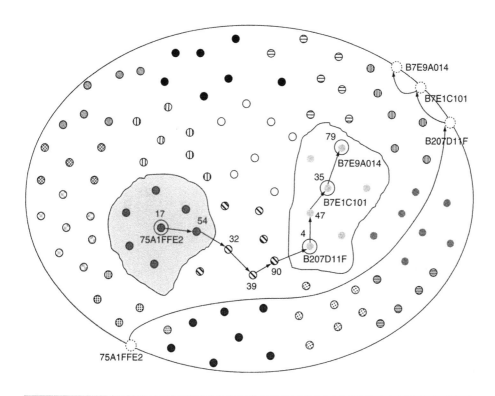

FIGURE 13.12 Routing from overlay and MANET perspectives in MADPastry. Reprinted from [461], © 2008, with permission from Elsevier.

corresponding to that landmark, nodes in the destination cluster use their leaf set entries to forward the message to the destination.

This two-step routing model is illustrated in Figure 13.12, where a message from node 17 with overlay address 75A1FFE2 is sent to node 79 with overlay address B7E9A014. The message makes three overlay hops, from nodes 17 to 4, 35, and 79. Each overlay hop is one or more MANET hops. For example, overlay hop from node 17 to 4 takes MANET hops from node 17 to 54, 43, 39, 90, and 4.

Other P2P MANET Designs

A large number of designs have been proposed for implementing P2P overlays in MANETs. Table 13.2 summarizes the key features of a number of proposals. The MANET routing algorithms used in these systems include Dynamic Source Routing (DSR), Optimized Link State Routing (OLSR), AODV, and Simple Multicast and Broadcast (SMB).

Table 13.2 Summary of P2P Overlay Designs

System	MANET Routing Algorithm	P2P Overlay	Lookups	Evaluation Size (Nodes)	Node Speed (m/s) and Range
MHT[575]	GPSR	None	Key maps to node's path	1000 to 100,000	10–15 m/s 2000×2000 m^2
Ekta[590]	DSR	Pastry	Prefix key-based	50	1–19 m/s 1500×300 m^2
MPP[586]	Extended DSR	Gnutella	Flooding	50…200	0–5 m/s $\leq 2000 \times 2000$ m^2
XL-Gnutella[594]	OLSR	Gnutella	Flooding with superpeers	50	≤ 15 m/s not stated
MADPastry[577,595,597]	AODV	Pastry	Prefix key-based with clustering around landmarks	100 and 250	1.4 m/s 1000×1000 m^2
FastTrack over AODV[596]	AODV	FastTrack	Flooding with superpeers	50	0–20 m/s 1500×320 m^2
ORION[588]	Neutral, AODV and SMB	Unstructured	Flooding	40	0 to 2 m/s 1000×1000 m^2
ISPRP[585]	DSR	Chord	Key-based	1000	NA
Dynamic P2P Source Routing[598]	DSR	Pastry	DP2PSR	800	9–19 m/s NA

SUMMARY

This chapter discusses the mobility and heterogeneity of mobile nodes in P2P overlay networks. Mobility of peers in an overlay induces increased churn, and node lifetime can also be reduced due to other characteristics of mobile devices, such as energy limitations and device usage patterns. Several proposals to mitigate mobility churn caused by mobile nodes use routing indirection or keep the mobile peer outside the overlay routing mechanism. Routing indirection mechanisms include use of Mobile IP, a native layer solution, or using stationary peers in the overlay to proxy routing to mobile peers. In addition, multihoming may become an important feature of mobile peers in the future.

There are some similarities between P2P networking and MANETs, leading to proposals to design P2P overlays for MANETs. MHT and MADPastry are described and other designs are summarized.

FOR FURTHER READING

Several proposals for the future of the Internet use overlays that are tied into the network infrastructure and that support network services that include mobility, including SpovNet[462] and Service-Aware Transport Overlay (SATO).[408] In addition, the IETF Host Identity Protocol (HIP) WG[464] is designing HIP-Bone, which provides an overlay using HIP addressing. HIP-Bone is intended to leverage HIP features and includes mobility transparency. Global Environment for Network Innovations (GENI) is using overlays for testing future Internet architectures and may consider them as deployment tools as well.[463]

Zahn and Schiller[461] analyze the design requirements for P2P structured overlays in MANETs and propose a design to enable porting and direct deployment of structured overlays in MANETs. Bisignano et al.[465] review recent cross-layer design approaches to synergistically integrate a P2P-MANET system.

Security

14

Security is a fundamental issue for P2P overlays because peers reside in different domains without enforcement of mutual trust. In addition, existing mechanisms for enabling trust use server infrastructure, whereas P2P overlays seek a distributed mechanism. In addition to conventional security issues, P2P overlays have some specific security risks, including large-scale impersonation attacks, use as a distributed DOS platform, and file pollution. This chapter surveys and classifies the security issues and presents techniques for addressing them. The chapter concludes with case studies on security in Groove, a P2P groupware application, and pollution in P2P file-sharing systems.

INTRODUCTION

Security is an essential requirement and an important component of any communication and computing system. This is certainly true for a peer-to-peer system. In fact, security in P2P is an issue of particularly concern to many. With Napster's debut in 1999, P2P file sharing became immensely popular. The public's concern with information security has also increased tremendously in the past eight years. Web searches on keywords such as: *P2P security news*, *P2P security concerns*, and *P2P security story*; all return long lists of results with many news headlines. Interested readers can refer to Tiversa's Website[444] for some "P2P security incidents."

Many users wonder, "Am I leaking some private, especially financial, information when I use a P2P system?" Recent studies[478,479,480] focusing on information leakage and inadvertent disclosures through P2P file-sharing networks found a surprising number of threats to both corporate and individual security, including a large number of searches targeted to uncover sensitive documents and data. In their study,[478] P2P searches and files on three P2P networks Gnutella, Fast-Track, and eDonkey over a seven-week period (December 27, 2005, through February 13, 2006) were categorized. Sixteen thousand searches out of an estimated 800 million searches were found to be related to banking institutes.

319

Out of the 16,000 searches, 7,194 were found to be medium and high risk, where searches are directed for specific documents or data, such as account user information, passwords, and routing and personal identification numbers (PINs). These kinds of searches could fuel malicious activity and represent clear threats. For example, *USA Today*[482] reported a case of ID theft by file sharing. The offender reportedly used Limewire's file-sharing program to troll other people's computers for financial information, which he used to open credit cards for an online shopping spree. At least 83 victims were identified, "Most of whom have teenage children and did not know the file-sharing software was on their computer." It also pointed out the possibility of the number of people affected in the order of hundreds and the total amount lost in the order of hundreds of thousands of dollars.

"We believe that P2P file-sharing networks represent a significant and poorly understood threat to business, government, and individuals. Given the nature of the threat, we would argue that many individuals may be experiencing identity theft and fraud without ever knowing the source of their misfortune. Furthermore, we see many of the current P2P trends increasing the problem. We urge both corporate executives and government officials to educate themselves and their constituencies to the risks these networks represent," an author of these studies concluded in testimony before the Committee on Oversight and Government Reform of the United States House of Representatives.[481]

File sharing is just one of many types of applications of P2P networks. The increasing popularity of P2P applications, including P2P file sharing, P2P media streaming, P2PTV, and P2P gaming, could potentially instigate security risks that are more serious than those found in [479] and beyond the much discussed content security and copyright issues.[483] It could open up opportunities for cyber criminals to trawl the P2P network and steal or gather confidential information, to damage documents, content, or even devices, and to poison the network for criminal intents. It is believed that much of these vulnerabilities are rooted in the autonomous and decentralized nature of P2P systems and the relatively limited use of security techniques in existing P2P applications. In the following sections, we look at the security threats of P2P systems, discuss several existing solutions, and address some challenges in the P2P security domain.

SECURITY RISKS AND ATTACKS
Classifications of Attacks

Attacks on P2P systems can be classified based on various criteria. Some common criteria include functional target, communication mechanism, propagation mechanism, effect on victims, and impact. Figure 14.1 lists four types of classifications. Here, as examples, we look at three of those (Figures 14.1A, 14.1B, and 14.1C) in more detail.

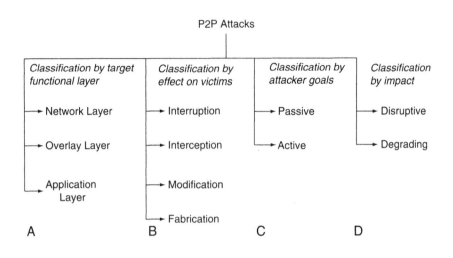

FIGURE 14.1 Classification of attacks on P2P systems.

Classification by Target Functional Layer

Attacks on P2P systems can be targeted on different layers (see Figure 14.2), including the overlay network layer and the application layer. Application layer security largely depends on the guarantees provided at the overlay network layer, whereas security at the overlay layer relies on the assurance offered at the network layers.

Security breaches that take place on the application layer assume direct user-to-network interaction through application interfaces. Although file sharing has been the most discussed application for security concerns in P2P networks, risks and threats do exist in regard to other P2P applications as well. P2P file storage systems and P2P media streaming, for example, are concerned with information leakage and copyright protection as well.

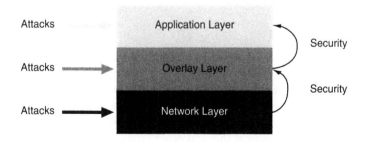

FIGURE 14.2 Attacks and security in a P2P network.

At the overlay layer, attacks target overlay layer operation primitives to alter or impair P2P communication. In structured P2P overlays, a major threat is malicious routing, whereby attackers exploit the vulnerability of the DHT routing mechanism, since peers rely on each other's routing table to function properly. This can be the weakest point of the overlay. When some or a substantial number of routing tables in the P2P overlay are compromised, the functionality of any P2P application that is built on top of the overlay may be degraded or even disrupted.

At the network layer, P2P overlay protocols are susceptible to existing conventional attacks that affect many other networked applications. These attacks include interception of packets, manipulation of packet contents, and mis-routing of packets.

Classification by Effect on Victims

As in conventional networked applications, the overlay messaging is also susceptible to four classes of attack:[484]

- *Interruption.* Unauthorized disruption.
- *Interception.* Unauthorized access.
- *Modification.* Unauthorized tampering.
- *Fabrication.* Unauthorized creation.

These attacks can be passive or active. Through exchange of information with other peers as well as through embedding attack mechanisms in the peer application software itself, a peer may easily be exposed to viruses, worms, Trojan horses, adware, or spyware. Intrusion, eavesdropping, espionage, sniffing, substitution or insertion, jamming, overload, spoofing, sabotage, spamming, reverse engineering, cryptanalysis, theft, scavenging, and denial of service are just some of the many forms of attack existing today.

Classification by Attacker Goals

Goals of attacks in a P2P overlay, besides *active* intent such as theft of data, theft of resources, tampering with devices and networks, and disruption of services, also include *passive* intent such as traffic analysis and signal analysis.

The P2P Security Gap

One unique characteristic of some P2P aggravated attacks is the collective use of resources to achieve malicious means. For example, a conspiracy of nodes may act in concert to attack a victim peer. A malicious peer may exploit a large amount of resources over the P2P network and use that to attack the victim. A Sybil attack,[485] forging of multiple identities for malicious intent, is representative of the type. To fight against this and other types of attack, some conventional solutions may be adopted in semidecentralized P2P systems. However, in a fully decentralized P2P system, decentralized security administration is expected.

Using a Sybil attack as an example, in the absence of an identification author-ity, a local peer's ability to discriminate among distinct remote peers depends on the assumption that an attacker's resources are limited. Peers have to issue resource-demanding challenges to validate identities, and peers must collectively pool the identities they have separately validated. To achieve these goals, it is required[485] that (1) all peers operate under nearly identical resource constraints; (2) all presented identities are validated simultaneously by all peers, coordinated across the system; and (3) when accepting identities that are not directly validated, the required number of vouchers exceeds the number of systemwide failures. These goals, however, are very difficult to achieve in a large-scale P2P sys-tem. That is, today decentralized security mechanisms are not in full place, whereas traditional network manager server-based security schemes do not offer suitable means for fully decentralized P2P network protection. This P2P security gap amplifies the risks and hinders the application of P2P networks.

One security problem that is of significant concern in many organizations is shown in Figure 14.3. To share data, files, or resources on your device and system and to access data and files or utilize resources on other peer devices within a P2P network, you may have to open a specific TCP port through the firewall (see Figure 14.3) for the peers to communicate. This TCP port becomes an "opportunity" for malicious attacks and increases the risk of malicious traffic at the peers.

Sample Attacks and Threats

Theft is an example of an interception attack. Theft attacks can be targeted at the network, overlay, or application layer with a simple goal of stealing confiden-tial information from others. Theft is the major attack discovered in studies of file sharing system security,[479,480,481] in which adversaries took advantage of information leakage and inadvertent disclosures to access confidential information.

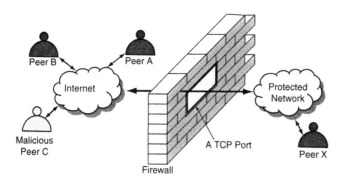

FIGURE 14.3 A security gap in a P2P system.

Wrapster,[486] a free utility software initially designed for Napster users, was released in 2000. It can be used as a tool to enable information leakage in P2P file sharing systems. Wrapster is used to transform any file, such as a program, video, or text, into a file in MP3 format to disguise it. An individual then shares the transformed file as an MP3 file using a P2P file sharing system. A receiving peer uses Wrapster to convert the file to its original format. Thus, using Wrapster together with file sharing software on the company's network, a malicious insider could covertly bypass the company security mechanisms and policies, and leak confidential information to anyone participating in the P2P file sharing system.

The most well-known attack is illegal copy and distribution of multimedia content and software. Copyright protection has been a nonstop battle for the Motion Picture Association of America (MPAA) and Recording Industry Association of America (RIAA). According to recent reports[487], U.S. movie studios lose $447 million annually due to online piracy. Placing copyrighted content online and sharing them freely via P2P file sharing applications has been a key attractor of P2P file sharing and streaming. As a result, MPAA and RIAA have targeted P2P networks as a potential threat. One of the most famous lawsuits perhaps is the *RIAA v. Napster* case, which led to injunction and shutdown of the original Napster service. The legal controversy has continued beyond Napster, however. For example, in *Elektra v. Barker*, RIAA put individual users on the stand. The goal is to prevent unauthorized copying and online distribution of music files.

Bandwidth clogging, an example of an interruption class of attack, has been a concern of many corporations and universities. It is especially serious for P2P content distribution applications. The rich multimedia (audio and video) files that P2P users share are usually large in size. Consequently, P2P multimedia download and streaming always cause heavy traffic, which clogs an organization's network and affects response time and performance of normal business correspondence. The damage escalates when adversaries manipulate peers to issue multimedia download or streaming simultaneously. This is the reason that many corporations and universities are banning the use of P2P file-sharing or streaming applications.

Denial of service (DoS) is another important type of interruption attack. Almost any attack that obstructs availability can be categorized as a DoS attack. DoS attacks could cause service breakdown through disruption of physical network components; consumption of resources such as storage, computation, or bandwidth resources; obstruction of communications; and interference with configuration and state information. For example, a DoS attacker may use malware to max out a user's CPU time or crash a system by triggering errors in instructions.

P2P networks further open up various possibilities for *distributed DoS* (DDoS) attacks,[488,489,490] networked DoS attacks whereby nodes work together to prevent a system from performing its task. For example, an attacker registers with a P2P overlay, gains access to multiple peer devices, plants zombie processes[488] (daemons that perform the actual attack) on those peer devices, and launches an attack with all the zombies on a target device or service at a predetermined time. With hundreds or thousands of zombies located on a P2P network working together, the victim's network bandwidth could be easily drained, causing denial of services.

On May 14, 2007, Prolexic Technologies, a network security vendor specializing in protecting web sites from DoS attacks, issued an alert[491] because the company observed an increase in the number and frequency of P2P-based DDoS attacks, which can cause a major local network disruption. "The popularity of peer-to-peer networks has now gained the interest of cyber criminals who see these networks as a huge potential for distributing malware and launching DDoS attacks by convincing 100k+ computers to attack on their behalf. Recently, attackers have found a way to pull off this type of attack anonymously, and with ease, flooding victims with far more connections than they can handle," the article stated. According to Prolexic, the most aggressive P2P-DDoS attack is a so-called DC++[492] attack, which employs the popular DC++ open-source client for Windows using a Direct Connection network. In a DC++ attack, the adversary acts as a puppet master, instructing peers of a P2P network to connect to a victim's Website. With a P2P network of size N peers, and each peer opening m connections simultaneously, the victim's site could potentially be hit with up to mN connections in short order. Prolexic reported very large DC++ attacks of over 300k ($N > 300,000$) IP addresses in its article,[491] which shows how the DDoS problem constantly evolves. Today, an increasing number of P2P-DDoS attacks are targeting Websites. In these attacks, peers (P2P network client computers, for example) are tricked into requesting a file from the victim's site, allowing the adversary to use the P2P network to overwhelm the victim's site and disrupt its availability. To an adversary, the major advantages of using a DDoS attack include (1) more attack traffic with a large number of distributed or peer resources and (2) more difficulty for the victim to track and shut down the attacking sources or zombies.

DDoS attacks appear in various forms. Mirkovic and Reiher[489] classify DDoS attacks based on degree of automation, communication mechanism, scanning strategy, propagation mechanism, exploited vulnerability, attack rate dynamics, and impact. For example, based on degree of automation, these attacks can be categorized into manual attacks, semiautomatic attacks, and automatic attacks; random, hit list, topological, permutation, and local subnet are several classes that exist in scanning strategy-based classifications. Alternatively, the attacks can be grouped into central, back-chaining, and autonomous subsets according to their propagation mechanism.

Later in this chapter we look at how P2P overlay networks can be taken advantage of by adversaries to issue DDoS attacks. Some available methods to defend against DoS attacks are also discussed.

The term *virus* refers to a program that reproduces by introducing a copy of itself and infecting another computer or device without permission or knowledge of the user. Often the virus is appended to the end of a file or the program header is modified to point to the virus code. A virus, as we all know, can cause severe damage to a system or device. A P2P network offers an attractive platform for attackers to spread viruses. A piece of code, the virus, could appear to be a popular file-sharing program and subsequently when downloaded and accessed could unknowingly affect many peers in the P2P overlay. The virus gains access to the peers' devices, modifies data and files on the devices, changes user password or access information, destroys the file system, and more, causing an interception, an interruption, a modification, and/or a fabrication class of attack.

These examples are merely an illustration of the security threats existing in P2P networks. Interested readers can refer to [493] and [494] for more discussion.

Overlay Layer Attacks

Unlike some other applications, P2P applications are built on top of overlay networks, which can introduce an additional layer of attack. At the overlay network layer, current P2P overlays in the literature provide limited security for message dissemination. Hence, a malicious peer has many opportunities to corrupt P2P communication at the overlay level. Assuming that the underlying network layer is reliable and secure, attacks on the overlay, such as attacks on peer identification mapping schemes, attacks on routing table entries or updates, lookup attacks, DoS attacks, attacks on data placement schemes, and attacks on message forwarding, can all potentially hinder the functionality of a P2P system. Using structured overlays (Chapter 4) as an example, let's look at several typical overlay layer attacks.

NodeId *Attacks*

A nodeId attack[496] can occur in a structured overlay when one node or a coalition of malicious nodes are able to obtain a specific nodeId (node identification) that maximizes its probability to appear in a victim peer's routing table or be closer to an object key. It could potentially compromise the integrity of a structured P2P network without the malicious party controlling a large fraction of nodes. For instance, one attacker may choose the closest nodeIds to all replica keys (objects) for a particular content object to gain control of access to that object. NodeId attacks would give the attacker the ability to mediate the victim peer's access to the overlay or censor the object.

Sybil Attacks

A Sybil attack is defined in [485] as a small number of entities counterfeiting multiple peer identities so as to compromise a disproportionate share of the system. In other words, an adversary tries to get a large number of nodeIds, which may or may not be randomly generated, to appear and function as distinct nodes. With multiple identities, the adversary can get closer to a certain object or many objects in the P2P overlay. It increases the opportunity to intercept message routing and overlay network operation. It can even enable a malicious party to take control of the P2P overlay network. The Sybil attack is named after the book *Sybil*,[495] a case study of a woman with multiple personality disorder. In [485], Douceur shows that, without a logically centralized authority, Sybil attacks are always possible except under extreme and unrealistic assumptions of resource parity and coordination among entities.

Routing Table Attacks

Routing table attacks include those attacks that manipulate routing table entries for malicious intent. Adversaries could take advantage of routing table updates to feed false updates and thus introduce faulty routing table entries to other peers. The effect cascades after subsequent updates. This could potentially trigger many problems in the P2P network. The routing poisoning-based DDoS attack discussed later in the chapter is a representative case of an attack via routing table manipulation.

Message-Forwarding Attacks

In the absence of faults, messages in structured P2P networks are delivered from the source to the destination node after an average of h hops. Even if the probability of a routing table being controlled by attackers is minimized, an adversary can still reduce the probability of a message being successfully delivered by simply not forwarding a message or by altering the routing algorithm. When one or more peer nodes or routes between two nodes are compromised, a message might be dropped, modified, or diverted. This is called a message-forwarding attack in [496] and [497].

More on DDoS

In [490], Naoumov and Ross describe two approaches to create a DDoS engine out of a P2P system: poisoning the distributed index in peers and poisoning the routing tables in peers. In index poisoning-based DDoS attacks, the attacker inserts bogus records into the P2P index system. In the index system, the location of one or more popular files, say $F1$, $F2$, ..., Fn, are replaced with the victim (target)'s IP address IPa and port number PNa. The victim could be a mail server, a Web server, or a user's desktop. It might not even be a client of the P2P system. When peers later search for $F1$, $F2$, ..., Fn, the targeted port PNa of the targeted host IPa is returned to the peers from the index. The peers then connect with the target and attempt to download $F1$, $F2$, ..., Fn. In a large P2P network, this could potentially overwhelm the target server with fully open TCP connections or by filling up the number of allowed connections and preventing legitimate users from obtaining services.

In a routing poisoning-based DDoS attack, the attacker attempts to poison the routing tables in the P2P nodes. As we discussed, the cascade effect can be extremely significant. Using updates or other methods, the adversary could try to poison the routing table entry of many peers and make the target a neighbor of many peers in the P2P overlay. When those peers forward a query or other messages, it may select the target from its neighbor set and send the message directly to the target. In a large P2P system, if a significant fraction of the peers have their routing tables poisoned, the target host can potentially receive a flood of query, publish, and maintenance traffic and hence be the victim of a bandwidth DDoS attack.

Naoumov and Ross used Overnet[498] as a vehicle to exploit the two types of P2P-DDoS attacks and measure the impact of these attacks. For a 45-minute period, bogus locations were advertised and location messages were sent to crawled peers. With little effort, Overnet was used to attack a victim that is not a client on the Overnet. For the entire duration of the attack, the victim received traffic from 340,274 peers from 22,484 autonomous systems (ASs) in their measurement. This illustrates the highly distributed nature of these attacks. This distributed nature makes it extremely hard to defend against DDoS attacks and makes filtering by source IP addresses difficult if not impossible.

SECURITY MECHANISMS

Given the vulnerabilities of existing P2P overlays and the attacks we've described, can we still make a P2P overlay secure and dependable? Defending against the threats against P2P overlays requires careful planning and selection of P2P infrastructure and security mechanisms. Security policies are the foremost requirement in building a secure system. The set of rules defines and governs the control, use, and action entities of a system. With security policies in place, it is then possible to design suitable security mechanisms to enforce the security policies and ensure the security of the system.

Cryptographic Solutions

Cryptographic schemes offer the most effective solutions for many information security issues. They are also essential to security in P2P. Among various crypto tools, encryption and authentication are two fundamental and the most frequently used crypto primitives.

Encryption is the process of disguising a message in such a way that its content is hidden and cannot be revealed without a proper decryption key. This is a fundamental security tool that implements confidentiality with coding. Symmetric key and asymmetric key encryptions are the two types of encryption algorithms. *Symmetric key encryption* algorithms, also called *private key encryption* algorithms, are a class of encryption algorithm that uses identical keys for both encryption and decryption. Popular examples of symmetric key encryption algorithms include Data Encryption Standard (DES) and Advanced Encryption Standard (AES), which are standardized by the National Institute of Standards and Technology (NIST) and are widely adopted by many applications. *Asymmetric key encryption* algorithms, a.k.a. *public key encryption* algorithms, such as the RSA encryption algorithm, are another class of encryption algorithm that employs different keys at encryption and decryption. Note that in general, asymmetric key algorithms are much more computationally intensive than symmetric algorithms.

Encryption can play many positive roles in P2P security. It makes it difficult for attackers to carry out interception and modification classes of attack. If all confidential information is encrypted, even if some is shared or leaked over some insecure P2P file-sharing communication channels, adversaries would have a hard time decrypting the information without a proper key. The security risks will be subsequently reduced. Therefore, in the ID theft case discussed early in this chapter, the offender would not have been able to get access to others' financial information that easily. The number of victims would have been greatly reduced in that case.

Authentication, another essential security tool in computer systems, is the process of verifying whether an object is in fact who or what that object declares itself to be. A one-way hash that is nonreversible, sensitive to input changes, and collision resistant is used for authentication as well as data integrity verification. Authentication can also play many positive roles in P2P security. For example, combining secure authentication of each peer with message encryption, a P2P system can prevent eavesdropping attacks. With content authentication, information substitution and insertion attacks can not easily be realized.

DoS Countermeasures

The most popular countermeasures of DoS attacks include service/host backup, reactive detection, rate limiting, and filtering. Having a separate emergency block of IP addresses, for example, can be invaluable in surviving a DoS attack. Pattern detection is often helpful by storing the signature of known attacks in a database. Rate-limiting mechanisms impose a rate limit on a stream that has been characterized as malicious by the detection mechanism. These are often used as a response technique when a detection mechanism cannot characterize the attack stream. Effective filtering is another way to protect against DoS and DDoS attacks. For example, attacks originating from or going to bogus IP addresses can be filtered using Bogon filter (a bogus IP filter). Filtering traffic based on access control lists (ACLs), rate limiting of IP addresses, or ranges of IP addresses can also be employed. Some switches today offer deep packet inspection capability and Bogon filtering. These can help defend against DoS and DDoS attacks.

TCP splicing, also called *delayed binding*, is another widely used mechanism to prevent DoS attacks. By postponing the connection between the client and the server, sufficient information to make a routing decision can be obtained. Many application switches and routers implement this capability today. Delay-binding the client session to the server until the proper handshakes are complete can prevent DoS attacks.

Firewalls have been used to defend against many types of attacks. Today advanced firewalls have built-in capabilities for differentiating good traffic from DoS attack traffic. For example, Cisco PIX (Private Internet Exchange)[499] uses stateful inspection to confirm TCP connections before proxying TCP packets to service networks. Certainly most simple firewalls have limited capabilities for differentiating good traffic from DoS attack traffic, making it difficult to defend against DoS attacks, let alone DDoS attacks.

Recall that Naoumov and Ross[490] show the distributed nature of two types of P2P-DDoS attacks, which lead to the ineffectiveness of IP address filtering in defending such types of attack. Although pattern detection and advanced filtering mechanisms may be helpful in detecting these types of P2P-DDoS attack, the eruption of new types and large P2P-DDoS attacks make this type one of the toughest to defend against.

Sia[500] also exploited the DDoS vulnerability of the current BitTorrent (BT) protocol. Allowing a user to arbitrarily specify its own IP is one significant cause of the BT protocol vulnerability to DDoS attacks. Sia suggested fixing this issue using more strict protocols with source authentication and pattern-matching packet filtering mechanisms.

Mirkovic and Reiher[489] summarize DDoS defense mechanisms into a series of categories. For example, resource accounting and resource multiplication are preventive types of defense, whereas pattern detection, anomaly detection, hybrid detection, third-party detection, agent identification, rate limiting, filtering, and reconfiguration are reactive defense types. Most notably, deploying comprehensive protocol and system security mechanisms can substantially help improve resilience to DDoS attacks. Additionally, enforcing policies for resource consumption and ensuring that abundant resources exist can both help reduce the impact of DDoS attacks so that legitimate clients will not be affected. For a comprehensive list and discussion of DDoS defense mechanisms, readers are encouraged to reference Mirkovic and Reiher's survey and taxonomy.[489]

Secure Routing in Structured P2P

In [496], Castro et al. define a secure routing primitive that ensures that when a nonfaulty node sends a message to a key, the message reaches all nonfaulty members in the set of replica roots with very high probability. Secure routing guarantees that even with the existence of malicious peers (nodes) that may corrupt, drop, modify, replace, or misroute the message, the correct message will eventually be delivered to the intended receiver with high probability.

Castro et al.[496] and Wallach[497] identify three categories of secure routing requirements in structured overlays such as Chord,[501] Pastry,[502] and Tapstry,[503] namely: (1) secure assignment of node identifiers, (2) secure routing table maintenance, and (3) secure message forwarding. Secure `nodeId` assignment ensures that a malicious node, a node in the P2P overlay network that uses the network improperly, whether deliberately or not,[496] will not be able to choose its ID maliciously and a coalition of malicious nodes cannot allocate a collection of nodeIds illegitimately so as to control a specific content object or to maximize their chances of controlling a victim's routes or the network. Secure routing table maintenance deals with attacks on routing tables, such as imposing bad routing table entries to divert a victim's message routes. Secure nodeId assignment and secure routing table maintenance may guarantee that the probability of a routing table being controlled by attackers is minimized. However, an adversary can still reduce the probability of a message being successfully delivered by simply not forwarding a message or by altering the routing algorithm.[504] When one or more peer nodes or routes between two nodes are compromised, a message might be dropped, modified, or diverted. To ensure that at least one correct copy of a message sent to a peer reaches the correct peer with high probability, secure message forwarding mechanisms are needed.

Secure nodeId *Assignment*

The most straightforward scheme for secure nodeId assignment is to establish a centralized certificate authority to issue nodeIds[496] and bind the nodeId to the IP address. In enterprise system or private networks, user authentication is already in place. Hence, central authority-based nodeId certification can be a preferred choice. Furthermore, imposing a nodeId certificate fee or physical identify bound nodeIds will greatly reduce the risk of Sybil attacks. Many believe, though, that trust is an important issue to improve a P2P system's capability to fight Sybil attacks.

A distributed nodeId binding scheme is another possible means to avoid malicious nodes inserting themselves at multiple nodeId locations with a single IP address. Every time a node accepts a particular binding <node id, IP address> from another node, it stores the binding information in the overlay using the IP address as the key. Before storing this binding, it checks to see whether another binding for the same IP address is stored. If such a binding with a different nodeId exists in the overlay, the current request to establish a new binding is rejected. If, however, an existing binding in the overlay contains the same nodeId, the current request is accepted. If there is no existing binding information for that particular IP address in the overlay, again the current binding is accepted.

Noticeably, without additional measures this scheme is vulnerable to DoS attack, whereby a malicious node simply inserts random bindings for different IP addresses, preventing those IP hosts from joining the overlay. To avoid this problem, a return routability test, similar to the one developed for Mobile IPv6, can be employed. A return routability test should be conducted every time a binding is stored on the overlay, to ensure the validity of the binding. Obvious extensions to this solution in terms of adding redundancy and verifying the source IP address ensure that a single node (with single IP address) cannot hog a large portion of the nodeId space. Although there is additional cost in terms of the return routability message exchange, we believe that it is justified for the same rationale behind the adoption of such a solution in Mobile IPv6.[505]

Secure Routing Table Maintenance

Castro et al.[496] suggests imposing strong constraints on the set of nodeIds that can fill each slot in a routing table to maintain routing table security. A two-table solution was given in [496]. In two-table routing, one guarantees performance while the other is constrained such that the probability of it being manipulated is minimized. Authentication is another way to reduce routing table attacks. However, additional cost is expected and may reduce the performance of the P2P application, especially delay-bounded applications.

A hybrid P2P architecture (see Figure 14.4) can also potentially help reduce the risks of routing table attack, assuming that all supernodes can be guaranteed trustworthy. Since ordinary nodes communicate through the supernodes, the probability of routing table manipulation by a malicious peer, an ordinary node, is greatly reduced.

Secure Message Forwarding

Since peer-to-peer overlays rely solely on other peers for message routing, a message has to be properly routed without modification in transit. An adversary may try to alter the message when routing the message to its receiver, alter its routing table to disrupt the message forwarding, or take advantage of locality to control some routes. Secure message forwarding ensures that at least one copy of a message sent to a peer reaches the correct peer with high probability.

An obvious way to trade performance for security is to use multiroutes to send duplicated messages from the source to the destination. However, in a bandwidth-intensive application, message duplication will burden the system. An improvement on the scheme is to utilize message authentication. Only when a message fails an authenticity check, redundant routing is invoked to reforward a correct copy of the message from one or more different routes. Although this is not helpful in streaming media applications due to the real-time and continuous playback requirement, it can be used otherwise. In streaming media applications, instead of redundant duplication, multiple substreams through multiple-route forwarding can be introduced. With a stream-splitting algorithm such as multiple description coding, a media stream can be split into multiple substreams. A receiver can still play back the media without interruption when receiving only some of all the

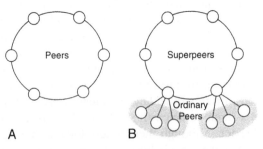

FIGURE 14.4 (A) Fully decentralized versus (B) hybrid P2P architecture.

substreams, although with degradation of quality. In this case, a fine-grained scalable message encryption and authentication scheme can help improve the security in streaming message forwarding, with minimal additional cost. One tradeoff of the stream-splitting scheme, though, is the added control cost in terms of multiple distribution routes (trees.)

Carefully designed overlay routing algorithms may also help reduce security risks in the overlay layer. Assuming that there are an average of h routing hops in message delivery from the sender to the destination peer, the percentage of faulty nodes is γ, so between the sender and receiver, the probability of routing successfully to a correct destination peer is $p = (1-\gamma)^h$. Obviously, the smaller h is, the higher p may be. This suggests that routing algorithms with fewer hops increase the probability of routing accuracy and hence reduce the probability of security risks at the overlay layer due to faulty message forwarding.

The hybrid P2P architecture (see Figure 14.4B) that comprises supernodes in the P2P overlay may also help improve secure message forwarding. If only trusted nodes can be promoted as supernodes, those supernodes can serve as filers or servlets. Trusted messaging between supernodes can be established. Further, a supernode can serve as a "centralized" authority to those ordinary nodes connected to it or message filters. This adds another layer of protection.

Fairness in Resource Sharing

Many researchers have observed the problem of fairness in P2P overlay-based applications. In one study,[506] 70% of free riders were reported. It is unfair to other peers in the overlay if some peers only want to use other peers' resources without fair contribution of their own resources. From a security point of view, this kind of behavior can be characterized as resource theft under the interception class of attack. Furthermore, with a large number of free riders in a P2P network, such as the 70% reported in [506], the rest of the peers more easily become congested or come under attack.

Auditing and Incentives

Incentives are one way to improve the situation; a peer gets an "incentive" to use other resources by contributing its own resources on a pay-more/get-more base. A centralized broker or trusted centralized quota authority that monitors all transactions could accomplish the goal of fairness in resource sharing. However, scalability is a major limitation of this kind of scheme. The centralized broker can quickly become a bottleneck in applications with frequent requests. In this case, distributed mechanisms are needed. A quota manager[507] approach, for example, is one distributed approach. For each peer in the P2P network, a manager set with a set of nodes, perhaps neighbors of the peer, acts as the quota manager. Each manager records the amount of resources consumed by the peers it manages. A remote node, when requesting a fair sharing, would seek an agreement with a majority of the managers of the peer agreeing that a given request is authorized. If a hybrid P2P network architecture is employed, the supernodes can naturally act as quota managers. In a fully distributed P2P network, though, selecting peers to act as quota managers is a challenging problem. Clearly, in either case, the process of approval can cause long latency.

Another class of distributed mechanism is distributed auditing. One approach is to ask each peer in the P2P network to maintain a record of its own usage and to publish it in the overlay. Other peers can audit these records to achieve fair sharing. In the case of a hybrid P2P network, auditing can be done in two ways: having the supernodes act as auditing authorities and collaboratively publish the auditing records, or making supernodes take on the task of auditing monitoring, whereby all peers publish records of their own, with the supernodes monitoring the publishing and auditing of peers. Of course, techniques to ensure that all peers will publish their records are needed, and this is most challenging in the fully distributed P2P network. Incentives are one way to achieve this goal.[507,508]

Micropayment systems may also help improve the fairness issue. It is unclear, though, whether any existing micropayment system or simple auditing scheme could scale well to support large P2P overlay and/or high churn applications. Mojo Nation, an already tested P2P system, tried to use a credit and incentive-based scheme to improve fair sharing. It was a pseudo-currency micropayment-based system. In Mojo Nation, if you provided resources, computational, storage, or bandwidth, to the system, you earned Mojo, a kind of digital currency. If you consumed resources, you spent the Mojo you'd earned. This system was intended to keep freeloaders from consuming more than they contributed to the system. But if users are heavily consuming resources, it does not pose a real threat to most existing P2P system users, so Mojo Nation never really worked. Today, designing a P2P system that can take advantage of incentive-based mechanisms with efficient auditing is still a challenging problem that is being studied by many researchers.

TRUST AND PRIVACY ISSUES

One important aspect of a P2P system is the way a peer trusts another peer in the system.[509,510] The level of trust is the level of confidence of one peer toward another peer with which it is communicating. A P2P system relies heavily on a set of distributed peers working properly and fairly together. In a small P2P system, especially one that involves only known entities, establishing and maintaining trust between peers is easily achievable. However, today's P2P system can be tens of thousands to millions of peers in size, with peers interacting with many unknown peers. Unfortunately, free riders are a common phenomenon in P2P applications.

As we saw earlier in this chapter, adversaries actively try to subvert or take advantage of the system to obtain confidential information for illegal financial gain. As such, performing peer authentication and authorization and thus establishing and maintaining reliable trust between peers play central roles in many aspects of P2P security. The main goal is to avoid interactions with nodes that do not lead to security risks. Noticeably, trust is not merely an issue of peer-to-peer trust. Content and resource trust, being able to authenticate the content and resource of an accessing peer, is also an obvious security issue.

Architecture

Figure 14.5 illustrates three different architectures of P2P trust management systems. For ease of discussion, let's assume that trust between two entities Ea and Eb (i.e., Ea and Eb have ascertained a trust relationship with each other) is established when the two entities are authenticated with each other. In Figure 14.5A, a centralized trust management architecture, a central authority is used to manage trust. Assuming a network size of N, the number of operations to establish and maintain trust is $O(N)$.

In a fully decentralized architecture (Figure 14.5B), a naive scheme whereby a peer has to perform authentication with each and every peer in the network will have a cost of $O(N(N-1)/2) = O(N^2)$, which imposes high overhead on the network.

In a hybrid P2P (Figure 14.5C) in which supernodes can act as trusted entities, the cost to establish and maintain trusts can be greatly reduced. Assume that we have Ns supernodes and all supernodes have to authenticate each other to establish trust. An ordinary node, however, will treat the supernode as a central authority. In this simple case, the number of operations to establish and maintain trust will be $O(Ns(Ns-1)/2+(N-Ns)) = O(Ns^2+N) \ll O(N^2)$ when Ns is small.

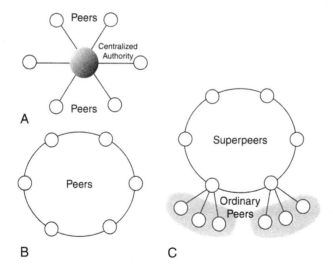

FIGURE 14.5 Three different architectures for trust management.

From a security point of view, a centralized system tends to be vulnerable to single point of attack at the centralized authority, which is subject to DDoS and many other types of attack. The hybrid architecture does not offer a single point for attacks. However, without an intelligent management scheme, the network can quickly become impaired when attacks target several supernodes simultaneously.

Reputation

One notable facet of research focuses on trust value establishment.[511,512,513] The key idea is to use previous interactions to determine the reputation and thus the trustworthiness of a particular user in the P2P network. Reputation is the memory and summary of behavior from past transactions. Reputation score is the numerical representation of reputation. It can be calculated either via a centralized reputation server or distributedly using local or global trust metrics. Trust value can be a function of the reputation score that acts as a guide for peers to make choices in selecting transaction partners or neighbors in a P2P network. It also serves as an incentive for those peers that have good reputation scores.

According to Despotovic and Aberer, reputation systems can be split into those using probabilistic estimation and those based on social networks.[514] The former considers only a small proportion of the globally available feedback concerning a node's behavior, using probabilistic methods to assess its trustworthiness. The latter aggregates all the feedback available to assess trustworthiness. The two solutions were found to have varying degrees of effectiveness depending on the nature of collusion that occurs within the P2P network. For example, the social networking technique was found to be most effective when the peer population was split into a group of colluding peers and a group of noncolluding peers of equal size, with probabilistic estimation performing better otherwise. The implementation cost in terms of message exchanges of the probabilistic method was found to be $O(\log N)$ in structured networks with logarithmic search costs and $O(E)$ for unstructured networks, where N represents the number of nodes and E the number of edges in the overlay. For social networks the entire network must be flooded, and the cost is therefore $O(N)$ and $O(E)$ for structured and unstructured networks, respectively.

In general, reputation requires mapping information about past transactions to peers and a metric that can bind the mapping to trustworthiness. When a peer solicits reputation information about a particular peer from other peers of the network, it faces the problem of trust; should the peer trust the reputation information provided by other peers? Obviously, if any peer can easily refresh or modify its reputation score, the value of the reputation-based scheme degrades to negative. This implies that a reputation scheme needs to be secure to prevent it from turning into the weakest link. Today this is still a challenging problem.

Privacy

Many P2P networks today do not have built-in privacy mechanisms. Users of these P2P networks can be tracked or identified by others, including attackers. Johnson's testimony[481] and the ID theft case discussed early in the chapter are perfect examples of the gravity of privacy risks in P2P file sharing. Obviously, user education, better software practice, and more secure protocols and system architecture can help reduce the risks. Adding privacy technology to a P2P network can also help offset this disadvantage. Goldberg[515] believes that reputation interacts well with privacy-enhanced technologies since reputation can be calculated without disclosing private information of a peer. His view is shared by Kinateder and Pearson.[516] They use a network of trusted agents on each client platform that exploit Trusted Computing Platform Alliance[517] (TCPA) technology. A trusted agent forms recommendations and decides what is appropriate to send out, depending on who is asking for it. This, or another such trusted agent, can be used to formulate queries asking for recommendations from others in a peer-to-peer network and process the responses. Furthermore, the system is designed such that the agents are independent and may be trusted by entities other than the owner of the platform on which they are running, and the integrity of these agents is protected by the trusted platform against unauthorized modification.

Another approach attempts to improve privacy with anonymous communication. If a communication protocol can guarantee that the sender is indistinguishable from other peers in network to a receiver, and vice versa, sender and receiver anonymity can be achieved. P^5 [518] achieves this goal via a broadcast-based protocol. It allows secure anonymous connections between a hierarchy of progressively smaller broadcast channels and allows individual users to trade off anonymity for communication efficiency.

Free Haven[519] uses cryptographic techniques to protect the identity of all parties, such as the reader, the server, the author, the document, and the query, involved in the P2P system. This actively prevents any party other than the authorized one to read or link information. Although it uses a simple routing structure, its technique to protect anonymity is very sophisticated.

Tarzan[520] serves as transport layer anonymizer. Each node selects a set of peers to act as mimics. Initial node discovery and subsequent network maintenance are based on a gossip model. Mimics are selected randomly but in some verifiable manner from the available nodes. Each node exchanges a constant rate of cover traffic of fixed size packets with its mimics using symmetric encryption. The relays' public keys are used to distribute the symmetric keys. Actual data can now be interwoven into the cover traffic without an observer detecting where a message originates. A sender randomly selects a given number of mimics and wraps the message in an "onion" of symmetric keys from each node on the path. The sender passes the packet—indistinguishable from cover traffic—to the first node in the chain, which removes the outermost wrapper with its private key and then sends it along to the next node. With the exception of the last node, each node in the chain is aware of the node before and after it in the chain but cannot tell where it is in the chain itself.

The final node in the chain of mimics acts as the Network Address Translator for the transport layer and sends the packet to its final destination through the Internet. This final node gets the content and destination but has no information about the sender. Nodes store a record for the return path, so a reply can be received by the final node in the chain, rewrapped with its private key, and sent back to the penultimate hop. The message is then passed back through the chain, with each node adding another layer of encryption. The originating node can use the public keys of each node to unwrap the layers and read the message. Since it is the only node to know the public keys of each hop along the path, the content is secure.

CASE STUDY: GROOVE

Groove[521,494] is a P2P groupware tool for workspace collaboration. In Groove, documents, data, and messages are shared confidentially and unaltered among peers, that is, group members. Groove is capable of data synchronization among all peers, even incremental changes. Groove builds on permanent secure connections with all shared space data encrypted on hard disks as well as in communications. Groove uses authentication to bind a user's identity to specific actions. Either out-of-band fingerprinting or a certificate authority management server is used to authenticate members of a workspace. Data are authenticated in Groove, with messages signed using 2048 bits RSA keys. Trust is established via physical world trust between peers and through out-of-band communication at join. Groove also provides access control using a hierarchical management peer structure. The P2P nature and rigid set of security policies protects Groove workspaces from many types of attack. It is one of the best-protected P2P systems on the market today.

CASE STUDY: POLLUTION IN FILE-SHARING SYSTEMS

Content security and copyright protection have brought a constant battle between the content industry and P2P content-sharing companies and users in the last several years. On one hand, many users are enjoying free content distributed via P2P file-sharing and streaming applications. On the other hand, content creators and their representatives are trying to stop unauthorized sharing. While taking file-sharing companies and individuals to court, the content industry also learned to take advantage of the distributed resources and other characteristics of P2P networks to sabotage P2P file-sharing systems themselves.

One of the techniques they used is called *pollution*. The goal is to stop P2P file sharing by causing user frustration. The basic idea is to create bogus content, especially popular content, and store it in a P2P file-sharing system. When peers search for files on these systems, they could be directed to the bogus ones. The chaining effect of such sharing will result in a large number of peers getting constant bogus content so that they become frustrated with the system and thus abandon it voluntarily.

Content pollution and metadata pollution are the two most popular types used in these attacks on file-sharing systems. With content pollution, the actual content of a music or video files is modified significantly to generate a bogus copy. Metadata pollution alters the metadata of a fake copy of the content and makes the metadata resemble the metadata of the target music or video. Because many P2P systems do not have effective mechanisms to prevent pollution attacks, these attacks have become successful tools for the content industry to use in its fight against illegitimate content sharing over P2P networks. Overpeer,[522] for example, is such a tool that uses pollution attacks to help content creators and distributors minimize sharing over P2P networks. Based on a measurement study conducted by Liang et al.[523] over KaZaa,[524] 50% of the copies of many popular songs were polluted at the time of the study. This shows the success of polluting file-sharing systems for copyright protection.

Pollution is used for copyright protection in the preceding case; it can also be used for other purposes as well. To defend against pollution attacks, we can adopt many mechanisms discussed in this chapter. Authentication and fingerprinting may be used for peers to acquire only authenticated copies of data and thus reduce the probability of downloading bogus contents. Trust and reputation systems can also help reduce the spread of bogus files.

SUMMARY

In this chapter we addressed some possible security risks and some sample isolated solutions. Although many stories have been told here, these obviously still do not cover all the aspects of P2P security. Making P2P systems secure is a big challenge due to their distributed nature and the wide availability of replicated objects. Peers on P2P networks may be easily exposed to distributed viruses, worms, Trojan horses, or spyware. They might even disclose sensitive information unknowingly, as indicated in several studies.[479,480,481] One significant cause of these security threats is that users are not well educated about the existing security risks in today's P2P-based applications. Certainly, many P2P systems today, at their immature stage of adoption, still have many security flaws that are subject to many types of attacks This is another important cause of the threat. A third important root of the problem is the P2P security gap. For instance, to share files on your device and to access files on other peer devices within a P2P network, you must open a specific TCP port through the firewall through which the P2P software can communicate. This increases the risk of malicious traffic at the peers.

Many P2P systems today are application specific. It is important to define the security goals and adopt security schemes that are application and system driven. Designing suitable protocols and systems with appropriate security policies and enforcement mechanisms can get you off to a good start and help you prevent and defend against various attacks.

FOR FURTHER READING

To further understand the security risks of P2P networks, "Why File Sharing Networks Are Dangerous," by Johnson, McGuire, and Willey[480] is a good place to start.

Managed Overlays

Physical networks are managed by their operators to assure that network services perform as expected. Although overlays are self-organizing, experience with deployed overlays indicates that additional management mechanisms are needed in some cases. This chapter compares the traditional network management functions with the requirements for managing large-scale overlays and outlines a general approach for integrating an external management agent with an overlay. In addition, we review current trends in addressing the impact of P2P traffic on ISP networks.

INTRODUCTION

In August 2007 the Skype P2P telephony service experienced a two-day outage due to a large number of users simultaneously attempting to re-login to the service.[525] The massive restart was reportedly triggered by the update feature on Microsoft Windows in which a user's computer automatically downloads and installs recent software updates, followed by a reboot of the host computer. Those peers performing the reboot almost simultaneously exited the Skype network. Large numbers of supernodes in particular were then no longer available to proxy regular nodes' connections to the Skype network. A diminished population of supernodes likely led to service disruption for regular nodes that rely on the supernodes. As the rebooting hosts attempted to reconnect to the Skype network, their requests flooded the Skype infrastructure, exposing a previously unknown bug in resource management in the Skype infrastructure. At the overlay level, any peers leaving the network due to normal usage were not being replaced by other peers joining the network due to the login services being swamped, reducing the critical mass of supernodes needed to maintain the overall population of the overlay.

Although exact details of the problem have not been released, we make a few observations about this particular outage before considering the general issues of service assurance for P2P overlays. Since Windows updates occur on a regular basis, the fact that similar outages had not occurred previously suggests either that the scale of requests reached a level not seen before or that the reported resource allocation bug was introduced relatively recently. If the former were the case, it is reasonable to expect that the Skype operators had in the past monitored the peer join and leave rate and would have noticed spikes of demand that they needed to be able to satisfy.

More important, the fact that the outage lasted for up to two days is probably due to factors such as these:

- *Time to recognize that a problem was occurring.* This is complicated by the normally volatile nature of the overlay population, the distributed nature of the peers making status costly to obtain, and the difficulty in forming a global view of the P2P network.

- *Time to identify the root cause of the problem.* In conventional network management, this is also a significant problem; there is a flood of events (called *faults*) that occur and there is a variety of explanations as to the cause of these events that the network operators must diagnose and resolve. Was the problem a DoS attack, a side effect of virus propagation among the client population, a bug in the Skype client software, a bug somewhere in the infrastructure, an ISP failure, or some combination of faults?

- *Time to fix the problem and potentially update and restart the software.* This could stress the bootstrap mode of the P2P overlay, that is, the mechanisms used to initially form the overlay. Since the Skype overlay typically operates in steady-state churn mode, it is reasonable to expect that the bootstrap mode would be less reliable and a relatively untested part of the system.

The Skype outage is a compelling motivation for the need to be able to manage large-scale P2P overlays, but these factors enumerated here are general issues facing any overlay deployment. It is with these types of questions we are concerned in this chapter. Further, what makes this problem different from traditional application management and why it is a relatively unexplored problem in the P2P community is that P2P overlays are inherently self-organizing. This raises the question: What is the appropriate boundary between self-organization and overlay operator management?

It is convenient to draw a parallel between the role of service provider in conventional telecommunications networks and the operator of a P2P overlay. The overlay operator is an entity that develops an application layer overlay to provide peer-to-peer services to end users and a service delivery platform for third parties. As discussed elsewhere in this book, such services include personal communications, file sharing, storage, and content delivery. In the peer-to-peer overlay paradigm, the overlay operator designs into the overlay some degree of self-management, adaptivity to network problems, and coordination with other peers. In today's overlays, the role of an operator is usually not visible and may be distributed across an open-source development community. In most cases there is no real-time operational view of the overlay or comprehensive data collection by which to plan performance upgrades. Instead, the overlay operator primarily provides and maintains the software implementation users install on their computing devices. For the overlay operator to take on the role of monitoring and potentially control aspects of the operation of the overlay to ensure that service levels are met, the following capabilities are needed:

- Periodic collection of operational statistics and status at each peer
- A scalable architecture for management agents and/or peers to receive peer status and statistics
- Means by which new resources and peer capabilities can be provisioned
- Ability for a management agent to remotely change peer configuration parameters

Since overlays are designed to operate without central control, questions naturally arise as to the nature and scope of a managed overlay. What is the boundary between self-managed and centrally managed? Does a managed overlay differ from an unmanaged or self-managed one, and if so, how? Which if any overlay algorithms are more suited to management? Is a managed overlay better able to offer different grades of service? What are the typical overlay failure modes? Which operating parameters of an overlay can be configured dynamically? Which performance parameters are important for collecting statistics? What management mechanisms can be designed that are independent of the overlay algorithm?

These are for the most part still open questions, but a pragmatic approach[527] retains the self-organization and peer coordination properties of the overlay and its services while using the management function to monitor exceptional conditions and provision resources to provide expected service quality levels. Assuming that there is sufficient bandwidth and appropriate overlay routing for the overlay manager to have a global real-time view, the manager can intervene where the distributed algorithms of the overlay are insufficient. This boundary is likely to change as the design of overlays advances.

MANAGEMENT OF OVERLAYS VS. CONVENTIONAL NETWORKS
Overlay Dimensions Impacting Manageability

A number of important protocols are widely used in enterprise and carrier networks for managing network elements, including Simple Network Management Protocol (SNMP), Common Management Information Protocol (CMIP), and Transaction Language 1 (TL1). In these environments, there is typically one administrative domain that controls the network elements. These elements—such as routers, switches, and gateways—are deployed and provisioned by the operator, have well-known operating characteristics, and have limited downtime. In carrier environments, there may be special dedicated networks that are used to manage the network elements. The communication latency from the management system to the network elements is under the control of the network operator.

On the other hand, peer-to-peer overlays have characteristics that are somewhat different than managed networks and that limit the use of conventional management protocols and techniques:[527]

- They are operated on a scale involving millions of hosts and distributed over the global network. It might be difficult or expensive to deploy distributed management agents in close proximity to all parts of the overlay. This leads to large volumes of management traffic and long delays between detection of a condition and the response.

- As discussed in Chapter 5, the population of peers is dynamic and with mean lifetimes that may be as low as one hour. The extent of any particular peer's participation is unpredictable and the operator cannot control the time window of peer participation in the overlay. In most overlay algorithms a peer knows the identity of only a fraction of other peers in the overlay. Consequently, it is difficult for a management agent to know the identity and state of all peers at any time.

- Peers run on end users' machines in separate administrative domains. The overlay management agent doesn't generally have authorization to administer either the host or the network in these different networks.

- As discussed in Chapters 6 and 13, peers may be behind NATs or may be mobile and might not be directly reachable.

- To apply conventional management techniques might involve deploying management agents in different regions of the Internet. The cost of deploying these agents could exceed the cost of the overlay itself.

- Fundamentally, the introduction of central control is contrary to the design philosophy. It may also increase the vulnerability of the overlay to security threats, since the penetration of a management agent might permit an intruder to control or disrupt the overlay using the management interface. Even excluding central control, performance monitoring is still useful to inform the designers of areas of potential improvement.

A managed overlay should retain its inherent self-organizing and peer-to-peer operational model, and the management function should supplement the intrinsic self-organizing features where necessary. First, some portion of a peer's bandwidth budget should be available on a continuous basis for management functions. This depends on the frequency of monitoring and control messages and whether the management agent needs to communicate with all peers in the overlay or a subset. Later in this chapter we describe some designs for broadcast messaging in overlays.

Second, when the distributed algorithms of the overlay reach an operating point at which they are known to substantially degrade, such as a high churn rate or request load, the monitoring and control mechanisms should be enabled. Further, unusual operating conditions such as sudden partitioning of the overlay, DoS, and other large-scale security attacks[535] should also trigger communication with the management agent.

Managed Overlay Model

Let's assume that the monitoring and control messages between the management agent and peers in the overlay are routed in the overlay rather than as separate connections at the native layer. This means that any peer that is reachable in the overlay is also reachable by some management agent. This also requires that each management agent be a member of the overlay.

The set of messages for peer management depends on which management functions we want to include. For monitoring only, some way to retrieve a set of measurement variables is needed, and the ability to subscribe to periodic measurement reports could reduce polling overhead. For configuration control, the ability to get and set operating parameters of a peer is needed. These functions are not unique to peers, and one implementation option is to encapsulate part or all of an existing protocol such as SNMP into the overlay messaging. For discussion purposes here, we avoid these details and focus on a generic description of message functions, with the understanding that an actual implementation could be mapped to an existing management protocol, either directly as messages in the overlay or via a gateway between the overlay's management agent and a conventional network management system. In addition, in practice, the management state of a peer could be represented as a management information base (MIB).

Following [527], a P2P overlay in some time interval t_i is a set of peers P with a set of attributes A. Each attribute has current state s and history h. History includes attribute-related messaging with other peers. The set of attributes $A = \{a, c, r, l, v\}$ contains the following:

- a. The peer's overlay address in the overlay address space and its network address.
- c. The peer's capability (peer capability determination is discussed in Chapter 6), a vector of the peer's system and network resource properties that determine its role.
- r. The overlay routing behavior for this peer. This includes overlay-related states such as a routing table, successor/predecessor references, and a list of neighbor peers. It might also include messaging between peers for routing table maintenance and overlay join/leave operations.
- l. One or more roles from the functional roles of peers in the overlay (example roles are described in Table 15.4).
- v. The list of overlay services provided by this peer such as file storage, multicasting, and content-based retrieval.

In practice there would be limitations on the amount of state and history information that could be stored at a peer or sent via the overlay to the management agent. Most information focuses on the peer's behavior and state. The misuse of peer monitoring and configuration should be avoided, such as gathering information about other applications running on the same host.

In a managed overlay it must be possible for a management agent to be able to initiate and receive messages with any peer in the overlay. In addition, the operations in Table 15.1 are supported between a management agent m and a set of peers P in

Table 15.1 Generic Management Operations

Operation	Result
s = get(P,x,m)	Returns the state s of attribute x to node m
h = get(P,x,t,m)	Returns the history h of attribute x in interval t to node m
set(P,x,s,s1)	Sets the state s of attribute x to s1
subscribe(P,x,e,m)	Subscribes node m to event m for x
unsubscribe(P,x,e,m)	Unsubscribes node m to event e for x
cmd(P,d,m)	Performs command d and sends result to node m
notify(p1,p2,e)	Sends notification from peer p1 to peer(s) p2 of event m

the overlay. A managed overlay may also support these operations from other non-management agents. There might also be means for other parties, such as the ISP or a vendor that deploys services on the overlay, to connect their own management agents to peers in the overlay. In this notation, P is the set of peers, s is the state identifier, h is history, t is an interval, and x is one of the attributes {a,c,r,l,v}.

The collection of peers with which the management agent needs to communicate varies depending on the overlay operational state. An important configuration change might need to be communicated to all peers. A network problem in a particular region of the Internet might involve only a subset of peers. Other peer sets could be recently joined peers, peers in a given geographic or network or overlay region, peers offering a specified service, and peers acting in a specified role. If the overlay provides a group address mechanism, groups could be defined for each such case. If not, the management agent must explicitly address each peer in the target set.

MANAGED OVERLAYS AND OVERLAY OPERATORS
Role of the Overlay Operator

There are clear parallels between the network service provider (NSP) role in telecommunications networks and the concept of an overlay operator, also referred to as an *overlay ISP*[383] or overlay service provider.[390] In the future NSPs could also take on the role of deploying and managing overlays to provide services that extend beyond their network operating regions. It is important for managed overlays to leverage the significant investment and capability in management systems that exists in enterprise and telecommunications network environments.

The Telecommunications Management Network (TMN) model is a network management model standardized by ITU-T that is often used to explain the key functions of network management. TMN divides the functions into four layers: business management, service management, network management, and element management. Within the lower layers, the management functions are further divided into fault, configuration, accounting, performance, and security. This set of functions is usually referred to by the abbreviation FCAPS. At the service layer, concepts such as service creation, service directories, and service provisioning have emerged. In general the service layer provides higher-level capability that represents a market need rather than a network element feature. Services at this layer may also cross or aggregate multiple network technologies, which might be separately managed at lower layers.

In this framework, an overlay is viewed as a service, and creation and configuration of the overlay are service creation and service provisioning steps. This perspective supports both the case in which an overlay operator manages a single overlay as well as the overlay operator that operates many overlays.

Service Creation

The overlay operator identifies an application that can be supported by an overlay. Peer software is developed or preexisting peer software is reused. The overlay operator makes the peer software available to the user community, deploys infrastructure peers (if any), and provides a suitable bootstrap mechanism so that users can connect to the overlay. The peer software is designed using P2P principles described in previous chapters so that peers self-organize and automatically connect to other peers in the overlay. In addition, the peer software collects operational statistics and status to deliver to the overlay operator's management agent, which monitors the overlay operation.

The operator controls the intrinsic services of the overlay and may provide a service advertisement and discovery mechanism by which third parties can add new services. For third-party services, the overlay operator can provide service assurance capability to the third party for operations carried by the overlay. The overlay operator should be able to monitor service-use statistics where service invocation uses the overlay for messaging. Service usage records are needed for billing.

Service Provisioning

In conventional network services, a customer selects service options and service quality levels. The service provider in turn configures the necessary network resources and activates the service. In the P2P overlay context, service options and quality levels are determined by the host running the peer software, as well as the collective resources of the current set of connected peers. The overlay operator may deploy high-capacity peers to enhance service quality, such as superpeers, relays, multicast proxies, and gateways. These deployments might be made for specific classes of overlay users, in specific regions of the network, or for specific types of overlay services.

Service Assurance

The service provider enforces the service quality levels agreed on with the customer and sets configuration and monitoring mechanisms in place to enforce these levels. The configuration mechanism relies on the configuration management component of FCAPS. The monitoring mechanism relies on the fault and performance management components of FCAPS.

The P2P overlay is adaptive by design, and peers select the best connection or path from the currently available set by periodically measuring the various links. Mechanisms such as dead node detection and replication are used to avoid information loss. Peer functionality can be upgraded when the operator updates the peer software algorithms and provides updates to existing peers via automatic software download. The overlay operator monitors in real time any faults in the overlay and maintains performance statistics. As in conventional fault management, the operator is concerned with failure conditions at each peer and with correlating these across peers to identify conditions that might cascade into larger regions over the overlay or that indicate a coordinated attack on the operation of the overlay. As in conventional performance management, the overlay operator is also concerned with performance conditions, such as those that violate thresholds for the service class, that indicate problems with the overlay design, or that require provisioning of additional overlay resources.

Accounting

Service costs in telecommunications networks can be packaged in a variety of ways, including by base rate, by usage, and by class of service. In addition, the service-level agreement (SLA) may have penalties to the service provider if the service quality falls below agreed-on levels.

In a P2P overlay, usage-based charging is feasible if each use is securely associated with its source and the amount of use can be reliably and securely measured. For example, a basic service might permit a number of indexing operations per day, and a peer performing beyond this level of indexing operations might either be charged or required to contribute more resources to the overlay. Subscription-based use is less demanding in terms of measuring use but requires subscription management and enforcement of subscriber-only use.

Examples

Table 15.2 illustrates overlay management scenarios for both service assurance and service provisioning. For each example there is a brief description and operations illustrating the use of the operators described. Next we look at scenarios involving specific types of overlays such as resilient overlay networks (discussed in Chapter 11) and P2P storage systems.

Managing a Resilient Overlay Network

A Resilient Overlay Network (RON) is an overlay network that routes application traffic by finding low-latency and available paths that might not be identified by the usual routing protocols. Most RONs have a small peer population, connect all peers in a mesh, and exchange their link measurements with all other peers in the RON. To monitor the operation of the RON, the management agent can be added as a

Table 15.2 Example Management Scenarios

Category	Example	Operation
Service assurance	Peer notifies management agent (MA) that its DHT storage capacity has exceeded a threshold	`notify (p,m,e)` e = threshold exceeded event
Service assurance	MA uses remote control of a peer to perform a diagnostic latency measurement to another peer	`cmd(p,d,m)` d = latency measurement
Service assurance	Peer forwards routing table statistics to MA, such as size of routing table, average age, distribution by region of overlay	`notify (p,m,e)` e = performance report
Service assurance	A peer notifies MA that an object inserted into the DHT is determined to be invalid due to mismatch of digital signature and public key	`notify (p,m,e)` e = object invalid
Service provisioning	MP broadcasts the list of peers that are identified as vehicles for a Sybil attack	`set (P,r,r-list, r-list1)` P = all peers in overlay *r-list* = type of state is blocked peer list *r-list1* = list of blocked peers

Service provisioning	1. MP collects response time history from a set of peers P in a given region to their neighbors
	 2. MP uses remote control at the peers P to determine response time to peers outside the region
	 3. MP provisions superpeers in adjacent regions to reduce end-to-end delay
	 4. MP configures peers P with an updated superpeer list
		`get (P,r,h,t,m)`
		 h = history
		 t = most recent
		 `cmd(p,d,m)` d = measure index operation response time to specified peers
		 `get(P,r,rly-list,m)`
		
		 `set(P,r,rly-list,rly-list2)`
		 rly-list = state is superpeer list
		 rly-list1 = updated superpeer list

well-known RON peer and can take on the special role of management agent. This role allows the peer to connect with other peers in the overlay and receive status messages without having to actively participate in flow routing. The overhead of participating in the operation of the overlay could interfere with its management agent role.

Following the FCAPS model, let's divide the management parameters into configuration, performance, and fault categories (Table 15.3). *Configuration* refers to operational settings of peers that can be set either by the management agent or the peer itself, using its self-organizing algorithms. *Performance* refers to variables that can be measured and that are significant to the function of the overlay.

Table 15.3 Example FCAPS Variables of Interest for Overlay Management by Type of Overlay

Overlay Type	Configuration	Performance	Fault
Generic DHT	Peer membership Overlay topology Object max size Max request rate Max number of objects	Churn rate Inbound and outbound bandwidth usage per peer Number of superpeers Average connection degree	Lookup rate > threshold Insert rate > threshold Churn rate > threshold
RON	Infrastructure peer status	Latency topology Per-flow measurements Statistics for path switching	Overlay path quality < native path quality
Distributed storage	Replication level Storage partition capacity	Storage partition usage Read/write bit rate	Replication level < threshold Read/write bit rate > threshold
File sharing	Proactive caching Cache size	Number of lookups by file Number of inserts by file File length and signature	Corrupted object inserted Object size > threshold
VoP2P	Feature peers Relay peers Media codecs	Feature usage load Relay quality Session lifetime	Voice quality < threshold Midcall relay failure

For example, for most overlays churn rate is an important parameter and could be calculated by having the management agent track join and leave events. *Fault* refers to functional failures or performance thresholds being exceeded.

The topology of the overlay is an important configuration parameter to monitor, since it can be used to determine load distribution and detect overlay partitions. For a RON, the network measurements that each peer collects and distributes to the other peers can also be sent to the management agent. Current values can be displayed with the topology to visualize bottleneck and low-capacity paths. Historic values can be used for trend detection or variation by workload or time of day. The RON also maintains periodic per-flow measurements. These measurements can be evaluated against a threshold so that a fault is generated to the management agent when the path the RON selects is not meeting the performance available to the native path. To evaluate and improve the behavior of the overlay, it's important to collect statistics for switching to alternate paths.

Managing a Distributed File Storage Service

A P2P distributed file storage service can be constructed using the secondary storage areas of peers in the overlay. A number of designs have been proposed, including PAST,[539] which runs on Pastry, and CFS,[541] which runs on Chord. In PAST, each user has a quota for the amount of storage that can be used in the overlay. Files are stored using the hashed file name as the key. Thus two different files from the same owner are likely to be stored at different sets of peers in the overlay. Each file is stored at the k closest peers in the overlay. Since peer addresses are generated randomly, there is a high probability that the k nodes are geographically dispersed.

CFS provides a distributed read-only file system and stores files in the overlay by dividing each file into blocks. The blocks for popular files will be spread over many servers. Each block is identified using a hash of its contents as the key. Each block is replicated k times in the overlay, with replicas at the peers immediately after the block's successor in the Chord ring. A peer sends a request for a block as a DHT lookup of the block's key. Each peer along the lookup path checks its cache to see whether the block is present. If it is, the block is immediately returned. If the request reaches the primary peer, the block is returned to the requesting peer, which then sends a copy to each peer along the lookup path to add to its cache.

Figure 15.1 illustrates the role of the management agent in monitoring the service quality of a distributed file store that is similar to the PAST model. A peer stores a file by the hash of its filename. The peer that receives the request forwards it to the $k-1$ closest peers in the overlay address space for replication. The management agent is notified that the distributed file service has accepted a file with a specified identifier. Later one of the peers storing the replica leaves the overlay. This generates a replication-level exception to both the peer that inserted the file and the management agent. If the primary storing peer fails to add another replica peer within a given time window, the management agent may intervene.

In addition, the management agent can monitor the uptime and storage integrity of each peer. The software for each peer can perform periodic file system integrity checks and send negative results to the management agent. A notification is also sent when the file system usage exceeds the threshold.

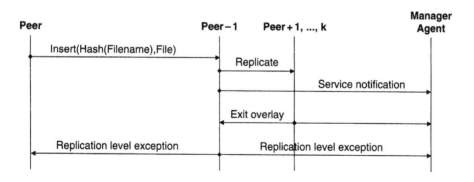

FIGURE 15.1 Overlay messages between peers storing file replicas and the manager agent.

OVERLAY MANAGEMENT ARCHITECTURE
Integration with Peer State and Event Detection

The management function should be organized to leverage the existing self-organization and peer coordination mechanisms intrinsic to the overlay. In addition, the peers and the management agent need to communicate. In the next section we discuss the various types of management messaging and how to accomplish them over the overlay.

Each peer has internal state, including routing tables and storage for data objects. It can instrument its state to collect statistics without interfering with the operation of the overlay. For example, statistics about the size of the routing table and the freshness of routing table entries can be calculated from time to time.

In addition, some peers may take on additional roles such as those shown in Table 15.4. These roles may require specific capacity, and the peer is likely to manage additional internal state information to perform these roles. Table 15.4

Table 15.4 Roles of Peers and Corresponding State Information for Performance Management

Role	Description	State Information
Superpeer	A peer that mediates NAT traversal for other peers	Client peers
Media relay, mixer, or transcoder	For streaming applications, a peer that acts an intermediary and may perform media processing for a streaming media session	Number of relayed sessions Data rate per session Latency measurements for endpoints
Multicast proxy	An infrastructure peer for improving the performance of application layer multicasting	Number of multicast sessions Node degree per session Data rate per session
Quarantined peer	A peer that is restricted to client status until its lifetime reaches a minimum value	Operational statistics of quaranteed peers
Client	A node that is not part of the overlay but that can use the overlay services	Operational statistics of clients
Virtual home agent	A peer with a static IP address that mediates overlay messages for one or more mobile peers	Number of mobile peers Roaming handoff statistics
Gateway	A peer that processes messages between peers in two or more different overlays; translating between protocols as needed	Message rates Message histograms

shows example state information related to these roles. This state information is likely to be of interest to the management agent, and collection of current and historic statistics should be supported by the management architecture.

Peers may encounter unexpected conditions, sudden capacity reductions, anomalous behavior from their neighbors, and performance problems. More examples of overlay fault conditions are shown in Table 15.5. These fault conditions should be reported to the management agent. A means to transmit notification messages from any peer to the management agent is needed. When it receives a fault notification, the management agent can correlate it with faults from other agents. The management agent can also evaluate it in the context of historical fault information. The management agent can more easily construct a global view of fault conditions and may have access to information about underlying network conditions that might not be available to peers.

Table 15.5 Fault Notifications

Category	Example	Management Agent Response
Routing table entry error	Can't reach a peer Timeout in peer's keepalive	Correlate with other peer timeouts
Invalid message	Duplicate overlay address detected Invalid overlay address Unrecognized request	Detect and disable illegal peer
Capacity constraint	Incoming message rate exceeds threshold	Check for DOS attack
Capacity constraint	Churn rate exceeds threshold	Check for underlying network cause
Capacity constraint	Too many keys to store	Check load balancing
Capacity constraint	Too many values for a key	Check whether object indexing popularity exceeds capability
Capacity constraint	Object too large to store	Count occurrences to identify DOS attempt
Capacity constraint	Number of clients exceeds threshold	Check whether there are insufficient superpeers in region
Security	Failure to authenticate peer	Count authentication failures
Integrity	Object corrupted Message or message field corrupted	Correlate to detect pollution attack Correlate with network link errors

Security Considerations

The introduction of a central point of control in the overlay is a potential security vulnerability. Malicious peers may spoof the management agent and try to use management agent message types to control other peers. If the overlay supports message broadcast for management messages, this can be abused by flooding the overlay with messages.

Thus, it is important that the management agent messages be directly authenticated and the management agent and the message mechanism not be compromised. There are additional requirements for the overlay itself, including security of peer identity, ability to authenticate any peer and verify that a message is from a given peer, and ability to prevent the interception of messages by other entities. The techniques for securing the overlay described in Chapter 14 are applicable here.

Generality for Various Types of Overlay

In conventional telecommunications networks, the management protocols and frameworks discussed earlier have been widely used in a variety of networking technologies and with network equipment from many different vendors. Large carriers routinely deploy a large number of legacy and new network technologies. Their networks include technologies such as wireless, cellular, ATM, SONET, Frame Relay, optical networks, IP, satellite, and microwave links. The flexibility of the management frameworks is important since it future-proofs a service provider's investment in management systems and enables higher-level service management and business management functions.

There are likely to be many types of overlays deployed in the future. Thus it is desirable that overlay management mechanisms be general purpose so that they can be easily reused across different overlay types. This requires a common management messaging protocol with common types for events, configuration parameters, state, performance metrics, and historical data.

OVERLAY MESSAGING FOR MANAGEMENT OPERATIONS
Reaching All Peers

For some management operations the management agent might need to send a message to all peers in the overlay. For example, to counteract a Sybil attack, a list of blocked addresses can be circulated to all peers. A software security patch for all peers to download and install could also be sent to all peers. The number of overlay messages needed for such broadcasts is $\Omega(N)$ assuming that every peer receives exactly one message. If, in addition, all peers in the overlay use broadcast messaging for application purposes such as global search, at least N^2 messages are sent. Thus overlay broadcast is impractical for large overlays as a general messaging mechanism, but in limited use it is feasible.

An overlay broadcast mechanism can be used to send a message to all peers. In overlay broadcast, a message is propagated to all peers using the overlay routing algorithm. Overall broadcast does not necessarily mean flooding as used in early unstructured overlays. Several broadcast topologies have been developed for structured overlays for overlay maintenance and these are suitable for overlay broadcast. For example, as described in Chapters 4 and 5, O(1)-hop overlays One-Hop and D1HT[531] maintain a fixed topology for routing table maintenance (Figure 15.2). Carrying a broadcast message over these topologies requires that the overlay routing algorithm be modified to use a new broadcast message type and to forward this message type using the maintenance connections. In addition, a peer should check to see that the message hasn't been previously forwarded. These changes are straightforward to accommodate.

Some overlay broadcast-messaging mechanisms have been proposed for multi-hop overlays. A blind search technique for Chord and Pastry uses a broadcast topology[534] by leveraging the finger tables and adjacent peer links. Instead of sending a request to only a single neighbor, the request is forwarded to a subset of neighbor links. The request is tagged to mark the region of the overlay to which the request is to be propagated, to avoid duplicate messages. This blind search message routing can be adapted to send a broadcast message.

In earlier work, El-Ansary et al.[529] present a similar broadcast mechanism for structured overlays for general use, which recursively divides the address space to which the message is forwarded. The approach is based on viewing the routing tables as forming a k-ary tree connecting all the nodes in the overlay, with the node initiating the broadcast as the root of the tree.

It is preferred that the broadcast topology distribute the load uniformly among all the peers and take advantage of proximity of peers in the network. In general, due to churn and the inconsistent state of routing tables, these designs do not guarantee that a message reaches all peers in the overlay.

If message broadcast is not available, peers can be programmed to periodically poll a specific overlay address or Website for global messages.

Aggregating Data Collection for Performance Management

Performance information can be collected from the peers in the overlay in the form of variables, historical data, and statistics. This information can be used for trend analysis, for example, to identify areas of the overlay where resource saturation might occur. It can also be used by the overlay operator to evaluate the settings of configuration parameters, algorithm design, and the potential for new services. Generally, performance data are not as time critical as fault information except in applications in which quality of service must be enforced. On the other hand, performance data collection can generate large volumes of information that could easily overwhelm both the overlay and the management agent when aggregated over all the peers. Two methods to manage the information flow are to control the rate at which performance data are sent and to have multiple collection points for different areas of the overlay to report to.

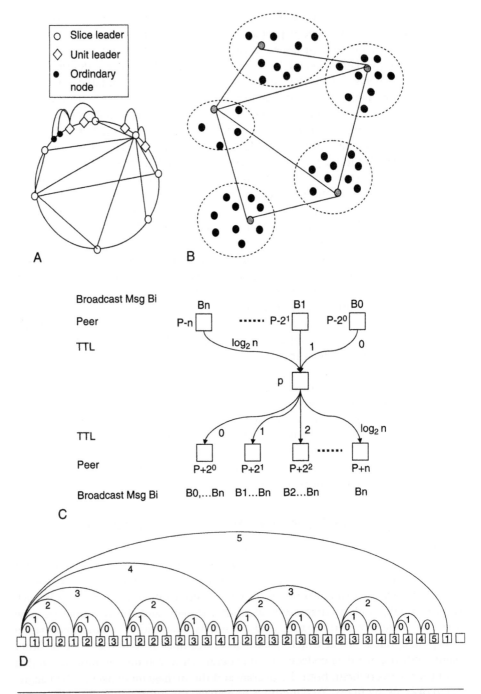

FIGURE 15.2 Broadcast topologies for overlays: (A) subdivision of overlay used in OneHop, (B) connected clusters according to network topology, and (C,D) message broadcast using overlay fingers in D1HT.

Performance data can be sent to the management agent on request or by subscription, in which case a peer publishes the information at some update interval. The broadcast topologies described earlier can be used in the reverse direction for peers to forward performance data to the management agent. A bottom-up algorithm for constructing aggregation and broadcast trees is described in [543]. This scheme differs from the broadcast mechanisms described earlier in that it doesn't reuse the routing table links to form the tree. Instead, it defines a parent(x) function that each peer x uses to determine its parent in the tree. This approach has the flexibility that the tree can have different characteristics such as a larger out-degree compared to the overlay's own inherent tree structure. However, additional overhead is required to build and maintain the bottom-up tree, and if more than one tree is needed, each must be separately constructed.

Multicast

Most communication between peers and the management agent does not require message broadcast. Data collection and configuration changes can be scoped by peer role, geographic location, neighbors of a peer, region of the overlay, region of the native network, or proximity to an infrastructure resource. Let's assume that the management agent can determine a set of peers and their overlay addresses that are to receive a message. If the set is small, the management agent can send each peer an individual message. Otherwise, to send a single message to a set of peers is a type of scope-broadcast or overlay multicast. The broadcast tree described earlier could be used for scoped broadcasts. For example, [530] and [544] use TTL values to approximately control a k-node broadcast in an overlay spanning tree. However, this technique may not be able to address the correct set of k-nodes and cannot constrain the set of nodes reached by the message to exactly k. If the set of peers is stable and messaging to this set is repeated over a suitable time window, a multicast tree can be constructed with the management agent as the root. Algorithms for implementing such multicast trees in overlays are described in Chapter 9.

MANAGING THE IMPACT OF THE OVERLAY TRAFFIC ON THE ISP NETWORK

P2P Traffic in the ISP Network

In addition to managing the overlay's service quality, both the design of the overlay and its management are important to the underlying physical networks. Each overlay relies on the services of these networks, which are operated by many different ISPs. The impact of the overlay on the underlying network has become a major issue due to the dramatic growth of P2P traffic in recent years. As a result of this growth, P2P applications have become a dominant portion of network traffic in ISP networks. High levels of traffic increase ISP costs and cause network congestion, potentially affecting other applications and users. The problem is complicated by a number of factors, including the popularity of P2P applications with end users, the desire of content owners to limit the use of P2P applications, and regulatory policies for network neutrality in some jurisdictions, such as the United States. In addition, some ISPs have reported that high network use is due to a small percentage of P2P application users in the customer population.

Approaches to Managing P2P Traffic

There are several proposals for addressing the problems due to P2P application use in ISP networks. Most of these are independent of the overlay itself or an ability to manage the overlay. These proposals include:

- *Restrict each user's bandwidth usage or define different classes of use so that high-volume users pay more.* This approach has the effect of throttling the P2P traffic, thus reducing congestion, without requiring much investment from the ISP. The perceived performance of P2P applications is likely to be affected.

- *Block P2P traffic.* No P2P traffic would be permitted. This solves the ISP's traffic problem but is unlikely to please its customers and may be difficult to enforce, since peer protocols can be encapsulated in other protocols to avoid detection. A good overview of current approaches to blocking and P2P application countermeasures to blocking is provided in [549].

- *Enable local peers to find resources in the ISP's network.* The idea is to help P2P file-sharing applications route more of their file transfers to peers in the local network. This makes the overlay more efficient but might not be appealing to every ISP. It also won't help other types of P2P applications such as VoP2P. An example of this approach is P4P, discussed in the following section.

- *Add P2P content caches similar to Web caches in the ISP network.* Then a request for a piece of content could go first to the local cache, saving network bandwidth. An ISP operating such a cache could face legal claims from content owners whose content is served by the cache.

- *Upgrade the network equipment with higher bandwidth connections and higher-capacity routers.* The ISP might not have a means to recover this investment, and it could lead to higher network costs for all users, even those who don't use P2P applications. In addition, more capacity can't eliminate all congestion.

P4P

Proactive Network Provider Participation for P2P (P4P) is an ISP mechanism by which nearby peers in an ISP network can more easily locate each other for the purposes of keeping traffic in the ISP's network that might otherwise be routed to an arbitrary peer anywhere in the world.[547,548] P4P is an industry group organized by DCIA.[546] Most ISPs organize their networks into tiers of routers, with the edge routers being closest to customer connections and a border router connecting with other ISPs' networks. In between are regional routers. Routing becomes more expensive for the ISP as packets move from edge routers to regional routers to border routers. If a peer can locate the required content at another peer at the same edge router, the packets will not reach the next regional router. Peers in the same ISP network are likely to perform transfers more quickly, improving performance for end users.

In the P4P approach, the ISP installs a server called an iTracker in its network. The server contains information about the network organization, such as preferred routes and congested links. Each peer queries the local iTracker and uses the information to connect to peers that are closer or preferred from an ISP standpoint. For peers participating in torrents, the torrent tracker can also obtain information about the ISP's iTracker. The torrent tracker uses this information to include a list of local peers.

SUMMARY

P2P applications can simplify the deployment of new distributed applications because of their limited dependence on new infrastructure. But it is likely that as P2P applications become a mainstream phenomenon, user expectations for service quality will increase. Methods for managing conventional networks and applications can be considered for managing future P2P overlays. But some distinct differences require adaptation, including the self-organizing characteristics of the peers, that most peers are in domains and run on hosts that are outside the control of an overlay operator, and the goal of limiting management infrastructure deployment costs.

Today's P2P applications are best-effort ones, but in the future they may offer different classes of service with multiple pricing levels. Supporting such service models requires real-time monitoring of service usage and the ability to provision new resources to improve performance. Usage monitoring and billing are also important if P2P service overlays are to attract third-party service providers. In addition, some service plans require accurate monitoring and billing of service usage.

The popularity of P2P overlays has caused substantial growth in ISP network traffic, increasing congestion and raising concerns about suitable methods for managing P2P traffic. The issues include traffic fairness, customer satisfaction, public policy, and ISP revenue.

FOR FURTHER READING

The concept of an overlay operator is called an *overlay ISP* in [383] and an *overlay service provider* in [390].

Detailed information about telecommunications and network management can be found in [533] and [532]. Service management is covered in [537] and [538]. Examples of service management are described in [536].

Buford[527] introduces and gives an overview of managed overlays and evaluates the messaging costs compared to those for overlay maintenance in different types of structured overlays.

Autonomic computing considers how properties of self-management, self-diagnosis, and self-healing can be added to existing systems to make them easier to manage. Principles of autonomic computing are relevant to improving the manageability of P2P overlays.

P2P overlays are also being considered as tools for network management, and some recent results are found in a special issue of the *Journal of Network and Systems Management* on "Peer-to-Peer Technologies in Network and Service Management" (Vol. 15, No. 3, September 2007, Springer Netherlands). SELFMAN[545] is a research project that uses a self-managing overlay to manage higher-level services.

Standardization of solutions for managing P2P traffic in ISP networks is being considered in the IETF. An overview of the potential technical work is provided in [550].

Bootstrap   (1) The process by which a peer which intends to join an overlay locates one or more peers that are connected to the overlay and through which the joining peer can perform the join protocol. (2) The process by which a new overlay is initially created.

Churn   The arrival and departure of peers to and from the overlay, which changes the peer population of the overlay.

A related concept is mobility-induced churn, which occurs when a roaming node departs and rejoins the overlay due to a network address change after a network-layer roaming transition.

Content-Addressable Network (CAN)   A type of distributed object location and routing system in which objects can be located either by identifier or by some other representation of the content of the object.

Content locality   In an overlay that spans multiple administrative domains, data inserted by peers within one administrative domain or in the same local area network are stored physically at peers within the same administrative domain or located on the same LAN.

Distributed hash table (DHT)   A structured overlay that uses key-based routing for put and get index operations and in which each peer is assigned to maintain a portion of the DHT index.

Distributed Object Location and Routing   A method for storing and finding an object placed arbitrarily in a distributed set of networked hosts using an identifier of the object. An example DOLR is key-based routing.

Eclipse attack   An attack on an overlay network in which the attacker controls a large fraction of neighboring nodes.

Federated overlay   An overlay that is implemented by multiple administrative domains, which may use different routing algorithms and addressing mechanisms in each domain.

Free rider   A peer that uses resources of a P2P system significantly in excess of the amount of resources it contributes to the P2P system.

Gossip protocol   A protocol by which a node randomly selects and exchanges information with other nodes in the network.

Half-life   The time it takes for a peer-to-peer network to replace half its nodes through departures and arrivals [38].

Hierarchical overlay   An overlay architecture that uses multiple overlays arranged in a nested fashion, and the nested overlays are interconnected in a tree. A message to a peer in a different overlay is forwarded to the nearest common parent overlay in the hierarchy.

Hop In the path in which an overlay message is carried from a source peer to destination peer, a hop is each direct transmission of the message from one peer to another peer in the path.

Internet coordinate system (ICS) An ICS maps network position to an arbitrary dimension Euclidean space with a distance function such that the distance between two Internet hosts can be accurately estimated by the distance between their respective ICS coordinates.

Key-based routing A set of keys is associated with addresses in the address space such that the nearest peer to an address stores the values for the associated keys, and the routing algorithm treats keys as addresses.

Managed overlay An overlay that can be dynamically configured and continuously monitored for operational parameters so as to continuously enforce performance, administrative, and security policies, where such policies can be changed by the overlay operator.

Multihop structured overlay A structured overlay in which messages from source peer to destination peer on average require multiple hops. An important category of multihop overlays includes those in which the number of hops is bounded by $O(\log N)$ hops, where N is the number of peers in the overlay.

Multicast A means of point-to-multipoint communication in which the same message is sent to multiple destinations such that duplicate messages are carried by the network only when routing paths for some subset of the destinations diverge.

Network address translator (NAT) A device that converts network addresses in packets as they are transmitted between two different address domains. Typically a NAT is used to convert between a private address space and a public address.

NAT traversal A mechanism to create a connection to a host that is behind a NAT.

One-hop structured overlay A structured overlay in which messages from source peer to destination peer on average require a constant number, that is, O(1), of hops, regardless of the size N of the overlay.

Overlay address An identifier in an address space for the overlay in which each peer has at least one unique identifier. The overlay address is used to route messages in the overlay toward a destination peer.

Overlay multicast (OM) (1) Hosts participating in a multicast session form an overlay network and only utilize unicast among pairs of hosts for data dissemination. The hosts in overlay multicast exclusively handle group management, routing, and tree construction, without any support from Internet routers. This is also commonly known as Application Layer Multicast (ALM) or End System Multicast (ESM).

(2) A backbone overlay is constructed by deploying special intermediate proxies that create multicast trees among themselves. End hosts communicate with proxies via unicast or native multicast.

Overlay network or overlay   An application layer virtual or logical network in which endpoints are addressable and that provides connectivity, routing, and messaging between endpoints. Overlay networks are frequently used as a substrate for deploying new network services or for providing a routing topology not available from the underlying physical network. Many peer-to-peer systems are overlay networks that run on top of the Internet.

Overlay operator   An entity that develops an overlay to provide peer-to-peer services to end users and a service delivery platform for third parties.

Path locality   In an overlay that spans multiple administrative domains, queries for objects that are available at peers in the same administrative domain are only routed to peers in the same administrative domain.

Peer   An end system, node, or host that is a member of a peer-to-peer system.

Peer capability   The available resources at a peer relevant to its role in a peer-to-peer overlay, specified as a set of capacities and system attributes.

Peer software   Application software provided by the overlay, which peers use to participate in the overlay. The peer software may be extendable by third parties. It may be instrumented to enable management of the peer function in the overlay.

Peer-to-peer (P2P)   "A distributed network architecture may be called a peer-to-peer network, if the participants share a part of their own hardware resources (processing power, storage capacity, network link capacity, printers). These shared resources are necessary to provide the Service and content offered by the network (e.g. file sharing or shared workspaces for collaboration). They are accessible by other peers." [25]
"Peer-to-peer systems are distributed systems consisting of interconnected nodes able to self-organize into network topologies with the purpose of sharing resources such as content, CPU cycles, storage and bandwidth, capable of adapting to failures and accommodating transient populations of nodes while maintaining acceptable connectivity and performance, without requiring the intermediation or support of a global centralized server or authority." [107]

Prefix-based routing   Each peer in the overlay forwards messages to the next hop based on the next sequence of address elements (the prefix) in the overlay address. First used in PRR, Tapestry, Pastry, P-Grid, Cycloid, and Z-Grid are systems that use prefix-based addressing.

Proximity-based overlay   Peers select adjacent nodes based on proximity of the nodes in the network.

Proximity neighbor selection (PNS)   An overlay maintenance strategy in which each node biases its selection of nodes in its routing table to those with which it has low latency.

Proximity route selection (PRS)   An overlay maintenance strategy in which a peer operates to increase the size of its routing tables so as to have as many nodes to choose from when routing.

Quarantine   A mechanism to reduce churn in an overlay in which a joining peer remains only a client of the overlay until the quarantine period has passed, after which it is promoted to a normal peer. Quarantine benefits from the node lifetime following a heavy-tailed distribution.

Routing table   A method to organize overlay routing information that contains a mapping between overlay addresses and native addresses and may contain other information such as the capabilities of the peer, distance from the peer, and time of last communication with the peer.

Small-world network   A class of random graphs in which most nodes can be reached by every other node in a small number of hops.

Semantic overlay   An overlay network in which routing topology is organized according to the semantic associations and relationship of information being stored in the overlay.

Service overlay   The integration of an overlay with one or more network or application services, and which may include coupling the overlay with a service advertisement and discovery mechanism.

Service-oriented architecture   An information system architecture that uses service orientation as its basic design principle, including external interfaces defined as services with service description documents and typically service discovery and advertisement mechanisms.

Stealth node   A mechanism to avoid mobility-induced churn in which a mobile peer can send outgoing overlay requests but does not receive incoming overlay requests.

Stretch   An overlay performance metric that compares the network distance of the overlay route versus the direct underlay route between the endpoints. Specifically, if $d(x_i, x_j)$ denotes the time to send a message from x_i to x_j, the stretch of that path is $[d(x_1,x_2) + \ldots + d(x_{n-1},x_n)]/d(x_1,x_n)$.

Structured overlay   An overlay in which nodes cooperatively maintain routing information about how to reach all nodes in the overlay.

Superdistribution   The distribution of digital content from user to user such that the content is freely distributed but usage and content changes are controlled by the content owner.

Superpeer   A hierarchical overlay in which peers with public IP address perform the overlay operations on behalf of regular peers that are behind NATs.

Sybil attack   An attack on an overlay in which the attacker obtains multiple different overlay identities.

Unicast   A means of point-to-point communication where a message is delivered from a sender node to a single other node. If a node wants to send the same information to many destinations using unicast, it must perform replicated unicast and send N copies of the data to each destination in separate messages.

Unstructured overlay   An overlay in which a node relies only on its adjacent nodes for delivery of messages to other nodes in the overlay. Example message propagation strategies are flooding and random walk.

Variable-hop structured overlay   A structured overlay adapts the hop-count performance of the overlay according to the peer's network bandwidth budget so that at higher bandwidth budget the average hop count decreases and at lower bandwidth budget the average hop count increases.

Virtual node   The assignment of multiple peer addresses to a single node in an overlay, proposed in the design of the Chord DHT, to improve the distribution of keys in the overlay.

Whitewasher   A user who leaves a P2P system and rejoins it after acquiring a new identity to avoid reputational penalties.[690]

References

Chapter 1

[1] D. Clark, B. Lehr, S. Bauer, P. Faratin, R. Sami, and J. Wroclawski, Overlay networks and the future of the Internet, Communications & Strategies 63, 3Q2006.

[2] D. Clark, B. Lehr, S. Bauer, P. Faratin, R. Sami, and J. Wroclawski, The growth of Internet overlay networks: implications for architecture, industry structure and policy, 33rd Telecommunications Policy Research Conference, Sept. 2005, available at http://web.si.umich.edu/tprc/papers/2005/466/TPRC_Overlays_9_8_05.pdf.

[3] L. Peterson, T. Anderson, S. Shenker, and J. Turner, Overcoming the Internet impasse through virtualization, IEEE Computer, Apr. 2005, 62–69.

[4] J. Li, B. T. Loo, J. Hellerstein, F. Kaashoek, D. Karger, and R. Morris, On the feasibility of peer-to-peer Web indexing and search, 2nd International Workshop on Peer-to-Peer Systems (IPTPS 2003), Berkeley, CA, 2003.

[5] T. Suel, C. Mathur, J. Wu, J. Zhang, A. Delis, M. Kharrazi, X. Long, and K. Shanmugasundaram, ODISSEA: A peer-to-peer architecture for scalable Web search and information retrieval, 6th International Workshop on the Web and Databases (WebDB), June 2003.

[6] J. Buford and M. Rahman, Instant Messaging and Presence Service (IMPS), in: Wireless Multimedia: Technologies and Applications, A. Salkintzis, and N. Passas, (eds.), 2005.

[7] UPnP Forum, www.upnp.org.

[8] Peer-to-Peer Universal Computing Consortium, www.pucc.jp/en/index.html.

[9] DCIA, www.dcia.info.

[10] Sandvine Corp. Analysis of Traffic Demographics in Broadband Networks, IETF Workshop on Peer-to-Peer Infrastructure (P2Pi), May 2008.

Chapter 2

[11] S. Narayanan, D. Braun, J. Buford, et al., Peer-to-peer streaming for networked consumer electronics, IEEE Communications Magazine, June 2007.

[12] M. Jeronimo and J. Weast, UPnP Design by Example, Intel Press, 2003.

[13] Bluetooth Special Interest Group (2001a), Specification of the Bluetooth System—Core, Version 1.1.

[14] Bluetooth Special Interest Group (2001b), Specification of the Bluetooth System—Core, Version 1.1, SDP specification, vol. 1, part E.

[15] J. Buford, R. Kumar, and G. Perkins, Composition trust bindings in pervasive computing service composition, IEEE Workshop on Pervasive Computing and Communication Security (PerSec), Mar. 2006.

[16] D. Braun, J. Buford, et al., UP2P: a peer-to-peer, overlay architecture for ubiquitous communications and networking, IEEE Communications Magazine, Dec. 2008.

[17] Rüdiger Schollmeier, A definition of peer-to-peer networking for the classification of peer-to-peer architectures and applications, Peer-to-Peer Computing 2001.

[18] D. Stutzbach and R. Rejaie, Understanding churn in peer-to-peer networks, Proceedings of the 6th ACM SIGCOMM on Internet Measurement, Rio de Janeiro, Oct. 25–27, 2006, IMC '06, ACM Press, New York, 189–202.

[19] S. Krishnamurthy, S. El-Ansary, E. Aurell, and S. Haridi, A statistical theory of Chord under churn, in: 4th Annual International Workshop on Peer-to-Peer Systems (IPTPS'05), Feb. 2005, Ithaca, NY.

[20] K. Aberer, L. O. Alima, A. Ghodsi, S. Girdzijauskas, S. Haridi, and M. Hauswirth, The essence of P2P: a reference architecture for overlay networks, Proceedings of the Fifth IEEE International Conference on Peer-to-Peer Computing (P2P '05), Volume 00, Aug. 31–Sept. 2, 2005, IEEE Computer Society, Washington, DC, 11–20.

[21] M. Castro, M. Costa, and A. Rowstron, Debunking some myths about structured and unstructured overlays, Proceedings of the 2nd Conference on Symposium on Networked Systems Design & Implementation, Volume 2 (May 2–4, 2005), USENIX Association, Berkeley, 7–7.

[22] S. Wang, D. Xuan, and W. Zhao, Analyzing and enhancing the resilience of structured peer-to-peer systems. J. Parallel Distrib. Comput., 65(2):207–219, 2005.

[23] K. Gummadi, S. Gribble, S. Ratnasamy, S. Shenker, and I. Stoica, The impact of DHT routing geometry on resilience and proximity, Proc. of ACM SIGCOMM 2003, ACM Press, 2003.

[24] J. S. Kong, J. S. A. Bridgewater, and V. P. Roychowdhury. A general framework for scalability and performance analysis of DHT routing systems, Proc. of the International Conference on Dependable Systems and Networks (DSN '06), 2006.

[25] D. Loguinov, A. Kumar, V. Rai, and S. Ganesh, Graph-theoretic analysis of structured peer-to-peer systems: routing distances and fault resilience, Proceedings of the 2003 Conference on Applications, Technologies, Architectures, and Protocols For Computer Communications, Karlsruhe, Germany, Aug. 25–29, 2003, SIGCOMM '03, ACM Press, 395–406.

[26] J. Aspnes, Z. Diamadi, G. Shah, Fault-tolerant routing in peer-to-peer systems, Proceedings of the 21st Annual Symposium on Principles of Distributed Computing, July 21–24, 2002, Monterey, CA.

[27] X. Zhang, Q. Zhang, Z. Zhang, G. Song, and W. Zhu, A construction of locality-aware overlay network: mOverlay and its performance, IEEE Journal on Selected Areas in Communications, Vol. 22, No. 1, Jan. 2004.

[28] J. Xu, A. Kumar, and X. Yu, On the fundamental tradeoffs between routing table size and network diameter in peer-to-peer networks, IEEE Journal on Selected Areas in Communications, November 2003.

[29] S. Guha, N. Daswani, and R. Jain, An experimental study of the Skype peer-to-peer VoIP system, in: 5th Annual International Workshop on Peer-to-Peer Systems (IPTPS'06), 2006.

[30] K. Shudo, Y. Tanaka, and S. Sekiguchi, OverlayWeaver: an overlay construction toolkit, Computer Communications Review, Vol. 31, No. 2, 402–412, Feb. 2008.

[31] F. Dabek, B. Zhao, P. Druschel, J. Kubiatowicz, and I. Stoica, Towards a common API for structured peer-to-peer overlays, in: Proc. 2nd Annual International Workshop on Peer-to-Peer Systems (IPTPS'03), 2003.

[32] B. Biskupski, J. Dowling, and J. Sacha, Properties and mechanisms of self-organizing MANET and P2P systems, ACM Trans. Auton. Adapt. Syst. 2, 1 (March 2007), 34 pp.

[33] L. Alima, A. Ghodsi, and S. Haridi, A framework for structured peer-to-peer overlay networks, in: LNCS volume 3267 of the Post-proceedings of Global Computing 2004, Springer-Verlag, 2004, 223-250.

Chapter 3

[34] S. Bornholdt and H. G. Schuster (eds.), Handbook of Graphs and Networks, Wiley-VCH, 2003.

[35] B. Bollobás and O. Riordan, Mathematical results on scale-free random graphs, in: S. Bornholdt, H. G. Schuster (eds.), Handbook of Graphs and Networks, Wiley-VCH, 2003, 1-34.

[36] A.-L. Barabási and R. Albert, Emergence of scaling in random networks, Science 286, 1999, 509-512.

[37] A.-L. Barabási, R. Albert, and H. Jeong, Scale-free characteristics of random networks: the topology of the World Wide Web, Physica A 281, 2000.

[38] Jon Kleinberg, The small-world phenomenon: an algorithm perspective, Proceedings of the 32nd Annual ACM Symposium on Theory of Computing, May 21-23, 2000, Portland, Oregon, 163-170.

[39] D. J. Watts and S. H. Strogatz, Collective dynamics of "small-World" networks, Nature 393, 1998, 440-442.

[40] S. Milgram, The small world problem, Psychology Today 2, 1967, 60-67.

[41] L. A. Adamic, B. Humberman, R. Lukose, and A. Puniyani, Search in power-law networks, Phys. Rev. E, Vol. 64, 2001, 46135-46143.

[42] L. Li, D. Alderson, R. Tanaka, J. C. Doyle, W. Willinger, Towards a theory of scale-free graphs: definition, properties, and implications (extended version), Internet Mathematica, 2005.

[43] I. Clarke, A distributed decentralized information storage and retrieval system (unpublished report), Division of Informatics, University of Edinburgh, 1999, www.freenetproject.org.

[44] I. Clarke, O. Sandberg, B. Wiley, and T. W. Hong, Freenet: A distributed anonymous information storage and retrieval system, in: Proc. ICSI Workshop Design Issues in Anonymity and Unobservability, Berkeley, CA, June 2000.

[45] H.-E. Skogh, J. Haeggstrom, A. Ghodsi, and R. Ayani, FastFreenet: improving Freenet performance by preferential partition routing and file mesh propagation, in: Proceedings of the 6th International Workshop on Global and Peer-to-Peer Computing on Large-Scale Distributed Systems (CCGRID '06), IEEE Computer Society, 2006, 9.

[46] H. Zhang, A. Goel, and R. Govindan, Using the small-world model to improve Freenet performance, Comput. Networks 46, 4 (Nov. 2004), 555-574.

[47] I. Clarke, Freenet's Next Generation Routing Protocol, 2003.

[48] Y. Chawathe, S. Ratnasamy, L. Breslau, S. Shenker, and N. Lanham, GIA: Making Gnutella-like P2P systems scalable, ACM SIGCOMM 2003.

[49] Y. Qiao and F. E. Bustamante, Structured and unstructured overlays under the microscope: a measurement-based view of two P2P systems that people use, in: Proceedings of the

Annual Technical Conference on Usenix '06 Annual Technical Conference (Boston, MA, May 30–June 3, 2006), USENIX Association, Berkeley, CA, 2006, 31–31.

[50] M. Castro, M. Costa, and A. Rowstron, Debunking some myths about structured and unstructured overlays, Proc. of the 2nd Symposium on Networked Sys. Design and Impl. (NSDI) 2005.

[51] C. Xie, S. Guo, R. Rejaie, and Y. Pan, Examining Graph properties of unstructured peer-to-peer overlay topology, Global Internet Symposium, 2007.

[52] Gnutella2 Developer Network, http://g2.trillinux.org/index.php?title=Main_Page, retrieved Nov. 2007.

[53] J. Liang, R. Kumar, and K. Ross, The FastTrack overlay: a measurement study, Computer Networks, 50, 842–858, 2006.

[54] Krishna P. N. Puttaswamy and Ben Y. Zhao, A case for unstructured distributed hash tables, Proceedings of IEEE Global Internet Symposium, Anchorage, AK, May 2007.

[55] R. Morselli, B. Bhattacharjee, A. Srinivasan, and M. Marsh, Efficient lookup on unstructured topologies, in: Proceedings of the 24th Annual ACM Symposium on Principles of Distributed Computing, Las Vegas (July 17–20, 2005), PODC '05, ACM Press, New York, 77–86.

[56] A. Löser, S. Staab, and C. Tempich, Semantic social overlay networks, IEEE J. Sel. Areas. Communications 25 (1), 2007, 5–14.

[57] C.-J. Lin, Y.-T. Chang, S.-C. Tsai, and C.-F. Chou, Distributed social-based overlay adaptation for unstructured P2P networks, 10th IEEE Global Internet Symposium, 2007.

[58] J. Pouwelse, et al., Tribler: A social-based peer-to-peer system, Proc. of the 5th International Workshop on Peer-to-Peer Systems (IPTPS '06).

[59] K. Sripanidkulchai, B. Maggs, and H. Zhang, Efficient content location using interest-based locality in peer-to-peer systems, 2nd Intl. Conf. of the IEEE Computer and Communications Societies (INFOCOM), 2003.

[60] G. Mangioni, V. Carchiolo, M. Malgeri, and V. Nicosia, Evaluating the dynamic behaviour of PROSA P2P network, International Symposium on Parallel and Distributed Processing and Applications, ISPA'06, 2006.

[61] G. Mangioni, V. Carchiolo, M. Malgeri, and V. Nicosia, Self-organisation of resources in PROSA P2P network, in: Self-Managed Networks, Systems, and Services, Proceedings of Second IEEE International Workshop, SelfMan 2006, Dublin, No. 3996 in LNCS, 2006, 172–174.

[62] O. Landsiedel, A. Pimenidis, and K. Wehrle, Dynamic multipath onion routing in anonymous peer-to-peer overlay networks, IEEE Globecom 2007.

[63] F. Dabek, B. Zhao, P. Druschel, J. Kubiatowicz, and I. Stoica, Towards a common API for structured peer-to-peer overlays, Proc. Intl. Workshop on Peer-to-Peer Systems (IPTPS '03), 2003.

[64] Albert-László Barabási, The Physics of the Web, July 1, 2001, 33–38, http://physicsworld.com/cws/article/print/100;jsessionid=393E49109C5C7789A248362FF597D16E.

[65] B. Carlsson and R. Gustavsson, The rise and fall of Napster: an evolutionary approach, in: Proceedings of the 6th International Computer Science Conference on Active Media Technology, (Dec. 18–20, 2001) J. Liu, P. C. Yuen, C. H. Li, J. K. Ng, and T. Ishida (eds.), Lecture Notes in Computer Science, Vol. 2252, Springer-Verlag, 347–354.

Chapter 4

[66] D. Milojicic, V. Kalogeraki, R. Lukose, K. Nagaraja, J. Pruyne, B. Richard, S. Rollins, Z. Xu. Peer-to-peer computing, HP Labs Technical Report, HPL-2002-57R1, July 14, 2003.

[67] S. Androutsellis-Theotokis and D. Spinellis, A survey of content distribution technologies, ACM Computing Surveys, Vol. 36, No. 4, Dec. 2004.

[68] E. K. Lua, J. Crowcroft, M. Pias, R. Sharma, and S. Lim, A survey and comparison of peer-to-peer overlay network schemes, IEEE Communications Surveys and Tutorials, Vol. 7, No. 2, 2Q2005.

[69] L. Alima, A. Ghodsi, and S. Haridi, A framework for structured peer-to-peer overlay networks, in: LNCS, Vol. 3267 of the Post-proceedings of Global Computing 2004, Springer-Verlag, 223-250.

[70] K. Aberer, L. Alima, A. Ghodsi, S. Girdzijauskas, M. Hauswirth, and S. Haridi, The essence of P2P: A reference architecture for overlay networks, Fifth IEEE International Conference on Peer-to-Peer Computing, Konstanz, Aug. 31-Sept 2, 2005.

[71] J. Risson, T. Moors, Survey of research towards robust peer-to-peer networks: search methods, Computer Networks 50, 17 (Dec. 2006), 3485-3521.

[72] S. El-Ansary, S. Haridi, An overview of structured P2P overlay networks, in J. Wu (ed.), *Handbook on Theoretical and Algorithmic Aspects of Sensor, Ad Hoc Wireless, and Peer-to-Peer Networks*, Auerbach Publications, 2006, 665-683.

[73] C. Qu, W. Nejdl, M. Kriesell, Cayley DHTs: a group-theoretic framework for analyzing DHTs based on Cayley graphs, ISPA 2004, 914-925.

[74] A. Tannenbaum, *Computer Networks*, 4th ed., Prentice Hall, 2002.

[75] W. Litwin, M.-A. Neimat, and D. A. Schneider, LH: linear hashing for distributed files, ACM SIGMOD Record, Vol. 22, No. 2, June 1, 1993, 327-336.

[76] W. Litwin, M.-A. Neimat, and D. A. Schneider, LH: a scalable, distributed data structure, ACM Transactions on Database Systems (TODS), Vol. 21, No. 4, Dec. 1996, 480-525.

[77] R. Devine, Design and implementation of DDH: a distributed dynamic hashing algorithm, Proceedings of the 4th international Conference on Foundations of Data Organization and Algorithms, Oct. 13-15, 1993, D. B. Lomet (ed.), Lecture Notes in Computer Science, Vol. 730, Springer-Verlag, 101-114.

[78] D. Karger, E. Lehman, T. Leighton, R. Panigrahy, M. Levine, and D. Lewin, Consistent hashing and random trees: distributed caching protocols for relieving hot spots on the World Wide Web, Proceedings of the 29th Annual ACM Symposium on theory of Computing, El Paso, Texas, May 4-6, 1997, STOC '97, ACM Press, 654-663.

[79] C. G. Plaxton, R. Rajaraman, and A. W. Richa, Accessing nearby copies of replicated objects in a distributed environment, Proceedings of the 9th annual ACM symposium on parallel algorithms and architectures, Newport, RI, June 23-25, 1997, 311-320.

[80] X. Li and C. G. Plaxton, On name resolution in peer-to-peer networks, in: *Proceedings of the Second ACM international Workshop on Principles of Mobile Computing*, Toulouse, France, Oct 30-31, 2002, POMC '02, ACM Press, 82-89.

[81] I. Stoica, R. Morris, D. Karger, M. Kaashoek, and H. Balakrishnan, Chord: A scalable peer-to-peer lookup service for Internet applications, in: ACM SIGCOMM 2001, San Diego, CA, 2001, 149-160.

[82] I. Stoica, R. Morris, D. Liben-Nowell, D. R. Karger, M. F. Kaashoek, F. Dabek, and H. Balakrishnan, Chord: a scalable peer-to-peer lookup protocol for internet applications, IEEE/ACM Trans. Netw. 11, 1 (Feb. 2003), 17-32.

[83] L. O. Alima, S. El-Ansary, P. Brand, and S. Haridi, DKS(N,k,f): A family of low communication, scalable and fault-tolerant infrastructures for P2P applications, Proc. 3rd IEEE/ACM Int'l. Symp. Cluster Comp. and the Grid, Monterey, CA, 2003, 344-50.

[84] L. O. Alima, S. El-Ansary, P. Brand, and S. Haridi, DKS(N, k, f): A family of low communication, scalable and fault-tolerant infrastructures for P2P applications, The 3rd International workshop on Global and P2P Computing on Large Scale Distributed Systems (CCGRID 2003), Tokyo, May 2003.

[85] B. Carton, V. Mesaros, and P. Van Roy, Improving the scalability of logarithmic-degree DHT-based peer-to-peer networks, in: Proc. of Euro-Par, Aug.-Sept. 2004.

[86] T. Schütt, F. Schintke, and A. Reinefeld, Structured overlay without consistent hashing: Empirical results, in: Proceedings of the Sixth IEEE International Symposium on Cluster Computing and the Grid (Ccgrid'06), Vol. 00, CCGRID, IEEE Computer Society, Washington, DC, May 16-19, 2006, 8.

[87] T. Schütt, F. Schintke, and A. Reinefeld, Range queries on structured overlay networks, in: Computer Communications, Vol. 31, No. 2, 280-291, Feb. 2008.

[88] Antony I. T. Rowstron and Peter Druschel, Pastry: Scalable, decentralized object location, and routing for large-scale peer-to-peer systems, Proceedings of the IFIP/ACM International Conference on Distributed Systems Platforms, Heidelberg, Nov 12-16, 2001, 329-350.

[89] K. Hildrum, J. Kubiatowicz, S. Rao, and B. Y. Zhao, Distributed object location in a dynamic network (expanded journal version of SPAA 2002 paper), Theory of Computing Systems, Mar. 2004, No. 37, 405-440.

[90] S. Ratnasamy, P. Francis, M. Handley, R. Karp, and S. Shenker, A scalable content-addressable network, Proceedings of the 2001 conference on applications, technologies, architectures, and protocols for computer communications, San Diego, CA, Aug. 2001, 161-172.

[91] S. Ratnasamy, M. Hanley, R. Karp, and S. Shenker, Topologically aware overlay construction and server selection, in: Proceedings of the 21st Annual Joint Conference of the IEEE Computer and Communications Societies (INFOCOM), June 2002.

[92] K. Aberer, A. Datta, and M. Hauswirth, Efficient, self-contained handling of identity in peer-to-peer systems, IEEE Transactions on Knowledge and Data Engineering 16(7), July 2004.

[93] K. Aberer, P. Cudré-Mauroux, A. Datta, Z. Despotovic, M. Hauswirth, M. Punceva, and R. Schmidt, P-Grid: A self-organizing structured P2P system, SIGMOD Record, 32(2), Sept. 2003.

[94] S. Rhea, B. Godfrey, B. Karp, J. Kubiatowicz, S. Ratnasamy, S. Shenker, I. Stoica, and H. Yu, OpenDHT: A public DHT service and its uses, *Proceedings of ACM SIGCOMM 2005*, Aug. 2005.

[95] P. Maymounkov and D. Mazieres, Kademlia: A peer-to-peer information system based on the xor metric, in: Proc of IPTPS02, Cambridge, MA, Mar. 2002.

[96] F. Kaashoek and D. R. Karger, Koorde: A simple degree-optimal hash table, IPTPS, Feb. 2003.

[97] A.-T. Gai and L. Viennot, Broose: a practical distributed hash table based on the de Bruijn topology, in: Fourth International Conference on Peer-to-Peer Computing, 2004, Aug. 2004, 167–174.

[98] A. Kumar, S. Merugu, J. Xu, and X. Yu, Ulysses: A robust, low-diameter, low-latency peer-to-peer network, in Proc. of IEEE ICNP 2003.

[99] J. Xu, A. Kumar, and X. Yu, On the fundamental tradeoffs between routing table size and network diameter in peer-to-peer networks, IEEE Journal on Selected Areas in Communications, Vol. 22, No. 1, Jan. 2004, 151–163.

[100] D. Malkhi, M. Naor, and D. Ratajczak, Viceroy: a scalable and dynamic emulation of the butterfly, in: Proceedings of the 21st Annual Symposium on Principles of Distributed Computing, Monterey, CA, July 21–24 183–192, 2002, PODC '02, ACM Press, 2002, 183–192.

[101] H. Shen, C.-Z. Xu, and G. Chen, Cycloid: A constant-degree and lookup-efficient P2P overlay network, in: Proc. of the 18th IEEE International Parallel and Distributed Processing Symposium (IPDPS), New Mexico, Apr. 2004.

[102] H. Shen, C.-Z. Xu, and G. Chen, Cycloid: A scalable constant-degree lookup-efficient P2P overlay network, Journal of Performance Evaluation's Special Issue on Peer-to-Peer Networks (6/29), 2005.

[103] G. Manku, M. Bawa, and P. Raghavan, Symphony: Distributed hashing in a small world, in: 4th USENIX Symposium on Internet Technologies and Systems, 2003, 127–140.

[104] Q. Lian, Z. Zhang, S. Wu, and B. Y. Zhao,. Z-Ring: Fast prefix routing via a low maintenance membership protocol, in: Proceedings of the 13TH IEEE international Conference on Network Protocols (Icnp'05) - Volume 00 (Nov. 6–9, 2005), ICNP, IEEE Computer Society, Washington, DC, 2005, 132–146.

[105] R. Rodrigues and C. Blake, When multi-hop peer-to-peer routing matters, Proceedings of the 3rd International Workshop on Peer-to-Peer Systems (IPTPS04), San Diego, CA, Feb. 2004.

[106] I. Gupta, K. Birman, P. Linga, A. Demers, and R. van Renesse, Kelips: building an efficient and stable P2P DHT through increased memory and background overhead, Proceedings of the 2nd International Workshop on Peer-to-Peer Systems (IPTPS '03), 2003.

[107] K. P. Birman, et al., Bimodal multicast, ACM Trans. Computing Systems, 17:2, May 1999, 41–88.

[108] B. Leong, B. Liskov, and E. D. Demaine. EpiChord: Parallelizing the Chord lookup algorithm with reactive routing state management, Computer Communications, Vol. 29, 1243–1259

[109] A. Gupta, B. Liskov, and R. Rodrigues, Efficient routing for peer-to-peer overlays, Proceedings of the 1st Symposium on Networked Systems Design and Implementation (NSDI 2004), 2004, 113–116.

[110] L. Monnerat and C. Amorim, D1HT: A distributed one hop hash table, in: Proc of the 20th IEEE Intl Parallel & Distributed Processing Symposium (IPDPS), Apr. 2006.

[111] J. Buford, A. Brown, and M. Kolberg. Analysis of an active maintenance algorithm for an O (1)-hop overlay, IEEE Globecom 2007, Nov. 2007.

[112] J. Buford, A. Brown, and M. Kolberg, Exploiting parallelism in the design of peer-to-peer overlays, Journal of Computer Communications, Special Issue on Foundations of Peer-to-Peer Computing, Vol. 31, No. 3, 452–463, Feb. 2008.

[113] J. Li, J. Stribling, T. M. Gil, R. Morris, and F. Kaashoek, Comparing the performance of distributed hash tables under churn, Proc. of the 3rd Intl. Workshop on Peer-to-Peer Systems (IPTPS'04), 2004.

[114] J. Li, J. Stribling, R. Morris, M. F. Kaashoek, and T. M. Gil, A performance vs. cost framework for evaluating DHT design tradeoffs under churn, Infocom 2005.

[115] C. Shui, H. Wang, P. Zhou, and Y. Jia: Cactus: A new constant-degree and fault tolerant P2P overlay, PRIMA 2006: 386–397.

[116] P. Fraigniaud and P. Gauron, D2B: a de Bruijn based content-addressable network, Theor. Comput. Sci. 355, 1 (Apr. 2006), 65–79.

[117] D. Li, X. Lu, and J. Wu, FISSIONE: a scalable constant degree and low congestion DHT scheme based on Kautz graphs, Proc. IEEE 24th Annual Joint Conference of the IEEE Computer and Communications Societies (INFOCOM 2005), Mar. 13-17, 2005, Vol. 3, 1677-1688.

[118] G. Wepiwé and P. L. Simeonov, HiPeer: A highly reliable P2P system, IEICE - Trans. Inf. Syst. E89-D, 2 (Feb. 2006), 570–580.

[119] H. Rostami, J. Habibi, and A. Rahnama, Semantic HyperCup, in: Proceedings of the 39th Annual Hawaii international Conference on System Sciences, Vol. 9 (Jan. 4-7, 2006), HICSS. IEEE Computer Society, Washington, DC, 223.

[120] I. Abraham, A. Badola, D. Bickson, D. Malkhi, S. Maloo, and S. Ron, Practical locality awareness for large-scale information sharing, The 4th Annual International Workshop on Peer-to-Peer Systems (IPTPS '05), 2005.

Chapter 5

[121] P. Maymounkov and D. Mazieres, Kademlia: A peer-to-peer information system based on the xor metric, in: Proceedings of the IPTPS02, Cambridge, MA, Mar. 2002.

[122] D. Liben-Nowell, H. Balakrishnan, and D. Karger, Analysis of the evolution of peer-to-peer systems, in: Proceedings of the ACM PODC, Jul. 2002.

[123] S. Rhea, D. Geels, T. Roscoe, and J. Kubiatowicz, Handling churn in a DHT, in: Proceedings of the Annual Conference on USENIX Annual Technical Conference, Boston, Jun. 27-Jul. 2, 2004.

[124] J. Li, J. Stribling, T. M. Gil, R. Morris, and F. Kaashoek, Comparing the performance of distributed hash tables under churn, in: Proceedings of the IPTPS, 2004.

[125] B. Y. Zhao, et al., Tapestry: A resilient global-scale overlay for service deployment, IEEE JSAC, 22(1):41-53, Jan. 2004.

[126] K. Hildrum, J. D. Kubiatowicz, S. Rao, and B. Y. Zhao, Distributed object location in a dynamic network, in: Proceedings of the SPAA, 2002.

[127] M. Castro, M. Costa, and A. Rowstron, Performance and dependability of structured peer-to-peer overlays. Technical Report MSRTR- 2003-94, Microsoft, 2003.

[128] M. F. Kaashoek and D. R. Karger, Koorde: A simple degree-optimal distributed hash table, in: Proceedings of the 2nd IPTPS, Berkeley, CA, Feb. 2003.

[129] N. De Bruijn, A combinatorial problem, in: Proc. Koninklijke Nederlandse Akademie van Wetenschappen, Vol. 49, 1946, 758-764.

[130] A. Kumar, S. Merugu, Jun Xu, and Xingxing Yu, Ulysses: a robust, low-diameter, low-latency peer-to-peer, in: Proceedings of the 11th IEEE International Conference on Network Protocols 2003, Nov. 4-7, 2003, 258-267.

[131] H. Shen, C. Xu, and G. Chen, Cycloid: a constant-degree and lookup-efficient P2P overlay network, Perform. Eval., Vol. 63, Issue 3, Mar. 2006, 195-216.

[132] M. Kolberg, F. Kolberg, A. Brown, and J. Buford, A Markov model for the Epichord peer-to-peer overlay in an XCAST enabled network, in: Proceedings of the IEEE International Conference on Communications (ICC), 2007.

[133] J. Buford, A. Brown, M. Kolberg, Analysis of an active maintenance algorithm for an O(1)-hop overlay, in: Proceedings of the IEEE Global Telecommunications Conference, (IEEE GLOBECOM 2007), Nov. 26–30, 2007, 81–86.

[134] L. R. Monnerat and C. L. Amorim, D1HT: a distributed one-hop hash table, in: Proceedings of the 20th International Parallel and Distributed Processing Symposium 2006 (IPDPS 2006), Apr. 25–29, 2006.

[135] P. Kersch, R. Szabo, L. Cheng, K. Jean, and A. Galis, Stochastic maintenance of overlays in structured P2P systems, Elsevier Journal in Computer Communications, Special Issue: Foundation of Peer-to-Peer Computing, Volume 31, Issue 3, Feb. 2008, 603–619.

[136] K. Aberer, et al., The essence of P2P: a reference architecture for overlay networks, in: Proceedings of the 5th IEEE International Conference on Peer-to-Peer Computing, 2005.

[137] A. Shaker and D. S. Reeves, Self-stabilizing structured ring topology P2P systems, in: Proceedings of the 5th IEEE International Conference on Peer-to-Peer Computing, Konstanz, Germany, Aug. 2005, 39–46.

[138] M. Castro, P. Druschel, A. Kermarrec, and A. Rowstron, One ring to rule them all: service discovery and binding in structured peer-to-peer overlay networks, in: Proceedings of the 10th Workshop on ACM SIGOPS European Workshop, 2002.

[139] L. Garc es-Erice, et al., Hierarchical peer-to-peer systems, in: Proceedings of the International Conference on Parallel and Distributed Computing (Euro-Par 2003), 2003.

[140] G. Wepiwe, and P. L. Simeonov, A concentric multi-ring overlay for highly reliable P2P networks, in: Proceedings of the 4th IEEE International Symposium on Network Computing and Applications, July 27–29, 2005.

[141] M. Kleis, E. K. Lua, and X. Zhou, Hierarchical peer-to-peer networks using lightweight superpeer topologies, in: Proceedings of the 10th IEEE Symposium on Computers and Communications, 2005 (ISCC 2005), June 27–30, 2005, 143–148.

[142] E. K. Lua and X. Zhou, Network-aware superpeers-peers geometric overlay network, in: Proceedings of 16th International Conference on Computer Communications and Networks, 2007 (ICCCN 2007), Aug. 13–16, 2007, 141–148.

[143] K. W. Ross, Hash-routing for collections of shared Web caches, IEEE Network Magazine, Vol. 11, 7, Nov.–Dec. 1997, 37–44.

[144] D. Karger, et al., Web caching with consistent hashing, in: Proceedings of the Eighth International World Wide Web Conference, May 1999.

[145] P. L. Simeonov. Waraan: A higher-order adaptive routing algorithm for wireless multimedia in wandering networks, in: Proceedings of the WPMC, 1385–1389, 2002.

[146] D. Stutzbach and R. Rejaie, Understanding churn in peer-to-peer networks, in: Proceedings of the 6th ACM SIGCOMM Conference on Internet Measurement Conference 2006 (IMC 2006), Oct. 25–27, 2006.

Chapter 6

[147] G. Giaccio, Stoica, A pretty flexible API for generic peer-to-peer programming, IEEE International Parallel and Distributed Processing Symposium, IPDPS 2007, Mar. 26–30, 2007, 1–8.

[148] F. Dabek, B. Zhao, P. Druschel, J. Kubiatowicz, and I. Stoica, Towards a common API for structured peer-to-peer overlays, in Proc. of the 2nd International Workshop on Peer-to-Peer Systems (IPTPS03), Berkeley, CA, 2003.

[149] Gnutella Protocol Specification, available at http://wiki.limewire.org/index.php?title=GDF.

[150] T. Klingberg and B. Manfredi, Gnutella Protocol 0.6. June 2002. Available at http://rfc-gnutella.sourceforge.net/src/rfc-0_6-draft.html.

[151] R. Fielding, et al., Hypertext Transfer Protocol: HTTP/1.1. IETF RFC 2616, June 1999.

[152] B. Cohen, The BitTorrent protocol specification, www.bittorrent.org/beps/bep_0003.html, Feb 2008.

[153] A. Loewenstern, DHT protocol, available at www.bittorrent.org, Jan. 2008.

[154] B. Cohen, Incentives build robustness in BitTorrent, in: Proc. of IPTPS, 2003.

[155] M. Izal, et al., Dissecting BitTorrent: Five months in a torrent's lifetime, in: *5th Annual Passive & Active Measurement Workshop*, Apr. 2004.

[156] D. Qiu and R. Srikant, Modeling and performance analysis of BitTorrent-like peer-to-peer networks, in Proc. of SIGCOMM, 2004.

[157] A. Bharambe, C. Herley, and V. Padmanabhan, Analyzing and improving a BitTorrent network's performance mechanisms, in Proc. of INFOCOM, 2006.

[158] A. Legout, G. Urvoy-Keller, and P. Michiardi, Rarest first and choke algorithms are enough, in Proc. of IMC, 2006.

[159] M. Piatek, et al., Do incentives build robustness in BitTorrent? 4th USENIX Symposium on Networked Systems Design & Implementation (NSDI 07), Apr. 2007, 1–14.

[160] A. Klemkin. Unofficial eDonkey protocol specification, unpublished manuscript, 2004; available at http://internap.dl.sourceforge.net/sourceforge/pdonkey/eDonkey-protocol-0.6.2.

[161] Y. Kulbak and D. Bickson, The eMule protocol specification, unpublished manuscript, Jan. 2005.

[162] K. Shudo, Y. Tanaka, and S. Sekiguchi, Overlay Weaver: An overlay construction toolkit, Computer Communications Review, to appear.

[163] Overlay Weaver project Website, http://overlayweaver.sourceforge.net/.

[164] I. Baumgart, B. Heep, and S. Krause, OverSim: A flexible overlay network simulation framework, Proceedings of 10th IEEE Global Internet Symposium (GI '07) in conjunction with IEEE INFOCOM 2007, Anchorage, AK, May 2007.

[165] OverSim project Website: www.ovesim.org.

[166] S. Baset, H. Schulzrinne, and M. Matuszewski, Peer-to-Peer Protocol (P2PP), IETF draft-baset-p2psip-p2pp-01, work in progress, Nov. 2007.

[167] US National Institute of Standards, Federal Information Processing Standards (FIPS) 180-2 Secure Hash Standard (SHS), Feb. 2004.

[168] S. Rhea, B. Godfrey, B. Karp, J. Kubiatowicz, S. Ratnasamy, S. Shenker, I. Stoica, and H. Yu, OpenDHT: A public DHT service and its uses. Proceedings of ACM SIGCOMM 2005, Aug. 2005.

[169] S. Rhea, B. G. Chun, J. Kubiatowicz, and S. Shenker, Fixing the embarrassing slowness of OpenDHT on PlanetLab, Proceedings of USENIX WORLDS 2005, Dec. 2005.

[170] B. Ford, P. Srisuresh, and D. Kegel, Peer-to-peer communication across network address translators, Proceedings of the 2005 USENIX Annual Technical Conference, Anaheim, CA, Apr. 2005.

[171] H. Khlifi, J.-C. Gregoire, and J. Phillips, VoIP and NAT/firewalls: issues, traversal techniques, and a real-world solution, IEEE Communications Magazine, 44(7). July 2006, 93–99.

[172] Illuminati, http://illuminati.coralcdn.org/, accessed Sept. 2007.

[173] B. Carpenter, and S. Brim: Middleboxes: Taxonomy and issues, IETF RFC 3234, Feb 2002.

[174] P. Srisuresh, et al., Middlebox communication architecture and framework, RFC 3303, Aug. 2002.

[175] M. Stiemerling, J. Quittek, and C. Cadar, NEC's simple Midbox Control Protocol, IETF RFC 4540, May 2006.

[176] UPnP Forum, Internet Gateway Device (IGD) Standardized Device Control Protocol v. 1.0, Nov. 2001.

[177] J. Rosenberg, J. Weinberger, C. Huitema, and R. Mahy, STUN: Simple Traversal of User Datagram Protocol (UDP), IETF RFC 3489, Mar. 2003.

[178] J. Rosenberg, Interactive Connectivity Establishment (ICE): A protocol for Network Address Translator (NAT) traversal for offer/answer protocols, IETF MMUSIC WG. draft-ietf-mmusic-ice-17, work in progress, July 2007.

[179] J. Rosenberg, Session traversal utilities for (NAT) (STUN), draft-ietf-behave-rfc3489bis-06, work in progress, Mar. 2007.

[180] J. Rosenberg, Obtaining relay addresses from Simple Traversal Underneath NAT (STUN), draft-ietf-behave-turn-03, work in progress, Mar. 2007.

[181] Microsoft Corporation, Peer Name Resolution Protocol, Sept 2006, accessed July 2008 at http://technet.microsoft.com/en-us/library/bb726971.aspx.

[182] Microsoft Corporation, Introduction to Windows peer-to-peer networking, Sept 2006., accessed July 2008 at http://technet.microsoft.com/en-us/library/bb457079.aspx.

[183] M. Castro, P. Druschel, A-M. Kermarrec, and A. Rowstron, One ring to rule them all: Service discover and binding in structured peer-to-peer overlay networks, SIGOPS European Workshop, France, Sept. 2002.

[184] M. Jelasity, A. Montresor, and O. Babaoglu, The bootstrapping service, Proceedings of International ICDCS Workshop on Dynamic Distributed Systems (ICDCS-IWDDS'06), Lisbon, Portugal, IEEE Computer Society, July 2006.

[185] J. Strauss, D. Katabi, and F. Kaashoek, A measurement study of available bandwidth estimation tools, The Internet Measurements Conference, Florida, 2003.

[186] F. Templin, T. Gleeson, M. Talwar, D. Thaler, Intra-Site Automatic Tunnel Addressing Protocol (ISATAP), IETF RTC 4214, Oct. 2005.

[187] B. Carpenter and R. Moore, Connection of IPv6 domains via IPv4 clouds, IETF RFC 3056, Feb. 2001.

[188] C. Huitema, Teredo: Tunneling IPv6 over UDP through Network Address Translations (NATs), IETF RFC 4380, Feb 2006.

Chapter 7

[189] Merriam-Webster's Online Dictionary, available at www.m-w.com/dictionary/search.

[190] http://en.wikipedia.org/wiki/Napster

[191] iMesh Professional 5.0. 2005, iMesh Inc., available at www.imesh.com.

[192] The Gnutella Protocol Specification v0.4. 2001, Gnutella, available at www9.limewire.com/developer/gnutella_protocol_0.4.pdf.

[193] BearShare, available at www.bearshare.com.

[194] Shareaza, available at www.shareaza.com.

[195] LimeWire, available at www.limewire.com/english/content/home.shtml.

[196] I. Clarke, O. Sandberg, B. Wiley, and T. Hong, Freenet: a distributed anonymous information storage and retrieval system, in: Proceedings International Workshop on Design Issues in Anonymity and Unobservability, Springer, 2001.

[197] J. Mache, et al., Request algorithms in Freenet-style peer-to-peer systems, in: Proceedings of the Second IEEE International Conference on Peer to Peer Computing, Sept. 5-7, 2002, Linkoping, Sweden.

[198] A. Z. Kronfol, FASK: a fault-tolerant adaptive scalable distributed search engine, Master's Thesis, Princeton University, available at www.cs.princeton.edu/~akronfol/fasd/.

[199] G. Salton, A. Wong, and C. S. Yang, A vector space model for automatic indexing, Communications of the ACM Archive, 18(11) Nov. 1975, 613-620.

[200] G. Salton and M. McGill, Introduction to Modern Information Retrieval, McGraw Hill, 1983.

[201] H. Cai and J. Wang, Exploiting Geographical and Temporal Locality to Boost Search Efficiency in Peer-to-Peer Systems, IEEE Transactions on Parallel and Distributed Systems, 2006, 17(10): 1189-1203.

[202] X. Li and J. Wu, Searching techniques in peer-to-peer networks, Handbook of Theoretical and Algorithmic Aspects of Ad Hoc, Sensor, and Peer-to-Peer Networks, J. Wu (ed.), Auerbach Publications, 2006, 617-642.

[203] J. Eberspacher, R. Schollmeier, S. Zols, and G. Kunzmann, Structured P2P networks in mobile and fixed environments, in: Proceedings 2nd International Working Conference on Performance Modelling and Evaluation of Heterogeneous Networks, 2004, West Yorkshire, UK.

[204] F. Dabek, E. Brunskill, F. Kaashoek, and D. Karger, Building peer-to-peer systems with Chord, a distributed lookup service, in: Proceedings of the 8th Workshop on Hot Topics in Operating Systems, 2001, Germany: IEEE Computer Society, 81-86.

[205] S. Ratnasamy, P. Fancis, M. Handley, and R. Karp, A scalable content-addressable network, in: Proceedings ACM SIGCOMM annual conference of the Special Interest Group on Data Communications, 2001, San Diego, CA, ACM Press, 161-172.

[206] A. Rowstron and P. Druschel, Pastry: Scalable, distributed object location and routing for large-scale peer-to-peer systems, in: Proceedings IFIP/ACM International Conference on Distributed Systems Platforms (Middleware), 2001, Heidelberg, ACM Press, 329-350.

[207] B. Zhao, L. Huang, J. Stribling, S. Rhea, A. Joseph, and J. Kubiatowicz, Tapestry: a resilient global-scale overlay for service deployment, IEEE Journal on Selected Areas in Communications, 22(1), 2004, 41-53.

[208] D. Loguinov, A. Kumar, and S. Ganesh, Graph theoretica analysis of structured peer-to-peer systems: routing distances and fault resilience, in: Proceedings the 2003 Conference on Applications, Technologies, Architectures, and Protocols for Computer Communications, Karlsruhe, Germany, Aug. 25-29, 2003, 395-406.

[209] N. D. de Bruijin, A combinatorial problem, Koninklijke Netherlands: Academe Van Wetenschappen, Vol. 49, 1946, 758–764.

[210] KaZaA, available at www.kazaa.com.

[211] L. Gong, JXTA: A network programming environment, IEEE Internet Computing, 2001, 5(3): 88–95.

[212] M. A. Traversat and E. Pouyoul, Project JXTA: A loosely-consistent DHT rendezvous walker, 2003.

[213] S. Li, JXTA 2: A high-performance, massively scalable P2P network, available at www.ibm.com/developerworks/java/library/j-jxta2/#2.0.

[214] B. Yang and H. Garcia-Molina, Efficient search in peer-to-peer networks, in: Proceedings the 22nd International Conference on Distributed Computing, 2002.

[215] Q. Lv, P. Cao, E. Cohen, K. Li, and S. Shenker, Search and replication in unstructured peer-to-peer networks, in Proceedings the Sixteenth ACM International Conference on Supercomputing, 2002.

[216] A. Crespo and H. Garcia-Molina, Routing indices for peer-to-peer systems, in Proceedings of the 22nd IEEE International Conference on Distributed Computing Systems, Vienna, July 2002, 23–32.

[217] V. Kalogeraki, D. Gunopulos, and D. Zeinalipour-yazti, A local search mechanism for peer-to-peer networks, in Proceedings of the 11th ACM Conference on Information and Knowledge Management, 2002.

[218] D. Tsoumakos and N. Roussopoulos, Adaptive probabilistic search in peer-to-peer networks, in: Proceedings the 2nd International Workshop on Peer-to-Peer Systems, 2003.

[219] C. Yang and J. Wu, A dominating set based routing in peer-to-peer networks, in Proceedings the 2nd International Workshop on Grid and Cooperative Computing, 2003.

[220] R. Ahmed and R. Boutaba, Distributed Pattern Matching: A Key to Flexible and Efficient P2P Search, IEEE Journal on Selected Areas in Communications, 2007, 25(1): 73–83.

[221] J. Risson and T. Moorsa, Survey of research towards robust peer-to-peer networks: Search methods, Computer Networks, Vol. 50, No. 17, Dec. 2006, 3485–3521.

[222] Y. Zhu and Y. Hu, Semantic Search in Peer-to-Peer Systems, Handbook of Theoretical and Algorithmic Aspects of Ad Hoc, Sensor, and Peer-to-Peer Networks, J. Wu (ed.), Auerbach Publications, 2006, 643–664.

[223] A. Bharambe, M. Agrawal, and S. Seshan, Mercury: supporting scalable multi-attribute range queries, in Proceedings ACM SIGCOMM2004, Aug. 30–Sept. 3, 2004, Portland, USA.

[224] A. Y. Levy, A. O. Mendelzon, Y. Sagiv, and D. Srivastava, Answering queries using views (extended abstract), in Proceedings of the 14th ACM SIGACT-SIGMOD-SIGART Symposium on Principles of Database Systems, ACM Press, 1995, 95–104.

[225] G. Gupta, D. Agrawal, and A. E. Abbadi, Approximate range selection queries in peer-to-peer systems, in: Proceedings of the First Biennial Conference on Innovative Data Systems Research, Asilomar, CA, 2003.

[226] A. Andrzejak and Z. Xu, Scalable, efficient range queries for grid information services, in: Proceedings of the Second IEEE International Conference on Peer to Peer Computing, Linkoping University, Sweden, Sept. 2002.

[227] C. Zhang, A. Krishnamurthy, and R. Y. Wang, SkipIndex: Towards a scalable peer-to-peer index service for high dimensional data, available at www.cs.princeton.edu/~chizhang/skipindex.pdf.

[228] M. W. Berry, A. Drmac, and E. R. Jessup, Matrices, vector spaces, and information retrieval, SIAM Review, 41(2), 1999, 335-362.

[229] C. Tang, Z. Xu, and S. Dwarkadas, Peer-to-peer information retrieval using self-organizing semantic overlay networks, in Proceedings of ACM SIGCOMM, Karlsruhe, Germany, Aug. 2003, 175-186.

[230] Y. Zhu and Y. Hu, ESS: Efficient Semantic Search on Gnutella-like P2P systems, technical report, Department of ECECS, University of Cincinnati, Mar. 2004.

[231] Y. Zhu, H. Wang, and Y. Hu, Integrating semantics-based access mechanisms with P2P file systems, in: Proceedings of the 3rd International Conference on Peer-to-Peer Computing, Linkping, Sweden, Sept. 2003, 118-125.

[232] K. Yang and J. Ho, Proof: A DHT-based peer-to-peer search engine, in: Proceedings the IEEE International Conference on Web Intelligence, 2006, Hong Kong: IEEE Computer Society, 702-708.

[233] R. Ahmed and R. Boutaba, Distributed pattern matching: A key to flexible and efficient P2P search, IEEE Journal on Selected Areas in Communications, Vol. 25, No. 1, 2007, 73-83.

[234] W. Wang and L. Xiao, An effective P2P search scheme to exploit file sharing heterogeneity, IEEE Transactions on Parallel and Distrubuted Systems, 2007, 18(2): 145-157.

[235] M. Castro, M. Costa, and A. Rowstron, Should we build Gnutella on a structured overlay?, ACM SIGCOMM Computer Communication Review, 34(1), 2004, 1331-1336.

[236] B. T. Loo, R. Huebsch, I. Stoica and J. M. Hellerstein, The case for a hybrid P2P search infrastructure, in: Proceedings the 3rd International Workshop on Peer-to-Peer Systems, San Diego, CA, Feb. 26-27, 2004.

[237] D. Kundur, M. Merabti, Z. Liu, and H. Yu, Advances in peer-to-peer content search, in: Proceedings IEEE International Conference on Multimedia and Expo 2007, July 2007, Beijing.

[238] D. Gibbon, Z. Liu, and B. Shahraray, The MIRACLE Video Search Engine, CCNC 2006, Las Vegas, Jan. 8-10, 2006.

[239] M. Christel and R. Conescu, Addressing the challenge of visual information access from digital image and video libraries, JCDL'05, Denver, June 7-11, 2005.

[240] C. Tang, Z. Xu, and M. Mahalingam, PeerSearch: Efficient information retrieval in peer-peer networks, Hewlett-Packard Labs: Palo Alto, 2002.

[241] J. Lu and J. Callan, Content-based retrieval in hybrid peer-to-peer networks, Proceedings of ACM CIKM'03, New Orleans, Nov. 2003.

[242] C. Yang, Peer-to-peer architecture for content-based music retrieval on acoustic data, WWW 2003, Budapest, May 20-24, 2003.

Chapter 8

[243] Gnutella, available at www.gnutella.com.

[244] KaZaa, available at www.kazaa.com.

[245] BitTorrent, available at www.bittorrent.com.

[246] O. Heckmann and A. Bock, The eDonkey 2000 Protocol, KOM Technical Report 08/2002, Ver. 0.8, Dec. 2002, available at ftp://ftp.kom.e-technik.tu-darmstadt.de/pub/papers/HB02-1-paper.pdf.

[247] V. N. Padmanabhan, H. J. Wang, P. A. Chou, and K. Sripanidkulchai, Distributing streaming media content using cooperative networking, in: Proceedings, the 12th international Workshop on Network and Operating System Support for Digital Audio and Video, Miami Beach, FL, May 2002.

[248] X. Hei, C. Liang, J. Liang, Y. Liu, and K. W. Ross, Insights into PPLive: A measurement study of a large-scale P2P IPTV system, in: Proceedings, Workshop on Internet Protocol TV (IPTV) services over World Wide Web in conjunction with WWW2006, Edinburgh, May 2006.

[249] PPLive, available at www.pplive.com.

[250] UUSee, available at www.uusee.com.

[251] M. Castro, P. Druschel, A.-M. Kermarrec, and A. Rowstron, SCRIBE: A large-scale and decentralized application-level multicast infrastructure, IEEE Journal on Selected Areas in Communications (JSAC), Special Issue on Network Support for Group Communication, Vol. 20, No. 8, Oct. 2002, 1489–1499.

[252] M. Castro, et al., Splitstream: Highbandwidth multicast in cooperative environments, in: Proceedings, the 20th ACM Symp. on Operating Sys. Principles (SOSP 2003), Oct. 2003.

[253] M. Castro, M. Costa, and A. Rowstron, Peer-to-peer overlays: structured, unstructured, or both?, Technical Report MSR-TR-2004-73, Microsoft Research, 2004, available at http://research.microsoft.com/~antr/MS/Structella-tr.pdf.

[254] F. Dabek, E. Brunskill, F. Kaashoek, and D. Karger, Building peer-to-peer systems with Chord, a distributed lookup service, in: Proceedings the Eighth Workshop on Hot Topics in Operating Systems, Germany: IEEE Computer Society, 2001, 81–86.

[255] S. Ratnasamy, P. Fancis, M. Handley, and R. Karp, A scalable content-addressable network, in: Proceedings ACM SIGCOMM annual conference of the Special Interest Group on Data Communications, San Diego, CA, ACM Press, 2001, 161–172.

[256] A. Rowstron and P. Druschel, Pastry: Scalable, distributed object location and routing for large-scale peer-to-peer systems, in: Proceedings IFIP/ACM International Conference on Distributed Systems Platforms (Middleware), Heidelberg, ACM Press, 2001, 329–350.

[257] B. Zhao, et al., Tapestry: a resilient global-scale overlay for service deployment, IEEE Journal on Selected Areas in Communications, 22(1), 2004, 41–53.

[258] J. Lan, X. Liu, P. Shenoy, and K. Ramamritham, Consistency maintenance in peer-to-peer file sharing networks, in: Proceedings, the 3rd IEEE Workshop on Internet Applications, June 2003, 90–94.

[259] S. Podlipnig and L. Böszörmenyi, A survey of Web cache replacement strategies, ACM Computing Surveys (CSUR), Vol. 35, No. 4, Dec. 2003, 374–398.

[260] P. Cao and S. Irani, Cost-aware WWW proxy caching algorithms, in: Proceedings, the USENIX Symposium on Internet Technologies and Systems, 1997, 193–206.

[261] C. C. Aggarwal, J. L. Wolf, and P. S. Yu, Caching on the World Wide Web, IEEE Transactions on Knowledge and Data Eng., Vol. 11, No. 1, Jan. 1999, 94–107.

[262] C.-Y. Chang, T. Mcgregor, and G. Holmes, The LRU* WWW proxy cache document replacement algorithm, in: Proceedings, the Asia Pacific Web Conference, 1999.

[263] B. Krishnamurthy and C. E. Wills, Proxy cache coherency and replacement—towards a more complete picture, in: Proceedings, the 19th International Conference on Distributed Computing Systems. IEEE Computer Society, Piscataway, NJ, 1999, 332–339.

[264] J. Wang, A survey of Web caching schemes for the Internet, ACM Comput. Commun. Rev., Vol. 29, No. 5, Oct. 1999, 36–46.

[265] H. Bahn, K. Koh, S. L. Min, and S. H. Noh, Efficient replacement of nonuniform objects in Web caches, IEEE Comput., Vol. 35, No. 6, June 2002, 65–73.

[266] M. Rabinovich and O. Spatscheck, Web caching and replication, Addison-Wesley, 2002.

[267] P. Kalnis, et al., An adaptive peer-to-peer network for distributed caching of OLAP results, in: Proceedings, the 2002 ACM SIGMOD international conference on management of data, Hong Kong, 2002, 25–36.

[268] J. Liang, R. Kumar, and K. W. Ross, The FastTrack overlay: A measurement study, Computer Networks, Vol. 50, No. 6, Apr. 2006, 842–858.

[269] A. Wierzbicki, N. Leibowitz, M. Ripeanu, and R. Wozniak, Cache replacement policies for P2P file sharing protocols, European Transactions on Telecommunications, Vol. 15, No. 6, Nov. 2004, 559–569.

[270] A. Wierzbicki, N. Leibowitz, M. Ripeanu, and R. Wozniak, Cache replacement policies revisited: the case of P2P traffic, in: Proceedings, IEEE International Symposium on Cluster Computing and the Grid, Apr. 2004, 182–189.

[271] M. Zhang, J.-G. Luo, L. Zhao, and S.-Q. Yang, A peer-to-peer network for live media streaming using a push-pull approach, in: Proceedings of the 13th Annual ACM International Conference on Multimedia, Singapore, 2005, 287–290.

[272] M. Khambatti, K. Ryu, and P. DasGupta, Push-pull gossiping for information sharing in peer-to-peer communities, in: Proceedings, International Conference on Parallel and Distributed Processing Techniques and Applications (PDPTA), Las Vegas, June 2003, 1393–1399.

[273] K. Aberer, et al., Advanced peer-to-peer networking: The P-Grid system and its applications, PIK - Praxis der Informationsverarbeitung und Kommunikation, Special Issue on P2P Systems, Vol. 26, No. 3, 2003.

[274] X. Zhang, J. Liu, B. Li, and T. P. Yum, Coolstreaming/donet: A data-driven overlay network for peer-to-peer live media streaming, in: Proceedings, 24th Annual Joint Conference of the IEEE Computer and Communications Societies INFOCOM, Miami, FL, 2005.

[275] K.-A. Skevik, V. Goebel, and T. Plagemann, Design of a hybrid CDN, Lecture Notes in Computer Science, Vol. 3311/2004, Interactive Multimedia and Next Generation Networks, Springer, Oct. 2004, 206–217.

[276] K.-A. Skevik, V. Goebel, and T. Plagemann, Analysis of BitTorrent and its use for the design of a P2P based streaming protocol for a hybrid CDN, Technical Report, Universitetet I Oslo, June 2004, available at www.ifi.uio.no/forskning/grupper/dmms/papers/129.pdf.

[277] D. Xu, S. Kulkarni, C. Rosenberg, and H.-K. Chai, A CDN-P2P hybrid architecture for cost-effective streaming media distribution, available at www.cs.purdue.edu/homes/dxu/pubs/MMCN03-enhanced.pdf.

[278] D. Xu, S. Kulkarni, C. Rosenberg, and H.-K. Chai, Analysis of a hybrid architecture for cost-effective streaming media distribution, in: Proceedings, SPIE/ACM Conference on Multimedia Computing and Networking (MMCN 2003), Santa Clara, CA, Jan. 2003.

[279] D. Xu, S. Kulkarni, C. Rosenberg, and H.-K. Chai, Analysis of a CDN-P2P hybrid architecture for cost-effective streaming distribution, ACM/Springer Multimedia Systems Journal, 11(4), 2006.

[280] A. Choonhwa Lee Helal, N. Desai, V. Verma, and B. Arslan, Konark: A system and protocols for device independent, peer-to-peer discovery and delivery of mobile services, IEEE Transactions on Systems, Man and Cybernetics, Part A, Vol. 33, No. 6, Nov. 2003, 682–696.

[281] R. Buyya, M. Pathan, and A. Vakali, Content delivery network, Springer, Apr. 2008.

[282] G. Held, A practical guide to content delivery networks, Auerbach, Sept. 2005.

[283] S. Hull, Content delivery networks: Web switching for security, availability, and speed, McGraw-Hill, Feb. 2002.

[284] D. C. Verma, Content distribution Nnetworks: An engineering approach, John Wiley & Sons, Dec. 2001.

[285] P. Venkatesh, S. D. Sivanandam, and R. Venkatesan, A review of consistency mechanisms for QoS aware content distribution networks, Academic Open Internet Journal, Vol. 14, June 2005, 8, available at www.acadjournal.com/2005/v14/part6/p8/.

[286] S. Saroiu, et al., An analysis of Internet content delivery systems, in: Proceedings, 5th Symposium on Operating Systems Design and Implementation, Boston, Dec. 2002, 315–328.

[287] J. Dilley, et al., Globally distributed content delivery, IEEE Internet Computing, Vol. 6, No. 5, Sept. 2002, 50–58.

[288] A. Vakali and G. Pallis, Content delivery networks: status and trends, IEEE Internet Computing, Vol. 7, No. 6, Nov. 2003, 68–74.

[289] J. Li, On peer-to-peer (P2P) content delivery, Peer-to-Peer Networks and Applications, an International Journal, Vol. 1, No. 1, Feb. 2008.

[290] S. Androutsellis-Theotokis and D. Spinellis, A survey of peer-to-peer content distribution technologies, ACM Computing Surveys (CSUR) archive, Vol. 36, No. 4, Dec. 2004, 335–371.

[291] D. Stolarz, Mastering Internet video: A guide to streaming and on-demand video, Addison-Wesley Professional, Aug. 2004.

[292] W. Simpson, Video Over IP: A practical guide to technology and applications, Focal Press, Sept. 2005.

Chapter 9

[293] PPLive, available at www.pplive.com.

[294] UUSee, available at www.uusee.com.

[295] SopCast, available at www.sopcast.com.

[296] QQLive, available at http://tv.qq.com.

[297] PPStream, available at www.ppstream.com.

[298] Feidian, available at www.feidian.com.

[299] TVAnts, available at www.tvants.com.

[300] J. Liebeherr, and M. El Zarki, Mastering Networks: an Internet lab manual, Addison-Wesley, Aug. 2003.

[301] J. Liebeherr, Overlay networks lecture notes, available at www.cs.virginia.edu/~cs757/slidespdf/757-09-overlay.pdf.

[302] S. Fahmy, and M. Kwon, Characterizing overlay multicast networks and their costs, IEEE/ACM Transactions on Networking, in: Proceedings, 11th IEEE International Conference on Network Protocols, 2003.

[303] H. Yu, and J. Buford, Peer-to-peer overlay multicast, in: Encyclopedia of Wireless and Mobile Communications, Auerbach Publications, January 2008.

[304] J. Chuang and M. Sirbu, Pricing multicast communications: A cost-based approach, Journal of Telecommunication Systems, Vol. 17, No. 3, July 2001, 281–297.

[305] Y.-H. Chu, S. G. Rao, S. Seshan, and H. Zhang, A case for end system multicast, IEEE Journal on Selected Areas in Communications (JSAC), Special Issue on Network Support for Group Communication, Vol. 20, No. 8, Oct. 2002, 1456–1471.

[306] X. Hei, C. Liang, J. Liang, Y. Liu, and K. W. Ross, Insights into PPLive: A measurement study of a large-scale P2P IPTV system, in: Proceedings, Workshop on Internet Protocol TV (IPTV) services over World Wide Web in conjunction with WWW2006, Edinburgh, May 2006.

[307] B. Zhang, et al., Universal IP multicast delivery, Computer Networks, Vol. 50, No. 6, Apr. 2006, 781–806.

[308] Q. He and M. Ammar, Dynamic host-group/multi-destination routing for multicast sessions, Journal of Telecommunication Systems, Vol. 28, 2005, 409–433.

[309] Y. Chawathe, S. Maccanne, and E. A. Brewer, RMX: Rliable multicast for heterogeneous networks, in: Proceedings, IEEE Nineteenth Annual Joint Conference of the IEEE Computer and Communications Societies INFOCOM, Mar. 2000.

[310] S. Q. Zhuang, et al., Bayeux: An Architecture for scalable and fault-tolerant wide-area data dissemination, in: Proceedings, the 11th International Workshop on Network and Operating System Support for Digital Audio and Video, June 2001.

[311] J. Jannotti, et al., Overcast: reliable multicasting with an overlay network, in: Proceedings, the Symposium on Operating Systems Design and Implementation, Oct. 2000.

[312] D. Anderson, H. Balakrishnan, F. Kaashoek, and R. Morris, Resilient overlay networks, in: Proceedings, IEEE Nineteenth Annual Joint Conference of the IEEE Computer and Communications Societies INFOCOM, Mar. 2000.

[313] Z. Li, Y. Shin, and P. Mohapatra, A survey of overlay multicasting technologies, course project, available at http://networks.cs.ucdavis.edu/~lizhi.

[314] M. Castro, P. Druschel, A.-M. Kermarrec, and A. Rowstron, SCRIBE: A large-scale and decentralized application-level multicast infrastructure, IEEE Journal on Selected Areas in Communications (JSAC), Special Issue on Network Support for Group Communication, Vol. 20, No. 8, Oct. 2002, 1489–1499.

[315] A. Rowstron and P. Druschel, Pastry: Scalable, distributed object location and routing for large-scale peer-to-peer systems, in: Proceedings, the ACM/IFIP/USENIX International Middleware Conference, Nov. 2001.

[316] I. Stoica, R. Morris, et al., Chord: A scalable peer-to-peer lookup protocol for Internet applications, IEEE/ACM Transaction on Networking, Vol. 11, No. 1, 2003, 17–32.

[317] S. Ratnasamy et al., A scalable content-addressable network, in: Proceedings, ACM SIGCOMM, 2001, 161–72.

[318] B. Y. Zhao et al., Tapestry: A resilient global-scale overlay for service deployment, IEEE Journal on Selected Areas in Communications, Vol. 22, No. 1, Jan. 2004, 41–53.

[319] P. Maymounkov and D. Mazieres, Kademlia: A peer-to-peer information system based on the XOR metric, Springer Lecture Notes in Computer Science, Peer-to-Peer Systems, Vol. 2429, Feb. 2002, 53–65.

[320] F. Kaashoek and D. Karger, Koorde: A simple degree-optimal hash table, in: Proceedings, 2nd International Workshop on Peer-to- Peer Systems (IPTPS'03), Berkeley, CA, Feb. 2003.

[321] Overview of Overlay Weaver, available at http://overlayweaver.sourceforge.net/, Apr. 8, 2007.

[322] D. Moen, Overview of overlay multicast protocols, available at http://netlab.gmu.edu.

[323] V. N. Padmanabhan, H. J. Wang, P. A. Chou, and K. Sripanidkulchai, Distributing streaming media content using cooperative networking, in: Proceedings, the 12th International Workshop on Network and Operating System Support for Digital Audio and Video, Miami Beach, FL, May 2002.

[324] M. Castro, et al., Splitstream: Highbandwidth multicast in cooperative environments, in: Proceedings, the 20th ACM Symp. on Operating Sys. Principles (SOSP 2003), Oct. 2003.

[325] J. Li, P. A. Chou, and C. Zhang, Mutualcast: an efficient mechanism for content distribution in a P2P network, in: Proceedings, Acm Sigcomm Asia Workshop, Beijing, Apr. 2005.

[326] V. K. Goyal, Multiple description coding: compression meets the network, IEEE Signal Processing Magazine, Vol. 18, No. 5, Sept. 2001, 74–93.

[327] M. Zhang, L. Zhao, J. G. Luo, and S. Q. Yang, A peer-to-peer network for live media streaming using a push-pull approach, in Proceedings, ACM Multimedia 2005, Singapore, Sept. 2005, 287–290.

[328] S. Banerjee, B. Bhattacharjee, and C. Kommareddy, Scalable application layer multicast, in: Proceedings, ACM SIGCOMM2002, Sept. 2002.

[329] S. Shi and J. Turner, Routing in overlay multicast networks, in: Proceedings, IEEE Twenty-First Annual Joint Conference of the IEEE Computer and Communications Societies INFOCOM, June 2002.

[330] S. Banerjee, C. Kommareddy, K. Kar, B. Bhattacharjee, and S. Khuller, Construction of an efficient overlay multicast infrastructure for real-time applications, in: Proceedings, IEEE Twenty-Second Annual Joint Conference of the IEEE Computer and Communications Societies INFOCOM, Apr. 2003.

[331] Y. Chawathe, Scattercast: an architecture for Internet broadcast distribution as an infrastructure service, Ph.D. thesis, University of California, Berkeley, Dec. 2000.

[332] L. Lao, J.-H. Cui, M. Gerla, and D. Maggiorini, A comparative study of multicast protocols: Top, bottom, or in the middle? in: Proceedings, 8th IEEE Global Internet Symposium (GI'05) in conjunction with IEEE INFOCOM'05, Miami, FL, Mar. 2005.

[333] M. Castro, et al., An evaluation of scalable application-level multicast built using peer-to-peer overlays, in: Proceedings, IEEE Twenty-Second Annual Joint Conference of the IEEE Computer and Communications Societies INFOCOM, Apr. 2003.

[334] Y. K. Dalal and R. Metcalfe, Reverse path forwarding of broadcast packets, Communications of the ACM, Vol. 21, No. 12, Dec. 1978, 1040–1048.

[335] A. El-Sayed, V. Roca, and L. Mathy, A survey of proposals for an alternative group communication service, IEEE Network, Vol. 17, No. 1, Jan./Feb. 2003, 46–51.

[336] C. Abad, W. Yurcik, and R. H. Campbell, A survey and comparison of end-system overlay multicast solutions suitable for network centric warfare, in: Proceedings, SPIE, Vol. 5441, 215, April 2004.

[337] Z. Anwar, W. Yurcik, R. H. Campbell, A survey and comparison of peer-to-peer group communication systems suitable for network-centric warfare, in: Proceedings, SPIE, Vol. 5820, 2005, 33–44.

Chapter 10

[338] T. Henderson, Observations on game server discovery mechanisms, in: Proceedings of the ACM SIGMULTIMEDIA NetGames 2002: First Workshop on Network and System Support for Games, Apr. 2002.

[339] H. Zheng, E. K. Lua, M. Pias, and T. G. Griffin, Internet routing policies and round-trip times, in: Proceedings of the Passive Active Measurement Workshop 2005 (PAM 2005), Mar. 30–Apr. 1, 2000.

[340] E. K. Lua, J. Crowcroft, and M. Pias, Highways: Proximity clustering for scalable peer-to-peer networks, in: Proceedings of the 4th IEEE International Conference on Peer-to-Peer Computing (IEEE P2P 2004), Aug. 25–27, 2004, 266–267.

[341] T. S. Eugene Ng and H. Zhang, Predicting Internet network distance with coordinates-based approaches, in: Proceedings of the IEEE INFOCOM 2002, New York, June 2002.

[342] Marcelo Pias, et al., Lighthouses for scalable distributed location, in: Proceedings of the 2nd International Workshop on Peer-to-Peer Systems (IPTPS 2003), Feb. 2003.

[343] L. Tang and M. Crovella, Virtual landmarks for the Internet, in: Proceedings of the ACM SIGCOMM Internet Measurement Conference (IMC 2003), Miami, FL, Oct. 2003.

[344] H. Lim, J. Hou, and C. Choi, Constructing Internet coordinate system based on delay measurement, in: Proceedings of the ACM SIGCOMM Internet Measurement Conference (IMC 2003), Miami, FL, Oct. 2003.

[345] Y. Mao and L. K. Saul, Modeling distances in large-scale networks by matrix factorization, in: Proceedings of the 4th ACM SIGCOMM conference on Internet Measurement, 2004, 278–287.

[346] M. Costa, M. Castro, A. Rowstron, and P. Key, PIC: Practical Internet Coordinates for distance estimation, in: Proceedings of the 24th IEEE International Conference on Distributed Computing Systems (ICDCS' 04), Tokyo, Mar. 2004.

[347] F. Dabek, R. Cox, F. Kaashoek, and R. Morris, Vivaldi: A decentralized network coordinate system, in: Proceedings of the ACM SIGCOMM 2004, Portland, OR, Aug. 2004.

[348] Y. Shavitt and T. Tankel, Big-bang simulation for embedding network distances in Euclidean space, in: Proceedings of the IEEE INFOCOM 2003, San Francisco, Apr. 2003.

[349] Y. Shavitt and T. Tankel, On the curvature of the Internet and its usage for overlay construction and distance estimation, in: Proceedings of the IEEE INFOCOM 2004, Hong Kong, Mar. 7–11 2004.

[350] Y. Shavitt and T. Tankel, Hyperbolic embedding of internet graph for distance estimation and overlay construction, IEEE/ACM Transactions on Networking (TON), Volume 16, Issue 1, Feb. 2008, 25–36.

[351] P. Pietzuch, J. Ledlie, and M. Seltzer, Supporting network coordinates on PlanetLab, in: Proceedings of the 2nd Workshop on Real, Large Distributed Systems (WORLDS 2005), Dec. 2005.

[352] P. Druschel and A. Rowstron, Pastry: Scalable distributed object location and routing for large-scale peer-to-peer systems, in: Proceedings of the 18th IFIP/ACM Middleware 2001, Nov. 2001.

[353] I. Stoica, et al., Chord: A scalable peer-to-peer lookup service for Internet applications, in: Proceedings of the ACM SIGCOMM Technical Conference 2001, San Diego, Aug. 2001.

[354] F. Dabek, M. F. Kaashoek, D. Karger, R. Morris, and I. Stoica, Wide area cooperative storage with CFS, in: Proceedings of the 18th ACM Symposium on Operating Systems Principles (SOSP 2001), Chateau Lake Louise, Banff, Canada, Oct. 21-24, 2001.

[355] M. Kleis, E. K. Lua, and X. Zhou, Hierarchical peer-to-peer networks using lightweight superpeer topologies, in: Proceedings of the IEEE Symposium on Computers and Communications (ISCC 2005), La Manga del Mar Menor, Cartagena, Spain, June 27-30, 2005, 143-148.

[356] E. K. Lua, X. Zhou, J. Crowcroft, and P. V. Miegham, Hierarchical geometric overlay multicast network, in: Proceedings of the 25th IEEE INFOCOM Conference 2006 Posters and Demo, Barcelona, Apr. 25-27, 2006.

[357] E. K. Lua, X. Zhou, J. Crowcroft, and P. V. Mieghem, Scalable multicasting with network-aware geometric overlay, Elsevier Journal of Computer Communications, Special Issue of Disruptive Networking with Peer-to-Peer (P2P) Systems, Vol. 31, Issue 3, Feb. 25, 2008, 464-488.

[358] P. Pietzuch, et al., Network-aware operator placement for stream-processing systems, in: Proceedings of the 22nd International Conference on Data Engineering (ICDE 2006), Apr. 2006.

[359] J. Ledlie, P. Pietzuch, and M. Seltzer, Stable and Accurate Network Coordinates, in: Proceedings of the 26th IEEE International Conference on Distributed Computing Systems (ICDCS 2006), July 04-07, 2006.

[360] J. Bourgain, On Lipschitz embedding of finite metric spaces in Hilbert space, Israel J. Math, 52(1-2):46-52, 1985.

[361] W. B. Johnson and J. Lindenstrauss, Extensions of Lipschitz mappings into a Hilbert space, Amer. Math. Soc., 1984, 46-52.

[362] J. A. Nelder and R. Mead, A simplex method for function minimization, The Computer Journal, 7(4):308-313, 1965.

[363] S. Floyd, V. Jacobson, C.-G. Liu, S. McCanne, and L. Zhang, A reliable multicast framework for light-weight sessions and application level framing, IEEE/ACM Trans. Netw., 5(6):784-803, 1997.

[364] D. R. Karger and M. Ruhl, Finding nearest neighbors in growth-restricted metrics, in: Proceedings of the 34th Annual ACM symposium on Theory of Computing, 2002, 741-750.

[365] M. Castro, P. Druschel, Y. C. Hu, and A. Rowstron, Exploiting network proximity in peer-to-peer overlay networks, Microsoft Research Technical Report, MSR-TR-2002-82, May 2002.

[366] S. Halabi and D. McPherson, Internet routing architectures, 2nd ed., Cisco Press, 2000.

[367] J. B. Kruskal and M. Wish, Multidimensional scaling, technical report, Sage University Series, 1978.

[368] J. W. Cannon, W. J. Floyd, R. Kenyon, and W. R. Parry, Hyperbolic geometry, Flavors of geometry, Cambridge University Press, 1997.

[369] W. P. Thurston, Three-dimensional geometry and topology, Princeton Mathematical Series 35, Princeton University Press, 1997.

[370] J. W. Anderson, Hyperbolic geometry, Springer, 2001.

[371] B. Wong, A. Slivkins, and E. G. Sirer, Meridian: a lightweight network location service without virtual coordinates, SIGCOMM Comput. Commun. Rev. 35, 4, Oct. 2005, 85-96. http://doi.acm.org/10.1145/1080091.1080103

[372] E. K. Lua, et al., On the accuracy of embeddings for internet coordinate systems, in: Proceedings of the ACM SIGCOMM-Usenix Internet Measurement Conference 2005 (IMC 2005), Oct. 19-21, 2005.

[373] H. Zheng, E. K. Lua, M. Pias, and T. G. Griffin, Internet routing policies and round-trip-times, in Proceedings of the Passive Active Measurement Workshop 2005 (PAM 2005), Mar. 30-Apr. 1, 2005.

[374] P. Pietzuch, J. Ledlie, M. Mitzenmacher, and M. Seltzer, Network-aware overlays with network coordinates, in: Proceedings of IWDDS 2006, Lisbon, Portugal, July 2006.

[375] S.-J. Lee, et al., Measuring bandwidth between PlanetLab nodes, in: PAM, Boston, Mar. 2005.

[376] D. Oppenheimer, D. A. Patterson, and A. Vahdat, A case for informed service placement on PlanetLab, Technical Report 04-025, PlanetLab, 2004.

[377] M. Szymaniaka, D. Presottob, G. Pierrea, and M. V. Steen, Practical large-scale latency estimation, Elsevier Journal of Computer Networks, Vol. 52, Issue 7, May 15, 2008, 1343-1364.

Chapter 11

[378] J. Pang, et al., Availability, usage, and deployment characteristics of the domain name system, in: Proceedings of the 4th ACM SIGCOMM Conference on internet Measurement, Taormina, Italy, Oct. 25-27, 2004, IMC '04, ACM, 1-14.

[379] R. Cox, A. Muthitacharoen, and R. Morris, Serving DNS using a peer-to-peer lookup service, in Revised Papers From the First international Workshop on Peer-to-Peer Systems, Mar. 7-8, 2002, P. Druschel, M. F. Kaashoek, and A. I. Rowstron (eds.), Lecture Notes in Computer Science, Vol. 2429, Springer-Verlag, 2002, 155-165.

[380] J. Jung, E. Sit, H. Balakrishnan, and R. Morris, DNS performance and the effectiveness of caching, in: Proceedings of the ACM SIGCOMM Internet Measurement Workshop '01, San Francisco, Nov. 2001.

[381] V. Pappas, D. Massey, A. Terzis, L. Zhang, A comparative study of current DNS with DHT-based alternatives, IEEE INFOCOM 2006, Apr. 2006.

[382] V. Ramasubramanian and E. Sirer, The design and implementation of a next generation name service for the Internet, in: Proceedings of the 2004 Conference on Applications, Technologies, Architectures, and Protocols for Computer Communications, Portland, OR, Aug. 30-Sept. 3, 2004, SIGCOMM '04, ACM, 331-342.

[383] D. G. Andersen, H. Balakrishnan, M. F. Kaashoek, and R. Morris, Resilient overlay networks, Proc. 18th ACM Symposium on Operating Systems Principles (SOSP), Banff, Canada, Oct. 2001, 131-145.

[384] D. Andersen, A. Snoeren, and H. Balakrishnan, Best-path vs. multipath overlay routing, Proceedings of the 3rd ACM SIGCOMM conference on Internet measurement (IMC'03), 2003.

[385] S. Qazi and T. Moors, Scalable resilient overlay networks using destination-guided detouring, Proc. IEEE International Conference on Communications (ICC), June 2007.

[386] Y. Zhu, C. Dovrolis, and M. Ammar, Proactive and reactive bandwidth driven overlay routing: A simulation study, Computer Networks, 50(6):742-762, Apr. 2006.

[387] Sung-Ju Lee, S. Banerjee, P. Sharma, P. Yalagandula, and S. Basu, Bandwidth-aware routing in overlay networks, IEEE INFOCOM 2008, 27th Conference on Computer Communications, Apr. 13-18, 2008, 1732-1740.

[388] R. Braden, D. Clark, and S. Shenker, Integrated services in the Internet architecture: An overview, IETF RFC 1633, June 1994.

[389] S. Blake, et al., An architecture for differentiated services. IETF RFC 2475.

[390] L. Subramanian, I. Stoica, H. Balakrishnan, and R. H. Katz, OverQos: an overlay based architecture for enhancing internet Qos, in: Proceedings of the 1st Conference on Symposium on Networked Systems Design and Implementation, Vol. 1, San Francisco, Mar. 29-31, 2004, USENIX Association, Berkeley, CA, 2004, 6-6.

[391] Z. Li and P. Mohapatra, QRON: QoS-Aware routing in overlay networks, IEEE J. Selected Areas in Comm., Vol. 22, No. 1, 2004, 29-40.

[392] Z. Duan, Z. Zhang and Y. Hou, Service overlay networks: SLAs, QoS, and bandwidth provisioning, IEEE/ACM Transactions in Networking 11(6), 2003, 870-883.

[393] Institute for Electrical and Electronics Engineers, IEEE P1903 Standard for Next Generation Service Overlay Networks, http://grouper.ieee.org/groups/ngson/.

[394] M. Balazinska, H. Balakrishnan, and D. Karger, INS/Twine: A scalable peer-to-peer architecture for intentional resource discovery, Proceedings of Pervasive 2002.

[395] C. Bettstetter and C. Renner, A comparison of service discovery protocols and implementation of the service location protocol, Proceedings EUNICE 2000, Sept 2000.

[396] W. B. Bradley and David P. Maher, The NEMO P2P service orchestration framework, Proceedings of the 37th Hawaii International Conference on System Sciences, 2004.

[397] J. Buford, A. Brown, and M. Kolberg, Meta service discovery, 4th IEEE International Conference on Pervasive Computing and Communications (PerCom), 3rd IEEE International Workshop on Mobile Peer-to-Peer Computing (MP2P'06), Pisa, Italy, 2006, 124-129.

[398] C. Lee and S. Helal, Protocols for service discovery in dynamic and mobile networks, Intl. J. of Computer Research, Vol. 11, No. 1, 2002, 1-12.

[399] G. G. Richard III, Service advertisement and discovery: Enabling universal device cooperation, IEEE Internet Computing, Vol. 4(5), Sept./Oct. 2000.

[400] G. G. Richard III, Service and device discovery: Protocols and programming, McGraw-Hill, 2002.

[401] C. Schmidt and M. Parashar, A peer-to-peer approach to Web service discovery, World Wide Web Journal, Vol. 7, Issue 2, June 2004.

[402] F. Zhu, M. Mutka, L. Ni, Classification of service discovery in pervasive computing environments, MSU-CSE-02-24, Michigan State University, 2002.

[403] Todd D. Hodes, et al., An architecture for secure wide-area service discovery, *Wireless Networks*, 8(2/3):213-230, 2002.

[404] V. Ramasubramanian and E. Sirer, Beehive: O(1) lookup performance for power-law query distributions in peer-to-peer overlays, in: Proc. of Networked System Design and Implementation (NSDI), Mar. 2004.

[405] X. Gu, K. Nahrstedt, and B. Yu, SpiderNet: An integrated peer-to-peer service composition framework, in: Proceedings of the 13th IEEE international Symposium on High Performance Distributed Computing (Hpdc'04), Vol. 00, June 4-6, 2004, Washington, DC, 2004, 110-119.

[406] D. Clark, et al., Overlay networks and the future of the Internet. Communications & Strategies, No. 63, 3rd quarter 2006.

[407] R. Bless, O. P. Waldhorst, and C. P. Mayer, The spontaneous virtual networks architecture for supporting future internet services and applications, June 2008.

[408] Ambient Networks Deliverable, System Design of SATO & ASI, www.ambientnetworks. org/Files/deliverables/D12-F.1_PU.pdf, Sept. 2007.

[409] J. Buford, A. Wang, X. Hei, Y. Liu, and K. Ross, Discovery of in-band streaming services in peer-to-peer overlays. IEEE Globecom 2007, Nov. 2007.

[410] I. Stoica, et al., Chord: a scalable peer-to-peer lookup protocol for internet applications, IEEE/ACM Trans. Netw. 11, 1, Feb. 2003, 17–32.

[411] J. Byers, J. Considine, and M. Mitzenmacher, Simple load balancing for distributed hash tables, in Proceedings of IPTPS, Berkeley, CA, Feb. 2003.

[412] A. Rao, et al., Load balancing in structured P2P systems, in: Proceedings of IPTPS, Berkeley, CA, Feb. 2003.

[413] S. Surana, et al., Load balancing in dynamic structured peer-to-peer systems, Perform. Eval. 63, 3, Mar. 2006, 217–240.

Chapter 12

[414] J. Rosenberg, et al., SIP: Session Initiation Protcol, IETF RFC 3261, June 2002.

[415] H. Sinnreich and A. B. Johnston, Internet communications using SIP: Delivering VoIP and multimedia services with Session Initiation Protocol, 2nd ed., Wiley, 2006.

[416] ITU-T, Packet-based multimedia communications systems, Rec. H.323 v6, May 2006.

[417] 3GPP, Technical Specification Group Services and System Aspects, IP Multimedia Subsystem (IMS), Stage 2, V5.15.0, TS 23.228, 3rd Generation Partnership Project, 2006.

[418] Gonzalo Camarillo and Miguel-Angel García-Martín, The 3G IP Multimedia Subsystem (IMS): Merging the Internet and the cellular worlds, John Wiley & Sons, 2006.

[419] J. Buford, A. Wang, X. Hei, Y. Liu, and K. Ross, Discovery of in-band streaming services in peer-to-peer overlays. IEEE Globecom 2007, General Symposium track on P2P Networking, Nov. 2007.

[420] Y. Liu, et al., Application level relay for high-bandwidth data transport, First Workshop on Networks for Grid Applications (GridNets), San Jose, Oct. 2004.

[421] TeleGeography Report and Database, International carriers' traffic grows despite Skype popularity, Retrieved on Sept. 20, 2007, www.telegeography.com/cu/article.php?article_id=15656&email=html.

[422] H. Max and T. Ray, Skype: The definitive guide, Que, 2006.

[423] S. Ren, L. Guo, and X. Zhang, ASAP: An AS-aware Peer-relay protocol for high quality VoIP with low overhead, in: Proceedings of 26th International Conference on Distributed Computing Systems (ICDCS'06), Lisbon, Portugal, July 4–7, 2006.

[424] J. Zhou, J. Buford, K. Dhara, M. Kolberg, V. Krishnaswamy, and X. Wu, Discovery and composition of communication services in peer-to-peer overlays, IEEE Workshop on Service Discovery and Composition in Ubiquitous and Pervasive Environments (SUPE'07), Nov. 2007.

[425] A. Johnston, et al., Session Initiation Protocol Service Examples, IETF Internet draft, draft-ietf-sipping-service-examples-12 (work in progress), Jan 2007.

[426] S. Baset and H. Schulzrinne, An analysis of the Skype peer-to-peer Internet telephony protocol, Columbia University, Department of Computer Science, Technical Report cucs-039-04, 2004.

[427] S. Guha, N. Daswani, and R. Jain, An experimental study of the Skype peer-to-peer VoIP system, in: IPTPS, 2006.

[428] T. Hoßfeld, Measurement and analysis of Skype VoIP traffic in 3G UMTS systems, 4th International Workshop on Internet Performance, Simulation, Monitoring and Measurement, IPS-MoMe 2006, Salzburg, Feb. 2006.

[429] K. Suh, D. R. Figueiredo, J. Kurose, and D. Towsley, Characterizing and detecting Skype-relayed traffic, in: Proceedings of IEEE Infocom (Infocom 2006), Barcelona, Apr. 2006.

[430] H. Xie, Y. Yang, A measurement-based study of the Skype peer-to-peer VoIP performance, The 6th International Workshop on Peer-to-Peer Systems. IPTPS 2007, Feb 2007.

[431] E. Cooper, A. Johnston, and P. Matthews, A distributed transport function in P2PSIP using HIP for multi-hop overlay routing, draft-matthews-p2psip-hip-hop-00, IETF P2P-SIP WG, work in progress, June 2007.

[432] R. Moskowitz and P. Nikander, Host Identity Protocol (HIP) architecture, IETF RFC 4423, May 2006.

[433] R. Moskowitz, P. Nikander, P. Jokela, and T. Henderson, Host Identity Protocol, IETF HIP WG, work in progress, draft-ietf-hip-base-08, June 2007.

[434] F. Al-Shraideh, Host Identity Protocol, International Conference on Networking, ICN/ICONS/MCL 2006, Apr. 2006, 203.

[435] C. Jennings, J. Rosenberg, and E. Rescorla, ASP: Address Settlement by Peer-to-Peer, draft-jennings-p2psip-asp-00. IETF P2P-SIP WG, work in progress, July 2007.

[436] International Engineering Consortium, Voice over Internet Protocol, www.iec.org/online/tutorials/int_tele.

[437] B. Ford, P. Srisuresh, and D. Kegel, Peer-to-peer communication across network address translators, Proceedings of the 2005 USENIX Annual Technical Conference, Anaheim, CA, Apr. 2005.

[438] H. Khlifi, J.-C. Gregoire, and J. Phillips, VoIP and NAT/firewalls: issues, traversal techniques, and a real-world solution, IEEE Communications Magazine, 44 (7), July 2006, 93–99.

[439] V. Kumar, M. Korpi, and S. Sengodan, IP telephony with H.323: Architectures for unified networks and integrated services, Wiley, 2006.

[440] A. Liotta and L. Lin, IP Multimedia Subsystem: The operator's response to P2P service demand, IEEE Communications Magazine 45 (7), July 2007, 76–83.

[441] P2P-SIP, www.p2psip.org.

[442] B. Karacali, M. J. Karol, A. S. Krishnakumar, P. Krishnan, and J. Meloche. Simple On-Demand Overlays for Reliable Real-Time Traffic in Enterprise Networks. International Conference on Internet Computing 2006: 224–229.

[443] C. Jennings, B. Lowekamp, E. Rescorla, S. Baset, and H. Schulzrinne. IETF REsource LOcation And Discovery (RELOAD). Work in progress. draft-ietf-p2psip-reload-00. July 2008.

[444] R. Barbosa, et al., Performance evaluation of P2P VoIP applications, NOSSDAV 2007.

Chapter 13

[445] S. Gurun, P. Nagpurkar, and B. Y. Zhao, Energy consumption and conservation in mobile peer-to-peer systems, in: Proceedings of the 1st international workshop on Decentralized resource sharing in mobile computing and networking, Los Angeles, Jul. 25–25, 2006.

[446] K. Christensen, B. Nordman, and R. Brown, Power management in networked devices, IEEE Computer, Aug. 2004, 91–93.

[447] H. Hsiao, and C. King, Mobility churn in DHTs, in: Proceedings of the 1st international Workshop on Mobility in Peer-teer Systems (MPPS), Volume 08, ICDCSW, IEEE Computer Society, Washington, DC, 2005, 799–805.

[448] J. Li, et al., A performance vs. cost framework for evaluating DHT design tradeoffs under churn, in: Proceedings of the 24th IEEE Infocom, Mar. 2005.

[449] H. Pucha, S. M. Das, and Y. C. Hu, How to implement DHTs in mobile ad hoc networks, in: Proceedings of the 10th ACM International Conference on Mobile Computing and Network (MobiCom 2004), Sept. 2004.

[450] A. MacQuire, A. Brampton, I. Rai, and L. Mathy, Performance analysis of stealth DHT with mobile nodes, in: Proceedings of the 4th IEEE International Conference on Pervasive Computing and Communications Workshops (PERCOMW 2006), Mar. 2006.

[451] C. Perkins, IP Mobility Support for IPv4, RFC 3344 (Proposed Standard), Aug. 2002.

[452] H.-C. Hsiao and C.-T. King, Bristle: A mobile structured peer-to-peer architecture, in: Proceedings of the Parallel and Distributed Processing Symposium (IPDPS'03), 2003.

[453] H.-C. Hsiao and C.-T. King, Tornado: Capability-aware peer-to-peer storage networks, in: Proceedings of the International Parallel and Distributed Processing Symposium, Apr. 2003.

[454] B. Y. Zhao, L. Huang, A. D. Joseph, and J. D. Kubiatowicz, Rapid mobility via type indirection, in: Proceedings of the 3rd International Workshop on Peer-to-Peer Systems (IPTPS'04), San Diego, Feb. 2004.

[455] J. Li, et al., A performance vs. cost framework for evaluating DHT design tradeoffs under churn, in: Proceedings of the 24th IEEE Infocom Mar 2005.

[456] J. Li, J. Stribling, R. Morris, and M. F. Kaashoek. Bandwidth-efficient management of DHT routing tables, in: the Proceedings of the 2nd USENIX Symposium on Networked Systems Design and Implementation (NSDI '05), Boston, 2005.

[457] A. Gupta, B. Liskov, and R. Rodrigues, Efficient routing for peer-to-peer overlays, in: Proceedings of the 1st USENIX Symposium on Networked Systems Design and Implementation (NSDI '04), Mar. 2004.

[458] M. Gerla, C. Lindemann, and A. Rowstron, P2P MANET's – New Research Issues, Perspectives Workshop: Peer-to-Peer Mobile Ad Hoc Networks: New Research Issues, Schloss Dagstuhl, Germany, 2005.

[459] O. Landsiedel, S. Götz, and K. Wehrle, Towards scalable mobility in distributed hash tables, in 6th International IEEE Conference on Peer-to-Peer-Computing, Cambridge, UK, Aug./Sept. 2006.

[460] B. Karp and H. T. Kung, GPSR: greedy perimeter stateless routing for wireless networks, in: Proceedings of the 6th Annual international Conference on Mobile Computing and Networking, MobiCom '00, Boston, Aug. 6–11, 2000, ACM, 2000.

[461] T. Zahn and J. Schiller, Designing structured peer-to-peer overlays as a platform for distributed network applications in mobile ad hoc networks, Computer Communications, Vol. 31, No. 3, Feb. 2008.

[462] The SpoVNet Consortium, SpoVNet: An architecture for supporting future Internet applications, www.spovnet.de.

[463] T. Anderson, L. Peterson, S. Shenker, and J. Turner, Overcoming the Internet impasse through virtualization, GDD-05-01, Geni Project Office, Global Environment for Network Innovations (GENI), www.geni.net, Apr. 2005.

[464] IETF HIP WG, End-host mobility and multihoming with the Host Identity Protocol (HIP), IETF RFC5206, Apr. 2008, http://tools.ietf.org/html/rfc5206.

[465] M. Bisignano, G. Di Modica, O. Tomarchio, and L. Vita, P2P over Manet: a comparison of cross-layer approaches, in: 18th International Conference on Database and Expert Systems Applications, 2007 (DEXA '07), Sept. 3–7, 2007, 814–818.

[466] R. Stacey, IEEE 802.11n emerging wireless standards discussion., presentation at IEEE Globecom 2006, Nov. 2006.

[467] D. Leeper, Ultrawideband (UWB) wireless technology, presentation at IEEE Globecom 2006, Nov. 2006.

[468] Ambient Networks Deliverable, System design of SATO & ASI, www.ambientnetworks. org/Files/deliverables/D12-F.1_PU.pdf, Sept. 2007.

[469] C. Cramer and T. Fuhrmann, ISPRP: A message-efficient protocol for initializing structured P2P networks, in: Proc. 24th IEEE International Performance, Computing, and Communications Conference (IPCCC 2005), 2005, 365–370.

[470] I. Gruber, R. Schollmeier, and W. Kellerer, Performance evaluation of the mobile peer-to-peer service, in: Proceedings IEEE CCGrid 2004, 2004, 363–371.

[471] A. Klemm, C. Lindemann, and O. Waldhorst, A special-purpose peer-to-peer file sharing system for mobile ad hoc networks, in: Proceeding Workshop on Mobile Ad Hoc Networking and Computing (MADNET 2003), 2003, 41–49.

[472] H. Pucha, S. Das, and Y. C. Hu, Ekta: An efficient DHT substrate for distributed applications in mobile ad hoc networks, Proc. 6th IEEE Workshop on Mobile Computing Systems and Applications (WMCSA), 2004, 163–173.

[473] M. Conti, E. Gregori, and G. Turi, A crosslayer optimization of Gnutella for mobile ad hoc networks, in: Proc. of the 6th ACM international symposium on Mobile ad hoc networking and computing (MobiHoc05), ACM Press, 2005, 343–354.

[474] T. Zahn and J. Schiller, MADPastry: A DHT substrate for practicably sized MANETs, in: 5th Workshop on Applications and Services in Wireless Networks (ASWN2005), Paris, June 2005.

[475] B. Tang, Z. Zhou, A. Kashyap, and T. Chiueh, An integrated approach for P2P file sharing on multi-hopwireless networks, in: Proc. of the IEEE Int. Conf. on Wireless and Mobile Computing, Networking and Communication (WIMOB'05), Montreal, Aug. 2005.

[476] T. Zahn and J. Schiller, Designing structured peer-to-peer overlays as a platform for distributed network applications in mobile ad hoc networks, Compute Communications, Vol. 31, Issue 2, Feb. 5, 2008, 643–654.

[477] H. Pucha, S. M. Das, and Y. C. Hu, Imposed route reuse in ad hoc network routing protocols using structured peer-to-peer overlay routing, IEEE Trans. Parallel Distrib. Syst. 17, 12, Dec. 2006, 1452–1467.

Chapter 14

[478] News and Events, Triversa, www.tiversa.com/news/.

[479] M. Eric Johnson, and Scott Dynes, Inadvertent disclosure: Information leaks in the extended enterprise," Proceedings of the 6th Workshop on the Economics of Information Security, Carnegie Mellon University, June 7–8, 2007.

[480] M. Eric Johnson, Dan McGuire, and Nicholas D. Willey, Why file sharing networks are dangerous, available at http://reform.democrats.house.gov/documents/20070724140635.pdf.

[481] M. Eric Johnson, Inadvertent file sharing over peer-to-peer networks, testimony of Professor M. Eric Johnson before the committee on oversight and government reform, US House of Representatives, July 24, 2007, available at http://oversight.house.gov/documents/20070724103956.pdf.

[482] G. Johnson, Arrest in case of ID theft by file-sharing, USA Today, Sept. 07, 2007, available at www.usatoday.com/tech/news/computersecurity/infotheft/2007-09-07-id-theft-file-sharing_N.htm#uslPageReturn.

[483] S. Moskowitz, Introduction: digital rights management, Multimedia Security Technologies for Digital Rights Management, Zeng, Yu, and Lin (eds.), Elsevier, 2006.

[484] W. Stallings, Network and internetwork security, Prentice Hall, 1995.

[485] J. R. Douceur, The Sybil attack, in: Proceedings, the 1st International Workshop on Peer-to-Peer Systems (IPTPS '02), Cambridge, MA, Mar. 2002.

[486] Wrapster, www.unwrapper.com.

[487] S. McBride and G. A. Fowler, Estimate of film-piracy cost soars: Hollywood loss is put at $6.1 billion a year, The Wall Street Journal Europe, May 4, 2006, www.lek.com/about/newsarchive.cfm.

[488] L. Garber, Denial of service attacks rip the Internet, Computer, Vol. 33, No. 4, 2000, 12–17.

[489] J. Mirkovic and P. Reiher, A taxonomy of DDoS attack and DDoS defense mechanisms, Computer Communications Review, Vol. 34, No. 2, Apr. 2004.

[490] N. Naoumov, and K. Ross, Exploiting P2P systems for DDoS attacks, in: Proceedings, the 1st international conference on Scalable information systems, Hong Kong, 2006.

[491] Prolexic distributed denial of service attack alert, Prolexic Technologies Inc., May 14, 2007, available at www.prolexic.com/news/20070514-alert.php.

[492] DC++, http://dcplusplus.sourceforge.net/features/.

[493] R. R. Brooks, Disruptive security technologies with mobile code and peer-to-peer networks, CRC Press, 2005.

[494] L. Divac-Krnic and R. Ackermann, Security-related issues in peer-to-peer networks, Chapter 31, P2P Systems and Applications, Steinmetz and Wehrle (eds.), Springer-Verlag, 2005, 529–545.

[495] F. R. Schreiber, Sybil, Warner Books, 1973.

[496] M. Castro, et al., Secure routing for structured peer-to-peer overlay networks, in: Proceedings, 5th Symp. on Operating Sys. Design and Impl., Boston, Dec. 2002, 299–314.

[497] D. Wallach, A survey of peer-to-peer security issues, in: Proceedings, International Symposium on Software Security – Theories and Systems, Tokyo, Nov. 2002, 42–57.

[498] Overnet, www.overnet.com.

[499] Cisco PIX 500 series security appliances introduction, Cisco, available at www.cisco.com/en/US/products/hw/vpndevc/ps2030/.

[500] K. C. Sia, DDoS vulnerability analysis of the Bittorrent protocol, UCLA Technical Report, June 2006, available at http://oak.cs.ucla.edu/~sia/cs239spring06.pdf.

[501] I. Stoica, R. Morris, et al., Chord: A scalable peer-to-peer lookup protocol for internet applications, IEEE/ACM Transaction on Networking, Vol. 11, No. 1, 2003, 17–32.

[502] A. Rowstron and P. Druschel, Pastry: Scalable, distributed object location and routing for large-scale peer-to-peer systems, in: Proceedings, the ACM/IFIP Int. Middleware Conf., Nov. 2001.

[503] B. Y. Zhao, et al., Tapestry: A resilient global-scale overlay for service deployment, IEEE Journal on Selected Areas in Communications, Vol. 22, No. 1, Jan. 2004, 41–53.

[504] H. Yu, J. Buford, and M. Meratbi, Improving messaging security in structured P2P overlay networks, in Proceedings, IEEE International Conference on Multimedia and Expo, Beijing, July 2007.

[505] P. Nikander, et al., Mobile IP Version 6 route optimization security design background, IETF RFC4225, Dec. 2005, available at www.ietf.org/rfc/rfc4225.txt.

[506] E. Adar, and B. Huberman, Free riding on Gnutella, First Monday, Vol. 5, No. 10, 2000.

[507] T. Ngan, D. Wallach, and P. Druschel, Enforcing fair sharing of peer-to-peer resources, in: Proceedings, 2nd International Workshop on Peer-to-Peer Systems (IPTPS), Berkeley, CA, Feb. 2003.

[508] A. Nandi, et al., On designing incentive comptabile peer to peer systems, in: Proceedings, 2nd Bertinoro Workshop on Future Directions in Distributed Computing, Bertinoro, Italy, June 2004.

[509] K. Aberer and Z. Despotovic, Managing trust in a peer-2-peer information system, in: Proceedings, the tenth international conference on Information and knowledge management, 2001.

[510] A. Abdul-Rahman and S. Hailes, Supporting trust in virtual communities, in: Proceedings, the 33rd Hawaii International Conference on System Sciences, 2000.

[511] L. Xiong and L. Liu, A reputation-based model for peer-to-peer communities, in: Proceedings, IEEE International Conference on Distributed Computing Systems, Providence, RI, May 2003.

[512] J. Camp, and A. Friedman, Peer-to-peer security, in: Proceedings, Telecommunications Policy Research Conference, Washington DC, Sept. 2003.

[513] K. Wongrujira, T. Hsin-Ting, and A. Seneviratne, Avoidance routing to misbehaving nodes in P2P by using reputation and variance, in: Proceedings, 6th Int. Conf. on Adv. Comm. Tech.: Broadband Convergence Network Infrastructure, South Korea, Feb. 9–11, 2004.

[514] Z. Despotovic, and K. Aberer, P2P reputation management: Probabilistic estimation vs. social networks, Computer Networks, Vol. 50(4), Mar. 15, 2006, 485–500.

[515] I. Goldberg, Privacy-enhancing technologies for the Internet, II: five years later, Privacy Enhancing Technologies, Springer, 2003.

[516] M. Kinateder and S. Pearson, A privacy-enhanced peer-to-peer reputation system, E-commerce and Web technologies, Springer, 2003.

[517] Trusted Computing Platform Alliance: TCPA main specification, version 1.1, 2001, available at www.trustedcomputing.org.

[518] R. Sherwood, B. Bhattacharjee, and A. Srinivasan, P5: A protocol for scalable anonymous communication, Journal of Computer Security, Vol. 13, No. 6, 2005, 839–876.

[519] The Free Haven Project, www.freehaven.net.

[520] M. J. Freedman and R. Morris, Tarzan: a peer-to-peer anonymizing network layer, in: Proceedings, ACM Conference on Computer and Communications Security, Washington, DC, 2002.

[521] Groove, www.groove.net.

[522] Overpeer, www.overpeer.com.

[523] J. Liang, R. Kumar, Y. Xi, K. W. Ross, Pollution in P2P file sharing systems, in Proceedings, Infocom 05, Miami, 2005.

[524] KaZaA, www.kazaa.com.

Chapter 15

[525] Associated Press, Skype service outage caused by software problems, Aug 16, 2007.

[526] S. A. Baset and H. Schulzrinne, An analysis of the Skype peer-to-peer Internet telephony protocol, Columbia University Technical Report CUCS-039-04, 2004.

[527] J. Buford, Management of peer-to-peer overlays, International J. of Internet Protocol Technology, Special Issue on Management of IP Networks and Services, Vol. 3, No.1, 2008, 2–12.

[528] J. Buford, Telecommunication services and service management challenges, J. Universal Computer Science, Special Issue for the Future of Computer Science Symposium (FOCSS), June 2001.

[529] S. El-Ansary, L. O. Alima, P. Brand, and S. Haridi, Efficient broadcast in structured P2P networks, 2nd International Workshop on Peer-to-Peer Systems (IPTPS'03), Berkeley, CA, Feb. 2003.

[530] M. Lue, C. King, and H. Fang, Scoped broadcast in structured P2P networks, in: Proceedings of the 1st international Conference on Scalable information Systems, Hong Kong, May 30–June 01, 2006, InfoScale '06, Vol. 152, ACM Press, 2006, 51.

[531] L. R. Monnerat and C. L. Amorim, D1HT: A distributed one-hop hash table, Proc. of the 20th IEEE Intl Parallel & Distributed Processing Symp. (IPDPS), Apr. 2006.

[532] W. Stalling, SNMP, SNMPv2, SNMPv3, and RMON 1 and 2, 3rd ed., Addison-Wesley, 1998.

[533] K. Terplan, OSS essentials: Support system solutions for service providers, John Wiley, 2001.

[534] V. Vischnevsky, A. Safonov, M. Yakimov, E. Shim, and A. Gelman, Scalable blind search and broadcasting in peer-to-peer networks, 6th IEEE International Conference on Peer-to-Peer Computing, Sept. 2006.

[535] H. Yu and J. Buford, Improving messaging security in structured P2P overlay networks, Proc. 2007 International Conference on Multimedia and Expo., to appear.

[536] J. Buford, Telecommunication services and service management challenges, J. Universal Computer Science, Special Issue for the Future of Computer Science Symposium (FOCSS), June 2001.

[537] L. Lewis, Managing business and service networks, Kluwer Academic Publishers, 2001.

[538] L. Lewis, Service level management for enterprise networks, Artech House, 1999.

[539] P. Druschel and A. Rowstron, PAST: A large-scale, persistent peer-to-peer storage utility, HotOS VIII, Schoss Elmau, Germany, May 2001.

[540] J. Kubiatowicz, et al., OceanStore: an architecture for global-scale persistent storage, SIGPLAN Not. 35, 11, Nov. 2000, 190–201.

[541] F. Dabek, et al., Wide-area cooperative storage with CFS, in: Proceedings of the 18th ACM Symposium on Operating Systems Principles, Banff, Canada, Oct. 21–24, 2001, SOSP '01, ACM, 2001, 202–215.

[542] Athicha Muthitacharoen, Robert Morris, Thomer M. Gil, and Benjie Chen, Ivy: A read/write peer-to-peer file system, 5th Symposium on Operating Systems Design and Implementation (OSDI), Boston, Dec. 2002.

[543] J. Li, K. Sollins, and D. Lim, Implementing aggregation and broadcast over distributed hash tables, SIGCOMM Comput. Commun. Rev. 35, 1 Jan. 2005, 81–92.

[544] Hung-Chang Hsiao and Chung-Ta King, Scoped broadcast in dynamic peer-to-peer networks, 29th Annual International Computer Software and Applications Conference, 2005, COMPSAC 2005, July 26–28, 2005, Vol. 2, 533–538.

[545] P. Van Roy, Self-management for large-scale distributed systems based on structured overlay networks and components, retrieved from www.ist-selfman.org/wiki/index.php/SELFMAN_Project, July 2008.

[546] DCIA, Proactive network Provider Participation for P2P (P4P). Retrieved from www.dcia.info/activities/#P4P, July 2008.

[547] H. Xie, et al., P4P: Provider Portal for (P2P) applications, IETF P2P Infrastructure Workshop (P2Pi), May 2008.

[548] H. Xie, et al., P4P: Provide portal for (P2P) applications, in: Proceedings of ACM SIGCOMM, Seattle, Aug. 2008.

[549] E. Rescorlak, Notes on P2P blocking and evasion, IETF P2P Infrastructure Workshop (P2Pi), May 2008.

[550] E. Marocco, et al., Peer-to-peer infrastructure: A survey of research on the application-layer traffic optimization problem and the need for layer cooperation, IETF P2P Infrastructure Workshop (P2Pi), May 2008.

Page numbers followed by "f" indicate figures
page numbers followed by "t" indicate tables.

Printed and bound by CPI Group (UK) Ltd, Croydon, CR0 4YY

03/10/2024

01040314-0013